Business and Personal Law

Gordon W. Brown J.D.

Paul A. Sukys J.D.

Mc
Graw
Hill
Education

Educational Reviewers

We wish to acknowledge the contributions of the following reviewers:

Barbara Beadle
Program Specialist, Business
Indiana

Katherine Bullard
Middleton High School
Tampa, FL

Cheryl Cooper
Southeast Career Center
Columbus, OH

Joy Davis
Delaware Area Career Center
Delaware, OH

Linda Gallo
Sickles High School
Tampa, FL

Karol Gotte
Largo High School
Largo, FL

Brian Gray
Myers Park High School
Charlotte, NC

Colleen Hunt
Iowa State Department of Education
State Business Education Department

John Husinka
East Bay High School
Gibsonton, FL

Vivian King
Independence High School
Columbus, OH

Connie Meek
CCSD
Coordinator, Business Education
Nevada

Elaine Metcalf
Chairperson/Career & Tech Education
  Facilitator
Missouri

Vanessa Moorhead
Alonso High School
Tampa, FL

Jennifer Morley
Blake High School
Tampa, FL

Barb Motley

Deanna Peck
David W. Butler High School
Matthews, NC

Terri Phillips
H. B. Pant High School
Tampa, FL

Janet Richards
Riverview High School
Riverview, FL

Josephine Rumore
Tampa Bay Tech High School
Tampa, FL

Natalie Schaublin
Westerville North High School
Westerville, OH

Michelle See
East Mecklenburg High School
Charlotte, NC

Rebecca Seher
ROP District
Long Beach, CA

Julie Smith
Southeast Career Center
Columbus, OH

Jaclyn Soles
East Bay High School
Tampa, FL

Glenn Stamm
Osceola High School
Seminole, FL

JoeAnn Streeter
Supervisor, Business Technology
Tampa, FL

Eileen Wascisin
Lynden High School
Lynden, WA

Liz Watt
North Education Center High School
Columbus, OH

Legal Reviewer:

Mark Mathiasen, J.D., Esq.,
Middleton, ID

Contributing Writers:

Jane A. Brown
Groveland, MS

Donna Lee Sirkis, MBA, MAEd,
CMS-Myers Park High School, Charlotte, NC

We wish to acknowledge the National Business Education Association for the development of national business law standards which this book was developed to meet. We also thank the National Council of Teachers of English, the national Council of Teachers of Mathematics, and the national Council for the Social Studies for allowing the use of their national standards in this textbook.

Treasure Hunt

Business and Personal Law: Real-World Connections contains practical information about the U.S. legal system. The trick is to know where to look to access all the information in this book. If you go on the treasure hunt with your teacher, you will discover how this textbook is organized and how to get the most out of your reading and study time. Let's Start!

❶ How many units and chapters does this textbook have?

❷ What part of the textbook will help you practice your essay-writing skills?

❸ Where can you find out about the rights of minors?

❹ What are the three book features that give you real court case examples?

❺ Where can you learn about your rights and duties when you rent an apartment?

❻ Where can you find out about business laws in foreign countries?

❼ What academic skill will you practice in Chapter 4, Section 4.1, Assessment?

❽ Where can you access additional *Business and Personal Law* resources as you study?

Table of Contents

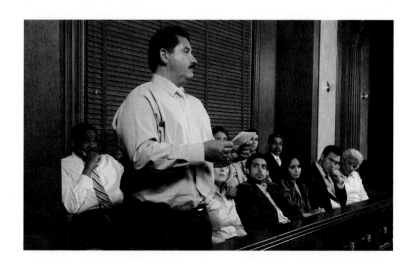

Table of Contents

Table of Contents

Table of Contents

Table of Contents

Table of Contents

Table of Contents

Table of Contents

Table of Contents

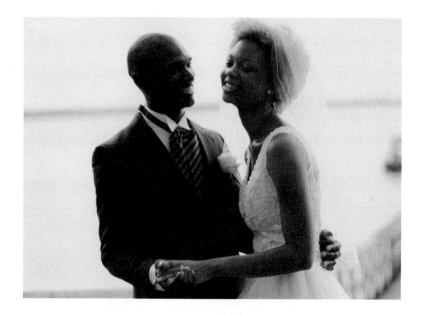

Study law with real cases: Step out of the classroom and into the world.

Studying law is about learning concepts and rules. It is also about understanding how the rules apply in real life. *Business and Personal Law* shows you how the law works with real court cases in every chapter and unit.

Preview the Cases

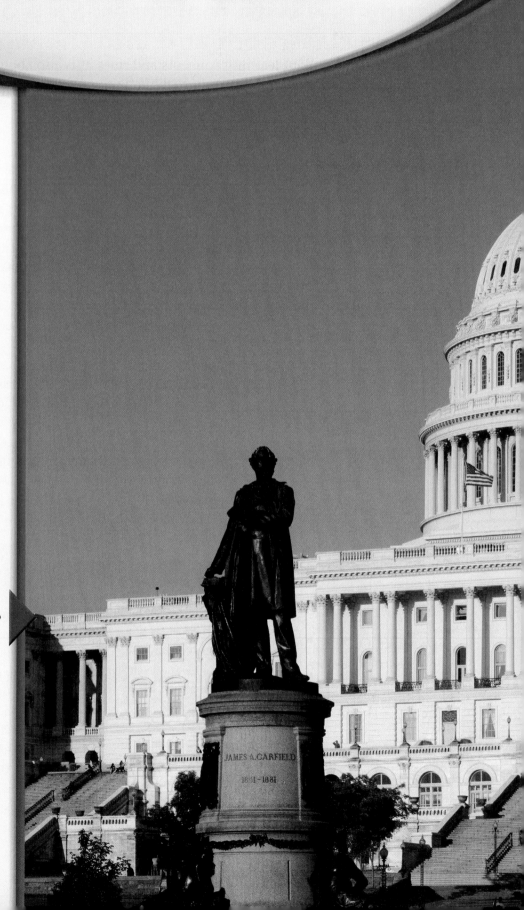

Separation of Powers
There are three branches of the U.S. government: the executive, the judicial, and the legislative. The executive branch is headed by the President and has the power to carry out the law. The judicial branch consists of the courts and has the power to interpret the law. *What is the legislative branch?*

Thematic Project Preview

Small Claims Suits

As you read this unit, use this checklist to prepare for the unit project:

- ✓ List terms and concepts commonly used in small claims court.
- ✓ Determine what type of preparation is needed for a small claims case.
- ✓ Evaluate whether the facts are sufficient enough to make a decision in the small claims case you create.

Legal Portfolio When you complete the Unit Thematic Project, you will have a guide for filing an action in your state's small claims court to add to your portfolio.

Ask AN EXPERT   Invest Your Money Wisely

Q: What is a typical investment scam, and what can I do to avoid it?

A: A common way investors lose money is through penny stock scams. Penny stocks are highly risky stocks that sell for under one dollar. In a penny stock scam, a scammer buys a large amount of cheap stock in a worthless company. The scammer then drums up interest in the stock with hot tips spread by word of mouth and over the Internet. As people buy up the stock, thinking they are getting in on a great deal, it drives up demand for the stock—and the price. By the time investors discover the stock is worthless and demand dries up, the scammer has sold all the stock at a tidy profit. Consider the source of a stock tip, treat every tip with doubt, and resist peer pressure. Most importantly, do not get greedy. Always heed the old saying, "If it sounds too good to be true, it probably is." Thoroughly investigate investment opportunities you are considering. Conduct research or consult with an investment professional.

Legal Briefs

For These Laws You Need a Sense of Humor

Some laws might surprise you.

Is that an uncaged bear in your car? Don't drive through Missouri. It's illegal. It's a good idea to cage a bear if you have one in your car, but does it require a law?

Laws are necessary. They protect us and help create fairness in our country. There are laws, however, that regulate activities that seem harmless, unnecessary, and outdated—such as that uncaged bear.

In Austin, Texas, it's illegal to carry wire cutters in your pocket. Landowners who wanted open ranges cut the barbed wire of those who wanted fences, but unless caught in the act, no one knew who did the crime.

In Idaho, candy shop owners beware. A man can only give his girlfriend a box of candy that weighs less than 50 pounds. A pickle is a pickle only if it bounces in Connecticut, a state where it's also illegal to walk across the street on your hands. In Maine, businesses take heed. You have to take your Christmas decorations down before January 14, and in Alaska, you can't wake a sleeping bear to take its picture.

Trial by Jury A defendant has a right to be tried before either a judge or a jury. *What are the steps in a jury trial?*

The Foundations of Law

What You'll Learn

- Explain how ethical decisions are made.
- Identify the different ethical character traits.
- Describe how the law relates to ethics.
- Explain the importance of the law.
- Identify the parts of the Constitution.
- Explain the components of common law.
- Explain the purposes of statutory law.
- Identify the ways that the courts make law.

Why It's Important

Knowing where laws come from will help you understand your own legal rights and responsibilities.

Reading Guide

Before You Read

Connect Have you ever been tempted to cheat on an exam? If you have, you have faced an ethical decision.

Focus on Ideas

The law is a set of rules developed over centuries from many different sources. It develops as society changes.

Take Notes

Go to connectED.mcgraw-hill.com to download a graphic organizer you can use to take notes as you read this section.

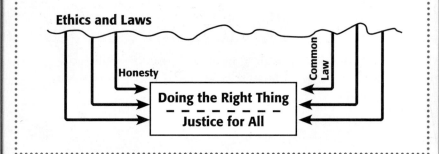

Ethics and Laws

Honesty

Common Law

Doing the Right Thing

Justice for All

Key Terms

You will learn these legal words and expressions in this chapter. You can also find these terms in *Black's Law Dictionary* or in an online legal dictionary.

- morality
- ethics
- justice
- law

- constitution
- common law
- statute
- administrative law

Academic Vocabulary

You will find these words in your readings and in your tests. Look them up in a dictionary and familiarize yourself with them.

- empathy
- permissible
- prevalent

What Are Ethics and Morality?

Do you think choosing between right and wrong always involves rules?

Determining the difference between right and wrong can be difficult. People use different methods to decide on the right thing to do in any given situation. **Morality involves the values that govern a group's ideas about right and wrong. Ethics refers to the rules used to determine the difference between right and wrong.** In this book, the words *ethics* and *morality* will be used for both ideas.

What Does Ethics Come From?

Using ethical rules will help you deal with big and small moral questions.

The Greatest Good One way to decide about right and wrong is to apply the greatest good idea. This examines whether the action will cause the greatest good for the greatest number of people. The more good that results, the more right the action. It is used incorrectly when people think only of their own good, or if a person sees only the good created for a small group.

The Golden Rule The Golden Rule says, "Do unto others as you would have them do unto you." Many people prefer this rule because it works in many situations. The heart of the Golden Rule is **empathy.** Empathy means putting yourself in another person's position. One way to test whether an action is right or wrong under the Golden Rule is to ask, "Would I want to be treated this way?" If your answer is no, then the action breaks the Golden Rule.

Real-World Ethics Real-world ethics says that there are moral rules that most people know instinctively, without thinking. For example, lying is wrong. However, real-world ethics says that there are rare times when a person might have to lie. For example, it might be **permissible** to lie to save somebody's life. This does not mean what you have done is right. It means that what you have done is less wrong. If you lie to save a life, you know that the lie is still wrong, but you also know that it is less wrong than saying something that leads to someone's death.

As You Read

Predict How do you know you are making the right ethical decision?

Vocabulary You can find vocabulary definitions in the **Key Terms** glossary and Academic Vocabulary glossary in the back of this book.

➡️ **Hammurabi's Code** One of the earliest written set of laws is the Code of Hammurabi, which was carved in stone. *Who was Hammurabi and how long ago was his code of law written?*

Reading Check

Explain *Is an ethical decision always the correct legal decision?*

Ethical Character Traits

In difficult cases where moral rules and legal guidelines do not help, specific character traits become a compass you can use. For example, think of a situation in which you have to decide whether to tell the truth, knowing that the truth will get you and others into trouble.

Honesty Honesty is a character trait of someone who is truthful in dealings with others.

Justice Justice **means treating people fairly and equally.** That means everyone, not just relatives and friends. A just person will see that everyone gets his or her fair share.

Compassion Compassion means caring about other people and the situation they are in. Compassionate people understand other people's mistakes and motivations.

Integrity Integrity is a willingness and determination to do the right thing. People with integrity stand up for their convictions, even when many people are against them.

The Relationship between Ethics and Law

What does the law have to do with right and wrong?

If people used ethics all the time to guide their behavior, there would be no need for law. In the real world, people sometimes do the wrong thing. This happens even when they know better. In order to develop and live both an ethical and a legal lifestyle, you must follow the law and incorporate ethics into your life.

Why Is Law Necessary?

Ethics tell you what you ought to do. However, people do not always do what they are supposed to, so governments create laws. **Law is a system of rules of conduct established by a country's government to maintain stability and justice according to the values that are relevant to that country.** The law defines the legal rights and responsibilities of the people. Under the different types of laws, the government can require certain actions, or it can forbid others. Laws create specific responsibilities for people. In the United States, the law is a way to enforce the rights and duties of everyone through the police, the courts, the legislature, and regulatory agencies. It is everyone's responsibility to obey the law.

The law has the power to punish people for acting illegally. Consider the contrast between a dishonest but legal business transaction and one that is both dishonest and illegal. If you tell a friend that you have no money to lend him when, in fact you have a lot of money and could easily lend him what he needs, your action is perfectly legal. However, no matter which ethical theory you use, you will have to admit that you have lied, which is clearly dishonest. The law cannot force you to tell the truth in this situation. On the other hand, if you steal money to lend to your friend, you have done something that is both dishonest and illegal. The law can clearly punish you for stealing.

Many new laws are created as a response to a person's or a company's unethical practices. For example, in the late 1990s some American corporations lied about their finances before they went bankrupt and many people lost money they had invested in the corporations on the stock market. As a result, the U.S. Congress established a new set of laws that made corporations more accountable to the public.

Ethical and Legal Conflicts

Ethics and the law affect each other. Changes in ethical standards can help us make new laws, or get rid of old laws. Changes in the law can help people adjust their ideas on morality. The conflict between social forces has led to such changes in the United States. For example, desegregation laws have changed the way many people act toward one another.

The Five Main Sources of the Law

What document is the basis of all U.S. laws?

In general, law in the United States today comes from five main sources.

Constitutional Law

A **constitution** is a country's formal document that spells out the principles by which its government operates. In our country, the most basic law is the U.S. Constitution.

The Constitution of the United States The United States Constitution describes the three branches of the U.S. government and their roles. It sets up the limits within which the federal and state

Business ETHICS

Home Sale

Suppose you are an attorney for a construction company. While reviewing plans for a new dormitory your company is building, you realize the dormitory will be built next to a house you are selling. Someone has offered to buy the house for exactly the amount you want. You know that as soon as the college announces where the dormitory will be located, prices for surrounding property, including yours, will drastically fall. You must now call the person interested in buying your property with your decision on the offer.

Critical Thinking: What ethical issues are involved and what should you tell the interested party? Explain.

governments may pass laws. The Constitution also sets down the rights of the people. The Constitution was created upon a basic value system the Founding Fathers felt was appropriate to all Americans.

Article I sets up the legislative branch of government, the Congress, which is responsible for passing laws for the country, and lays out duties and requirements for serving in the federal government. Article II creates the executive branch. The executive branch includes the President and all of the different departments within the government, such as the State Department and the Department of Defense. The executive branch is responsible for ensuring that the laws passed by Congress are upheld and followed. Finally, Article III describes the judiciary branch of government, which is responsible for interpreting the laws passed by Congress and adjudicating criminal cases in federal matters and disputes between parties.

These initial three Articles form a system of checks and balances, so that one branch is not more powerful than another. No one branch has the sole authority to pass laws, enforce laws, and adjudicate laws. These responsibilities are divided among the three branches.

Article IV requires each state to give full faith and credit to the laws of all other states. This means that each state must accept the laws of all the other states. Article V tells how laws may be added to the Constitution—by creating amendments.

Article VI contains the supremacy clause. This clause states that the U.S. Constitution and the laws of the United States are the highest laws in the country. Article VII, the last article, explains how to approve the Constitution. This event took place in 1787.

The Constitution now has 27 amendments. The first ten amendments were approved in 1791. They are called the Bill of Rights. They limit the powers of the government. The basic goal of the Bill of Rights is to protect our individual rights and freedoms. For example, the First Amendment protects some very important rights, such as freedom of speech, religion, assembly, and freedom of the press. No law may be passed by Congress, or any state, that would limit these individual rights and freedoms. Other important amendments include the 13th Amendment, which abolished slavery in the U.S.; the 19th Amendment, which gave women the right to vote; and the 26th Amendment, which lowered the voting age to 18 years of age.

State Constitutions Each state has its own constitution. State constitutions are not the same as the United States Constitution. Although state constitutions usually include a number of similarities, such as three branches of government and the protection of certain basic rights, state constitutions are often longer and more detailed than the United States Constitution. Duties and requirements for serving in state and local governments are determined by the individual states.

Legal Talk

Precedent: *n* An earlier occurrence. From Latin *praecedere:* prior in time.

Integrity: *n* Firm adherence to a code of moral or artistic values, the quality of being undivided. From Latin *integritas:* entire.

Vocabulary Builder List three words that have the same origin as *precedent* and three words that have the same origin as *integrity*. Define and name parts of speech for each word.

Common Law

In the early days of England's history, the king tried to centralize the English court system. Judges traveled around the country deciding cases. Because there was no written law, judges made decisions based on the customs and traditions of the people. Judges shared their decisions with one another so that the same laws would be applied everywhere in the country. This practice formed the basis of common law.

The common law is a set of laws made by the courts which provide a series of consistent rules that later courts must follow. The early American colonists came from England, so it was natural for them to use the common law of England in their new land.

Eventually, these court decisions were written down and a body of cases developed. Judges could then refer to past cases when making their decisions. These past cases came to be known as precedent. A precedent is a past case that a court follows when making a present decision.

The process of relying on past court cases is called stare decisis. This means "let the decision stand." English common law is not used today as much as it was in the past. However, parts of the common law are still used in some states.

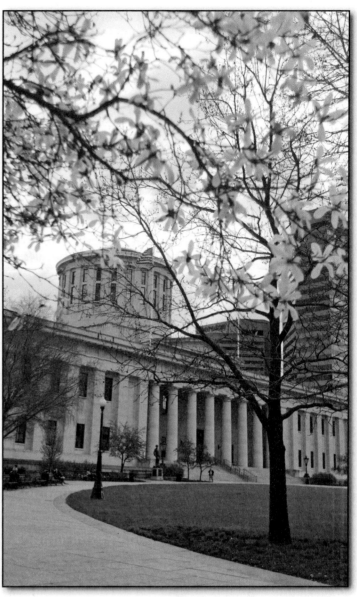

Statutes and the Civil Law System

The origin of civil law can be traced back to the Roman Empire during the 6th century when Emperor Justinian I called for the collection of all the different laws created by previous Roman emperors. This is the basis of the civil law system that is **prevalent** in Europe and the state of Louisiana.

Unlike common law, civil law is law based on statutes, rather than court decisions. **A statute is a law passed by a government body that has been made for the purpose of creating laws.** A government body that has been set up to pass statutes is called a legislature. A statute can declare the law on an issue. Statutes may also order people to do something. For example, a statute might say people have to pay taxes or wear seat belts. Other statutes say that people cannot do something. This is what a criminal statute does when it says murder is a crime.

A statute is created when legislature passes a proposed law, or bill. After the bill is passed, it is sent to the President or the

Law at the State Level
State legislatures and state courts play an important role in the U.S. legal system. Legislatures vote on statutes and create laws. State courts review and interpret statutes and also create case law. *Where is your state's supreme court located? Where is your state legislature located?*

Governor, depending on whether it is a federal law or a state law, to sign the bill into law. A law does not go into effect until the President or Governor signs it.

Federal Statutes Laws that are passed by the U.S. Congress and signed by the President are called federal statutes. The United States Congress is a legislature. It has the job of making statutes under the powers given to the federal government by the Constitution. These powers include such things as the power to spend, tax, and borrow money.

Commerce Clause One important clause in the constitution is the commerce clause. The commerce clause gives Congress the power to make laws pertaining to interstate commerce, or commerce between the states. Congress has used this clause to pass laws that affect American businesses on various topics such as civil rights and interstate trucking.

Global Law

International Sources of Law

Countries throughout the world have many sources of law: national constitutions, religious texts, court-created case law, and voter-initiated propositions. Even within the United States, diversity abounds. Louisiana, for example, uses a code-based legal system inherited from the French tradition, whereas most other states follow a case law system that originates in England.

European systems of law were adopted by many countries around the world. France and the United Kingdom were very influential. The United States created a legal system that incorporates parts of both French and British law.

The United States has four primary sources of law:

1. The U.S. Constitution
2. International treaties
3. Statutes passed by the U.S. Congress
4. Case law created by the U.S. Supreme Court

France, on the other hand, has three sources of law with no case law:

1. The French Constitution
2. International treaties
3. The *Code civil des français,* or French Civil Code

Finally, the United Kingdom also has only three sources of law, with no constitution:

1. International treaties
2. Statutes passed through the Houses of Parliament
3. Case law created by the House of Lords in its holdings

Across Cultures: What's a lawyer called in England?

In England lawyers are divided into two categories based on the legal work that they do. Barristers engage in trial work and often prepare trial briefs, and solicitors handle office work. Barristers count on solicitors to provide them trial work because they are not allowed to do it on their own.

Critical Thinking: *What are the advantages (or disadvantages) of having a supreme court that can create law? What about a constitution?*

As noted earlier, the U.S. Constitution is the supreme law of the land. This means that Congress cannot pass laws that conflict with the U.S. Constitution, including the Bill of Rights. The Supreme Court may declare any statute that does go against the Constitution to be unconstitutional. This means that the statute is invalid.

State Statutes Each state also has its own legislature. Like Congress, the state legislatures cannot pass statutes that conflict with the U.S. Constitution or their own constitutions.

> **Example** Lawmakers in Massachusetts wanted to have a graduated income tax that would very much be like the federal income tax. A graduated tax requires people with larger income to pay a higher tax rate than people with smaller incomes. Such a tax could not be passed because the Massachusetts constitution requires all people to be taxed at an equal percentage rate.

As a way of lessening confusion and creating similar statutes in all the states, there are many different uniform codes. One of the best known examples is the Uniform Commercial Code, or UCC. Every state has passed a version of the UCC, which means that statutes relating to commerce are essentially the same in all the states, and people do not have to worry about knowing 50 different sets of law with regard to business transactions.

Ordinances Most local governments, like cities and towns, have the power to create laws that affect their citizens. These laws are known as ordinances and can apply to topics such as parking fines and noxious weed control.

Court Decisions

Most people are surprised to learn that courts make law. Court-made law is often called case law, court decisions, or judge-made law. Courts make law in three ways: through the common law tradition, by interpreting statutes, and by judicial review.

Creating Laws Decisions made by the highest court of a state are the law of that state. These decisions must be followed by other courts in that state. These decisions continue to be law until they are changed by statute or a new court decision.

Interpreting Laws A second type of court decision involves interpreting statutes. When a statute is confusing, the court must figure out what the statute means. A judge cannot interpret a statute unless the statute is part of a case.

Judicial Review The courts can also decide whether laws conflict with the Constitution. Any laws or government actions that conflict with the Constitution are unconstitutional. The Supreme Court of the United States has the last word on whether a statute conflicts with the Constitution.

Administrative Regulations

The legislature must regulate many activities. This is true of Congress and of the state legislatures. However, legislators do not have knowledge in every field. They also do not have the time to do everything that they are charged with doing. For these reasons, legislatures will give the power to regulate certain activities to an administrative agency. For example, the Federal Communications Commission (FCC) has the power to regulate radio, television, and cable companies.

Administrative agencies are departments of government that are formed to carry out certain laws. These agencies can make and enforce rules directly related to the area of responsibility given to them by the legislature. **Administrative law is the body of rules created by government agencies.**

Administrative agencies have a lot of power. However, there are checks and balances that keep them from becoming too powerful. The legislature that created an agency has the power to end the agency or to change its power. A final decision by an agency can be reviewed by the courts.

International Law

Although not a major source of law in the United States, international law can be equally important. International treaties signed by the United States and other countries are held to the same level as federal statutes. Like a federal statute, everyone in the U.S. must follow any treaty that the U.S. has signed.

In addition to treaties, there are international agreements between countries, such as trade agreements, that are not binding on the countries, but provide recommendations for how countries should interact within the international community.

After You Read

Summarize What are the five main sources of the law?

SECTION 1.1 ASSESSMENT

Self Check

1. What is the difference between morality and ethics?

2. Why is the law necessary?

3. What are the possible purposes of a statute?

Academic Connection

Social Studies The Bill of Rights clearly spells out the immunities for the individual citizen. Why do you think the writers of the Bill of Rights were so concerned with this?

English Language Arts Using the Bill of Rights as a guide, write a bill of rights addressing student rights to a free education.

Critical Thinking

Software Downloading Suppose that your best friend had a way to hack into your math teacher's computer so that he could download the answers to your next test. Your friend offers to give you the answers for five dollars. Would you go along with your friend's tempting offer? Why or why not? What ethical rule would you use to make this decision?

The Court System and Trial Procedures

Reading Guide

Before You Read

Connect If a 16-year-old gets into legal trouble, does the case always go to a juvenile court?

Focus on Ideas

There are many different levels of the court system to deal with different types of legal problems.

Take Notes

Go to connectED.mcgraw-hill.com to download a graphic organizer you can use to take notes as you read this section.

Litigation

1. **Filing a Complaint** _____
2. _____
3. _____
4. _____

Key Terms

You will learn these legal words and expressions in this chapter. You can also find these terms in *Black's Law Dictionary* or in an online legal dictionary.

- jurisdiction
- appellate court
- alternative dispute resolution (ADR)
- arrest
- bail
- arraignment
- detention hearing

Academic Vocabulary

You will find these words in your readings and in your tests. Look them up in a dictionary and familiarize yourself with them.

- informal
- mediator
- jeopardy

What You'll Learn

- ◆ Define jurisdiction.
- ◆ Describe the structure of the federal court system.
- ◆ Explain the role of the United States Supreme Court.
- ◆ Determine the common structure of most state court systems.
- ◆ Identify alternative dispute resolution techniques.
- ◆ Differentiate between civil and criminal cases.
- ◆ Describe the steps in a civil lawsuit.
- ◆ Explain the rights of criminal defendants.
- ◆ List the steps in a criminal prosecution.

Why It's Important

Learning about the structure of the U.S. court systems will help you understand how the U.S. legal system works.

A Dual Court System

Are all the U.S. courts of justice the same no matter where you live?

As You Read

Predict Do all cases get resolved in court?

The United States has two major court systems: federal and state. Federal courts hear cases involving federal subjects. They also hear cases involving citizens from different states or from another country. According to the U.S. Constitution, powers not specifically granted to the federal government are reserved for the states. So states have their own courts with their own rules.

The Federal Court System

Jurisdiction is a court's power to hear a case and to make a judgment. Federal courts have jurisdiction over certain types of cases. These cases include:

1. Actions in which the United States or one state is a party, except those actions between a state and its citizens
2. Cases that raise a federal question, such as interpreting the Constitution
3. Cases, which involve citizens of different states and in which the amount of money in dispute exceeds $75,000
4. Admiralty cases, or those pertaining to the sea
5. Patent and copyright cases
6. Bankruptcy cases

Federal courts are arranged in three tiers. The first tier is the U.S. district court. Each state has at least one district court; many have more. The second tier consists of the U.S. courts of appeals and the highest tier is the U.S. Supreme Court (see **Figure 1.1,** page 17).

District Courts District courts have original jurisdiction over most federal civil and criminal cases. Original jurisdiction means that a court has the power to hear a case for the first time. Most federal cases begin in one of the U.S. district courts.

The Supreme Court The highest court in the land is the U.S. Supreme Court. Supreme Court justices have vast legal experience as lawyers and judges. *Who was the first African American appointed to the Supreme Court?*

Courts of Appeals U.S. courts of appeals are the appellate courts of the federal system. An appeal is a request to a higher court to reverse a lower court's decision. **An appellate court is a court that hears appeals and reviews cases from the lower courts.**

In the federal system, the courts of appeals are intermediate courts. An intermediate court is one that is between lower courts and the highest court of a system and has appellate jurisdiction. Appellate jurisdiction is the power to hear an appeal from a lower court.

Steven Petteway, Collection of the Supreme Court of the United States

Figure 1.1 Court Systems in the United States

U.S. Supreme Court
Hears appeals from federal and state courts; has original jurisdiction in cases in which a state is a party, and in cases involving American ambassadors, ministers, and consuls

Court of Appeals for the Federal Circuit
Hears cases on appeal from the U.S. Claims Court and the Court of International Trade; hears certain appeals from U.S. district courts

State Supreme Courts
Hear appeals from lower state courts; have original jurisdiction in cases in which the state is a party, and in cases that involve the state constitution

U.S. Claims Court
Hears cases from citizens involving claims against the federal government

U.S. Courts of Appeals
Hear cases on appeal from district courts and certain other federal courts

Intermediate Appellate Courts* Hear cases on appeal from general trial courts and lower trial courts

U.S. Court of International Trade
Hears civil cases concerning tariffs and import taxes

U.S. District Courts
Hear criminal and civil cases

General Trial Courts
District, County, Circuit, Common Pleas, or Superior Courts; hear major criminal and civil cases; may hear certain cases on appeal from lower courts

U.S. Tax Court
Hears cases dealing with tax laws

→ Indicates route of appeals
▬ Federal Court System
▬ State Court System

Territorial Courts
Hear cases dealing with territorial and federal laws in the territories of the United States

Lower Trial Courts
Justice, Magistrates, and Municipal Courts; hear misdemeanors and civil cases that involve small amounts of money

Court of Military Appeals Hears appeals of court martials

*Found in about two-thirds of the states

The courts in the United States are divided into federal and state systems.
In which court system would a criminal trial be heard?

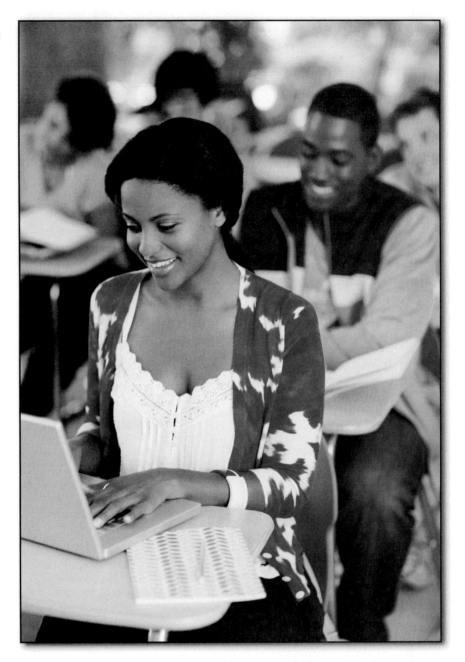

Who Gets to Be a Supreme Court Justice? A diverse student body representing the country's demographics is the goal of many colleges that train future lawyers, judges, and justices. *What do you think the most challenging part of studying law and becoming a lawyer is?*

The United States is divided into thirteen judicial circuits. Each circuit has several district courts and one court of appeals. A panel of three judges is responsible for rendering decisions in most appeals. No witnesses are heard, no evidence is presented, and no jury is present. Only questions of law can be raised on appeal, not questions of fact. Appellate courts only determine whether the lower court correctly applied the law in the case.

Special U.S. Courts Congress has set up several special federal courts. These courts have jurisdiction in certain kinds of cases. These cases include lawsuits that are brought by citizens against the federal government.

Supreme Court The United States Supreme Court is the highest court in the country. It consists of the Chief Justice of the United States and eight associate justices.

The President chooses the justices with the consent of the Senate. Like all federal judges, the justices who sit on the United States Supreme Court serve for life. The Court's main job is to hear appeals. The Court decides which appellate cases it will hear. This requires a vote of at least four of its nine justices. The Supreme Court will hear cases that affect a wide range of people and those that involve the Constitution. A case is also likely to reach the Supreme Court when several lower courts have faced the issue, but have disagreed on how to resolve it. The Supreme Court has original jurisdiction in all cases that involve ambassadors, consuls, and other public ministers. It also has original jurisdiction in cases that involve a state.

State Court Systems

Each state has its own court system. However, the general pattern is the same in all states.

Local Trial Courts Local courts are courts of limited jurisdiction. Limited jurisdiction means that a court handles minor matters. Such cases might involve disputes over small amounts of money which are heard in small-claims courts. Minor cases are also heard by traffic, police, or mayor's courts.

General Trial Courts In most states, each county has one general trial court, also called a court of general jurisdiction. Courts with general jurisdiction handle criminal and civil cases.

Juvenile Courts Juvenile courts deal with juvenile offenders and with children who need the protection of the state. These courts deal with children up until the age of majority, which is 18 in most states. They have special jurisdiction over delinquent, unruly, abused, and neglected children.

Procedures in juvenile courts differ from those in other courts. Most juvenile matters are sealed, meaning that unlike other court proceedings, they are not open to the general public. This is to protect the privacy of the minor. Hearings are often more **informal** than in other courts of law. Young people who appear before a juvenile court have no right to a trial by jury and no right to be released on bail. However, the Supreme Court has held that there must be proof beyond a reasonable doubt to convict a child as an adult.

Vocabulary You can find vocabulary definitions in the **Key Terms** glossary and Academic Vocabulary glossary in the back of this book.

Intermediate Appellate Courts Some states have intermediate appellate courts that hear appeals. Appeals may be made to a state intermediate court when the parties believe they did not have a fair trial in the lower court. They may also appeal to the intermediate court if the judge did not interpret the law correctly. State appellate courts hear appeals only on questions of law. No witnesses testify. Appeals judges hear arguments from attorneys. They also study the documents and records in the case.

State Supreme Courts The highest court in most states is the supreme court. A state's highest court decides matters of law appealed from lower courts. Supreme courts do not hold a second trial.

They do not look at the facts in the case. Instead, they decide whether the lower court made a mistake in interpreting or applying the law. At times, cases that have been decided by a state supreme court may be appealed to the United States Supreme Court.

Civil Trial Procedure

Suppose you are suing your neighbor for damaging your property. Will your case appear in the court as a criminal case?

The law can be divided into two very simple categories: substantive law and procedural law. Substantive law tells us what the law is. There are many different classifications of substantive law ranging from criminal law to business law, family law to bankruptcy law. Most of this book is devoted to substantive law.

Procedural law tells us how the law works. The two major divisions in this area of the law are civil procedure and criminal procedure. Criminal procedure and civil procedure are very different from one another.

The government brings criminal cases to court for offenses against the public. Criminal law is enacted to protect the public from harm. In contrast, individuals who believe they have been injured bring civil cases. Civil law is enacted to govern

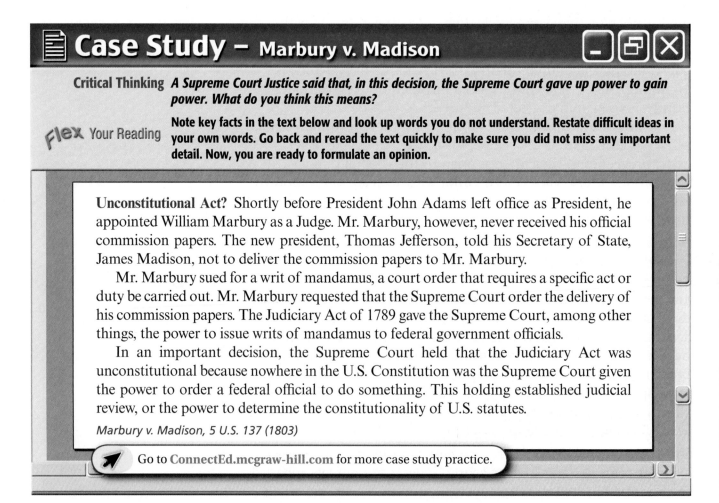

Case Study – Marbury v. Madison

Critical Thinking *A Supreme Court Justice said that, in this decision, the Supreme Court gave up power to gain power. What do you think this means?*

Flex Your Reading Note key facts in the text below and look up words you do not understand. Restate difficult ideas in your own words. Go back and reread the text quickly to make sure you did not miss any important detail. Now, you are ready to formulate an opinion.

Unconstitutional Act? Shortly before President John Adams left office as President, he appointed William Marbury as a Judge. Mr. Marbury, however, never received his official commission papers. The new president, Thomas Jefferson, told his Secretary of State, James Madison, not to deliver the commission papers to Mr. Marbury.

Mr. Marbury sued for a writ of mandamus, a court order that requires a specific act or duty be carried out. Mr. Marbury requested that the Supreme Court order the delivery of his commission papers. The Judiciary Act of 1789 gave the Supreme Court, among other things, the power to issue writs of mandamus to federal government officials.

In an important decision, the Supreme Court held that the Judiciary Act was unconstitutional because nowhere in the U.S. Constitution was the Supreme Court given the power to order a federal official to do something. This holding established judicial review, or the power to determine the constitutionality of U.S. statutes.

Marbury v. Madison, 5 U.S. 137 (1803)

Go to **ConnectEd.mcgraw-hill.com** for more case study practice.

the relationships between two individual parties, and does not normally involve the government. The injured person begins a lawsuit by filing a complaint with the court. Another name for bringing a civil lawsuit is litigation.

There are many advantages to litigation. One advantage is that, since litigation has a long history in our legal system, the courts have had a chance to develop rules that make the process as fair as possible. However, there are disadvantages too. For instance, when an individual brings a civil case to an attorney, the lawyer investigates the case. This investigation can be costly and time consuming. Unlike in criminal cases, a person in a civil lawsuit is not guaranteed or provided an attorney. Many people choose to represent themselves in court, and they are expected to follow the same specific rules that attorneys follow during litigation.

Important Civil Statutes

There are many reasons for civil litigation. For example, if someone is hit by a car and dies, the victim's family may sue the driver of the car for wrongful death. The family may get money to compensate for the pain of losing their loved one.

Survival statutes are written to ensure that when a plaintiff dies, a representative for the deceased can continue the case, or bring a new case on the deceased's behalf. Statutes of limitation are passed to provide time limits for when a plaintiff may sue a defendant. For example, the statute of limitation for bringing a wrongful death claim may be three years. In the above example, that means that the family of the victim has three years to begin a suit against the driver for their loss. There are different time limits for each separate claim.

Alternative Dispute Resolution

To cut costs and to save time, people have begun to explore substitutes for lawsuits. **Alternative dispute resolution (ADR) occurs when parties try to resolve disagreements outside of the usual court system.** Some ADR techniques are mediation, arbitration, conciliation, and negotiation.

Mediation Mediation occurs when parties to a dispute invite a **mediator** to help them solve the problem. This can be done voluntarily, or as required by a court. A mediator tries to persuade the parties to compromise. A major advantage to mediation is that the final decision remains in the hands of the parties. A disadvantage is that, if carried out too quickly, mediation can highlight the disagreement between the parties rather than the points of agreement.

Arbitration Sometimes, the parties give the power to settle their dispute to a third party. This process is called arbitration. The person who is hired to settle the case is the arbitrator. An advantage to arbitration is that it often results in a fair solution because the decision is in the hands of an independent, objective third party. A disadvantage is that the final decision does not remain in the hands of the people who have a dispute.

Reading Check

Enumerate *List the different types of federal courts and state courts.*

Conciliation Conciliation is similar to mediation and arbitration. In conciliation, however, the intermediary, who is generally referred to as the conciliator, does not bring the parties together in a face-to-face conversation. Instead, the conciliator shuttles back and forth between the parties seeking a consensus. An advantage to conciliation is that the parties are kept apart from one another. This reduces the possibility of an angry confrontation. A disadvantage is that conciliation takes more time because the conciliator must meet separately with everyone involved.

Negotiation In negotiation, each party appoints a spokesperson to represent him or her in the reconciliation process. The negotiators then meet to hammer out an agreement. Negotiation is just one step closer to litigation, which involves an actual lawsuit. An advantage to negotiation is that it permits the parties to determine the relative merits of their arguments without going to court. A disadvantage is that often negotiation simply leads to litigation, thus adding an extra step to an already long process.

Civil Case Procedures
How do court trials start?

Civil litigation begins with pleadings: formal papers filed with the court by the plaintiff and defendant. The plaintiff is the person bringing the lawsuit. The defendant is the person who the lawsuit is against. The complaint expresses the plaintiff's claims against the defendant. The answer is the defendant's official response to the claims in the complaint.

Methods of discovery are used to bring facts out before trial. They include depositions, interrogatories, requests for documents and other evidence, physical and mental examinations, and requests for admission. If a case cannot be settled at that point, the court clerk places the case on the calendar, or court docket, for trial.

Pretrial Hearing Before the trial takes place, a pretrial hearing occurs. This hearing is an informal meeting before a judge. Sometimes, people settle the case at the pretrial hearing. If they do not settle the case, then they try to simplify things so the trial can run smoothly.

Steps in a Trial

When a case is filed, the parties must decide whether they want a jury trial or a court trial. With a court trial, there is no jury, and a judge makes all the decisions. If a jury trial is requested, then the trial begins by choosing the jury members. The trial then moves to opening statements. After the opening statements, the evidence is introduced. When there is no more evidence to show, the closing arguments begin. Then, the judge gives

Jury Duty People are summoned at random for jury duty. *How many people sit on a jury?*

© moodboard/Corbis

the jury its instructions. The jury then decides the case and brings a verdict. The verdict is followed by a judgment.

Selecting the Jury The judge calls the court to order. Then the judge has a jury drawn from a group of people who have been called to serve. The jury must determine the facts of the case. The jury also applies the law to those facts. The lawyers question each juror to predict whether a juror will be fair or unfair. The lawyers consider the juror's background, education, experience, relationships, attitudes, and employment.

Arguments and Evidence After jury members are chosen, the lawyers make opening statements. The opening statements explain what the lawyers intend to prove. The plaintiff's lawyer goes first. The defendant's lawyer goes next, or waits to give an opening statement until after the plaintiff's evidence has been presented.

The plaintiff's lawyer presents all of the plaintiff's evidence. Witnesses testify at this time, including expert witnesses. Expert witnesses give authoritative opinions on evidence in the case.

The defense lawyer has the chance to cross-examine the plaintiff's witnesses. The cross-examination is supposed to test the truth of a witness's statements. It might also bring out evidence that was not brought out on direct examination. When the plaintiff's lawyer is done, the defendant's lawyer presents evidence. The plaintiff's lawyer may then cross-examine. When both lawyers are done, they rest their cases.

The plaintiff's lawyer is the first to give a closing argument. This is followed by the defense lawyer. Each lawyer gives a summary of the evidence and suggests reasons why the judge or jury should find in favor of their client.

Instructions to the Jury The judge must explain the law to the jury. This is a process called jury instruction. Lawyers from both sides may suggest instructions.

Verdict and Judgment Jury members go to the jury room to talk about the case. After discussing the case, the jury will decide who has won the suit. This decision is called the verdict. States may allow a less than unanimous decision by jurors to agree on a verdict. Following the jury's verdict, the court issues a judgment. The judgment is the court's determination of liability in the case, or who is responsible for what. If there is no jury, the judge issues findings of fact, which are similar to a jury verdict, and then conclusions of law and a judgment.

The Witness Stand A witness testifies under oath at a trial (a deposition may be used in a trial if the witness is not available). The plaintiff or the defendant may be witnesses. Witnesses testify about what they have seen, heard, or experienced, or about the signing of a document such as a contract or a will. *What is the most important responsibility of a witness?*

Remedies When a defendant is found liable in a civil trial, the plaintiff is granted a remedy. Courts provide two types of remedies. One type is the payment of money. The other type requires some other action by the defendant. The plaintiff may want the defendant to keep a promise in a contract. This is called specific performance. Sometimes the plaintiff wants the defendant to stop doing something. In that case, the plaintiff seeks an injunction.

Execution of Judgment After the trial, the judgment of the court must be carried out. A judgment is enforced when the judge issues an execution order. The judge might order the sheriff to take some of the property that belongs to the losing party. The sheriff would then sell the property at an auction. The sheriff must use the money made at the auction to pay the winning party.

The Appeal Process

The parties are permitted to appeal the judgment of the court. The appeals process is different from trial. An appeal can only be based on a legal mistake by the judge. This is why attorneys object to certain procedures and to certain decisions made by the judge at the lower court level. There is no retrial at the appellate level. The lawyers argue their case before the appellate court, which then can affirm, reverse, or remand the case back to the lower court.

Criminal Trial Procedure

What happens when the police arrest a criminal suspect?

An arrest occurs when a person is legally deprived of his or her freedom. Criminal cases often start when the defendant is arrested. Defendants have a right to due process of law, or fair treatment according to established legal principles. The law requires a court hearing right away. This is supposed to protect the defendant's rights. The trial is planned for later to give both lawyers time to prepare their cases. The rules in criminal procedure must be followed exactly. In contrast, in a civil case, procedure can often be altered or changed by the agreement of the parties and judge. This is to protect the rights of the defendant.

Rights of the Defendant

The Supreme Court, in a case called Miranda v. Arizona, decided that people must be informed of their constitutional rights when they are arrested. The Miranda warnings require the police to tell people what crimes they are being arrested for. The police must also tell people they arrest that they have the right to a lawyer. If a defendant cannot afford a lawyer, the court must appoint one at no cost. The police must also tell people they arrest that they have the right to not say anything and that anything they do say can be used against them in court.

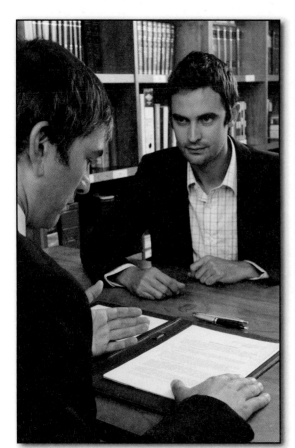

Lawyers and Clients Court decisions may be appealed. In appeals cases, lawyers prepare to make their arguments to an appellate court. *What is the main difference between an appeal case and a trial?*

A police officer may arrest a person at any time if the officer has a warrant. A police officer may arrest a person without a warrant if the officer believes the person has committed or is committing a crime in the officer's presence.

Bail A person who has been arrested can sometimes be released on bail. **Bail is money or other property that is left with the court to assure that a person who has been arrested, but released, will return to trial.** A judge determines bail.

Search and Seizure A police officer may search a person, car, house, or other building only if permission is given or if the officer has a search warrant. The search must only be the area mentioned in the warrant. An officer may conduct a limited search, or frisk, if the officer believes a person is carrying a weapon. When the search is over, the person must either be released or arrested. Persons who have been arrested may be searched without a warrant.

The Arraignment

The suspect is brought before the court as soon as possible after an arrest. At this brief hearing, the criminal defendant is informed of the complaint. The defendant is also made aware of his or her rights. At this time, the judge may find a reason to dismiss the complaint. The judge might also decide that there is probable cause that a crime was committed.

Grand Jury Depending upon the jurisdiction, the prosecuting lawyer either prepares an information or presents the case to the grand jury. An information is a set of formal charges drawn up by the prosecuting attorney. A grand jury is a jury made up of citizens who must decide whether there is enough evidence to justify accusing a person of a crime. A grand jury conducts its hearings in private to determine whether someone must stand trial. If jurors decide a crime has been committed, they issue an indictment, or written accusation charging the individual. This does not mean that the named person is guilty but that the grand jury believes there is a possibility the person is guilty.

Following the indictment, the accused is brought to court for arraignment. **An arraignment is a formal hearing during which the defendant is read the indictment or information and is asked to plead guilty or not guilty.** The accused is informed of his or her rights. If the person pleads guilty, the judge may then impose the sentence. If the person pleads not guilty, the case goes on to trial. A defendant may also plead guilty pursuant to a plea agreement. This is an agreement between the government and the defendant. Trial can be difficult, so the government may offer to change the charges to a crime with a lesser sentence if the defendant will plead guilty without a trial.

The Trial

If the defendant requests a jury trial, the jury members must be selected. Otherwise, the case is tried before the judge, which rarely

Legal Talk

Disposition: *n* Final arrangement or settlement. From Latin *dis* = apart + *ponere* = to arrange.

Adjudicatory: *adj* Relates to a judge's decision or sentence. From Latin *adjudicare*, to judge.

Vocabulary Builder List and define two words that begin with the prefix *dis*.

happens in criminal trials. The actual trial is similar to a civil trial. The lawyers make opening statements. They introduce evidence. The trial ends with each lawyer's closing statement. The closing statements are followed by the judge's instructions to the jury.

In a criminal case with a jury, the verdict must be unanimous. When a jury cannot unanimously agree, it is called a hung jury and a mistrial is called. A new trial may be held at the option of the prosecution. If the verdict is not guilty, the defendant is released. If the defendant is guilty, the judge imposes a sentence in the form of a fine, imprisonment, or both. In a criminal matter, if the defendant is guilty, that means that beyond all reasonable doubt, the defendant is the person who did the crime. In addition, for every crime, there is an element of intent, which means the defendant must have intended to break the law. A person who is found not guilty cannot be tried twice for the same crime in the same court. This is the principle of double **jeopardy** which is defined in the Fifth Amendment of the U. S. Constitution.

Sentencing

After a person has been convicted of a crime, the court will sentence that individual. This means the judge decides the punishment. The law provides certain sentencing guidelines and penalties. The penalties could include fines, imprisonment, and even death.

Fines A fine is the payment of money as a penalty for committing a crime. Fines are levied against a defendant when the crime is minor. However, fines can also be attached to more serious penalties, such as imprisonment.

Imprisonment States deal with imprisonment in different ways. In some states, the judge may hand down an indefinite sentence. This means that the judge orders a minimum and maximum amount of time that the convicted criminal may spend in prison, such as five to ten years. Other states make the judge state the exact period of time a criminal will spend in prison. Some states have made mandatory sentences for certain crimes which cannot be changed for any reason.

The Death Penalty Our Constitution says death penalty laws must include guidelines to ensure fair treatment. The U.S. Supreme Court has held that a jury, not a judge, must now decide whether a defendant deserves the death penalty. The United States Supreme Court has ruled that criminal defendants under 18 years of age and those who are mentally incompetent cannot be sentenced to death.

Disposition of Juvenile Cases

Cases involving juvenile offenders are handled by the juvenile court. As a first step, the judge usually holds a detention hearing. **A detention hearing is a court session during which the judge tries to learn whether there are good reasons to keep the accused in custody.** The court's probation department or a child welfare agency investigates the minor's background and home life. The judge might dismiss the charges after hearing the results of the investigation.

Adjudicatory Hearings If the charges are not dismissed, the judge conducts an adjudicatory hearing. This is the informal hearing of the case by the court. The judge may question the young person and the parents, listen to witnesses, or seek advice from the probation officer. After a hearing, the judge may decide the outcome of the case in one of three ways.

- The judge may allow the offender to return home on probation for a period of time, under the supervision of a probation officer.
- The judge may place the offender in an agency or foster home. The natural parents will then be required to pay what they can toward the offender's support.
- The judge may commit the offender to a training or reform school.

The judge can also order the juvenile offender to pay for the damages with money, work, or both. The parents of the offender may have to repay the victim. Sentences for youthful offenders are set with rehabilitation in mind. They are generally limited to probation under court supervision, confinement for not more than three years in a reformative institution, or another course of action designed to help, rather than to punish.

After You Read

Summarize List differences and similarities between civil and criminal court procedures?

SECTION 1.2 ASSESSMENT

Self Check

1. What is the difference between a civil and a criminal case?

2. What is the role of the United States Supreme Court?

3. Under what conditions can a police officer search a person?

Academic Connection

Mathematics Create a table listing which of the 13 original colonies were represented in the 39 signatures to the U.S. Constitution. Calculate the percent that

figure represents of the total participants.

CONCEPT **Number and Operations: Using Fractions, Decimals, and Rounding.** To figure out the problem, take the number for each category and divide by the total. For example, 8 ÷ 39 = .205. Then change the decimal to a percent by moving the decimal to the right two spaces and adding a percent sign. Round numbers of 5 or more up and numbers less than 5 down. For example, .2045 rounds to 20.5% and .2044 rounds to 20.4%.

 For more math practice, go to the Math Appendix.

Critical Thinking

Search and Seizure
Suppose that the principal of your school has decided that all students will be searched when they enter the school building in the morning and when they leave in the afternoon. Write a legal argument that you could present to the principal when you ask him or her to reconsider the new search policy.

Chapter 1 Review and Assessment

Summary

Section 1.1 The Foundations of Law

◆ Ethical decisions can be made by applying the greatest good principle, or by following the Golden Rule.

◆ Four ethical character traits are: honesty, justice, compassion, and integrity.

◆ Ethics may be subjective. Laws provide an objective standard of behavior.

◆ The U.S. Constitution, which consists of seven articles and 27 amendments, enumerates the fundamental rights of citizens, names the functions of the three branches of government, and creates a system of checks and balances.

◆ Common law is a set of laws that provide rules for courts of justice. It is the basis of the U.S. legal system. Statutory law is the body of laws derived from statutes.

◆ Legislatures form regulatory agencies, which have a wide range of powers to create, enforce, and adjudicate rules and procedures.

Section 1.2 The Court System and Trial Procedures

◆ Jurisdiction is the power and authority given a court to hear a case and make a judgment.

◆ Federal courts are arranged in three levels: U.S. district courts, U.S. courts of appeals, and the Supreme Court of the United States.

◆ State court systems consist of local trial courts, courts of general jurisdiction, appellate, and supreme courts.

◆ Mediation, arbitration, conciliation, and negotiation are examples of reactive Alternate Dispute Resolution (ADR).

◆ In civil court, the plaintiff sues the defendant for a remedy. In a criminal proceeding, the district attorney prosecutes on behalf of the government.

◆ The steps in a civil trial are: jury selection, opening statements, evidence, closing arguments, instructions to the jury, the jury verdict, and the court's judgment.

Vocabulary Builder

1 On a sheet of paper, use each of these terms in a sentence.

Key Terms

- morality
- ethics
- justice
- law
- constitution

- common law
- statute
- administrative law
- jurisdiction
- appellate court

- alternative dispute resolution (ADR)
- arrest
- bail
- arraignment
- detention hearing

Academic Vocabulary

- empathy
- permissible

- prevalent
- informal

- mediator
- jeopardy

Key Points Review

Answer the following questions. Refer to the chapter for additional reinforcement.

2 What are the four ethical character traits?

3 What are the parts of the U.S. Constitution?

4 What is common law?

5 How do the courts make laws? What is the structure of the federal court system?

6 What is the common structure of most state court systems?

7 What are some alternative dispute resolution techniques?

8 What are the steps in a civil lawsuit?

9 What rights does a criminal defendant have?

10 What are the steps in a criminal prosecution?

Standardized Test Practice

11 Read this excerpt of Senate Document 105-14 entitled "How Our Laws Are Made" and complete questions 1 and 2.

"Laws may be initiated in either chamber of Congress, the House of Representatives or the Senate. For this example, we will track a bill introduced in the House of Representatives.

When a representative has an idea for a new law, s/he becomes the sponsor of that bill and introduces it by giving it to the clerk of the House or by placing it in a box, called the hopper. The clerk assigns a legislative number to the bill, with H.R. for bills introduced in the House of Representatives and S. for bills introduced in the Senate. The Government Printing Office (GPO) then prints the bill and distributes copies to each representative."

1. The first step for a new law is

Ⓐ Get a sponsor

Ⓑ Create an idea

Ⓒ Give it to the House

Ⓓ Call the hopper

2. Laws can be initiated through

Ⓐ House of Representatives or Senate

Ⓑ Government Printing Office or House of Representatives

Ⓒ House of Representatives or President

Ⓓ President, Senate, or House of Representatives

Test-Taking Strategies Make sure you read all the answer choices, identify choices that are obviously wrong, and choose from answers that remain.

Apply and Debate

Read the following scenarios. Get together with other students in pairs or groups of three and take a position on each scenario. Debate your position in class with students taking the opposite position or prepare a written argument justifying your position.

12 Lost Wallet

As you walked down the street you found a wallet full of money on the ground. You placed an ad in the lost and found section of the local paper. After a month of running the ad no one has responded to it.

> **You Debate** *Is it your ethical duty to find the rightful owner?*

13 Eyewitness

Alex witnessed a mugging on his way home but did not stop to get involved. Other witnesses saw Alex leaving the area. Later Alex saw on TV that the police were asking for witnesses to the mugging to come forward and give a statement.

> **You Debate** *Can the law force Alex to give a statement?*

14 Free Speech

Rini is running for student council and has placed flyers on all the cars and inside the campus buildings. The principal suspended her for doing this without permission. Rini argued she is entitled to free speech under the First Amendment.

> **You Debate** *Does free speech extend to flyers posted for a student election?*

15 Plea Bargaining

Roberto is an accountant charged with stealing company funds from Haven's Landscaping. The district attorney offered Roberto a deal of one year in prison if he would plead guilty to the crime. Roberto accepted the deal.

> **You Debate** *Should punishment for a crime be lessened in exchange for the defendant pleading guilty without the expense of a trial?*

16 Entrapment

Manik has always been an upstanding citizen. A man came in to Manik's used electronics store and offered to sell him flat-screen TVs at an extremely low price. Manik did not question the low sales price. When Manik paid the man for the goods, he discovered that the man was an undercover police officer, who charged Manik with purchasing stolen goods.

> **You Debate** *Can Manik argue that the charge was entrapment?*

S. Olsson/PhotoAlto

Case Study Practice– Papaila v. Uniden America Corp.

17 Who Has Juridiction? Theodore Papaila, an American employee of Uniden America Corporation (UAC), a subsidiary of a Japanese company, sued UAC for racial discrimination. He claimed UAC treated 16 Japanese employees differently by giving them higher base salaries, fringe benefits, and job protection. Two laws apply to this case. U.S. Code statute 42 U.S.C. §2000e-2(a)(1) reads: "(a) Employer practices: It shall be an unlawful employment practice for an employer to fail or refuse to hire or to discharge any individual, or otherwise to discriminate against any individual with respect to his compensation, terms, conditions, or privileges of employment, because of such individual's race, color, religion, sex, or national origin." The Friendship, Commerce, and Navigation Treaty and Protocol Between the United States and Japan, 4 U.S.T. 2063 reads: "Nationals and companies of either Party shall be permitted to engage, within the territories of the other Party, accountants and other technical experts, executive personnel, attorneys, agents and other specialists of their choice."

Source: Papaila v. Uniden America Corp., 51 F.3d 54 (5th Cir. 1995)

Practice Which law should apply to this case? What are the ethical implications?

18 Ethics
←?→ Application

Guilty by Silence? As you enter the classroom, you see another student named Jonathan copying down the answers to today's test from the teacher's desk.
◆ What would be the ethical decision to make regarding this situation?

19 Think back to the Legal Briefs feature you read at the beginning of the chapter. Ask yourself why some of these unusual laws are still on the books. At one time, each law was written for a reason. What do you think those reasons were? Write one or more paragraphs to answer these questions.

Criminal Law

Legal Briefs

Expungement of Criminal Records
Reducing the consequences of past indiscretions.

Should your past mistakes follow you forever? Some states have laws that allow for expungement, sealing, or annulment of criminal records under certain circumstances. Records can be physically destroyed or public access to them limited. These laws can be important when someone is applying for a job or buying a home.

Some states do not allow anything in a person's record to be expunged. Other states allow juvenile records to be sealed, or arrests that do not result in convictions to be erased. Those laws, however, affect only the records in the legal system.

Online news services and newspaper archives still have stories about a crime, arrest, trial, or conviction on file. That means that if a prospective employer performs a Google search on a job applicant, the information that the court sealed may still pop up.

News outlets can put code in their online stories that keep them from appearing in Google searches, but not all of them do this. It's more common in Europe, where people are deemed to have "a right to be forgotten."

Crime Scene The elements of a crime are the criminal act and the required state mind. *What is the state of mind required for murder?*

Crimes and Criminal Justice

What You'll Learn

- Explain the differences between categories of crime.
- Distinguish federal from state criminal law.
- Describe the elements of a crime.
- Determine several defenses to criminal acts.
- Explain the differences between penalties for committing felonies and misdemeanors.

Why It's Important

Knowing the elements of a crime and the defenses to crimes will help you if you are ever accused of a crime or the victim of a crime.

Reading Guide

Before You Read

Connect You have may seen trials on television and in movies. In real life, what does a prosecutor have to prove to convict someone of a crime?

Focus on Ideas

There are different categories of crimes based on their level of seriousness.

Take Notes

Go to **connectED.mcgraw-hill.com** to download a graphic organizer you can use to take notes as you read this section.

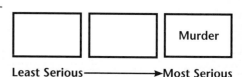

Least Serious ———————→ Most Serious

Classifications of Crimes

Key Terms

You will learn these legal words and expressions in this chapter. You can also find these terms in *Black's Law Dictionary* or in an online legal dictionary.

- crime
- defendant
- plaintiff
- prosecutor
- felony
- misdemeanor
- infraction

Academic Vocabulary

You will find these words in your readings and in your tests. Look them up in a dictionary and familiarize yourself with them.

- intent
- motive
- impulse

Classifications of Crimes

What types of crimes can you go to jail for?

A crime is an offense committed against the public good, or society. U.S. criminal law is very specific and the penalties for most criminal offenses are very serious. A person who is convicted of a crime can be fined, imprisoned, or sometimes even sentenced to death. The Constitution of the United States limits how the government can deal with people who have been accused of a crime to protect the innocent from unjust accusations or imprisonment.

A defendant is a person who is accused of a crime. The state or the federal government, representing the public, is the plaintiff. **A plaintiff is the party that accuses a person of a crime. The prosecutor is the government official who brings the case against the defendant.** In some states, the prosecutor is called a district attorney. The prosecutor represents the people, or the public, in a criminal case.

Felonies

A felony is a major crime. A person who commits a felony may be punished by a fine, or by imprisonment in a penitentiary, or both. Murder and robbery are examples of felonies. The most serious felony is murder. In some states, murder is punishable by death. Felonies may also be called high misdemeanors. People convicted of a felony may also be liable for a civil penalty awarded to the victim or the victim's family. For example, a rape victim may be able to sue the defendant to recover the costs of medical bills and counseling.

Misdemeanors

A misdemeanor is a less serious crime. A person who commits such a crime can also be punished by a fine, by jail time, or both. However, the maximum amount of time in jail is usually less than a year. Also, if a defendant gets jail time, it is usually served in a smaller, county jail, rather than in a state penitentiary. Driving an automobile without a license is an example of a misdemeanor.

Infractions

Both felonies and misdemeanors are punishable with imprisonment. **An infraction is a minor offense that is usually punishable with a fine and not with jail time.** Some states refer to these as minor misdemeanors, while others call them petty crimes. Minor traffic violations, such as speeding tickets, are considered infractions.

As You Read

Predict What is the difference between a serious crime and a petty crime?

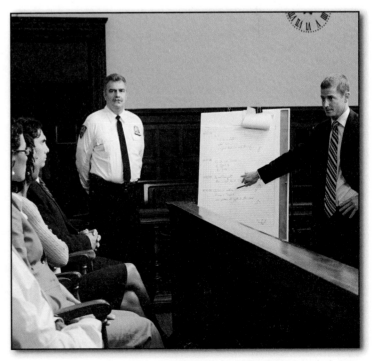

Criminal Cases Serious crimes are prosecuted in courts and rely on physical evidence and testimonies of witnesses and experts. *Is a misdemeanor a crime?*

© Ocean/Corbis

Criminal Law in the U.S. Legal System
Are all criminal law courts federal courts?

The American legal system is actually made up of two court systems: federal and state. The federal court system deals with laws on a national level. In addition, each state has its own court system. Both the federal and state courts have the power to make and enforce criminal laws. However, the powers of each are different.

Federal Criminal Law

The Constitution limits the powers of the federal government. For example, the federal government cannot make criminal laws. However, there are exceptions to this rule. For example, the federal government can make laws against counterfeiting money because money is printed by the federal government.

The federal government also has a police force. This police force is called the Federal Bureau of Investigation (FBI). The power to create this police force comes from a special clause in the Constitution known as the Commerce Clause. The Commerce Clause says that the U.S. Congress can regulate interstate commerce, or business that crosses state lines. This includes criminal activities that cross state lines. For this reason, federal criminal law usually involves commerce among the states.

State Criminal Law

Each state government has the built-in power to make criminal laws. That power is called the state's police power. Many states have criminal laws that are just like the criminal laws in other states. Still, the definitions and names of certain crimes are not exactly the same in every state. For example, a crime that is called theft in one state may be called stealing in another.

🔻 **Evidence** During the investigation of a crime, police collect as much evidence as possible. This evidence may be used in court to prove or disprove a defense to a crime. *What type of evidence might help prove self-defense?*

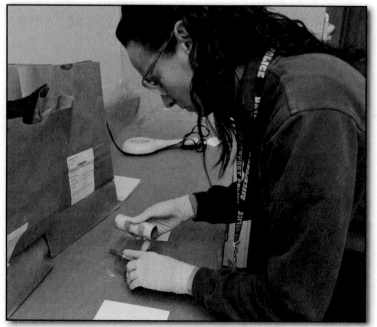

Elements of a Crime
Can you be convicted of a crime if the state cannot prove you had a motive?

A crime is made up of two elements. The first element is the criminal act. The second element is the required state of mind.

Criminal Act

Criminal laws must describe the specific conduct that the law forbids. For example, the definition of theft is stealing another person's property, while the definition of robbery is stealing another person's property through violence or the threat of violence. Some criminal laws make not doing something a crime. For example, not paying taxes that are owed is a crime.

Aaron Roeth Photography

Global Law

The International Criminal Court

The International Criminal Court (ICC) is an independent criminal court located in The Hague, Netherlands. It was created by treaty on July 1, 2002, 60 days after the final ratification of the treaty by 60 countries. The original treaty was signed by 120 countries, although only 60 had to ratify the treaty for it to go into effect. It is the first permanent, treaty-based international criminal court established to promote the international rule of law and ensure that the worst international crimes are prosecuted. It was created to be a complement to national criminal jurisdictions. The jurisdiction of the ICC is defined as follows:

1. The jurisdiction of the Court shall be limited to the most serious crimes of concern to the international community as a whole. The Court has jurisdiction in accordance with this Statute with respect to the following crimes:

   (a) The crime of genocide
   (b) Crimes against humanity
   (c) War crimes
   (d) The crime of aggression

Since its implementation on July 1, 2002, the ICC has taken three cases under consideration. Those three cases come from alleged violations in the Democratic Republic of Congo, the Republic of Uganda, and the Darfur region of Sudan. Five warrants for arrest have been issued in the Republic of Uganda case against commanders of a rebel group alleged to have committed numerous crimes against civilians in Uganda.

Across Cultures: Equality on the Court

The International Criminal Court is trying to be the first court founded on equality. Under the founding documents, the ICC must try to have an equal number of male and female judges and attorneys. Furthermore, there cannot be more than one judge from any country and each geographic region must be equally represented.

Critical Thinking *The United States has decided not to join the International Criminal Court, arguing that by joining the ICC the U.S. would allow its citizens to be prosecuted by an international organization that may not offer the same protections that the U.S. offers. Is this a good reason, or should the U.S. join the ICC?*

A criminal act must be voluntary; it cannot be a person's condition. For example, it is not a crime to be an alcoholic. This is because alcoholism is a condition, not an act. However, the government may create laws that make it a crime to operate a vehicle while under the influence of alcohol.

Required State of Mind

The second element of a crime is the required state of mind. The law defining murder forbids the intentional taking of a person's life. The required mental state is **intent**. The law defining involuntary manslaughter forbids the negligent taking of somebody's life. The required mental state is negligence. In both laws the criminal act is taking a person's life. In the law against murder, the mental state is intent, meaning the defendant must have intended to take another person's life. In the law against involuntary manslaughter, the mental state is negligence, meaning the defendant was negligent or careless, and because of this negligence, another person died.

Vocabulary You can find vocabulary definitions in the **Key Terms** glossary and Academic Vocabulary glossary in the back of this book.

Reading Check

Enumerate *Name the different people who play a role in a trial.*

Motive

In detective movies and television shows there is often a heavy emphasis on proving a defendant's **motive**. In reality, motive plays no part in proving that a person committed a crime. All that is needed is to prove that a defendant committed an act with the required state of mind. The motive does not matter. Motive only helps to explain why a defendant did what he or she did.

Defenses to Crimes

What are some reasons for pleading not guilty in a criminal case?

In any legal proceeding, civil or criminal, defendants have several possible defenses they may use to try and explain their actions. The main defenses for defendants in criminal cases, as shown in **Figure 2.1,** include insanity, entrapment, self-defense, and defense of family members.

Insanity

U.S. law says that people cannot be held responsible for their actions if they do not know what they are doing. This means that insanity can be a defense to criminal conduct.

The oldest legal test of insanity is called the M'Naghten Rule. This rule goes back to an 1843 English case. A man named Daniel M'Naghten was acquitted of killing the Prime Minister's secretary

Figure 2.1 Defenses to Crimes

An **insanity** defense requires that the person did not know the difference between right and wrong when he or she committed the crime.

Entrapment is when a law enforcement official tricks someone into committing a crime he or she would otherwise not have committed.

In a criminal case, the defense tries to show that the prosecution failed to prove the required elements of the crime. *What element of a crime does the insanity defense seek to eliminate?*

because he was insane and did not know what he was doing. Under this rule, a defendant must have a mental disease so serious that he or she does not know the difference between right and wrong when he or she commits the crime.

Another test used by some states is the irresistible **impulse** test. Under this rule, the defendant must have a mental disease that makes telling the difference between right and wrong impossible or makes the defendant unable to stop him- or herself from committing the crime.

The American Law Institute (ALI) has a more modern test for insanity. Under the ALI rule, the defendant must have a mental disease so serious that he or she lacks substantial capacity either to appreciate the criminality of his or her conduct or to conform his or her conduct to the requirements of law.

People who are found not guilty by reason of insanity do not go free. They must go to a mental institution to receive psychiatric treatment. These people are released only when they are found to be sane.

Entrapment

If a police officer talks a person into committing a crime, the person may have a defense. This defense is called entrapment. Entrapment means that a person was talked into or tricked by a police officer into committing a crime he or she would not otherwise have committed.

People can claim **self-defense** when they believe they were in imminent danger and had no choice but to use force to protect themselves.

With **defense of family members**, a person can use force to protect family members who are in danger of being hurt or killed.

Self-Defense

There are situations when people believe they are in danger of being hurt or killed. In such cases, they may use force to protect themselves. This is known as self-defense. In some states, the person using self-defense must try to run away first. Running away is not necessary if the person is in his or her own home. People cannot use self-defense in court if they started the confrontation or if they continued to use force even after the danger was gone.

Defense of Family Members

Sometimes, someone believes a family member is in danger of being hurt or killed. In such cases, the person may use force to protect the family member. This defense is called defense of family members. As in the case of self-defense, the rescuer must have a good reason to believe the victim was in danger of severe bodily injury or death.

People cannot use this defense if the crime occurs after the threat of harm has passed. For example, a parent cannot go after someone who hurt his or her child if that person has left the area and is no longer capable of hurting the child.

After You Read

Summarize Name and define the four main defenses to a crime.

SECTION 2.1 ASSESSMENT

Self Check

1. Where did the federal government get the power to create the Federal Bureau of Investigation (FBI)?

2. What is the oldest insanity test used in the United States and what does that test say?

3. What does the defense of entrapment involve?

Academic Connection

Social Studies The law of the land in the United States is based on the Constitution, which gave the federal government certain powers, and the Bill of Rights (passed in 1791), which amended the Constitution to protect the rights of individuals. How does the federal government keep up with changing values in American society? Give a couple of examples.

English Language Arts Amendments to the Constitution have to be carefully worded to address a specific right and to avoid misinterpretation. Write a 28th Amendment to the Constitution guaranteeing a specific right you think everyone should have.

Critical Thinking

When Does Self-Defense Become a Crime? Sam and Wade are walking home after school when they are attacked by two gang members. Sam and Wade overpower their attackers. Sam knocks his attacker to the ground and sits on him until the police arrive, but Wade keeps hitting his attacker in the head even after he is lying on the ground unconscious. Can Sam claim self-defense? Can Wade? Explain.

Types of Crimes

Reading Guide

Before You Read

Connect Crimes can affect both people and property. Can you name crimes that directly involve people as victims?

Focus on Ideas

Every criminal law must use specific language to describe the conduct that is forbidden by that law.

Take Notes

Go to connectED.mcgraw-hill.com to download a graphic organizer you can use to take notes as you read this section.

Key Terms

You will learn these legal words and expressions in this chapter. You can also find these terms in *Black's Law Dictionary* or in an online legal dictionary.

- murder
- manslaughter
- battery
- assault
- burglary
- larceny
- robbery
- vandalism

Academic Vocabulary

You will find these words in your readings and in your tests. Look them up in a dictionary and familiarize yourself with them.

- domestic
- malicious
- contempt

What You'll Learn

- ◆ Describe the different categories of crime.
- ◆ Identify several special crimes that involve the use of motor vehicles.
- ◆ Define different types of business crimes, such as arson, forgery, and embezzlement.

Why It's Important

Knowing how to distinguish among various crimes will help you understand criminal liability.

Crimes against People

What could you be charged with if you killed someone by accident?

Crimes can be categorized into crimes against people, property, business, government, society, and crimes involving motor vehicles. Common crimes against people include murder, manslaughter, assault, battery, kidnapping, and domestic violence.

Murder

Murder is the intentional killing of another person. First-degree murder involves one or more of the following circumstances: killing after making a detailed plan to kill; killing in an especially vicious way, such as by torture; and killing while committing another serious crime. If none of these conditions apply, the crime may be second-degree murder. The distinction between first-degree murder and second-degree murder is important because a person convicted of first-degree murder can receive the death penalty in some states.

Manslaughter

Manslaughter is killing another person without intending to do so. Manslaughter is either voluntary or involuntary. Voluntary manslaughter happens when someone kills a person while in a state of great distress and without a prior plan to kill. Involuntary manslaughter occurs when someone kills another person accidentally while committing an unlawful or reckless act.

Assault and Battery

Battery is the unlawful touching of another person. It involves the forceful use, however slight, of a person's hand, a weapon, or other instrument against another person. Battery

As You Read

Predict Name one or more categories of crimes.

Case Study – Deck v. Missouri

Critical Thinking *Do you believe the jury was negatively influenced? Why or why not?*

Flex Your Reading Note key facts in the text below and look up words you do not understand. Restate difficult ideas in your own words. Go back and reread the text quickly to make sure you did not miss any important detail. Now, you are ready to formulate an opinion.

A Bad Impression When Carman Deck appeared before the jury to be sentenced after a murder conviction, he was in chains and shackles. The jury sentenced him to death. Deck later appealed his sentenced arguing that the chains and shackles had negatively influenced the jury.

Deck v. Missouri, 544 U.S. 622

Go to **ConnectEd.mcgraw-hill.com** for more case study practice.

may be committed by ordering a dog to attack a person or even kissing someone who does not want to be kissed. **An assault is an attempt to commit a battery.** Waving a baseball bat at someone is assault. Hitting the person with the baseball bat is battery. Simple assault and battery are misdemeanors. Aggravated assault and battery are felonies. To be aggravated, the crime must be committed with a deadly weapon, or with the intent to commit murder, rape, or robbery.

Kidnapping

Kidnapping is the unlawful removal or restraint of a person against his or her will. Most state laws distinguish between simple kidnapping and more serious offenses, such as child stealing and kidnapping for ransom.

Sex Offenses

The crime of rape involves one person forcing another to have sexual intercourse. The law applies to both men and women. Statutory rape involves having sexual intercourse with a minor, with or without force. A minor can be prosecuted for having sex with another minor. Sexual assault by a friend or a date is a sexual offense, called date rape or acquaintance rape.

Domestic Violence

Any reckless form of physical or mental harm in a family or household is **domestic** violence. Domestic violence laws protect children, spouses, and other family members from neglect, mental abuse, or physical abuse by another member of the family or household. Children are protected by child endangerment and child abuse laws. Abused spouses may request a court order to stop an abusing spouse from coming near them.

Traffic Laws Young drivers do not get any special treatment when they violate traffic laws. *Can you get a ticket if you did not know you were driving past curfew hours?*

Vocabulary You can find vocabulary definitions in the **Key Terms** glossary and **Academic Vocabulary** glossary in the back of this book.

Crimes against Property

If someone breaks into a house and takes $2,000 worth of computer equipment, which crime was committed?

The most common crimes against property include burglary, robbery, arson, larceny, and vandalism. Crimes against property can be felonies or misdemeanors.

Vandalism To be guilty of vandalism you do not have to be the person who actually did the damage. *Is graffiti considered a form of vandalism?*

Burglary

Burglary, under common law, is breaking and entering into a house at night to commit a felony. State laws have expanded the definition of burglary to include daytime breaking and entering, breaking and entering places other than homes, and breaking and entering to commit a misdemeanor. If any part of the definition of burglary cannot be proven, the defendant cannot be found guilty.

Larceny

Larceny is the unlawful taking of someone's personal property with the intent to keep the property away from that person. In some states, larceny is called theft. Petty larceny, a misdemeanor, is stealing property of a small monetary value. The individual states usually set that value between $300 and $1,000. Grand larceny, a felony, is stealing property valued at more than a state's limit for petty larceny.

Robbery

Robbery is the wrongful taking of someone's property by threatening violence or using violence. The penalty for robbery is greater than the penalty for larceny.

Vandalism

Vandalism is willful or malicious damage to property. It is also called **malicious** mischief or criminal damage. To be guilty of vandalism, a person does not have to be the one who actually does the damage. Anyone who supports vandalism by being a lookout, for example, can also be charged.

Crimes Involving Business

Could you be charged with shoplifting before you actually leave a store with unpaid merchandise?

Crimes involving business are also called white collar crimes. Business crimes include embezzlement, shoplifting, fraud, money laundering, arson, and forgery.

Embezzlement

Embezzlement is the wrongful taking of property by someone lawfully entrusted with possession and control of that property. Embezzlement is often committed by an agent or employee of a business who has the power to write checks and to withdraw funds from the firm's bank accounts.

Reading Check

Explain *What is the difference between murder and manslaughter, and what is the difference between robbery and burglary?*

Dave Mover

Shoplifting

Shoplifting is stealing goods from a store. Shoplifting costs American consumers billions of dollars each year because prices of goods are raised to make up the loss. In some cases, people may be charged with shoplifting just for hiding merchandise in their pants or stuffing them under a baggy sweatshirt, even before they leave the store.

Fraud

Fraud is when a person or a business engages in some form of deception to obtain money or property. Fraud undermines the very foundation of the business world. Some types of fraud are federal offenses. Using the United States Postal Service to commit fraud is referred to as mail fraud. Using the telephone or other forms of electronic communication, such as the Internet, to commit fraud is called wire fraud.

Money Laundering

When criminals obtain large amounts of money illegally, they need to hide the money. They often do this by putting the money into legal businesses to launder it, as one would clean laundry to remove the dirt. The federal government has passed laws to prosecute any persons involved in money laundering even if they did not steal the money themselves.

Arson

Sometimes, business owners who find themselves on the verge of bankruptcy will destroy their own property to collect the insurance on it. They commit arson. Under common law rules, arson is defined as the willful and malicious burning of someone else's house. Today, most states define arson as the burning of any building.

Forgery

Forgery is placing a false signature on a check or other document with the intent to deceive someone in order to deprive that person of his or her property. It is a felony subject to a fine and imprisonment. Forgery does not require that the property actually change hands. Once the false signature is placed on the check, the signer has committed forgery.

Crimes against the Government

Is it a crime if you ignore an order to appear in court?

Crimes that involve direct offenses against the government itself include treason, perjury, obstruction of justice, contempt of court, and bribery.

Treason

Treason is defined in Article III, Section 3 of the United States Constitution as waging war against the United States, or giving aid and comfort to the enemies of the United States. Treason is the only crime that is mentioned by name in the U.S. Constitution.

Legal Talk

Embezzlement: *n* The crime of fraudulently appropriating money or property for one's own use. From Anglo-French *embesiller* = to make away with.

Allegedly: *adv* From Middle English *allegen* = to submit as justification; to assert without proof.

Vocabulary Builder The suffix *-ment* comes from the Latin root *-mentum*, and means the result of an action. List three words that end with *-ment* and define them.

Commonwealth v. Jaynes
65 Va. Cir. 355 (2004)

Jeremy Jaynes was charged by the Commonwealth of Virginia with violating a Virginia law governing the transmission of unsolicited bulk e-mail (spam). In a period of three days, Mr. Jaynes allegedly sent millions of spam e-mails to America Online (AOL) addresses using false or forged e-mail transmission or routing information. Mr. Jaynes had used fake e-mail addresses and falsified the transmission information, making it appear that the e-mails had originated in the country of Belize, not the United States.

Ruling and Resolution
Mr. Jaynes argued that the law disallowing him from sending spam e-mail was unconstitutional because it violated his right to free speech under the First Amendment of the U.S. Constitution. The Virginia court held, though, that the law prohibited e-mails using false or forged information, but did not prohibit people from sending bulk e-mails using a valid e-mail address from a valid computer.

Critical Thinking Do you think Mr. Jaynes has a right to send his e-mails to anyone from any e-mail address? If not, what do you think Mr. Jaynes's penalty should be?

Perjury, Obstruction of Justice, and Contempt of Court

Perjury, obstruction of justice, and **contempt** of court all involve offenses that undermine the administration of the courts. Perjury occurs when a person lies under oath during a court process or an administrative procedure. Generally, the lie must involve a fact that is material to the proceeding.

Obstruction of justice occurs when an individual does something that hinders the ability of the court to move forward in a judicial proceeding. It might involve suppressing evidence or shielding someone from arrest. Contempt of court occurs when an individual ignores a court order or shows a lack of proper respect for the integrity of the court.

Bribery

Bribery is giving money or property to a public official in exchange for a favor from that official. Both the person offering the bribe and the public official accepting the bribe are guilty of bribery. For instance, if a company executive offers a bribe to the chairperson of a government planning board in exchange for a vote approving his or her company's bid, that executive is guilty of paying a bribe. If the chairperson actually takes the bribe, he or she is guilty of accepting a bribe.

It is against the law to pay a bribe, to offer a bribe, or to accept a bribe. It is also against the law to ask for a bribe when none has been offered. This crime is called bribery solicitation.

Crimes Against Society

Can you be prosecuted for using racist language?

All criminal law statutes involve offenses against society. Some deserve special attention because they prohibit behavior that endangers the public peace.

Disorderly Conduct and Rioting

Disorderly conduct is an activity that threatens to disrupt the social order, to imperil public safety, or to jeopardize the health of the public at large. Rioting is an activity that generally requires a gathering of at least three individuals who threaten to harm people or to damage property, or who violently commit one or the other of those offenses.

Motor Vehicle Violations

Do you have a right to a driver's license?

A license to drive a motor vehicle is a privilege, not a right. If drivers abuse that privilege, they may lose it. All drivers who ignore traffic laws are treated the same. Young drivers do not get a break when they speed, drive recklessly, or run red lights. They may be tried in traffic court and they can be fined. They can also have their licenses suspended or taken away permanently. Many states outlaw drag racing and joyriding. Drag racing is racing two vehicles side by side or timing vehicles that separately run a prearranged course. Joyriding is taking a vehicle without the owner's permission. In both cases, everybody who joins in is liable.

After You Read

Summarize Give two examples of crimes in each category.

SECTION 2.2 ASSESSMENT

Self Check

1. What is the only crime specifically named in the U.S. Constitution?
2. What are the different ways an anti-bribery statute can be violated?
3. What are white collar crimes?

Academic Connection

Mathematics In the United States, there was an estimated 56,146 felony cases filed in the state courts of the 75 largest counties during May 2002. About a fourth of these felony defendants were charged with a violent offense, usually assault (12.7%) or robbery (5.4%). Those charged with murder (0.8%) or rape (1.8%) accounted for a small percentage of defendants overall. About three-fourths of defendants were charged with a nonviolent felony. The most frequently charged nonviolent offenses were drug trafficking (17.1%), other drug offenses (18.6%), theft (8.8%), and burglary (8.1%). Create a table showing this information in numerical versus percent form.

 For more math practice, go to the Math Appendix.

CONCEPT **Number and Operations: Using Fractions, Decimals, and Rounding.** Figure out the total number for each percent given. For example: $56{,}146 \times .127$ (12.7%) $= 7{,}130.5$ assaults. Remember to round numbers of 5 or more up and numbers less than 5 down. For example, .542 rounds to .5.

Chapter **2** Review and Assessment

Summary

Section **2.1** Crimes and Criminal Justice

◆ A crime is an act against the public good. Crimes are divided into felonies or misdemeanors. A felony is a major crime punishable by imprisonment or death. A less serious crime is called a misdemeanor.

◆ An infraction is a minor offense punishable by a fine.

◆ Both federal and state courts can make and enforce criminal laws.

◆ A crime is defined by two elements: the criminal act and the required state of mind.

◆ Criminal defendants can use the following defenses: insanity, entrapment, self-defense, and defense of family members.

Section **2.2** Types of Crimes

◆ Crimes against people include murder, manslaughter, assault, battery, kidnapping, sex offenses, and domestic violence.

◆ Crimes against property include burglary, larceny, embezzlement, robbery, arson, vandalism, and shoplifting.

◆ Business crimes include embezzlement, shoplifting, fraud, money laundering, arson, and forgery.

◆ Crimes against the government include treason, perjury, obstruction of justice, contempt of court, and bribery.

◆ Crimes against society include statutes that involve disorderly conduct, and statutes that prohibit rioting.

Vocabulary Builder

1 On a sheet of paper, use each of these terms in a sentence.

Key Terms

- crime
- defendant
- plaintiff
- prosecutor
- felony

- misdemeanor
- infraction
- murder
- manslaughter
- battery

- assault
- burglary
- larceny
- robbery
- vandalism

Academic Vocabulary

- intent
- motive

- impulse
- domestic

- malicious
- contempt

Key Points Review

Answer the following questions. Refer to the chapter for additional reinforcement.

2 What are the differences between a felony and a misdemeanor?

3 What are the elements of a crime?

4 What are the defenses to a crime?

5 What are the major crimes that can be committed against people?

6 What are the major crimes that can be committed against property?

7 What crimes can be committed directly against the government?

8 What crimes can be committed against society?

9 What are two crimes that involve the use of motor vehicles?

Standardized Test Practice

10 Read the following information provided by the Department of Motor Vehicles (DMV) and complete questions 1 and 2.

All states offer courses in defensive driving through the DMV. Passing a defensive driving course can often reduce the cost of your auto insurance. However, the key reason to take defensive driving should be to improve your driving skills. Some basic concepts of defensive driving include the following guidelines. Slow down, especially during inclement weather conditions or at night. Do not follow too closely. Concentrate on your driving at all times. Never drive if you are impaired by lack of sleep or are under the influence. Check your mirrors frequently. Assume that drivers will run through stop signs or red lights at intersections and be prepared to react. Keep a watchful eye on pedestrians and pets along the roadside. Incorporating these defensive driving tips into your everyday driving technique will help you become a better driver.

1. Defensive driving teaches drivers that

Ⓐ pedestrians do not walk on the sidewalk

Ⓑ they should assume some drivers may run a stop sign

Ⓒ accidents are caused by following too closely

Ⓓ there are more accidents when it rains

2. What are three of the recommendations given for defensive driving?

Ⓐ Do not follow closely, keep pets in a carrier, and be prepared to react.

Ⓑ Slow down, watch for pedestrians, and watch for intersections.

Ⓒ Concentrate, check mirrors frequently, and watch for pedestrians.

Ⓓ Slow down, keep radio volume low, and watch for pets.

 Test-Taking Strategies
If you are preparing for a multiple-choice test, find out whether points are deducted for each wrong answer.

Apply and Debate

⑪ Self-Defense

While cooking dinner, Jack and Rick got into a fight over Jack's girlfriend. Rick picked up a vase to hit Jack, so Jack grabbed a knife from the counter and stabbed Rick.

You Debate *Can Jack's actions be considered self-defense?*

⑫ Felony or Misdemeanor

Isabel intended to burn her house down when she set fire to it. As the house started to burn, however, she changed her mind and used a hose to put it out. Isabel is arrested and charged with arson.

You Debate *Should Isabel's crime be classified as a felony or a misdemeanor since she changed her mind and did less than $500 damage to her property?*

⑬ Burglary

Yolanda went over to a friend's house to visit. When she arrived, her friend was not home, but had left the door unlocked. Yolanda went inside the house and took a laptop before returning home.

You Debate *Should this be considered burglary since the house was left unlocked?*

⑭ Double Jeopardy

Lois was charged with embezzling money from her employer. She was tried in court before a jury who found her innocent of the crime. After the trial, the police found additional evidence clearly showing Lois was guilty of the crime.

You Debate *Since Lois cannot be charged with embezzlement again, can she be charged with stealing?*

⑮ Mischief or Vandalism

On Halloween night, John and several friends decided to pull some pranks at their school and damaged some of the classrooms. The next morning, school security officers reviewed the security videotapes to see who had done the damage. They arrested the students for vandalism.

You Debate *Since John and his friends are under the age of 18, was their Halloween behavior mischief?*

S. Olsson/PhotoAlto

Case Study Practice – State v. Ham

16 Who Has Valid Consent? Andrew Ham was 19 and lived with his mother in a two-bedroom apartment. In February, Andrew entered into an informal agreement with his mother to pay rent for his bedroom, which he shared with a younger brother. He paid the rent for February and March, but failed to pay rent in April. Since he did not pay the rent, Mrs. Ham told Andrew that he would have to move out. Prior to moving out, the police began to investigate Andrew in connection with a burglary. The police went to the Hams' apartment and asked Mrs. Ham whether they could search Andrew's bedroom, even though the police did not have a warrant to perform the search. Mrs. Ham consented. While searching the bedroom, the police found the stolen property in Andrew's closet.

Source: State v. Ham, 744 P.2d 133 (Id. Ct. App. 1987)

Practice Can Andrew's mother provide consent to the police to search Andrew's room? Does it make a difference whether Andrew paid rent to his mother?

17 Ethics
←?→ Application _____

Responsible Party You have been invited to a Friday night party with a group of your friends. Your family says it is okay for you to go as long as there is adult supervision and no underage drinking. When you arrive, you see that there are no adults present and a lot of the partygoers are drinking alcohol.

◆ Do you call your family to let them know what is happening at the party?

18 Think back to the Legal Briefs feature you read at the beginning of the chapter. Then ponder this scenario and write one or more paragraphs to answer these questions: A young woman is arrested for misdemeanor possession of marijuana. The charges are dropped when she attends a drug abuse education course. Years later, when she applies for a job as a teacher, the event resurfaces. Should the records have been available? Should they make a difference in her employment? What if she were applying to be a sales clerk?

Tort Law

Legal Briefs

Agreeing to Online Terms of Use

Understand your rights to arbitration.

Always read the fine print in a contract, so you don't give away an important right—that of filing a lawsuit. This is especially important online.

Many companies' websites include in their Terms of Use (TOU) a policy called "forced arbitration." If a customer has a problem with the company, both sides must go to arbitration instead of suing in a civil court.

What's so bad about that?

- The company can specify where the arbitration will be held, including in another state or country. You get hit with the cost of filing and travel.
- You lose your right to sue in a court of law or to bring a class action suit.

When you click the "I Agree" box—or sometimes merely visit a website—you may agree to forced arbitration. Some companies allow you to opt out, but most don't. If you opt out, you can still choose arbitration, if you wish, or file a lawsuit. It will be up to you.

As always, the best advice is to read before you sign—or click.

Intentional or Unintentional If you cause damage or injury through carelessness rather than deliberately, you have committed an unintentional tort. *What is another term for unintentional tort?*

Definition of a Tort

What You'll Learn

- ◆ Distinguish between a tort and a crime.
- ◆ Differentiate between and give examples of negligence and intentional torts.
- ◆ Explain a person's rights and duties in relation to tort law.
- ◆ Describe remedies available in tort law.
- ◆ List the main intentional torts against people and property.

Why It's Important

Knowing the difference between a tort and a crime will help you understand what your legal options are if you ever feel you have been victimized.

Reading Guide

Before You Read

Connect Has anyone ever intentionally embarrassed you, scared you, or victimized you? Did you think that there was any legal action you could take?

Focus on Ideas

A tort is not a crime against society. A tort is a wrong one person commits against another person.

Take Notes

Go to connectED. mcgraw-hill.com to download a graphic organizer you can use to take notes as you read this section.

```
                        ┌─────────────────────┐
                        │  Intentional Torts  │
                        └──────────┬──────────┘
              ┌────────────────────┴────────────────────┐
    ┌──────────────────┐                      ┌──────────────────┐
    │  Against Persons │                      │ Against Property │
    └──────────────────┘                      └──────────────────┘
    ┌──────────────────┐                      ┌──────────────────┐
    │     Assault      │                      │                  │
    │  ──────────────  │                      │  ──────────────  │
    │  ──────────────  │                      │  ──────────────  │
    │  ──────────────  │                      │  ──────────────  │
    │  ──────────────  │                      │  ──────────────  │
    │  ──────────────  │                      │  ──────────────  │
    └──────────────────┘                      └──────────────────┘
```

Key Terms

You will learn these legal words and expressions in this chapter. You can also find these terms in *Black's Law Dictionary* or in an online legal dictionary.

- tort
- tortfeasor
- intentional tort

Academic Vocabulary

You will find these words in your readings and in your tests. Look them up in a dictionary and familiarize yourself with them.

- compensate
- confidential
- distress

The Nature of Tort Law

If someone assaults you, is it a crime against you or against society?

Tort law is based on the idea that everyone in our society has certain rights. For example, the right to walk around freely without being falsely arrested, the right to privacy, or the right to one's good name and reputation. Along with having certain rights, everyone has the duty to respect the rights of others. The purpose of tort law is to enforce those rights and duties.

As You Read

Predict Name actions that can violate someone's rights.

What Is a Tort?

In law, **a tort is a private wrong committed by one person against another. A tortfeasor is a person who commits a tort.** A person who commits a tort interferes with another person's rights. There are three elements to any tort: (1) the possession of certain rights by an innocent party; (2) a violation of those rights by the tortfeasor; and (3) a resulting injury that somehow hurts the person whose rights were violated. The person injured is usually called the victim, the innocent party, or the plaintiff in a lawsuit. The tortfeasor is the defendant in a lawsuit.

Global Law

Tort Law in Mexico

Tort law in Mexico differs quite a bit from U.S. tort law. In the United States, if someone is injured in an accident, it is not uncommon for the victim to sue the person who caused the accident. In Mexico, however, such a procedure is less likely to occur.

Mexican culture, not the law, holds that a person who causes an accident should help pay for any costs incurred by the victim, including medical expenses and expenses to replace damaged property. The Mexican Federal Labor Act provides the calculation of lost wages so that the victim can be compensated for those as well. Mexican law does not provide for the recovery of punitive damages or compensation for pain and suffering. Although Mexican culture provides for the non-litigious resolution of most tort claims, there are two pieces of legislation that provide for tort claims in court.

Mexican Tort Legislation

1 The Mexican Civil Code

The Civil Code provides for tort claims arising out of contractual liability between two parties. It further has a section that covers objective liability, which is similar to strict liability in the United States.

2 The Mexican Federal Labor Act

The Federal Labor Act was passed by the Mexican Legislature in part to cover personal injury cases arising from accidents that occur while on the job.

Across Cultures: Historic Legal System

When Spain conquered Mexico in the 1500s, the Spanish found that the indigenous peoples had created a legal system that was so effective the Spanish maintained it for more than 300 years. When Mexico gained its independence, it created a new system.

Critical Thinking: *Should the Mexican Legislature change its laws to allow punitive damages or compensation for pain and suffering?*

The Difference between Criminal Law and Tort Law

Torts are different from crimes. A crime is a wrong committed against the public good. A tort is a wrong committed against a particular person or property. A tort is considered a civil or private wrong rather than a criminal wrong. However, sometimes a tort is also a crime. For example, an assault is both a tort and a crime because it not only hurts an individual, but poses a threat to all members of society. Slander is a tort but not a crime because it hurts only an individual and does not threaten society in general.

Penalties in Criminal Law The purpose of criminal law is to protect society from criminal offenders by punishing them. The penalties for most criminal offenses are very serious.

Remedies in Tort Law The purpose of tort law is to compensate the victim for injuries caused by the tortfeasor. Remedies in tort law usually consist of the court making the tortfeasor pay a fair amount of money—called damages—to the injured party. Damages can be awarded for pain and suffering, to pay medical expenses, to replace (or repair) damaged property, or to pay for lost wages. The court might also award punitive damages to punish a tortfeasor for especially serious acts.

Intentional Torts against Persons

Can you sue someone for telling lies about you?

Intentional torts are actions that deliberately hurt, embarrass, or scare people. Some intentional torts are much more serious than others. The most common intentional torts against people are assault, battery, false imprisonment, defamation, invasion of privacy, and the intentional infliction of emotional distress (see **Figure 3.1**).

Assault and Battery

Assault and battery are two separate torts. They can be committed together or by themselves. A person commits an assault by threatening to harm an innocent person. For example, if someone pulls a knife on you, you have been assaulted even if you manage to escape. The assault occurs as soon as you are afraid of immediate harm to your body.

Battery involves the unlawful, unwanted touching of another person. A battery is committed even if the physical contact is not harmful. Battery can also be touching something closely associated with a person's body, such as a backpack or cap, that causes harm. For example, if you pull the chair out from under someone before the person sits down, you have committed a battery.

False Imprisonment

People have a right to move around freely. If somebody interferes with this right, then that person has committed false imprisonment. For example, security guards in a store must have

Vocabulary You can find vocabulary definitions in the **Key Terms** glossary and Academic Vocabulary glossary in the back of this book.

Reading Check

Connect *What are two examples of intentional torts?*

Figure 3.1 Intentional Torts against Persons

Assault and Battery An assault occurs as soon as a person is afraid of immediate harm, even if the person is not physically touched. Battery is the unlawful touching of another person, even if the physical contact does not cause injury.

Prying into Other People's Lives Invasion of privacy is interfering with a person's right to be left alone and to be free from unwanted publicity. This includes using a person's name or likeness without the person's permission.

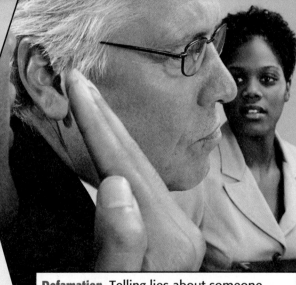

The Right to Move about Freely To detain someone without reasonable cause is called false imprisonment.

Defamation Telling lies about someone damages that person's reputation. Libel includes lies that are printed or broadcast.

A person who commits a tort interferes with another person's rights and can be sued for damages by that person. This figure shows four main types of torts.
What is a fifth main tort and what does it require?

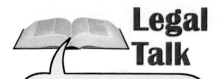

reasonable grounds to suspect shoplifting before they stop a customer. They must also hold the person in a reasonable way and only for a reasonable time.

Defamation

Defamation occurs when somebody lies about another person in a way that hurts the innocent person's reputation. There are two types of defamation: libel and slander.

Libel consists of lies about a person in written, printed, or recorded form, including television shows, magazine stories, Web sites, and e-mails. Slander consists of verbal or spoken lies that damage a person's reputation.

Movie stars, famous athletes, and politicians have a hard time winning libel suits because the Supreme Court ruled that public figures must prove that lies about them are told with actual malice. Actual malice means that the person who published the lie knew it was a lie and published it anyway. Actual malice could also mean that the person who published the lie thought it was true but did a poor job checking out the facts.

Invasion of Privacy

Invasion of privacy is interfering with a person's right to be left alone. This includes the right to be free from unwanted publicity. It also means that people must stay out of your private matters.

People who use **confidential** records in their jobs, such as doctors, nurses, lawyers, teachers, and counselors, have to be extremely careful with those records. A nurse may talk to another nurse about a patient if both nurses are taking care of that patient. The same nurse, however, cannot let outsiders see the patient's records or talk about them to outside people. It is also an invasion of privacy for somebody to use your photograph, likeness, or name without your permission for advertising, publicity, or marketing purposes.

Intentional Infliction of Emotional Distress

Someone can cause great emotional or mental **distress** to another person, even if there is no intent to cause physical harm. For example, one person might falsely convince another person that a close family member has died. In the past, the victim had no recourse to remedy. Today, you can sue for intentional infliction of emotional distress. The distress, however, must be caused by extreme and outrageous conduct.

Intentional Torts Against Property

Can you sue someone for borrowing something and not returning it?

Some intentional torts are actions that affect property. The most common intentional torts against property are trespass, conversion, nuisance, and disparagement.

Trespass

A trespass is interfering with somebody's real property. Real property is land. It also includes things built on the land, such as a storage shed, and things that are attached to the land permanently, such as a house or a tree. It can even include whatever might be under the property, such as minerals and oil.

Conversion

Conversion is interfering with a person's right to personal property. Suppose you lend a friend your cell phone. If your friend never returns it, your friend has converted your property to his or her own and interfered with your right of ownership.

Nuisance

Nuisance is anything that interferes with the enjoyment of property. Loud music at night, foul odors, or fumes coming from a nearby house are nuisances. If a nuisance affects only one person or household, it is a private nuisance. If it affects a lot of people, such as an entire neighborhood, it is a public nuisance.

Disparagement

Disparagement consists of lies about objects. The lies can be about quality or ownership. For example, if you try to sell your used car, which is in excellent condition, to a friend and someone claims your car is defective, that person has committed disparagement. In court, you must prove that you actually lost money as a result of the lie.

After You Read

Summarize List the main differences between crimes and torts.

SECTION 3.1 ASSESSMENT

Self Check

1. Is it possible for a wrongful act to be both a crime and a tort? Explain.

2. What is the definition of an intentional tort? Give an example.

3. What are the three elements of any tort?

Academic Connection

Social Studies The National Highway Traffic Safety Administration (NHTSA), under the U.S. Department of Transportation, was established by the Highway Safety Act of 1970 to carry out safety programs under the National Traffic and Motor Vehicle Safety Act of 1966 and the Highway Safety Act of 1966. Why do you think this agency was formed?

English Language Arts Go to connectED.mcgraw-hill.com and visit the NHTSA Web site to read what programs and benefits are available to consumers. Prepare an informational flyer to share with your class on the information you discover.

Critical Thinking

The Actual Malice Test Suppose you wrote an article for the school newspaper accusing the mayor of your town of corruption. The accusation turns out to be totally false. Can the mayor sue you, and possibly your school, for defamation? If so, will the suit be based on slander or libel? Will the actual malice test be applied by the court? Why or why not?

What You'll Learn

- Define negligence.
- Explain the concepts of the reasonable person test and proximate cause.
- Explain the concept of strict liability.
- Compare and contrast negligence, strict liability, and proximate cause.

Why It's Important

Understanding what negligence is will help you if you are ever the victim of an accident or the cause of an accident.

Reading Guide

Before You Read

Connect List all the careless things that you think you did during the past few months. Could the examples on your list have caused injury to another person or damage to property?

Focus on Ideas

Negligence involves a certain level of carelessness that people must avoid or they could suffer legal consequences.

Take Notes

Go to connectED.mcgraw-hill.com to download a graphic organizer you can use to take notes as you read this section.

Duty of Care

Elements of Negligence

Key Terms

You will learn these legal words and expressions in this chapter. You can also find these terms in *Black's Law Dictionary* or in an online legal dictionary.

- negligence
- proximate cause
- contributory negligence
- comparative negligence
- assumption of risk
- strict liability

Academic Vocabulary

You will find these words in your readings and in your tests. Look them up in a dictionary and familiarize yourself with them.

- reasonable
- objective
- foreseeable

Negligence

Can you be sued if you hurt someone by accident?

Negligence is a tort that results when one person carelessly injures another. It is an accidental tort. It is also the tort that occurs most often. In contrast to an intentional tort, it requires no actual intent by the tortfeasor. Negligence is being less careful than a **reasonable** person should be in the same situation. Negligence can occur in an automobile accident, in the meltdown of a nuclear power plant, or when someone slips on the ice.

Elements of Negligence

The law has tough standards for negligence. To succeed in a tort suit for negligence, the plaintiff must prove all of the following elements:

- The defendant owed the plaintiff a duty of care.
- The defendant breached that duty by being careless.
- The defendant's carelessness was the proximate cause of harm.
- The plaintiff was really hurt by the defendant's carelessness.

Remember, you have to prove all the elements. Fail to prove just one and you will not receive remedy from a defendant.

Duty of Care The law of torts is grounded in the concept of rights. Because every person has certain rights in our society, all of us have a duty to not violate these rights. This concept of duty is extremely important in negligence lawsuits. When plaintiffs cannot prove that the defendants owed a duty of care—the obligation to use a reasonable standard of care to prevent injury to others—the judge will throw out the case.

Breach of Duty You breach, or break, your duty to another person when you fail to use reasonable care in dealing with

As You Read

Predict Can you be sued for negligence even if no harm was caused?

Vocabulary You can find vocabulary definitions in the **Key Terms** glossary and Academic Vocabulary glossary in the back of this book.

Business ETHICS

Defective Cars

Suppose you are an attorney for a car manufacturer. A company engineer informs you that one in 1,000 of the company's new cars may suffer from a transmission failure if it idles too long at a stoplight. Your company has sold 50,000 of the new cars so far. To recall the cars would cost the company $5 million. It could cost a lot less to settle the 50 potential lawsuits that might result because of the defective cars.

Critical Thinking: What is your advice to the company?

Proximate Cause Proximate cause involves a negligent act that could lead to an injury or accident. *What do courts use to determine if proximate cause exists?*

that person. Just how careful do you have to be? To determine whether certain conduct is negligent, the law has developed a standard called the reasonable person test. The reasonable person test is an **objective** test. It does not change because the injured party changes.

According to the reasonable person test, you have to be as careful as a reasonable person would be in the same situation. A reasonable person considers how likely a certain act is to cause harm, how serious the harm would be, and the burden involved in avoiding the harm. For example, suppose the walkway leading to your home has some cracks in it that could cause someone to trip and fall. The likelihood that someone will trip is small and the harm would probably not be serious. The cost of replacing the walkway could be substantial compared to how unlikely it is to cause an accident. However, it would be reasonable to patch the worst cracks or post a warning sign to avoid the harm.

Proximate Cause It is not enough to show that a defendant's actions were unreasonable. The action or behavior must also be the proximate cause of the injury. **Proximate cause, also called legal cause, exists when the link between the negligent conduct and the injury is strong enough to be recognized by the law.** Without proximate cause, there would be no injury.

To determine if proximate cause exists, courts use the foreseeability test. The court asks whether the injury to the victim was **foreseeable** at the time of the negligent conduct. If the injury to the victim was foreseeable, then proximate cause exists, and the defendant is liable for negligence.

Actual Harm If a victim was not actually harmed, there can be no negligence. The victim must suffer an injury, have property destroyed, or lose a lot of money. Without actual harm, even the biggest mistake will not result in negligence.

Defenses to Negligence

You can defend yourself in a negligence suit by eliminating one of the four elements. For example, you could argue that you owed no duty to the plaintiff. You could also claim that you were as careful as a reasonable person would have been in the same situation. You could also state that your actions did not cause the victim's injury. Finally, you could try to prove that the victim was not really injured in the way that he or she claims.

A defendant who cannot get rid of at least one of these elements could be in serious trouble. However, that defendant is still not necessarily liable. There are three other defenses that a defendant could use against negligence.

Contributory Negligence Contributory negligence is a defense against negligence whenever the defendant can show that the victim did something that helped cause his or her own injuries. If the defendant can prove this, then the plaintiff loses the lawsuit. It does not matter how small the victim's negligence was. Many states no longer follow this doctrine. This is because it is unfair to plaintiffs who may have been only very slightly negligent. These states use another standard called comparative negligence.

Comparative Negligence Comparative negligence is a defense against negligence which is raised when the carelessness of each party is compared to the carelessness of the other party. The amount of money plaintiffs can receive in damages is reduced by the percent of their carelessness. Comparative negligence actually protects plaintiffs. This is because plaintiffs can still collect damages even if they were careless.

There is a condition, however, called the 50 percent rule. Most states use the 50 percent rule. According to the 50 percent rule, the plaintiff is allowed to receive some damages if the plaintiff's negligence is less than the defendant's. If the plaintiff's negligence is more than half, however, the plaintiff gets nothing.

Assumption of Risk Assumption of risk is a defense against negligence that is raised when the plaintiff knew of the risk involved and still took the chance of being injured. People who are injured while participating in extreme sports may also be unable to bring lawsuits for negligence. This is because they assume the risk involved with a dangerous sport. If you jump out of an airplane that is in good condition, you have assumed a risk of injury, even with the parachute on your back. The same is true if you bungee jump, skateboard, or windsurf.

Reading Check

Analyze *How does negligence relate to proximate cause?*

Critical Thinking *If you cause injury to yourself by spilling hot food, should you be able to sue the company that served you the food?*

Flex Your Reading   **Note key facts in the text below and look up words you do not understand. Restate difficult ideas in your own words. Go back and reread the text quickly to make sure you did not miss any important detail. Now, you are ready to formulate an opinion.**

Personal Responsibility? Stella Liebeck was a passenger in her grandson's car. They decided to go through their local McDonald's drive-thru. Ms. Liebeck purchased a cup of coffee and placed it between her legs to hold it while she tried to mix in cream and sugar. While the lid was off, the hot coffee spilled and Ms. Liebeck was burned severely.

Ms. Liebeck spent eight days in the hospital and suffered third-degree burns to her skin. Her treatment included several skin grafts to help repair the burned area. The burns left Ms. Liebeck scarred and disabled for more than two years. Before deciding to sue McDonald's, Ms. Liebeck offered to settle the case with the company for approximately $20,000 (the cost of her medical bills). McDonald's made a counteroffer of only $800, which Ms. Liebeck refused.

Liebeck v. McDonald's Restaurants, No. CV-93-02419 (N.M. Dist. Aug. 18, 1994)

➤ Go to **ConnectED.mcgraw-hill.com** for more case study practice.

Strict Liability

Who is liable if you are injured by a faulty product?

Strict liability is a legal doctrine that says that some activities are so dangerous that liability will always follow any injury that results from those activities. Some states call strict liability absolute liability. This rule applies only to ultrahazardous activities. These activities always involve a great risk to people and property. The risk is so great that no amount of care will eliminate it.

Using explosives and keeping wild animals as pets are both in this category. If you keep a pet rattlesnake in a shoe box and it escapes and bites somebody, you are liable no matter how careful you were when you placed the rattler in the box.

Product Liability

Strict liability has been applied in product liability cases. When people are injured by defective products, both the firm that manufactured the products and the seller of the products are liable for injuries. Fault does not matter.

Limits to Product Liability

Product liability has limits. It does not apply if the seller of the defective product does not usually sell such items. For example, a corporation that auctions off some machinery after one of its plants closes would not be liable for an injury caused by a defect in one of the machines. Product liability will also not apply if the only damage done by the product is damage to the product itself.

Tort Reform

If the injured party in a lawsuit dies, what happens to the lawsuit?

Some of the traditional rules of tort law are out of step with the real world. To solve this problem many state legislatures have passed new laws to reform tort law. Two such attempts involve survival statutes and wrongful death statutes.

Survival Statutes

In the past, under common law, when an injured person died, the right to sue also died. This meant that the defendant in a lawsuit was better off if the plaintiff died from injuries caused by the defendant. Most states now have survival statutes that say a lawsuit can continue even if both the plaintiff and the defendant die.

Wrongful Death Statutes

Also under common law, when an injured person died, the person's family forfeited, or gave up, the right to sue the party whose negligence caused the injury. This meant that, for example, a person who lost a spouse could not sue for damages even though he or she depended on the spouse's income for support. Wrongful death statutes now prevent this injustice and allow the relatives to bring a lawsuit even if the victim has died.

After You Read

Summarize Name the four elements of negligence.

SECTION 3.2 ASSESSMENT

Self Check

1. What does duty of care mean?
2. What does breach of duty mean?
3. What types of activities are involved in strict liability?

Academic Connection

Mathematics The projected tort-related costs in product liability lawsuits for each American citizen in 2005 was $1,000. In 1950 it was $12 per citizen. What percent change does the 2005 figure represent over the figure from 1950?

CONCEPT **Number and Operations:** To calculate the percent change, divide the amount of change by the base figure. In this problem, the amount of change is the amount in 2005 minus the amount in 1950, and the base figure is the amount in 1950.

Critical Thinking

Bad Brakes Suppose that you are driving to work after school and your brakes fail. All that happens is you glide to a stop in the parking lot. However, on two more occasions your brakes fail. You cannot afford to pay for repair costs yet so you decide to take your chances. Applying your knowledge of negligence, explain whether you could be held liable.

Summary

Section **3.1** Definition of a Tort

◆ A tort is a private wrong committed by one person against another. A tortfeasor is a person who commits a tort. A person who commits a tort interferes with another person's rights.

◆ The law of torts is grounded in rights. Under tort law, all people are entitled to certain rights simply because they are members of our society.

◆ The law imposes a duty on all of us to respect the rights of others.

◆ The major intentional torts that can be committed against people are assault, battery, false imprisonment, defamation, invasion of privacy, and intentional infliction of emotional distress.

◆ The major intentional torts against property are trespass, conversion, nuisance, and disparagement.

Section **3.2** Negligence and Liability

◆ Negligence is an accidental or unintentional tort. It is the tort that occurs most often.

◆ Negligence is the failure to exercise the degree of care that a reasonable person would have exercised.

◆ A suit for negligence must prove four elements: duty of care, breach of duty, proximate cause, and actual harm.

◆ People can defend themselves against negligence by eliminating one of the four elements. If the defendant cannot eliminate one of the elements, he or she may still be able to use contributory negligence, comparative negligence, or assumption of risk as a defense.

◆ According to the doctrine of strict liability, those who engage in ultrahazardous activities will be held liable for any injury or damage that occurs because of that activity, regardless of intent or care.

Vocabulary Builder

❶ On a sheet of paper, use each of these terms in a sentence.

Key Terms

- tort
- tortfeasor
- intentional tort

- negligence
- proximate cause
- contributory negligence

- comparative negligence
- assumption of risk
- strict liability

Academic Vocabulary

- compensate
- confidential

- distress
- reasonable

- objective
- foreseeable

Key Points Review

Answer the following questions. Refer to the chapter for additional reinforcement.

2 What are the three elements of a tort?

3 What is the difference between a crime and a tort?

4 What is the difference between libel and slander?

5 What are the main intentional torts against people?

6 What are the main intentional torts against property?

7 What is negligence?

8 What are the elements of negligence?

9 What are the major defenses to negligence?

10 What is strict liability?

Standardized Test Practice

11 Read the following information about the National Highway Traffic Safety Administration (NHTSA) and complete questions 1 and 2.

The NHTSA is responsible for reducing deaths, injuries, and economic losses resulting from motor vehicle crashes. This is accomplished by setting and enforcing safety performance standards for motor vehicles and motor vehicle equipment, and through grants to state and local governments to enable them to conduct effective local highway safety programs.

The NHTSA investigates safety defects in motor vehicles, sets and enforces fuel economy standards, helps states and local communities reduce the threat of drunk drivers, promotes the use of safety belts, child safety seats, and air bags, investigates odometer fraud, establishes and enforces vehicle anti-theft regulations, and provides consumer information on motor vehicle safety topics. (*Information excerpted from the NHTSA Web site.*)

1. How does the NHTSA accomplish reducing deaths, injuries and economic losses from vehicle crashes?

Ⓐ educational grants and incentives for drivers

Ⓑ building new interstate highways and rest stops

Ⓒ reducing the cost of GPS tracking systems

Ⓓ setting and enforcing safety performance standards

2. The purpose of NHTSA investigating motor vehicle safety defects is to

Ⓐ build less expensive cars to increase new car sales

Ⓑ install anti-theft devices to prevent vehicles from being stolen

Ⓒ mandate child safety seats and air bag standards

Ⓓ advertise employment possibilities at the NHTSA

 Test-Taking Strategies Try to include time at the end of the test to review your test before turning it in.

Apply and Debate

Read the following scenarios. Get together with other students in pairs or groups of three and take a position on each scenario. Debate your position in class with students taking the opposite position or prepare a written argument justifying your position.

12 Disturbing the Peace

To celebrate Kama's sixteenth birthday, 42 friends and family members gave her a surprise party. As the party went into the evening hours, her next door neighbors complained about the noise and the cars parked on the street.

You Debate *Under the tort of nuisance doctrine, are the neighbors justified in their complaint?*

13 Invasion of Privacy

Donna and Matthew share an office. Donna was balancing her checkbook when she was called away from her desk. Matthew saw the checkbook on her desk and went through it while she was away.

You Debate *Did Matthew's actions constitute invasion of privacy?*

14 Assault and Battery

Tania and Megan were arguing over which one of them should be homecoming queen. Tania told Megan that if she won the race she would cause her severe bodily injury. Megan told her parents of the threat and they contacted the police.

You Debate *Did Tania commit assault or battery or should the statement not be taken seriously because of the context in which it was said?*

15 Defamation of Character

Aisha wrote an unfavorable article about one of her teachers for her high school newspaper. She did not talk to the teacher to get the teacher's side of the story. As a result of the article, the teacher was put on suspension pending an investigation.

You Debate *Is Aisha's article slander or libel and can the teacher do anything about it?*

16 Assumption of Risk

Leslie went snowboarding with a group of friends at a local resort. As she slid down the mountain, she hit a trail marker sign, flipped off her board, and broke her leg.

You Debate *Can Leslie sue the resort for placing a sign where users might run into it and be injured?*

S. Olsson/PhotoAlto

Case Study Practice– Kolarik v. Cory International Corp.

⑰ Who Is Liable? Douglas Kolarik bought a jar of pitted olives. When he bit into one of the olives, Mr. Kolarik broke a tooth on a piece of olive pit or some other hard object in the olive. He sued the olive company on grounds of strict liability and negligence. Under the theory of strict liability, Mr. Kolarik claimed the jar of olives had left the processing plant in a defective condition and that the defect was dangerous to any consumer. Mr. Kolarik further claimed that he had used the olives in an ordinary manner and that if the olives had left the processing plant without defects, his injury would not have occurred. Mr. Kolarik also argued that the olive company was negligent in failing to remove all pits or hard objects from the olives or preventing them from entering the olives as they were processed. Prior to trial, the olive company moved to dismiss the case, arguing it was not liable for stray pits left in olives.

Source: Kolarik v. Cory Int'l Corp., LACV063821 (Ia. Dist. Ct. March 31, 2004)

Practice Should the court dismiss this case? Why or why not?

⑱ Ethics ←?→ Application

Duty to Disclose After listing your car for sale, you are sent a notice regarding a mechanical recall on your vehicle. This afternoon you have an interested buyer coming to look at the car. After seeing and test driving the car, the buyer makes you an immediate offer to pay what you are asking.

◆ What would be the ethical way to handle this situation?

⑲ Think back to the Legal Briefs feature you read at the beginning of the chapter. Then go online to a social media outlet, online game, or to the web site of a large company such as Amazon or eBay. Find the Terms of Use policy and read it carefully to find the arbitration clause. Make a list of the requirements for forced arbitration with that company—where it will be held, how long a customer has to make a claim, and so on. Write one or more paragraphs to summarize your findings.

Denise M. Howell

Counsel, Appellate Group
Publisher, BagandBaggage.com

What do you do at work?

"My specialty is appellate practice and procedure, which means I have devoted a good deal of time and study to the art of presenting cases to appellate tribunals, which differ greatly from the trial courts. Half the fun of being a litigator of any kind is the freedom it affords you to be a generalist (regarding subject matter). It's a rare case where I'm not learning about some area of the law with which I was not already very familiar. That said, my personal and professional interests mostly intersect in the ever-changing area of technology and intellectual property law."

What skills are most important to you?

"Effective and efficient information gathering and research techniques are especially important. It's also important to have the ability to analyze and tie sources together into a persuasive presentation."

What training do you recommend?

"The best training for appellate practitioners is to spend lots of time with other appellate practitioners, and let them shred your work—over and over again. It can be demoralizing, but it's effective. Whatever your area of legal expertise or interest, I recommend looking into the world of legal weblogs, or blogs. At the minimum, you will likely find free and informative writing by legal professionals who keep meticulously current on developments in your field. You might also find you have something to contribute to the discussion and analysis."

What is your key to success?

"Steve Jobs told a Stanford graduating class that it is best not to let many consecutive days pass by if you dislike what you are doing. Instead, change the course, select another option, move on, and find your passion. If you find that passion, you'll project the positive attitude, professional behavior, and personal responsibility so necessary for professional success."

Resume Builder

Academic Skills

- Strong ability to investigate and conduct research
- Analyze information gathered into meaningful pieces

Education and Training

Collegiate focus will vary based on the specialty of work chosen. The following high school and college courses will help develop the necessary background knowledge:

- English Language Arts
- Social Studies
- U.S. Government
- Introduction to Law (in high school)
- Basic law courses (in college)
- Business, contracts, and consumer law

Critical Thinking

How can appropriate business attire, respect for confidentiality, and ethical behavior help you to project a professional image?

Expository Writing Practice

What Happened, and What Is the Crime? Henry, a 78-year-old man, makes a right-hand turn onto a street temporarily closed because of the farmer's market, where hundreds of people mingle and buy produce and other goods. His car runs over the orange pylons and makeshift gates closing off the street. He continues to drive, allegedly accelerating through the market, injuring dozens of people and instantly killing six before his car runs into a vendor's tent and stops. Bystanders pull Henry from his car and proceed to shout at him. He seems dazed and confused at all the commotion. Police arrive at the scene, interview witnesses, and cover the bodies, as paramedics tend to the injured. The police take Henry into custody for questioning.

Assignments

Research Research what particular charges might be filed against Henry. Determine your state's rules for crimes against people.

Write Imagine you are a public defender assigned to the case, and there is still much unknown about what exactly happened. Consider the situation above and write an expository essay analyzing how and what you need to find out from Henry regarding his character and the day at the market. Describe in detail the information you know and the information you need to gather in order to create a picture of the day and the man.

Writing Tips Before you start writing your essay, read through the following composition review tips:

- ✓ Determine and define your audience.
- ✓ Define your purpose.
- ✓ Explain your main idea in a clear thesis statement.
- ✓ List facts as supporting details.
- ✓ Focus on cause-effect relationships between facts.

Essay Test Strategies The word expository is a derivative of the word expose, which means to make known or explain. Expository writing explains and informs. Make sure you can explain your position clearly and support it with facts.

Thematic Project

Small Claims Suits

For this project, you will use what you have learned to prepare a checklist and a guide for filing an action in one of your state's small claims courts.

Here is a checklist of the skills that you will need to complete this project and that your teacher will consider when evaluating your work.

Evaluation Rubric

Academic Skills

1.	Online and library research	1.	10 points
2.	Reading for information	2.	10 points
3.	Note-taking	3.	5 points
4.	Essay structure and outline	4.	10 points
5.	Grammar, spelling, and transitional and topic sentences	5.	10 points

Legal Skills

6.	Research of small court procedures	6.	15 points
7.	Requirements of a plaintiff and defendant in small claims cases	7.	15 points
8.	Analysis of the essential procedural information	8.	20 points
9.	Use of technology	9.	5 points
		Total 100 Points	

Step 1: Preparation

1. Create a vocabulary reference guide of terminology used in small claims court.
2. Use all you have learned in this unit, at the library, or on the Internet as tools.
3. Complete this project in a format acceptable for a portfolio addition.

Step 2: Procedure

❶ Review the text in this unit and make a list of the terminology with definitions.

❷ List the following subcategories: 1) small claims court; 2) what you cannot do in small claims court; 3) do you need a lawyer; 4) costs involved in filing a suit in small claims court; 5) small claims court terminology; and 6) small claims checklist.

❸ Write a guide using the categories above to use for gathering information to present a case in small claims. Use the Internet to download a copy of your state's small claims filing form. Make enough copies of your guide and checklist so your classmates can review and annotate your information.

❹ Describe a scenario that would require you to file a suit in small claims court using your guide as a reference. Present the facts to support your case to your class and have them act as the judge in determining if the information would be sufficient to make a decision in the case.

Step 3: Create an Analysis Report

As a class, compare the checklists and guides that are presented. Create a spreadsheet to list and summarize the best ideas of the projects presented. In reviewing your classmates' checklists and guides, answer the following questions:

❶ How many subcategories and items were presented in the checklists?

❷ Did all of the guides include all the necessary elements to file a suit?

❸ If not, how does the absence of the element(s) affect the validity of a suit?

❹ How was your guide similar to and different from the other guides presented?

Community Connection

Find information on small claims cases in your state or county. Also, find out from your district court administrator if there is a dispute resolution center in your area and what its jurisdiction is. Prepare an oral presentation to report your findings to your classmates.

Competitive Event Prep
Knowing about the Law

Situation Assume the role of an experienced employee at a deli counter that is a favored spot for nearby office workers to pick up lunch. Employees of the deli are allowed a 30 percent discount on the sandwiches and salads that they purchase for themselves. This discount does not extend to persons other than the employee. A new employee has been purchasing two sandwiches each day, then passing one of the sandwiches to a friend who eats lunch with the employee.

Activity You are to explain to the new employee (event judge) that this behavior is a violation of the employee discount privilege.

Landmark Case

Cipollone v. Liggett Group, Inc.
United States Supreme Court 505 U.S. 504 (1992)

Read Critically As you read the case, ask yourself the following questions:

1. Why did the jury deny Rose Cipollone's claim for compensation?
2. What defense did the cigarette manufacturers raise in this case?
3. What is the effect of the supremacy clause in the U.S. Constitution?
4. When does federal law preempt state law?

Assignment When you are done, write a short summary of the situation. Include the court's decision and a couple of sentences about why or how the court reached its decision.

Facts Health Problems from

Cigarettes After 42 years of smoking, Rose Cipollone died of lung cancer. During the last 15 years of her life, cigarette packages contained the following label: "WARNING: THE SURGEON GENERAL HAS DETERMINED THAT CIGARETTE SMOKING IS DANGEROUS TO YOUR HEALTH."

Rose and her husband brought suit in federal court against three cigarette manufacturers. They blamed the cigarette makers for Rose's cancer and sought compensation based upon New Jersey tort law.

Manufacturer's Response The manufacturers argued they were not liable for state law tort claims arising before 1966. They further argued that the Federal Cigarette Labeling and Advertising Act of 1965 and the Public Health Cigarette Smoking Act of 1969 preempted such claims.

Jury Verdict Rose died before trial. The jury ruled in favor of the manufacturers, stating that Rose had voluntarily assumed

the risks of smoking. However, the jury did award Rose's husband $400,000 as compensation for his losses, holding that Liggett, a cigarette manufacturer, had breached its express warranties that smoking was not hazardous. Both sides appealed.

Opinion Congressional Actions In

1965, Congress passed the Federal Cigarette Labeling and Advertising Act, which required cigarette packages to contain the following label: "CAUTION: CIGARETTE SMOKING MAY BE HAZARDOUS TO YOUR HEALTH." Congress later passed the Public Health Cigarette Smoking Act of 1969, which required a stronger label to be placed on cigarette packages: "WARNING: THE SURGEON GENERAL HAS DETERMINED THAT CIGARETTE SMOKING IS DANGEROUS TO YOUR HEALTH."

The Petitioner's Complaint The petitioner's complaint alleged that the cigarette makers were responsible for Rose's illness on the following grounds:

- **Design Defect** The cigarette manufacturers did not use a safer alternative design, and the dangers created by cigarettes outweighed their social value.
- **Failure to Warn** There was no adequate warning about the health dangers of cigarettes, and manufacturers were negligent when "they tested, researched, sold, promoted, and advertised" cigarette products.
- **Express Warranty** The cigarette makers expressly warranted that their cigarettes did not pose serious health dangers.
- **Fraudulent Misrepresentations** The cigarette manufacturers tried to negate federal health warning labels and ignored scientific evidence demonstrating the hazards of smoking.
- **Conspiracy to Defraud** The cigarette makers tried to deny scientific evidence about the hazards of smoking.

The Defendant's Reply The cigarette manufacturers replied that federal laws preempt New Jersey's tort laws.

According to the supremacy clause of the U.S. Constitution, if a state law conflicts with a federal law, the federal law overrules the state law.

The petitioner claimed that state tort law should apply in this case because, unlike the 1969 Act, state tort claims for damages do not impose "requirement[s] or prohibition[s]" by statutes or regulations. Instead, the petitioner seeks compensation based upon prior court decisions (common law).

The Relationship of Federal and State Law In its opinion, the Court rejected the petitioner's argument. It held that state common law tort actions are based on the existence of a legal duty, which imposes "requirements and prohibitions."

The Court also cited an earlier case in which it said "[state] regulation can be effectively exerted through an award of damages as through some form of preventative relief. The obligation to pay compensation can be, indeed is designed to be, a potent method of governing conduct and controlling policy."

Consequently, the Court rejected the petitioner's claim that common law tort claims brought by individuals do not constitute matters of state law, and therefore ruled that federal law could overrule them.

After clarifying the applicable law, the Court examined each of the petitioner's claims to determine if it was preempted by the federal law. To determine whether a state law is preempted, the Court said that it must look to the intent of Congress. It ruled that federal law does not preempt state law unless it is "the clear and manifest purpose of Congress" that a federal law supersedes a state law.

Holding The Court's Decision

The Court held that the 1965 Act did not preempt state tort claims because Congress did not intend that result. The Court further held that, although the 1969 Act preempted state claims based on failure to warn, it did not preempt claims based upon express warranty, intentional fraud and misrepresentation, or conspiracy.

TRIAL PREP

The National High School Mock Trial Association organizes competitions at the local, regional, and national levels where teams of high school or college students prepare and argue fictional legal cases before practicing attorneys and judges. Mock Trial team members are each assigned a role as either an attorney or witness. Each team must develop a courtroom strategy, legal arguments, and a presentation style.

UNIT 2

Contract Law

In This Unit You Will Find:

Owning Your First Car
This is a big step toward independence but also a big financial and civic responsibility. *What do you think is the most challenging aspect of owning a car?*

Writing a Driving Contract

As you read this unit, use this checklist to prepare for the unit project:

✓ List the elements needed to create a contract.

✓ Differentiate between classes of contracts.

✓ Compare the requirements of an offer and of an acceptance.

✓ Explain how offer and acceptance can create contractual rights and duties.

✓ Determine whether an agreement is definite enough to be enforced as a contract.

Legal Portfolio When you complete the Unit Thematic Project, you will have a real contract to add to your portfolio.

Ask AN EXPERT   Investing in Mutual Funds

Q: I have heard that mutual funds are a type of investment. What are they?

A: A mutual fund is a collective investment that pools money from many investors to buy and sell stocks, bonds, short-term money-market instruments, and other securities traded on stock exchanges around the world. A mutual fund operates by specific rules and while you do not have to sign a contract document, by entering a fund you effectively agree to follow its rules and pay its fees. What the fund invests in is called a portfolio. By law, you should receive a prospectus from the fund company before you invest in it. It tells you the goals of the fund and how it intends to achieve them. You will also find information about the fund's fees.

What Is a Contract?

Legal Briefs

The FTC Takes a Bite Out of Apple

Parents refunded for children's in-app purchases.

Parents won in a case against Apple to the tune of $32.5 million. In the 2012 settlement with the Federal Trade Commission, Apple not only had to pay up, they also had to modify their billing practices.

Apple had advertised their game apps as "free," but once parents signed onto the games to allow minors to play, they unknowingly agreed to allow them to incur charges while playing, some as high as nearly $340.

Apple argued that in question was the Terms of Service contract, which was signed by the parents. This meant that regardless of who used the game, the contract was with the person who signed it—and this person was legally responsible for payment.

Parents argued that the in-game purchases were a separate contract made between Apple and minors, and that contracts with minors may be nullified.

The court sided with the parents, forcing Apple to pay up and to modify billing practices. Apple now must obtain parents' expressed, informed consent prior to any charges being incurred, and they have the right to withdraw consent.

Legal Download An interest in movies may include building and maintaining your movie collection. *When is it legal to download movies off the Internet?*

Agreements and Contracts

What You'll Learn

- Explain the nature and importance of contracts.
- Identify the elements of a valid contract.
- Analyze the different classes of contracts.
- Differentiate between express and implied, unilateral and bilateral, and oral and written contracts.

Why It's Important

Knowing the elements and characteristics of a contract will help you determine whether an agreement is valid or not.

Reading Guide

Before You Read

Connect If you have ever agreed to conditions to enter a Web site, you have made a contract. What are some contracts you have made lately?

Focus on Ideas

For a contract to be valid, it must meet several requirements and have certain characteristics.

Take Notes

Go to connectED. mcgraw-hill.com to download a graphic organizer you can use to take notes as you read this section.

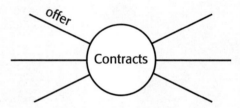

The Six Components of a Contract

Key Terms

You will learn these legal words and expressions in this chapter. You can also find these terms in *Black's Law Dictionary* or in an online legal dictionary.

- contract
- offer
- acceptance
- genuine agreement

- express contract
- implied contract
- bilateral contract
- unilateral contract

Academic Vocabulary

You will find these words in your readings and in your tests. Look them up in a dictionary and familiarize yourself with them.

- determine
- assume
- require

Understanding Contract Law

Do you think a contract always is a written document that needs to be signed?

If you bought your first car last year or sold your old video games at a garage sale, you might know that these activities involve contracts. Many common daily activities also involve contracts, from buying a fast food meal to filling your car with gas. Most people think a contract is a long, printed, formal document that they sign when buying a vehicle, selling their house, or purchasing insurance. Such formal documents represent only a small fraction of the contracts that you will make in your lifetime. The truth is that you create a contract any time you agree to exchange things of value.

As You Read

Predict Does a contract have to be in writing to be valid?

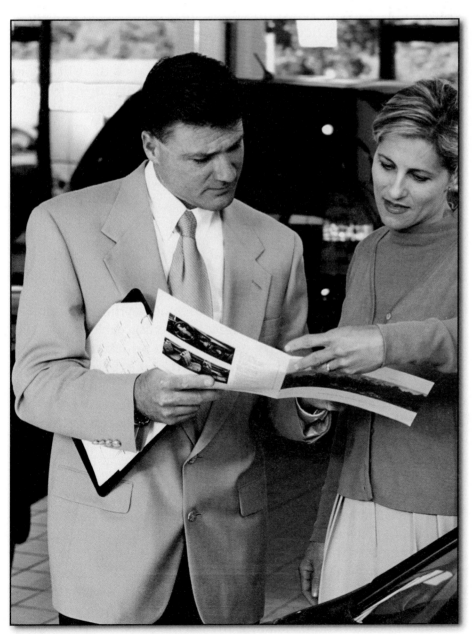

Contracts Are Everywhere
Contractual agreements are not always obvious, but they are everywhere in our lives. *Do you think a car manufacturer's claim of 36 miles per gallon gas consumption is a contract? Why or why not? When you have finished reading and studying this chapter, look at this ad again. Would you change your original answer? Explain how and why?*

The Nature of a Contract

Are all agreements you make contracts?

A contract is any agreement enforceable by law. You should never enter into a contract without understanding the legal responsibilities involved. Not all agreements are contracts. An informal promise to take out the trash is not a contract. In contrast, an ad in a newspaper offering a reward for a lost skateboard is a type of contract. If someone answers the ad and returns the skateboard, the person who placed the ad will owe the person who returned the skateboard what was promised as a reward in the ad.

The Three Theories of Contract Law

The legal responsibilities associated with contracts are based on what the parties involved do and say to one another. In the past, courts asked whether the parties to a contract exchanged things of equal value. This was called the equity theory of contract law. As industrial capitalism developed, the courts focused on the exercise of each party's will: they asked whether the parties really had agreed to the terms of an agreement. This was called the will theory of contract law. But, it was still very difficult to **determine** what the parties were thinking as they had entered into an agreement. The courts tried to determine if the parties had reached a meeting of the minds and, gradually, this led to a search for elements that consistently appeared in genuine agreements. The courts focused on the form of agreements. This became known as the formalist theory of contract law.

The Elements of a Contract

The six elements of a contract, as shown in **Figure 4.1,** are offer, acceptance, genuine agreement, consideration, capacity, and legality. To be legally complete, a contract must include all six elements. Notice that the list does not include anything written. Not all contracts have to be in writing to be enforceable.

An offer is a proposal by one party to another intended to create a legally binding agreement. An acceptance is the second party's unqualified willingness to go along with the first party's proposal. A genuine agreement means that an agreement is true and genuine: a valid offer is met by a valid acceptance. Circumstances such as fraud, misrepresentation, mistake, undue influence, and economic duress can destroy the genuineness of an agreement. The fourth element, capacity, is the legal ability to enter a contract. The law generally assumes that anyone entering a contract has the capacity, but this assumption can be disputed. The fifth element, consideration, is the exchange of things of value. In an offer to let someone borrow a car, there is no consideration in the agreement if nothing is offered in return. People cannot enter into contracts that include illegal acts. Legality, the sixth element, means that the contract does not entail violating any laws.

Vocabulary You can find vocabulary definitions in the **Key Terms** glossary and Academic Vocabulary glossary in the back of this book.

Figure 4.1 Elements of a Contract

Capacity The law presumes that anyone entering a contract has the legal capacity to do so. Minors are generally excused from contractual responsibility, as are mentally impaired people and individuals under the influence of drugs or alcohol.

Consideration Consideration is the thing of value promised to one party in a contract in exchange for something else of value promised by the other party. The mutual exchange binds the parties together.

Legality Parties are not allowed to enforce contracts that involve illegal acts. Some illegal contracts involve agreements to commit a crime or a tort. Others involve activities made illegal by statutory law.

Offer A proposal made by one party (the offeror) to another party (the offeree) indicating a willingness to contract.

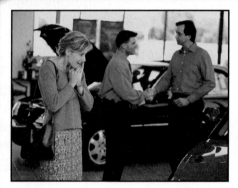

Acceptance The agreement of the offeree to be bound by the terms of the offer.

Genuine Agreement Offer and acceptance go together to create genuine agreement or a meeting of the minds. Agreement can be destroyed by fraud, misrepresentation, mistake, duress, or undue influence.

An agreement is not a contract unless it contains the six elements of a contract.
Of the six elements, which is the most crucial to setting up a valid contract?

Characteristics of a Contract

Now that you know about the different elements of a contract, can you think of different types of contracts?

Contracts can be created in different ways and can **assume** diverse forms. A contract can be described by any of the following characteristics:

- valid, void, voidable, or unenforceable
- express or implied
- bilateral or unilateral
- oral or written

Any contract can have characteristics from one or more of these four groups. That is, a contract can be valid, express, bilateral, and written. Let's take a closer look at what these characteristics indicate about a contract.

Valid, Void, Voidable, or Unenforceable Contracts

The word valid means legally good, thus a valid contract is one that is legally binding. On the other hand, a contract that is void has no legal effect. An agreement that is missing one of the previously discussed elements would be void, such as any agreement to do something illegal.

When a party to a contract is able to void or cancel a contract for some legal reason, it is a voidable contract. It is not void in

Case Study – Vokes v. Arthur Murray

Critical Thinking *Who do you think should win this case? Why?*

Flex Your Reading **Note key facts in the text below and look up words you do not understand. Restate difficult ideas in your own words. Go back and reread the text quickly to make sure you did not miss any important detail. Now, you are ready to formulate an opinion.**

Misled into a Contract? Audrey Vokes went to a dance party offered by the Arthur Murray, Inc., dancing school, where she was persuaded to sign a contract for a dance course. Ms. Vokes was told she was an excellent dancer with grace and poise, and was encouraged to take more dance lessons. She was repeatedly talked into taking more dance courses by assurances that she was rapidly improving and developing in her dancing skills, and that additional lessons would make her a beautiful dancer, capable of dancing with the most accomplished dancers. Over a period of 16 months, Ms. Vokes took a total of 14 dance courses at a cost of over $31,000. In fact, Ms. Vokes had no skill as a dancer and her dancing did not improve with lessons. When she finally realized this, she sued the Arthur Murray dance school, claiming it had misled her to get her to sign a contract.

Vokes v. Arthur Murray, Inc., 212 So.2d 906 (FL)

Go to **ConnectEd.mcgraw-hill.com** for more case study practice.

itself but may be voided by one or more of the parties. A contract between two minors could be voidable by either of them because minors have the right to get out of contracts (see Chapter 5).

An unenforceable contract is one the court will not uphold, generally because of some rule of law, such as the statute of limitations. If you wait too long to bring a lawsuit for breach of contract, the statute of limitations may have run its course, making the contract unenforceable.

Express or Implied Contracts

An express contract is a contract statement that may be oral or written. An implied contract is a contract that comes about from the actions of the parties. People often enter into implied contracts without exchanging a single word.

> **Example** Herb Schneider went to a self-service gas station that requires payment before the attendant will turn on the pumps. He handed the attendant $10, returned to his car, pumped $10 worth of gas into his tank, and drove off. Neither party spoke a single word, yet an implied contract arose from their actions.

Bilateral or Unilateral Contracts

Another characteristic of a contract to consider is whether it is bilateral or unilateral. See **Figure 4.2** for a visual representation of bilateral and unilateral contracts. A **bilateral contract is a contract that contains two promises.** One party promises to do something in exchange for the other's promise to do something else. Most contracts are created this way.

A **unilateral contract is a contract that contains a promise by only one person to do something, if and when the other party performs some act.** If your friend

Figure 4.2 How Parties Reach Agreement

Unilateral Contract

Offer
Promise by offerer

Agreement

Acceptance
Act performed by offeree at offeror's request

Bilateral Contract

Offer
Promise by offeror

Agreement

Acceptance
Promise made by offeree at offeror's request

A contract may be unilateral or bilateral. *In which type of contract do both parties, the offeror and the offeree, make promises?*

says, "I'll sell you my DVD player for $150 if you give me the cash before noon tomorrow," he or she will not be **required** to keep the promise unless you hand over the cash before noon on the following day.

A reward offer is one of the most common instances of a unilateral contract. The acceptance of the reward offer must precisely comply with the offer.

> **Example** Anne Chen placed an ad in the local newspaper offering a reward for the return of her lost laptop computer. Ms. Chen's offer of a reward alone did not create a contract. The contract would come into existence only when someone returns the laptop. Ms. Chen would then owe the finder the reward.

Oral or Written Contracts

An oral contract is created by word of mouth and comes into existence when two or more people form a contract by speaking to each other. One person usually offers to do something, and the other party agrees to do something else in return. Most contracts are oral contracts of this nature.

Sometimes, however, it is desirable to put contracts in writing. A written contract assures that both parties know the exact terms of the contract and also provides proof that the agreement was made. A law, the Statute of Frauds, requires that certain contracts must be in writing to be enforceable.

After You Read

Summarize List the components of a legal contract.

SECTION 4.1 ASSESSMENT

Self Check

1. What are the differences among valid, void, and voidable contracts?
2. What are the differences between express and implied contracts?
3. What is a unilateral contract?

Academic Connection

Mathematics You recently borrowed $500 from a friend. You signed a contract that requires you to pay back one third of the loan every month for three months. How much will you have to pay back each of the first two months? How much will you have to pay back the third month?

CONCEPT **Number and Operations: Using Fractions, Decimals, and Rounding** To figure out 1/3 of $500, divide 500 by 3 and round to the nearest cent. Remember to round numbers of 5 or more up and numbers less than 5 down. For example, $2.224 rounds to $2.22 and $2.226 rounds to $2.23. To get the payment for the third month, subtract the amounts for the first two months from 500.

 For more math practice, go to the Math Appendix.

Critical Thinking

Reward: Lost Backpack You lost your backpack and posted a $20 reward for it. If someone who did not know about the reward returned the backpack, would you be legally obligated to pay the reward?

How a Contract Begins

Reading Guide

Before You Read

Connect Businesses make offers to potential customers using a variety of methods. What are some ways you have received offers?

Focus on Ideas

A contract begins with a clear offer, which can be either accepted, changed, or terminated.

Take Notes

Go to connectED. mcgraw-hill.com to download a graphic organizer you can use to take notes as you read this section.

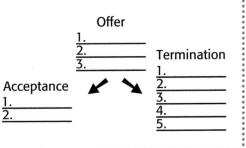

Offer
1. _____
2. _____
3. _____

Acceptance
1. _____
2. _____

Termination
1. _____
2. _____
3. _____
4. _____
5. _____

Key Terms

You will learn these legal words and expressions in this chapter. You can also find these terms in *Black's Law Dictionary* or in an online legal dictionary.

- invitations to negotiate
- mirror image rule
- counteroffer
- revocation
- rejection

Academic Vocabulary

You will find these words in your readings and in your tests. Look them up in a dictionary and familiarize yourself with them.

- definite
- specify
- impose

What You'll Learn

- ◆ Explain the requirements of a valid offer.
- ◆ Recognize the requirements of an acceptance.
- ◆ Distinguish the differences between an offer, an invitation to negotiate, an acceptance, and a counteroffer.
- ◆ Explain how offers are terminated.

Why It's Important

You need to know when an offer has been made and accepted for a contract to go into effect.

Requirements of an Offer

How do you know if an offer is real?

The six elements of a contract form the heart of contract law. Understanding the elements of offer and acceptance is necessary before moving on to other matters, such as which contracts must be in writing, how contract rights are transferred, how contracts end, and what happens when one party breaches a contract. An offer is a proposal by one party to another party to enter into a legally binding agreement. The person making the offer is the offeror, and the person who receives the offer is the offeree. An offer has three basic requirements. It must be:

- made seriously
- definite and certain
- communicated to the offeree

Serious Intent

An offer must be made with the intention of entering into a legal obligation. An offer made in the heat of anger or as a joke would not meet this requirement. For example, a friend complaining about her unreliable car might say, "Give me five dollars and it's yours." This statement may sound like an offer, but your friend cannot be forced to sell her car for five dollars.

Often an invitation to negotiate is confused with an offer. **Invitations to negotiate are invitations to deal, trade, or make an offer.** Sellers usually have limited merchandise to sell and cannot possibly sell an advertised product to everyone who sees an ad. For this reason, most advertisements in newspapers, magazines, and catalogs are not treated as offers but as invitations to negotiate. If customers say they would like to buy an advertised item, they are actually making an offer to buy the item at the advertised price. The storeowner is free to accept or reject the offer. There are exceptions to this rule.

As You Read

Predict Are most advertisements in newspapers and magazines offers to enter into a contract?

Invitation to Negotiate or Contract? This ad promotes a sale with a discount up to 70% off. *Is this ad an invitation to negotiate or a contract? Explain your answer.*

Michele Constantini/PhotoAlto/Corbis

The courts consider some advertisements as offers when they contain specific promises, use phrases such as "first come, first served," or limit the number of items that will be sold. In such cases, under the terms of the advertisement, the number of people who can buy the product becomes limited, making the advertisement an offer rather than an invitation to negotiate.

Price tags, signs in store windows and on counters, and prices marked on merchandise are treated as invitations to negotiate rather than as offers.

Definiteness and Certainty

An offer must be **definite** and certain to be enforceable. A landlord of an apartment with faulty plumbing might agree to pay a share of the cost if the tenant fixes the plumbing, but the court would not enforce the contract because it was not possible to determine what the parties meant by a share.

Vocabulary You can find vocabulary definitions in the **Key Terms** glossary and Academic Vocabulary glossary in the back of this book.

Communication to the Offeree

Offers may be made by telephone, letter, telegram, fax, e-mail, or by any other method that communicates the offer to the offeree.

Requirements of an Acceptance

How can you tell if an offer has been accepted?

The second element of a legally binding contract is acceptance of the offer by the offeree. As in the case of an offer, certain basic requirements must be met: the acceptance must be unconditional and must follow the rules regarding the method of acceptance.

CYBERLAW

American Airlines, Inc. v. FareChase, Inc.
Case No. 067-194022-02 (Texas, 67th Dist., Mar. 8, 2003).

FareChase, Inc., is a search engine whose customers are travel agencies. Its software scours—or scrapes—the Web sites of airlines, hotels, and car rental agencies to find the best rates. In February, 2003, American Airlines (AA) won an injunction against FareChase, alleging that FareChase scraped AA's site and took information without its permission. AA also claimed that FareChase violated the law of "trespass to chattels"—or interfering with someone's ownership of goods. Even though AA's Web site, AA.com, is a public site, its home page contains a statement restricting the use of the information on its site.

Ruling and Resolution
FareChase appealed the ruling on the grounds that the statement on AA's home page used a shrinkwrap or browsewrap agreement, which unfairly limits the use of facts. AA eventually settled with FareChase. According to the settlement, AA agreed to let FareChase search its site with some restrictions.

Critical Thinking Did FareChase have any type of contract with American Airlines? Do you think that FareChase did need a contract allowing the search of a public Web site? Why or why not?

Unconditional Acceptance

The acceptance must not change the terms of the original offer in any way according to the mirror image rule. **The mirror image rule means that the terms stated in the acceptance must exactly mirror or match the terms of the offer.** Any change in the terms of the offer means the offeree has not really accepted the offer but has made a counteroffer. **A counteroffer is a response to an offer in which the terms of the original offer are changed.** In that case, the original offeror is not obligated to go along, and no contract results. Instead, the offeror becomes an offeree and may accept or reject the counteroffer.

Contracts for the sale of goods are exceptions to the mirror image rule. These exceptions include contracts for personal property such as clothing, furniture, food, motor vehicles, appliances, and other items. The primary exceptions are created by the Uniform Commercial Code (UCC), which is a set of statutes that covers the law of sales as well as other areas of commercial law. It was drafted to make trade among the states easier and has been adopted with minor variations by 49 states. Only Louisiana has not adopted all of its provisions.

Methods of Acceptance

The time at which an acceptance takes place is important because that is when the contract comes into existence. When the parties are dealing face-to-face or on the telephone, no special problem exists. One party speaks, and the other listens and communicates the offer or the acceptance.

Special rules, however, govern acceptances that take place when the parties are separated by a distance and must communicate by letters, telegrams, or fax. According to common law, an acceptance that must be sent over long distances is effective when it is sent. Any method of communication that has been expressly or impliedly endorsed by the offeror would qualify. Common law also says that an acceptance is implied when the offeree accepts by the same or a faster means than that used by the offeror.

The authorization of an acceptance can also be implied by any reasonable means, including past practices between the parties, the usual method in the trade, or the customary means in comparable transactions. Naturally, the offeree must correctly address the acceptance so that it is delivered to the right place. If the address is faulty, the acceptance is not complete until delivery has been made to the offeror. It is also possible for the offeror to specify the time by which the acceptance must be received to be effective.

This rule applies to contracts for real estate and services. For sale-of-goods contracts under the UCC, the acceptance takes place when it is sent, as long as the method of communication is reasonable. Consequently, the acceptance of a mailed offer for goods would be effective when it is sent electronically, via fax, or through an overnight carrier. If the offeror states in the offer what method the offeree must use to accept, that method must be followed.

Reading Check

Explain *What are the characteristics of an offer?*

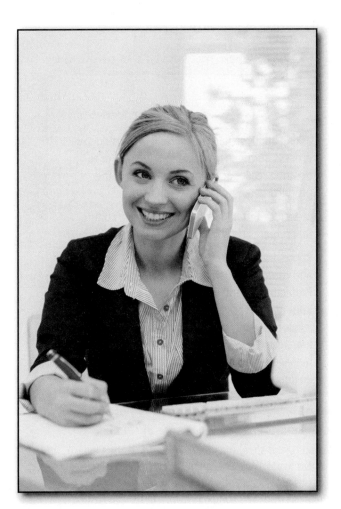

Long Distance Acceptance Problems may arise when the acceptance of a contract must travel over long distances. *How can people make certain that an acceptance is valid and effective when it must travel to a distant location?*

Sometimes, an offer specifies that it must be accepted by an action. In these cases, the action must take place before there is an acceptance. The offeror cannot **impose** silence on the offeree as the means of acceptance unless he or she has previously agreed to this condition or has allowed silence to signal acceptance in the past. In contrast, if the offeror has established silence as the means of acceptance, then he or she will have to live by that condition if the offeree accepts by remaining silent.

Termination of an Offer

Can you change your mind and withdraw an offer?

Even though an offer has been properly communicated to the offeree, it may be terminated. This termination may occur in any of five ways: revocation, rejection, counteroffer, expiration of time, and death or insanity.

Revocation

Revocation is the taking back of an offer by the offeror. The offeror has a change of mind or circumstances and decides to withdraw the offer before it has been accepted. Two important rules govern revocation: an offer can be revoked any time before it is accepted, and a revocation becomes effective when it is received by or communicated to the offeree.

Global Law

Entering Contracts in China

In the United States, a signed contract means that all parties know who will do what, with what level of quality, and by what deadline. Once the contract is signed, the parties move on to fulfill the contract, knowing that everyone will do their part. These rules do not exist in China. When people sign a contract there, they simply agree that they want to do business with one another, that the goals of the contract are desirable, and that the terms of the contract are reasonable. However, everyone knows that activities do not always happen as planned.

Camille Schuster, a consultant, speaker, and professor of marketing, international negotiations, and consumer-centered business practices, gives these guidelines for conducting business and managing contracts in China:

1 Maintain frequent, regular communication.

2 Asking "yes" or "no" questions will not generate useful information. You will be spared embarrassment, you will feel reassured, and you will know nothing. Instead of asking your Chinese contact if the production deadline will be met, try asking about significant events in the production process during the past week or month, or to describe recent activities of members of the production team.

3 Meet face-to-face. This is a relationship culture that requires personal, one-to-one commitment.

4 Represent all levels. Chinese culture is hierarchical and communication serves to preserve harmony. Problems are not freely discussed with superiors. Your team needs to include people at different levels of the hierarchy so that quality-control managers talk with other quality-control managers, and line engineers talk with other line engineers.

Across Cultures: The Importance of *Guanxi*

Guanxi (gwan-shee) means relationships. In the Chinese business world, personal connections are the basis for most business deals and contracts. It is very common for employees from one company to visit the residence of acquaintances from other organizations and bring gifts.

Critical Thinking: *What key contractual components are not included in Chinese contracts?*

Rejection

Rejection is a refusal of an offer by the offeree that brings the offer to an end. For example, if someone says to you, "I'll sell you my camera for $150," and you say, "I don't want it," then the offer has come to an end.

Counteroffer

A counteroffer ends the first offer. If someone says to you, "I'll sell you my camera for $50," and you say, "I'll give you $35 for it," no contract comes into existence unless the original offeror accepts your new offer. If you later say, "Okay, I'll give you $50 for the camera," you will be making a new offer, which the original offeror may accept or reject.

Expiration of Time

If the offeror sets a time limit for the acceptance of the offer, it must be honored. Assume that Bradley has offered to sell Franz his motorcycle for $1,745. Bradley tells Franz the offer will remain open until noon of the following day. To create the contract, Franz must accept within that time period.

If no time for acceptance is stated in the offer, it must be accepted within a reasonable time. Otherwise, no contract exists. What is a reasonable time depends on the circumstances. For example, a reasonable time to accept an offer for purchasing a truckload of ripe tomatoes would be different from a reasonable time to accept an offer for purchasing a house.

When an offeree pays money or other consideration to an offeror to hold an offer open for an agreed period of time, an option contract comes into existence. An option is a binding promise to hold an offer open for a specified period of time. It offers to the holder of the option the exclusive right to accept the offer within the agreed time, subject to the terms of the option. For example, you might offer a seller $50 to hold an offer open for two days. Such a contract is legally binding. For an entire contract to be completed, the option must be exercised by the person holding the option. This requires an absolute, unconditional, unqualified acceptance exactly according to the terms of the option.

Death or Insanity

If the offeror dies or becomes insane before the offer is accepted, the offer comes to an end. Although death ends an offer, it does not end a contract, except for contracts related to personal services.

After You Read

Summarize List the key requirements of an offer and of an acceptance.

SECTION 4.2 ASSESSMENT

Self Check

1. What are the requirements of an offer?

2. What are the requirements of an acceptance?

3. When is an offer terminated?

Academic Connection

English Language Arts
Now that you have learned why contracts are so important in business life, imagine that you work as an executive manager for a company that outsources the manufacturing of electrical components to a company in China. Make sure you read the Global Law feature on page 92 and research contractual and communication issues between U.S. and Chinese businesses. Draft an e-mail memo addressed to the five mid-level production and marketing managers who have been asked to travel to China next month to make sure component production is going according to plan. Outline specific instructions and general advice on how to handle potential problems during the upcoming trip. Make sure your e-mail follows appropriate memo format.

Critical Thinking

Identifying an Offer
Why is it important to be able to distinguish between an offer and an invitation to negotiate?

Summary

Section 4.1 Agreements and Contracts

◆ A contract is any agreement enforceable by law. The six elements of a contract are: offer, acceptance, genuine agreement, consideration, capacity, and legality.

◆ Valid contracts are legally binding. A void contract has no legal effect because at least one element is missing. A contract may be voided by one of the parties because of a defect.

◆ An express contract is stated in words. It may be written or oral. An implied contract is implied from the actions of the parties.

◆ Bilateral contracts are formed by promises that parties make to each other. A unilateral contract contains one party's promise that it will fulfill if and when the other party performs an act.

◆ Oral contracts are created when a party verbalizes a promise and the other party responds with a spoken promise. A written contract contains the promises in writing.

Section 4.2 How a Contract Begins

◆ An offer is a proposal by one party to another party to enter a contract. An offer must be (1) seriously intended, (2) definite and certain, and (3) communicated to the offeree.

◆ An invitation to negotiate may look like an offer, but it is not. Any such invitation cannot be made into an offer by agreeing to the terms of the invitation.

◆ An acceptance must meet two requirements: (1) it must be unconditional; and (2) it must follow the rules regarding the method of acceptance. Unconditional acceptances do not seek to change the terms of the original offer in any way.

◆ An offer must be accepted without change to its terms. If an offeree changes the terms of an offer, this is not an acceptance, but a counteroffer which the original offeree then may choose to accept or reject.

◆ An offer is terminated by revocation, rejection, counteroffer, expiration of time, death, or insanity.

Vocabulary Builder

1 On a sheet of paper, use each of these terms in a sentence.

Key Terms

- contract
- offer
- acceptance
- genuine agreement
- express contract
- implied contract
- bilateral contract
- unilateral contract
- invitations to negotiate
- mirror image rule
- counteroffer
- revocation
- rejection

Academic Vocabulary

- determine
- assume
- require
- definite
- specify
- impose

Key Points Review

Answer the following questions. Refer to the chapter for additional reinforcement.

2 Describe the formalist theory of contract law.

3 Explain the elements of legal contracts.

4 What are the exceptions to the mirror image rule?

5 When an acceptance is sent over a long distance, when does it become effective?

6 Under what circumstances is a contract voidable?

7 Why is it desirable to put some contracts in writing?

8 What two rules govern the revocation of contracts?

9 Explain the differences between bilateral and unilateral contracts.

Standardized Test Practice

10 Read this excerpt of the Uniform Commercial Code (UCC) and complete questions 1 and 2.

§ 1-103. Construction of UCC to Promote its Purposes and Policies: Applicability of Supplemental Principles of Law.

The UCC must be liberally construed and applied to promote its underlying purposes and policies, which are: (1) to simplify, clarify, and modernize the law governing commercial transactions; (2) to permit the continued expansion of commercial practices through custom, usage, and agreement of the parties; and (3) to make uniform the law among the various jurisdictions.

§ 1-105. Severability.

If any provision or clause of the UCC or its application to any person or circumstance is held invalid, the invalidity does not affect other provisions or applications of the UCC which can be given effect without the invalid provision or application, and to this end the provisions of the UCC are severable.

1. The purpose of the UCC is to

A simplify criminal law

B simplify and bring up-to-date the law that rules commercial transactions

C create different rules for different jurisdictions

D none of the above

2. The UCC section 1-105 on severability means that

A if one section of the UCC does not apply to a case, all sections of the UCC are invalid

B if a UCC provision does not apply, it can be severed and other provisions remain valid

C no provision or clause can ever be severed, or set aside, from the UCC

D all of the above

 Test-Taking Strategies Read the stem of the statement carefully, then read each of the answer options all the way through.

Apply and Debate

Read the following scenarios. Get together with other students in pairs or groups of three and take a position on each scenario. Debate your position in class with students taking the opposite position or prepare a written argument justifying your position.

⑪ Twin Pines

The Galaxy Research Center e-mailed an offer to the owners of Twin Pines, a farm in rural Arkansas. The e-mail message stated: "Please consider this our offer to purchase between 9,000 and 11,000 acres of your 15,000-acre tract of farmland near Twin Pines, Arkansas. Our offering price is between $15,000 and $19,000 per acre. Respond ASAP."

You Debate *Is this e-mail message a legally effective offer? Why or why not?*

⑫ Homecoming

Connie Adler agreed to go to the homecoming dance with Fred Wolfe. Later, Steve McNamara, the captain of the football team, asked Connie to be his date for homecoming. Connie broke her date with Fred to go to the dance with Steve.

You Debate *Does Fred have a legal claim against Connie? Why or why not?*

⑬ Pocket Calculator

Bob Goodman made a verbal agreement to buy a pocket calculator from Howard Hermann for $35. When Hermann delivered the calculator, Goodman refused to accept it, stating that he was not bound by his verbal agreement.

You Debate *Was Goodman correct? Why or why not?*

⑭ Waterbeds

Home Furniture Company advertised its waterbeds in a local newspaper. The newspaper mistakenly advertised the beds for $49 instead of $249.

You Debate *Must Home Furniture sell the beds at the advertised price? Defend your position by citing which legal principle is involved and how it applies.*

⑮ Revocation

Victor Archer mailed an offer to Sally Miles. Sally mailed a properly addressed and stamped letter of acceptance ten minutes before she received a revocation from Victor.

You Debate *Was the revocation effective? Defend your position by citing which legal principle is involved and how it applies.*

Case Study Practice – Heiman v. Parrish

⑯ Is an Agreement a Contract? In August of 1994, Jerod Heiman purchased a $9,033 diamond engagement ring. He then asked Heather Parrish to marry him. She said yes and took the ring. About a year later, in October 1995, Mr. Heiman broke off the engagement. Mr. Heiman asked Ms. Parrish to return the ring to him, but she refused. Mr. Heiman then sued her to retrieve the ring.

Ms. Parrish argued to the court that an engagement ring is a part of a contract between two parties to get married at a later date. She argued that Mr. Heiman broke off the engagement, breached the contract, and could not recover the ring.

Mr. Heiman argued that the proposal and engagement were not a binding contract but rather a statement that the parties would get married. The ring was a conditional gift to Ms. Parrish, which Ms. Parrish could keep if the two got married. Since the two did not get married, Mr. Heiman had a right to recover the ring.

Source: Heiman v. Parrish, 942 P.2d 631 (Kan. 1997)

Practice Was there a contract between Mr. Heiman and Ms. Parrish?

⑰ Ethics ←?→ Application _____

Reward or Not? Suppose you posted a reward notice that read, "Reward: $50 for the return of my lost iPod." Someone who did not know about the reward offer found your iPod and returned it to you.

◆ Would it be legal not to pay the reward money to the person who returned your iPod? Explain.

◆ Would it be ethical not to pay the reward money? Explain.

⑱ Think back to the Legal Briefs feature you read at the beginning of the chapter. Team up with a classmate to debate the issues described in the feature. One half of the class represents Apple, and the other half, the parents. Debate these points: Do in-game purchases made by minors qualify as contracts separate from the Terms of Service contract signed by the parents? Do the parents have the right to void contracts made by minors? Write one or more paragraphs to describe the experience and explain which side gave the best arguments.

5 Elements of a Contract

Legal Briefs

Non-Disclosure Agreements

Keeping private information private.

Want to start a business? You'll need a non-disclosure agreement. A non-disclosure agreement (NDA) is a legal contract that shows a confidential relationship between the business and its partners, including employees, contractors, and anyone who has proprietary information about your business.

If you signed a NDA with a former employer, you'll need to make sure that your new business does not conflict with that contract. Read over any NDA you signed before you move forward with your new business. It may have a time limit that has expired. If not, make sure your business does not conflict with your former employer's, or you might find yourself in court.

Most new entrepreneurs bounce their ideas off others. If someone steals that idea, it will go a long way in court if you show you've done your best to protect it by having potential partners and employees sign an NDA. Be specific when defining the proprietary information.

You want to protect your idea, but you don't want to scare off potential investors. Have your NDA ready, but use discretion as to when to present it.

Minors and Contracts Suppose you need to purchase a cell phone. *If you are under 18, can you sign an agreement, such as a wireless phone contract?*

© Paul Bradbury / age fotostock

Capacity and Legality

Reading Guide

Before You Read

Connect Does everybody have the same right to enter into any type of contract?

Focus on Ideas

Specific rules govern who can enter into contracts and whether a contract is legal, valid, or void.

Take Notes

Go to **connectED. mcgraw-hill.com** to download a graphic organizer you can use to take notes as you read this section.

Contractual Rights and Duties of Minors

Duties

Rights

Key Terms

You will learn these legal words and expressions in this chapter. You can also find these terms in *Black's Law Dictionary* or in an online legal dictionary.

- capacity
- minor
- majority
- emancipated

- disaffirm
- ratification
- public policy
- Statute of Frauds

Academic Vocabulary

You will find these words in your readings and in your tests. Look them up in a dictionary and familiarize yourself with them.

- assumption
- usury
- dispensing

Requirements of Capacity

Can you think of some people who might not be able to enter into contracts?

For a contract to be valid, offer, acceptance, genuine agreement, capacity, legality, and consideration are required. Whenever people negotiate the terms of a contract, they assume that everyone has the power or capacity to do so. **Capacity is the legal ability to enter into a contract.** The assumption that another person has the capacity to contract is called rebuttable presumption. The law allows some people to say after the fact that they did not have the capacity to enter into a contract.

Contractual Capacity Rules and Limitations

According to the law, several types of people may have the right to disaffirm a contract: minors, people with mental impairments, and people under the influence of drugs or alcohol.

People with Mental Impairments People with mental impairments can argue that they cannot be bound by contract. A mental impairment could be an injury. It could be a physical problem that someone has had from birth. It could also be a psychological problem that was recently diagnosed. The law only says that if a person had a mental problem when he or she entered a contract, then that person may not be bound to the contract. The mental problem must have made it impossible for the person to understand what was going on when the contract was made. The law requires doctors, not lawyers or judges, to determine if someone is mentally impaired.

As You Read

Predict Can minors cancel contracts to which they have agreed?

Contracts and Minors
Minors have rights and duties when it comes to contracts. They may, for example, change their minds and terminate a contract they have entered. However, they must be truthful about their age when making agreements. *How does this apply to buying movie tickets?*

Sometimes, people have a mental problem that is so severe they cannot take care of themselves. If the court decides that is the case, it will appoint a guardian for that person. The mentally impaired person's contracts are then declared void. This means that the person cannot make any contracts at all.

It is also possible that a contract made by a person with a mental impairment is perfectly valid. If the person was not suffering from the impairment when the contract was made or, if suffering from the impairment, the person still knew what he or she was doing at the time, then the contract is valid.

Minors Most of the time, minors are able to enter into and honor contracts. The law allows minors to get out of contracts. It considers them too inexperienced, immature, unknowledgeable, or naive to be permitted to enter into contracts without some sort of protection. If a minor does decide to get out of a contract, most adults choose not to fight it. To make contracts, there are a number of rules that minors must follow. Adults can also protect themselves from deceitful minors by refusing to enter into contracts with minors, unless parents also enter the contract. This approach is generally used for very expensive items such as cars. It protects the adult by obligating the parents if the minor tries to escape the contract.

A minor is a person who has not yet reached the age of adulthood. Sometimes we say that a person who is still not an adult is in his or her minority. A person who has reached the age of adulthood is said to have reached his or her majority.

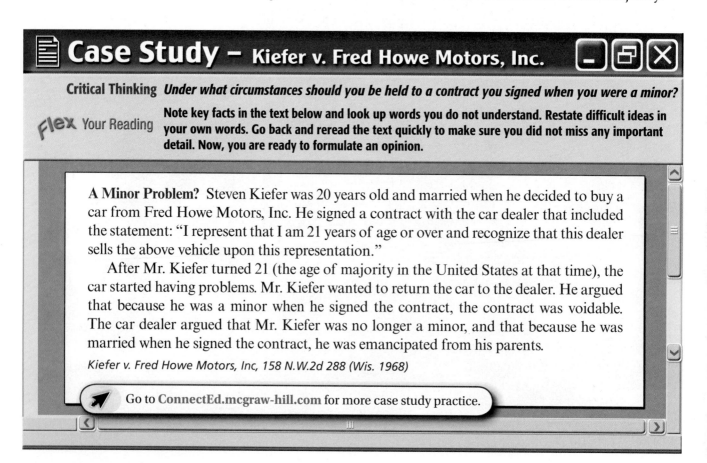

Case Study – Kiefer v. Fred Howe Motors, Inc.

Critical Thinking *Under what circumstances should you be held to a contract you signed when you were a minor?*

Flex Your Reading Note key facts in the text below and look up words you do not understand. Restate difficult ideas in your own words. Go back and reread the text quickly to make sure you did not miss any important detail. Now, you are ready to formulate an opinion.

A Minor Problem? Steven Kiefer was 20 years old and married when he decided to buy a car from Fred Howe Motors, Inc. He signed a contract with the car dealer that included the statement: "I represent that I am 21 years of age or over and recognize that this dealer sells the above vehicle upon this representation."

After Mr. Kiefer turned 21 (the age of majority in the United States at that time), the car started having problems. Mr. Kiefer wanted to return the car to the dealer. He argued that because he was a minor when he signed the contract, the contract was voidable. The car dealer argued that Mr. Kiefer was no longer a minor, and that because he was married when he signed the contract, he was emancipated from his parents.

Kiefer v. Fred Howe Motors, Inc, 158 N.W.2d 288 (Wis. 1968)

Go to **ConnectEd.mcgraw-hill.com** for more case study practice.

The age of majority is 18 in most states. Many states have made the drinking age 21, the age at which someone may legally purchase or consume alcohol. In most states, however, the age at which a person can legally purchase tobacco products is 18.

In the eyes of the law, people reach a particular age at the beginning of the day before their birthday. The law does not deal in fractions of days. One second after the clock strikes midnight means that the entire new day has been counted by the law. On your eighteenth birthday, you are legally considered eighteen and one day old.

An emancipated minor is one who is no longer under the legal control of his or her parents. Emancipated minors are responsible for their own contracts. Minors are automatically emancipated when they get married or set up their own households. Minors may also seek a court's permission for emancipation by suing for emancipation.

Minors who claim to be adults are committing fraud. In some states, when minors lie about their age and then insist on getting out of a contract, the other parties may sue for fraud. All five elements of fraud (see Chapter 6) must be proven for such a lawsuit to succeed. Other states still follow a much older rule that says minors cannot be sued for fraud, even if they lie about their age. These states still see it as a criminal offense when minors lie about their age to get age-restricted products, such as cigarettes and alcohol.

Intoxicated Persons People who are under the influence of drugs or alcohol can sometimes get out of a contract. Persons claiming intoxication must have been so impaired that they did not know what they were doing when they entered the contract. This decision is made by a judge or a jury.

Other Limits on Capacity In a few states, convicts have a limited capacity to contract. Aliens, citizens of other countries living in the United States, may also have limited contractual capacity. In wartime, foreign-born people identified as enemy aliens may be denied certain legal capacities.

The law makes exceptions when contracts involve necessaries such as food, clothing, shelter, medical care, and other things a person needs to live. It is up to a judge or a jury to decide whether a particular item is necessary.

Rights and Duties of Minors

Contracts made by minors are voidable by the minor. This means that minors have the right to disaffirm, or avoid their contracts if they choose. **To disaffirm a contract means to show the intent not to live up to the contract.** This intent can be shown by action or by statement. Minors can disaffirm contracts even when they have used poor judgment.

Returning Goods Minors who still have the goods they purchased when they disaffirm sales contracts must return those goods within a reasonable time. What reasonable time is, is decided by a judge or jury.

Reading Check

Enumerate *What statutes that affect capacity should you be aware of when entering a contract?*

The more perishable the goods, the less time will be considered reasonable. The minor can give back the goods by actually handing the goods over to the other party or by making an offer to do so. In some states an amount can be deducted for damaged, dirty, tattered, and torn items that the minor returns. Young people can also disaffirm a contract after becoming an adult. They must do this within a reasonable amount of time. Sometimes, even minors who no longer have the goods can get out of their agreements.

Disaffirming Contracts Minors cannot pick and choose the parts of the contract they want to keep and those they want to disaffirm. When two minors make a contract with each other, both of them can get out of the contract. Minors are, therefore, at risk when they enter a contract with another minor.

If an adult discovers that the other party is a minor, the adult has no right to get out of the contract for that reason alone. Sometimes, people buy goods from somebody who bought the goods from a minor. If the minor then decides to get out of the original contract, the ownership rights of the innocent third party are protected. This rule applies only to goods, not to land.

Ratification of a Minor's Contracts **Ratification is the act of agreeing to go along with a contract that could have been avoided.** A person can ratify a contract by words or actions. The words can be spoken or written. A minor can ratify a contract after becoming an adult. Once this is done, all the contractual privileges that the person had as a minor are gone. If a minor makes a payment that is due under a contract after becoming an adult, that minor has ratified the contract.

Returning Goods Special rules apply to minors when returning merchandise they have purchased. Suppose you have bought a video game and used it for a week. *Could you return it?*

Exceptions to the General Rule The law may use exceptions to the rule that lets minors get out of their contracts. For example, minors must pay the fair value of the necessaries. Some states will hold minors to contracts for things required by law, such as car insurance. Some states give limited capacity to minors who own businesses. Other states say that married minors are adults. Others treat an apartment rental agreement as a contract for a necessary. Minors also cannot get out of military enlistment agreements.

Minors as Drivers Driving is a privilege, not a right. As a privilege, it must be earned, and then kept under conditions of good behavior. Many states will not permit minors to earn a license until they reach the age of 16.

Gallo Images/Richard Kepp/Getty Images

Minors must also meet certain minimum requirements before earning a license. The requirements generally include a written test to qualify for a temporary driving permit, a driver's education course, and a final examination that consists of a road test and a vision exam. A minor with a driver's license generally has the same rights and responsibilities as an adult driver.

Minors as Students Students in a school setting may be searched if school officials have reason to suspect the law or a school rule has been broken. While adult speakers and writers are granted freedom in how they can express themselves in speech or in print, students may be restrained from printing certain matters in a school-sponsored newspaper.

The Rights and Duties of Parents and Guardians

Parents have certain rights under the law. They have the right to discipline their children and to manage their children's property. Adoptive parents have the same rights. Neither natural nor adoptive parents can abuse those rights.

The law protects children from abusive parents under the *parens patriae* doctrine. This doctrine holds that the state can act as a child's parent when natural or adoptive parents cannot or will not perform their parental duties.

The law also states that both natural and adoptive parents have the duty to provide their children with necessaries. If minors are forced to purchase the necessaries on their own, the parents will be liable for that contract. If a minor becomes emancipated, parental duties come to an end.

In their wills, parents may name guardians for their minor children. Two types of guardians can be appointed by the parents. Guardians of the child will act as the parents would act in relation to the child. Property guardians will handle the child's property. This right ends when the child reaches the age of majority.

Legality

Is a contract valid if one of its terms breaks the law?

Illegality can destroy an otherwise valid contract. It can also expose people who agree to the contract to potential charges of criminal conduct and other legal consequences. While most laws are widely known and understood, there are many laws against doing things that are not so obvious, such as having a yard sale without a license. These laws create what is called a hidden dimension of illegality.

Effect of Illegality

In general, a court will not help any party to an illegal contract. Instead, it will leave the parties where they put themselves. Neither party can enforce the agreement. Neither party can get help from the court. An exception is made when the parties are not equally at fault. In such cases, the court may help people who are less at fault in getting back any money or property they may have lost.

Legal Talk

Illegal: *adj* Against the law. From Latin *il* = not + *leg, lex* = law: not lawful.

In pari delicto: Latin adverbial phrase = in equal fault.

Vocabulary Builder *Il, im, in,* or *ir* at the beginning of a word (that is, as a prefix) often means not. List five words that begin with these prefixes and define them using the word not. For example, improper = not proper.

Illegality in Entire Agreement Sometimes, a contract cannot be divided into separate promises and different acts. If a contract cannot be divided, then anything illegal within the contract makes the entire contract illegal. The whole contract is, therefore, void. This is true even if sections of the agreement are legal.

***In Pari Delicto* and Divisible Contracts** If certain promises and actions in a contract can be performed by themselves, the contract is divisible. The courts may enforce parts of the agreement that are legal and cancel the parts that are not.

The parties are said to be in pari delicto (in equal fault) if they both know that the agreement is illegal. In that case, the court will not help either party. On the other hand, if one party is not aware of the illegality and had no intent to break the law, then the parties are not in pari delicto. The courts may grant relief to the innocent party.

Agreements That Break Statutes

State legislatures pass laws that make some agreements illegal because they violate the state's civil or criminal statutes, **usury** statutes, gambling statutes, licensing statutes, or Sunday statutes.

Civil and Criminal Statutes Agreements that require one party to commit a tort or a crime are illegal. Common torts are slander, libel, and fraud. Crimes include burglary, larceny, murder, and arson. An agreement is illegal if it is made to interfere with or to violate the rights of another person. Agreements to protect one party from the consequences of the torts or the crimes he or she has committed are also illegal.

Usury Statutes A contract to buy stolen goods or commit arson is obviously illegal. Usury, however, is an example of an activity that has the hidden dimension of illegality. Interest is the fee a borrower pays to a lender for using money. Usury is charging more than the maximum legal interest rate. Each state has a statute that sets a maximum interest rate that lenders can charge for loans. Charging whatever you want for interest is not only unfair, it is also illegal.

The Truth in Lending Act is one step the federal government has taken to make consumers aware of the cost of borrowing money. Under this law, the lender must clearly report the annual percentage rate (APR) to the borrower. Before you sign any loan agreement or credit card, look for the true rate of interest (APR).

Gambling Statutes Gambling statutes fall within the hidden dimension of illegality: Playing cards, betting on sports events, or entering an office pool for money may seem harmless, but they are illegal in many states. If you win money gambling but have trouble collecting, the court will not enforce the debt, and may consider you to be in violation of the law.

Today, many types of regulated gambling are legal. A state may legalize one form of gambling and outlaw others. One form of gambling might be legal in one state but not in another.

Giveaway games by stores or businesses for promotion are legal as long as you are not required to buy a ticket or product to participate. Betting at racetracks is allowed in New York, Illinois, California, Massachusetts, Ohio, and some other states. Lotteries, other than those run by the state government, are still illegal in many places. Many states have set up their own state-run lotteries to raise money.

Sunday Statutes In early colonial days, some American colonies passed special Sunday statutes, also called blue laws, that made agreements made on a Sunday void. An offer made on a day other than Sunday, but accepted on a Sunday, is void. If an offer is made on a Sunday but accepted on another day, the contract is valid because acceptance marks the creation of the contract. If an agreement is made on a Sunday, but a date other than Sunday is placed on the agreement, the contract is void. States that still observe Sunday laws often apply the same restrictions to legal holidays.

Licensing Statutes All states have statutes that require a license to do certain jobs. A license is a legal document that grants permission from the government to do a certain job. Licenses protect people from dealing with unqualified persons. Trade and professional people such as nurses, doctors, lawyers, funeral directors, barbers, and plumbers must be licensed. An agreement made with an unlicensed person working in such jobs is illegal. Some state statutes require licenses simply to raise money. Any person who pays the fee gets a license. A law requiring a vendor's (seller's) license is designed to raise revenue for the local government that issues the license. In these cases, agreements made with unlicensed people are valid. However, the unlicensed person might be fined.

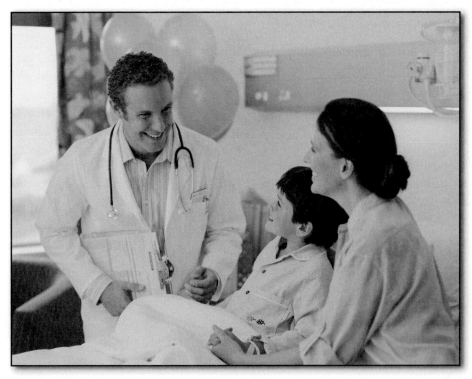

← **Special Statutes** Doctors and most people in medical professions have to obtain and display a license to practice medicine. *What is the purpose of licensing medical personnel?*

Agreements Contrary to Public Policy

Not all illegal agreements break statutes. Some agreements are illegal because they break public policy. The power to regulate the public's health, safety, welfare, and morals belongs to the government. The states have this power because they have governmental authority. The federal government has this power because of the U.S. Constitution. **Public policy is a legal principle that holds that nobody should be allowed to do something that harms the public.** Public policy allows the courts to get involved to protect the public welfare when other laws do not.

Agreements That Unreasonably Restrain Trade The law protects the right to make a living. If a contract takes away this right, the law will label the contract void. Restraint of trade agreements take away somebody's ability to do business with others. Three types of contracts circumvent this rule: agreements not to compete, agreements to fix prices, and agreements to defeat competitive bidding.

Agreements Not to Compete When someone buys a business, that person also buys the seller's goodwill not to compete. One way to ensure goodwill is to add a restrictive covenant to a sales contract. A restrictive covenant not to compete is an agreement in which the seller promises not to open a business that competes with the buyer within a certain area for a period of time.

Bidding for Public Works Contracts It is illegal for contractors to engage in any type of price fixing when bidding for public works contracts. *Why does this rule protect the public?*

A court will uphold this agreement, which keeps it out of the hidden dimension of illegality if it is reasonable in time, location, and type of business. If the restraint is unreasonable considering the nature of the business sold, then the restraint is illegal. Promises not to compete are also found in employment contracts. Employees agree not to work at similar jobs for a period of time after they leave this employment. Such contracts are enforced only as needed to protect the former employer.

Agreements for Price Fixing In the United States, some laws have been created to protect competition. Price fixing is when competitors agree to set prices within certain ranges. In some cases, competitors agree to sell a particular product or service at an agreed price. In other cases, manufacturers dictate the price at which retailers must sell a product. Price fixing hurts competition and keeps prices artificially high. Because they are contrary to public policy, the courts will not uphold price-fixing agreements. In fact, competitors who seek to fix prices may be prosecuted by state or federal agencies.

Agreements to Defeat Competitive Bidding A bid is an offer to buy or sell goods or services at a stated price. Laws often require governments to construct public works or buy goods and services through competitive bidding. In this process, competitors submit bids for a project, and the the lowest qualified bid wins the contract. If competitors agree not to bid lower than a certain price, then they are not bidding competitively. The agreements and the contracts are not enforceable.

Agreements to Obstruct Justice A contract that gets in the way of the **dispensing** of justice is illegal. Such contracts include protecting someone from arrest, encouraging lawsuits, giving false testimony, or bribing a juror. It also includes an agreement to pay a non-expert to testify at a trial. It could also include an agreement to take money to stop a legal action against a person who has committed a crime.

Agreements Inducing Breach of Duty or Fraud Many persons hold positions of trust and have a responsibility for the well-being of others. Your representative in Congress, your state senator, and all other public officials hold positions of trust. They owe a duty to work for the best interest of the public. Any contract that tries to influence these people for private gain is unenforceable. This rule also applies to private persons who are in positions of trust.

Agreements to Give Up the Right to Litigate or Arbitrate Contracts may include clauses that limit the ability of the parties to bring a lawsuit or to arbitrate a claim. Sometimes, such clauses are valid. However, they might be offered on a take-it-or-leave-it basis by the party with the most power. The clause must be fair. If it is not, the court might say it is unconscionable and strike it down as illegal.

Agreements Interfering with Marriage Contracts that discourage, damage, or destroy good family relationships are illegal. For instance, if Mr. Popson promises to give his daughter, Angela, $100,000 if she never gets married, the contract is void.

The Statute of Frauds

What happens if you want to make changes to a contract after you agreed to its terms?

In the past, under common law rule, a person accused of breaking a contract could not testify about it in court. Instead, only people who were not parties to the contract could testify. This encouraged bribery. To prevent this, the English Parliament passed a law in 1677 that required certain contracts to be in writing in order to be enforceable. The law was called An Act for the Prevention of Frauds and Perjuries.

Global Law

Contract Differences in Canada

The United States and Canada have a legal tradition based upon English common law. Many of their legal principles, including those dealing with contracts, are similar. Some differences have occurred since the two countries gained their independence from England. Two major differences relate to entering into noncommercial oral contracts and the elements of proving fraud in a contract dispute.

Oral Contracts

In the United States, oral contracts are considered as valid as written contracts for almost everything except the sale of real estate.

In Canada, however, there is a presumption that people do not enter into oral contracts for non-business, religious, or charitable reasons. This includes entering into contracts with family members and friends.

This is demonstrated in a case in which a Canadian court held that an agreement entered into by friends to share a set of season hockey tickets was not a valid oral contract because it was not for business reasons.

Fraud

Another contract law difference between the United States and Canada relates to fraud. In the United States, the parties must prove that the victim suffered an actual loss from the fraud in order to recover losses. In Canada, a loss is not required to recover damages against the perpetrator of the fraud. This can be especially advantageous when the victim wishes to rescind or cancel a contract before harm occurs.

Across Cultures: Quebec's Legal System

Most Canadian provinces have a common law system. However, Quebec has a civil code system inherited from the French; so does the state of Louisiana in the United States.

Critical Thinking *Would an oral agreement between neighbors for splitting the cost of a fence be considered a valid oral contract in Canada? In the United States?*

Today, most states in the United States have a Statute of Frauds. **A Statute of Frauds is a state law that requires that certain contracts be in writing.** This is so there is evidence that (1) the contact exists, and that (2) it has certain definitive terms.

Elements of a Written Contract

A written contract can be a letter, a sales slip, an invoice, or several words placed on a check. There are some specific requirements. The written contract must, for example, identify the place, date, parties, subject matter, price and terms, and intent of the parties. It should also contain the signature of the party who may be charged.

Interpretation of Contracts and Clashing Terms It may be necessary to make changes to a contract in handwriting because it is too inconvenient to print a whole new contract. The court will enforce handwritten terms. The court assumes that the handwritten changes were placed in writing after the contract was printed and represent the final intent of the parties. According to the law: (1) handwriting prevails over typewriting, preprinting, or word processing; (2) typewriting or word processing prevails over preprinting. The court will honor the amount on a check that is written in words.

When a written contract is filled with confusing language, the court will lean against the party who actually wrote the contract. Words, phrases, and sentences should be clear and unambiguous.

Contracts That Must Be in Writing

The Statute of Frauds adds a requirement to the six elements of a valid contract: offer, acceptance, genuine agreement, capacity, consideration, and legality. Certain contracts must be in writing to be enforceable. Be aware that the Statute of Frauds applies only to executory contracts (contracts that have not been fully performed).

Contracts to Pay Somebody Else's Debt A contract to pay someone else's debts must be in writing to be enforceable. The debtor still owes the money; the person promising to cover the debt does so only if the debtor fails to pay.

Contracts to Pay Debts of a Person Who Has Died When a person dies, somebody has to pay that person's debts and divide up the rest of his or her property among any remaining relatives. Executors and administrators handle such matters. The law says that executors and administrators are not personally responsible for the debts.

Often, executors are close relatives of the deceased. They may feel responsible for the deceased's debts when the estate runs out of money and agree to pay them. Later, the executor might have second thoughts about having made such a promise. To protect someone in such a vulnerable position, the law requires that such an agreement be in writing.

Real Estate Contracts Contracts that involve real estate sales must be in writing. *What is the exception to this rule?*

Contracts Requiring More Than a Year to Perform
Any contract that cannot be performed within one year must be in writing to be enforceable. The year begins to run when the contract is made, not when the performance is to start. Agreements in which the amount of time involved is uncertain do not have to be in writing.

Contracts in Consideration of Marriage
When two persons agree to marry, they enter into a contract. The promises they make to each other are consideration for the contract. Agreements to marry have never required a written contract. Under present-day law, an agreement between two people to marry is not enforceable. Either party can break the agreement. If one person agrees to marry another person for a third person's promise of money or property, the agreement must be in writing. A promise to adopt a child from a former marriage or to care for another relative in return for a promise of marriage must be in writing to be enforceable.

Contracts for the Sale of Goods
Although the Uniform Commercial Code (UCC) lists many exceptions to this rule, a contract for the sale of goods for $500 or more must be in writing.

Goods are movable items such as furniture, books, computers, PDAs, cultivated crops, clothing, vehicles, and MP3 players.

According to the UCC, a written agreement is valid if it indicates that a contract for sale has been made between the parties. The UCC does not require that all the terms of the contract be in writing.

Contracts to Sell Real Property   Contracts for the sale of real property must be in writing to be enforceable. Real property is land and anything permanently attached to the land. One important contract for real property you might enter into is the contract to buy or sell a home. The contract of sale, sometimes called a purchase and sale agreement, consists of an offer that is made by the buyer and accepted by the seller.

One major exception to the requirement that a contract for the sale of real property be in writing is called equitable estoppel. According to equitable estoppel, a party cannot claim the Statute of Frauds if the other party did something extreme, such as making excess improvements to the property, because of what the other party promised.

Special Rules for the Interpretation of Contracts

It is crucial to understand which contracts must be in writing to be enforceable in a court of law. There are also special rules for the interpretation of written contracts. These rules include the parol evidence rule and the best evidence rule.

The Parol Evidence Rule   A written contract should contain everything that was agreed upon between the parties so that neither party can go to court and claim a contract is incorrect or fails to show the parties' real intentions.

This long-established rule is called the parol evidence rule. Parol means word of mouth; evidence, in this instance, means anything presented as proof in a trial. The parol evidence rule says that evidence of oral statements made before signing a written agreement cannot be presented in court to change or add to the terms of that written agreement. The court presumes that a written contract contains all of the terms and provisions intended by the parties.

There are exceptions to this general rule. Parol evidence may be introduced to explain some point that is not clear in a written agreement. It may be used to show that certain terms were incorrectly placed in the written contract. It also may be presented to prove that one party was tricked by another.

The Best Evidence Rule   This rule requires that the original written agreement (rather than a copy) be used as evidence in court. The rule means a court does not want to look at photocopies or faxed copies of a written agreement. Copying a contract can make it easier for a dishonest person to hide alterations to the original. For this reason, when a contract is reduced to writing, each party receives an original version of the contract.

Duplicate originals are original versions of a contract that are signed by and provided to all of the parties to a contract.

Real-World Rules When you are asked to sign an order blank, sales slip, or other printed form, such documents may contain small print on the front or reverse side. The words are often difficult to read, and the language may be hard to understand. Often, the small print is not written in your favor. Follow these guidelines before you sign:

- Read the entire text of the document before you sign it.
- If you do not understand something or do not agree to it, cross it out before you sign. Do not be shy about having the other party initial the change too. The change is meaningless unless the other party has initialed it.
- Do not be afraid to make changes on a printed or word-processed form. If any extra-added promises are made to you, write them in.
- If a contract is for something major, such as the purchase of a house or car, and contains a lot of legal language—or legalese—you do not understand, have a lawyer review it before you sign.
- Refuse to sign a written contract if you do not agree with everything contained in the writing.

After You Read

Summarize What should you consider when you are evaluating a contract?

SECTION 5.1 ASSESSMENT

Self Check

1. What rights does a minor have in relation to contracts?
2. What happens when a minor becomes emancipated?
3. How are minors protected under the parens patriae doctrine?

Academic Connection

Mathematics As a part of your sales contract with Wilson Sporting Goods Company, you are entitled to a trade discount. The invoice is for $1,454.00 with the terms 6/15/n30, which means that if your bill is paid within 15 days of receipt you receive a 6% discount. If you take the full 30 days to pay, no discount applies. Calculate the discount and the amount due for the invoice.

THEORY **Number and Operations: Use Fractions, Decimals, and Rounding** To solve this problem use the following formulas:

$$\frac{\text{Cash}}{\text{Discount}} = \frac{\text{Net}}{\text{Price}} \times \frac{\text{Cash-}}{\text{Discount}}$$
$$\text{Rate}$$

$$\frac{\text{Cash}}{\text{Price}} = \frac{\text{Net}}{\text{Price}} - \frac{\text{Cash}}{\text{Discount}}$$

 For more math practice, go to the Math Appendix.

Critical Thinking

Contracts between Minors Suppose that you have purchased an MP3 player from a classmate. Can that classmate change his mind, ask you to return the player, and offer you a refund? Explain.

Consideration

Reading Guide

Before You Read

Connect If you agree to sell your MP3 player to your best friend for $50, what do you gain and what do you lose? What does your friend gain and lose?

Focus on Ideas

Consideration is a kind of exchange and it is a key element of a valid contract.

Take Notes

Go to **connectED. mcgraw-hill.com** to download a graphic organizer you can use to take notes as you read this section.

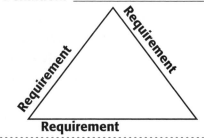

Consideration
Definition: _____

Requirement

Requirement

Requirement

Requirement

Key Terms

You will learn these legal words and expressions in this chapter. You can also find these terms in *Black's Law Dictionary* or in an online legal dictionary.

- consideration
- forbearance
- unconscionable contract
- adhesion contract
- accord and satisfaction
- promissory estoppel

Academic Vocabulary

You will find these words in your readings and in your tests. Look them up in a dictionary and familiarize yourself with them.

- contain
- indicating
- obligation

What You'll Learn

- ◆ Analyze the requirements for valid consideration.
- ◆ Define the different types of consideration.
- ◆ List exceptions to the requirements of consideration.
- ◆ Compare unconscionability and illegality.

Why It's Important

Understanding the concept of consideration will help you make sure that contracts you enter into are valid.

The Legal Concept of Consideration

Is ordering a taco at a street stand consideration?

Consideration is the exchange of benefits and detriments by the parties to a contract. A benefit is something that a party receives in the agreement. A detriment is something a party gives up in the agreement (see **Figure 5.1**). There are three types of detriments:

- Giving up something that you have the right to keep
- Doing something that you have the right not to do
- Not doing something that you have the legal right to do

The last type of detriment listed is also called forbearance. **Forbearance is not doing what you have the right to do.**

Requirements for Valid Consideration

The parties must bargain with each other if there is to be a contract. Each side in the agreement must give up something and get something in exchange. The exchange or the promise to exchange something of value is what binds the parties together. A date for Friday night or a promise to pick up a friend before school are not contracts because neither one **contains** consideration.

The Characteristics of Consideration

There are three characteristics of consideration:

- Consideration must involve a bargained-for exchange.
- Consideration must involve something of value.
- The benefits and detriments that make up consideration must be legal.

As You Read

Predict Does a contract have to include an exchange to be valid?

Vocabulary You can find vocabulary definitions in the **Key Terms** glossary and Academic Vocabulary glossary in the back of this book.

➡ **Consideration** Consideration is an exchange of benefits and detriments by the parties to an agreement. *Is consideration necessary to make a contract legally binding?*

Figure 5.1 Consideration

Benefit: The right to receive the money.

Promisor

I'll sell you my car for $3,500.

Legal Detriment: The promise to give up the $3,500.

Promisee

I'll buy it for that price.

Joseph Duffey
1122 Reeling Way
Flatwood, MO

PAY

THE BIG BANK
ANYPLACE, USA

Promisee

Legal Detriment: The promise to give up the car.

Promisor

Benefit: The right to receive the car.

Bargained-for Exchange A contract involves a bargained-for exchange when a promise is made in return for another promise. It also occurs when an act is exchanged for an act or a promise not to act. Bargaining means that a party will lose something if the other party does not come through as promised. Conversely, both parties gain something when the promises are kept or the acts are performed.

Something of Value Something of value to one person may be worthless to another. The law is not concerned with the value of consideration and does not set value in a contract. All that matters is that the parties agree freely on the value and the price, and that consideration be present and the parties agree to it.

The only time a court might look at the value of consideration is if it thinks that the consideration offered is so far from what it should be that it is grossly unfair. This type of contract is said to be unconscionable. **An unconscionable contract is an agreement in which the consideration is so out of line with the actual value of the subject matter and so unfair that it shocks the court's conscience.**

Two additional conditions must be present for a contract to be unconscionable:

- There must be uneven power between the parties.
- The party with all the power tells the other party to take it or leave it.

This is called an adhesion contract. **An adhesion contract is a take-it-or-leave-it offer made by a party who holds most of the power in a bargaining session.** When the courts are faced with this type of situation, they will do one of three things:

- Refuse to enforce the entire contract.
- Enforce the contract without the unconscionable clause (if possible).
- Limit the enforcement of that clause.

Legality and Unconscionability The law requires that the consideration that passes from one party to another be legal. If the consideration is illegal, the contract is void. For example, someone cannot give up something, such as a stolen bicycle, that he or she does not own. Illegality is not the same as unconscionability. Consideration may be legal, as when money is paid for an item, but unconscionable because the amount paid is so unfair that it shocks the conscience of the court.

Types of Consideration

If you agree to sell your laptop to a classmate, what do you think consideration could be?

There are very few limits on what consideration can be: it is what two parties agree it should be. Courts see some everyday things as consideration: money, property, services, promises not to sue, and promises made to a charity (see **Figure 5.2**).

Money as Consideration

Often, one party offers money in exchange for the other party's property or services. Sometimes, when costs get out of hand, the government might step in and control prices. There are also a few laws, like the Federal Fair Labor Standards Act, which sets a minimum wage for workers, that dictates the amount that can be offered in certain contracts.

Property and Services as Consideration

Service as consideration is part of a contract with some workers; for example, when your family hires a gardener to take care of the lawn or a plumber to fix a leaky pipe or when you buy the services of the hair stylist who cuts your hair. Property is also consideration. This is the type of agreement you enter whenever you go to the mall to buy CDs. Contracts for the purchase of a new house are another example. Property is consideration in barter agreements, such as when when you trade video games with your friends.

A Promise Not to Sue

Giving up the right to sue is a type of forbearance. Lawsuits are often settled when one party agrees not to sue the other party. The other party promises to pay a set amount of money in return. A signed agreement not to sue is called a release. This practice is so common that many insurance companies have preprinted forms that they use to settle cases before they even get filed.

Charitable Pledges

Charities depend on money from businesses and individuals. This has led the courts to uphold donation promises as if they were contracts, although there often is no consideration in the agreement. Courts uphold these pledges because charities provide services to society.

Figure 5.2 Types of Consideration

Service as consideration involves exchanging work or expertise for goods or money, such as when you contract someone to repair your computer or cut your hair.

Property as consideration involves the exchange of goods for money, services, or other goods. Exchanging goods for other goods, such as trading video games or CDs with a friend, is called barter.

Money as consideration, which can be in the form of credit or a paycheck, involves the exchange of money for goods or services.

Money, property, and services are the most common forms of consideration in a contract. *What are two other forms of consideration?*

Problems with Consideration

Sometimes, the parties to a contract disagree on how much money is due. There is a way out of such disagreements. The solution depends on whether there really is a genuine disagreement as to the amount that is owed.

Disputed Amounts If there is a genuine issue as to the amount owed, the parties can use accord and satisfaction to settle the argument. **Accord and satisfaction is a legal way to settle contractual disputes by which one party agrees to accept less than the amount due as full payment.** The acceptance by the creditor of less than what was billed is the accord. The agreed-to settlement as contained in the accord is the satisfaction. The dispute must be real and in good faith. Finally, the amount involved cannot be trivial.

> **Example:** Alison and Jeremy Brisbane made a contract with the Port Clinton Construction Company to put siding on their house in Lakeside, Ohio. The company charged $50 per hour for a job that lasted 200 hours. The final bill for labor was $11,250. When they looked at the bill, the Brisbanes saw that they had been charged an hour per day for travel time from the company's home base to their house. The Brisbanes thought it unfair for them to be charged for travel time. They deducted $1,250 from the bill (25 travel hours at $50 per hour). They sent a check for $10,000 to the company. On the check, they wrote, "In full payment for the siding placed on our summer home at 206 Jasmine, Lakeside, Ohio." When Port Clinton Construction cashed the check, they accepted the lesser amount as full payment.

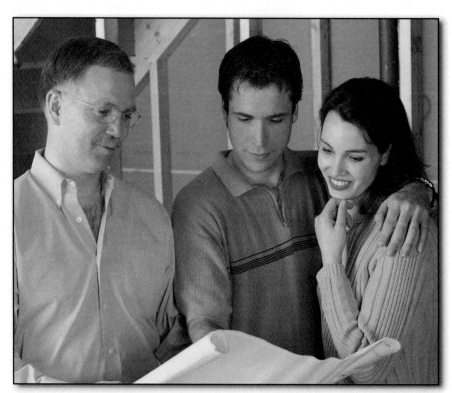

➡ **Amount Due Disagreement** A contractor and a homeowner might not agree on an amount due in exchange for work performed. *In what case could accord and satisfaction not be used to settle the issue?*

Ingram Publishing

Undisputed Amounts If the parties have agreed to a set amount of money in the contract, then accord and satisfaction does not apply. This is true even if the party who owes the money finds out that the product was on sale for a lesser amount somewhere else.

Exceptions to the Requirements of Consideration

Some agreements are valid even without consideration. Specific rules vary from state to state, but some agreements always fall into this group.

Promises Under Seal A seal is a mark or an impression placed on a written contract **indicating** that it is a formal agreement. Most states today do not require a seal. Those that do generally allow the word seal on the letters, L.S., or the phrase *locus sigilli* (place of the seal) after the signature. Contracts for goods do not require a seal. Some contracts for land do need a seal.

Promises After Discharge in Bankruptcy Sometimes, people who have had their debts discharged in bankruptcy court promise to pay the debts anyway. A court hearing is required when such promises are made. In the hearing, the debtor is told about the legal consequences of making such a promise. Some states do not require any consideration for this promise. The promise is supported by contractual intent. Some states say the promise must be in writing.

Debts Ended by the Statute of Limitations A statute of limitations sets up the time limit for suing somebody. Different states have different time limits. Such variations can run from three to ten years. The same state may also have different time limits for different types of contracts. For instance, the statute of limitations may set one time limit for oral contracts and a different one for written contracts. A time limit for a contract for goods may be different from a contract for the sale of real property.

Promises Enforced by Promissory Estoppel If someone making a promise should have reasonably expected the other person to rely on the promise, and the other person did rely on the promise and suffered a loss, the innocent party can use promissory estoppel to make the other party compensate him or her for the loss. The doctrine stops one party (the estoppel part) from denying that he or she made a promise that hurt the second party (the promissory part). **Promissory estoppel is the principle that a promise made without consideration may nonetheless be enforced to prevent injustice.** The following elements must be present:

- The promise was made about the innocent party's action (or lack of action).
- The innocent party gave no consideration in exchange for that promise.

Preexisting Duty

Preexisting duties cannot be made consideration in a new contract. *Why does the law prevent preexisting duties from being consideration in new contracts?*

- The innocent party relied on the promise and did something that changed his or her position in a major way (such as sold a car, moved out of an apartment, sold a house, or took a vacation).
- Injustice can be avoided only by enforcing the promise and making up for the loss.

Option Sometimes one person will pay another person money to keep an offer open for a set period of time. This is called an option. When the contract involves goods, the offer can be held open without the money payment. This is called a firm offer. A firm offer requires a written offer stating the period of time during which the offer will stay open. The time cannot go beyond three months. The person making the written offer must be a merchant who deals in the types of goods involved on an everyday basis.

Agreements without Consideration

Some agreements and promises seem to include consideration, but in reality they do not, and what passes for consideration is actually not enforceable by law.

Illusory Promises For a contract to be real, all the parties must be required to do something. Sometimes, a contract seems to require something when it really does not. For example, this happens when a restaurant agrees to buy all the apples it needs for the summer from a particular farmer. The promise seems real, but since the restaurant can simply say it did not need any apples that summer, the promise is not real. This is an illusory promise.

Future Gifts and Legacies A person's promise to give a gift to another person at some time in the future or to leave a legacy in a will cannot be enforced without consideration. This rule applies to promises of free services or to promise to lend somebody something.

Past Consideration The act of giving consideration must happen at the same time that the contract is made. Past consideration is something that was given or promised in the past that somebody tries to use again in a new contract. The courts do not accept past consideration. For example, suppose you help your older brother move into his college dormitory on Saturday. The next day, he promises to pay you $25 for helping. That promise is not binding because your consideration was given in the past.

Preexisting Duties The act of giving consideration requires a new promise for every new contract. A preexisting duty is an **obligation** that a person already has to do something and cannot be used again in a new contract. Suppose a person is already obligated to do something, such as mow the lawn every week. Then he or she cannot make it consideration in a new contract. If the courts allowed preexisting duties to bind a party in a new contract, they would be permitting one promise to do double duty.

Promise to Attend a Social Engagement All contracts are agreements, but not all agreements are contracts. A promise to take a friend to a concert would not be a legally binding agreement because the friend has given nothing in exchange for the promise: That agreement lacks consideration.

After You Read

Summarize What are contractual situations in which consideration does not apply?

SECTION 5.2 ASSESSMENT

Self Check

1. What are the characteristics of consideration?
2. What is an unconscionable contract?
3. What is forbearance?

Academic Connection

Mathematics Mikiko Iwayama purchased a vacuum cleaner for $299.99. She lives in Wisconsin where the sales tax is 5%. What is the total amount that she will pay for the appliance? Does this purchase constitute a contract? What is consideration in this case?

CONCEPT **Number and Operations: Computing Percentages** To solve this problem use the following formulas:

Sales Tax = Selling Price × Sales Tax Rate

Total Purchase Price = Selling Price + Sales Tax

 For more math practice, go to the Math Appendix.

Critical Thinking

Accord and Satisfaction Suppose that you make a contract to buy a skateboard for your friend, Hal. You then see the exact same skateboard on auction on eBay. You monitor the auction and discover that the winning bidder paid a lot less than you paid Hal. Can you use accord and satisfaction to pay the lesser amount for the skateboard? Explain.

Summary

Section 5.1 Capacity and Legality

- Capacity is the legal ability to enter a contract.
- People who lack contractual capacity are: minors, people with mental impairment, and intoxicated persons.
- The law makes an exception when the contract involves necessaries. Necessaries are food, clothing, shelter, and medical care.
- Minors who decide to get out of their contracts can do so. A minor is a person who has not yet reached the age of adulthood.
- An emancipated minor is no longer under the control of his or her parents. Emancipated minors are responsible for their own contracts.
- Minors who claim to be adults are committing fraud.
- Minors must disaffirm an entire contract. They cannot pick and choose the parts of the contract they want to keep and those they want to disaffirm.
- Ratification is the act of agreeing to go along with a contract that could have been avoided.

Section 5.2 Consideration

- Consideration is the exchange of benefits and detriments by the parties to a contract. A benefit is something received in the agreement. A detriment is a loss.
- Consideration must involve a bargained-for exchange. It must involve something of value.
- Consideration includes money, property, and services. Other forms of consideration include promises not to sue and promises made to a charity.
- Accord and satisfaction is a legal way to settle contractual disputes by which one party agrees to accept less than the amount due as full payment.
- Agreements valid without consideration: promises under seal, promises after discharge in bankruptcy, debts ended by statute of limitations, promises enforced by promissory estoppel, and options.
- Agreements not valid without consideration: illusory promises, promise of future gifts or legacies, promises based on past consideration or on preexisting duties, and agreements to attend social engagements.

Vocabulary Builder

❶ On a sheet of paper, use each of these terms in a sentence.

Key Terms

- capacity
- minor
- majority
- emancipated
- disaffirm
- ratification
- public policy
- Statute of Frauds
- consideration
- forbearance
- unconscionable contract
- adhesion contract
- accord and satisfaction
- promissory estoppel

Academic Vocabulary

- assumption
- usury
- dispensing
- contain
- indicating
- obligation

Key Points Review

Answer the following questions. Refer to the chapter for additional reinforcement.

2 Who determines whether a mental impairment compromised a person's ability to enter a contract?

3 What is the rule that determines if someone is so intoxicated that he or she cannot be held responsible for any contracts entered while in that state?

4 Can minors disaffirm part of a contract?

5 How can adults protect themselves from deceitful minors?

6 Why do the courts refuse to become involved trying to set the value of consideration?

7 Is it okay to agree to do something that might be considered illegal as consideration in a contract? Explain.

8 What ordinary things might be consideration in a contract?

Standardized Test Practice

9 Read the following information about the Census Bureau and complete questions 1 and 2.

The Census Bureau conducts many censuses and surveys. The most well known is the official population census of the United States, called the decennial census. It is conducted every ten years, most recently in April 2000. During each decennial census, the Census Bureau collects data from every household in the U.S. and its territories.

Besides the decennial census, the Census Bureau conducts nearly one hundred other surveys and censuses every year. By law, no one is permitted to reveal information from these censuses and surveys that could identify any person, household, or business. Individual records from each decennial census are made public 72 years after the census has been taken.

1. How often does the Census Bureau conduct the decennial census?

A every eight years
B every five years
C every six years
D every ten years

2. By law, what information cannot be revealed?

A identify any person, business, or income records
B identify any person, household, or business
C identify any person, household, or individual record
D identify any person, census taker, or business

 Test-Taking Strategies Read the stem of the question carefully, then read each of the possible answers all the way through.

Apply and Debate

Read the following scenarios. Get together with other students in pairs or groups of three and take a position on each scenario. Debate your position in class with students taking the opposite position or prepare a written argument justifying your position.

10 Emancipation

Kirsten is 17 and a senior in high school. For the past six months, she has not been getting along with her parents and wants to move out on her own. Her parents reject this idea, so Kirsten decides to emancipate herself from her parents.

You Debate — *In this situation, can Kirsten emancipate herself from her parents?*

11 Rescinding a Contract

Matthew is 17, a senior in high school, and in JROTC. A recruiter visits his school to recruit students for the navy. Matthew signs a contract to enlist without discussing it with his parents.

You Debate — *Since Matthew is a minor and did not discuss this with his parents, can he rescind the contract?*

12 Contract for Necessaries

Jordan is 16. While mowing his grass, he seriously cut his hand. His neighbor took him to the emergency room where he was treated and released. Two weeks later, Jordan received a bill from the hospital for $575. Jordan refused to pay the bill.

You Debate — *Since Jordan is a minor, can he still be held responsible for the hospital bill?*

13 Consideration

Shawn offered to paint Margaret's house in exchange for an old car she was selling for $4,000. Shawn failed to show up to finish painting the house or to contact Margaret. A week later, another person offered to purchase the car and Margaret sold it. The next day Shawn came by to finish painting the house and learned the car had been sold.

You Debate — *Can Shawn sue Margaret for breach of contract?*

14 Option

Malik offered to sell his condo to Gayathri for $70,000. Gayathri said she did not have the money right now, but would like an option to buy it at a later date. Malik did not specify a time limit on the offer. A month later Malik had the opportunity to sell the condo for $70,000. Malik informed Gayathri, and she reminded Malik that she had an option with no time limit.

You Debate — *Is Malik bound by this agreement with Gayathri?*

S. Olsson/PhotoAlto

Case Study Practice – Olsen v. Hawkins

⑮ A Case of Incompetence? Hobart Turner purchased a life insurance policy on his own life. He listed Marvin and Mercedes Olsen, his stepson and his stepson's wife, as the beneficiaries on his policy. Three years later, Mr. Turner changed the beneficiary to Charles Hawkins. Mr. Turner died two years later.

The Olsens sued Mr. Hawkins for the money, arguing that Mr. Turner was not competent to contractually change the beneficiary when he did because he was under the effects of alcoholism. There was no evidence that Mr. Turner was either drunk or insane at the time he changed the beneficiary, but he did suffer from chronic alcoholism. A jury agreed with the Olsens and held that Mr. Turner was incompetent when he changed the beneficiary to Mr. Hawkins because of his alcoholism.

Source: Olsen v. Hawkins, 408 P.2d 462 (Idaho 1965)

Practice Was the jury right in its findings?

⑯ Ethics
←?→ Application

Duty to Disclose? Shadonna typed up a simple agreement between Jonathan and herself for the sale of her computer equipment valued at $1000. When Jonathan read the agreement, he saw that Shadonna had made an error and typed the amount in at $100. Shadonna had already signed her name to the agreement without noticing the error, so Jonathan signed it then handed her $100.

◆ Is Jonathan required to point out the error in the amount to Shadonna before signing the contract?

⑰ Think back to the Legal Briefs feature you read at the beginning of the chapter. Then research what information should be in an Non-Disclosure Agreement. For example, the names of all involved parties should be included and your state under whose law the NDA is enforced. Make a list of the information. Beside each item, write a short description of what each means. If you do not understand any of the information that should be included, make a note and ask your teacher for an explanation or research further to learn the answer.

CHAPTER

6 How Contracts Come to an End

Legal Briefs

Attorneys' Fee Provisions

Protect yourself from legal fees you can't afford.

No business owner wants to go to court and lose—or to see a settlement shrunk by attorneys' fees.

Attorneys' fees seem inevitable—you hire a lawyer and expect to pay. In most cases that's true. The "American Rule" says that each side pays its own attorneys. However, there are ways to avoid this expense.

If you hire a lawyer on a contingency basis, the attorney is paid only if your side wins. Otherwise, you owe nothing. Of course, an attorney may not want to take your case on this basis. Also, the lawyer will still receive a percentage of what you collect if you do win.

You can also add a legal fees clause to any contract—one of two kinds:

- One states the customer pays all legal fees. Large corporations such as banks and insurance companies often do this.
- The other kind states that whoever loses the case pays the other side's legal fees.

You can also ask for a legal fees clause in contracts that someone else offers. State laws differ, so be sure to ask your attorney.

Delegation of Duties Contracts that require someone's personal skill and judgment cannot be delegated. *What are some types of jobs that cannot be delegated to someone else?*

Transferring and Ending Contracts

What You'll Learn

- ◆ Explain how and when contracts can be discharged.
- ◆ Analyze the concept of performance.
- ◆ Describe the rules that apply to transfers of rights and duties.
- ◆ Understand the difference between delegation and assignment.

Why It's Important

Knowing when a contract ends is crucial for determining when the rights and duties of the parties terminate.

Reading Guide

Before You Read

Connect If you have signed a contract with someone or with a company, what are the ways this contract could end?

Focus on Ideas

Contracts may end because all rights and duties have been fulfilled or because the agreement has been broken.

Take Notes

Go to connectED. mcgraw-hill.com to download a graphic organizer you can use to take notes as you read this section.

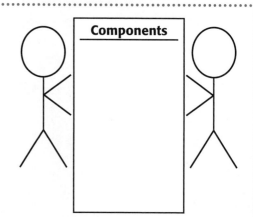

Components

Key Terms

You will learn these legal words and expressions in this chapter. You can also find these terms in *Black's Law Dictionary* or in an online legal dictionary.

- substantial performance
- tender
- discharge by agreement
- impossibility of performance
- statute of limitations
- breach of contract
- assignment
- delegation

Academic Terms

You will find these words in your readings and in your tests. Look them up in a dictionary and familiarize yourself with them.

- substituted
- expire
- affected

Ending a Contract

If you sign a contract with a personal trainer, and the trainer has an accident and cannot work with you, is your contract still valid?

A contract is discharged when it comes to an end. The parties to a contract may enforce their rights and must perform their duties, according to the terms of the contract, up to the time of discharge. The law tells us when contracts can end so that people will know when their rights and duties conclude. Contracts can be discharged voluntarily in two ways:

- by performance
- by agreement

Discharge by Performance

Most contracts are discharged by performance. Performance is a series of activities that fulfills the purpose of a contract. As long as all the terms of the contract have been followed properly and completely, the contract has been discharged. Complete performance represents a stage in the contract at which all the terms have been carried out properly.

Time for Performance The time for completing performance may be important to one or both of the parties. If the time for performance is not stated in a contract and there is a question of performance, the court will say that all duties under the contract must be completed in a reasonable time.

Reasonableness is determined by what is suitable, fair, and proper to the goal of the contract. A reasonable time for selling tomatoes, for instance, is not the same as a reasonable time for selling a house.

As You Read

Predict Think of three reasons why a contract would end.

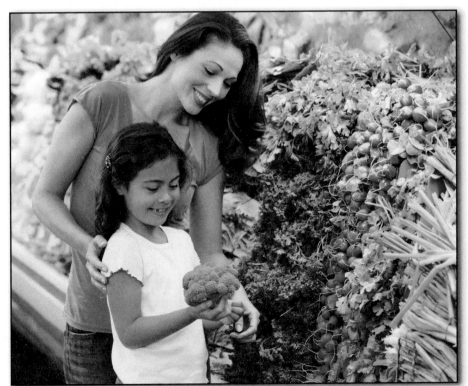

Time Is of the Essence A reasonable amount of time to sell produce is not the same as a reasonable amount of time to sell a car. *What are some types of goods or services in which time is of the essence in delivering or selling them?*

Design Pics / Monkey Business

If the parties state a time limit in the contract, the court may still give them more time if asked to do so by one of the parties. To avoid any kind of misunderstanding about time, the time limit should be included in the contract along with the words *time is of the essence.*

Satisfactory Performance The law requires that contractual services be done in a satisfactory manner. Sometimes, a contract says nothing about satisfaction; at other times, a contract may say that the work must be done in a satisfactory manner. In both situations, when one party believes the job is unsatisfactory, the dispute may end up in court.

In a lawsuit, the court uses the reasonable person test to measure whether the contract was performed in a satisfactory manner. This means the court asks whether a reasonable person would believe that the job was completed in a satisfactory manner. The jury generally gives the answer to this question. If there is no jury, the judge gives the answer. Occasionally one party will agree to perform services to the other party's satisfaction. In such a case, the other party must be satisfied to be held to the contract.

Substantial Performance Both parties must fully perform their duties for a contract to end by complete performance. Someone who has not fully performed his or her duties cannot, in most cases, win a lawsuit against the other party for money owed or for other damages.

An exception to this rule is known as the doctrine of substantial performance. **Substantial performance is a situation in which a party has, in good faith, completed the major requirements of a contract, leaving only a few minor details unfinished.** The court will allow that person to recover the amount agreed upon under the contract, minus the cost of completing the job. However, the court will allow recovery only if it can determine that it would be unfair to deny that recovery. The doctrine of substantial performance is often applied to construction contracts.

Tender of Performance A party can fulfill the terms of a contract by performing an act or by paying money. **A tender is an offer to do what you have agreed to do under a contract.** It is important to make tender even if you know the other party will not perform his or her part of the contract. In some states, making tender is necessary to test the other party's willingness and ability to perform. If neither party has made tender, then neither party can bring a lawsuit against the other.

If a person who must perform an act makes a tender of performance and that tender is rejected, that person is excused from fulfilling the contract. This principle does not apply to debts. An offer to pay a certain amount to fulfill a contract is a tender of payment. If a person makes a tender of payment and is rejected, that person is not excused from the debt. He or she is only excused from paying further interest on the amount of debt included in the tender of payment.

Critical Thinking *If there is an impossibility to perform a contract, who is liable?*

 Flex Your Reading — Note key facts in the text below and look up words you do not understand. Restate difficult ideas in your own words. Go back and reread the text quickly to make sure you did not miss any important detail. Now, you are ready to formulate an opinion.

Impossibility of Performance? The Opera Co. of Boston and the Wolf Trap Foundation entered into an agreement whereby the Opera Co. would perform an opera for four nights in a row at a theater operated by the Wolf Trap Foundation. In return, the Opera Co. would be paid $60,000, plus $53,000 for each performance. The Opera Co. performed on the first three nights without any problems. On the fourth night, however, an electrical storm knocked out power to the theater, and Wolf Trap had to cancel the performance. Because it did not perform, the Wolf Trap Foundation did not give the Opera Co. its final $53,000 payment. The Opera Co. sued to recover its last payment. Wolf Trap argued that it did not have to make the last payment because the contract was impossible to perform.

Opera Co. of Boston v. Wolf Trap Foundation, 817 F.2d 1094 (4th Cir. 1987)

Go to ConnectEd.mcgraw-hill.com for more case study practice.

The person offering to pay the required amount of money must offer legal tender. Under federal law, legal tender for debts, public charges, taxes, and dues is U.S. coins or currency.

Discharge by Agreement

Discharge by agreement means that people can end a contract by mutual agreement. This can be done by mutual release or by accord and satisfaction. A mutual release is an agreement between two parties to end a contract. Whatever the parties agree to do in the first place, they can later agree not to do. Otherwise, there would be no consideration for the promised release. A contract can also be discharged when one party agrees to accept a different performance from the other party. One contract is **substituted** for another. This is called accord and satisfaction. It is often used to settle an honest disagreement on an amount owed.

Involuntary Discharge

Some contracts are discharged involuntarily despite what the parties intend or what they actually do (see **Figure 6.1** on page 135). In these situations, the obligations under the contract may also **expire.** The two primary ways contracts are discharged in this way are:

- by impossibility of performance
- by operation of law

Vocabulary You can find vocabulary definitions in the **Key Terms** glossary and Academic Vocabulary glossary in the back of this book.

Figure 6.1 Involuntary Discharge of a Contract

A contract cannot be completed if the subject matter of the contract, such as a piece of property, is destroyed through no fault of the parties to the contract.

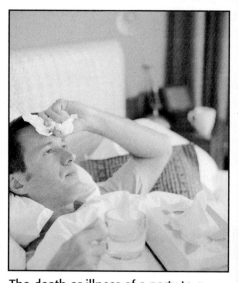

The death or illness of a party to a contract may end the contract if it required the personal service of that person.

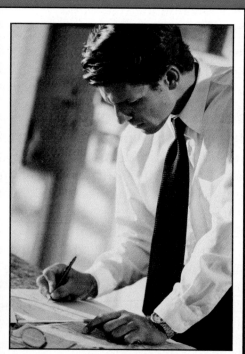

The law will discharge a contract if the Statute of Limitations for completing the contract runs out.

Despite what the parties intended to do, some contracts can be ended involuntarily for the reasons shown in the figure. *For what other reasons might an contract be ended involuntarily?*

Discharge by Impossibility of Performance

A contract that becomes legally impossible to perform generally may be discharged, and both parties may be released from the obligation. The courts allow a discharge for impossibility of performance. **Impossibility of performance may be allowed in case of death or illness that prevents the performance of a personal service contract; the destruction of the exact subject matter, or the means for performance; and illegality, or situations in which the performance of a contract becomes illegal.**

Death or Illness in a Personal Service Contract The death or illness of a party to a contract may be an excuse for nonperformance. This is true only if the contract requires the personal service of the person who has died or become ill.

Destruction of the Exact Subject Matter If the means or subject matter that is needed to perform the contract is destroyed through no fault of either party, the contract is discharged. The destruction must occur after the contract is entered, but before it is carried out.

Discharge by Operation of Law

At times, the best interests of society demand that a contract be terminated. Under these circumstances, the law declares contracts discharged by operation of law.

Wrongful Alteration One party's wrongful acts (such as altering or changing a contract) will discharge a contract by operation of law.

Statute of Limitations State laws specify how much time can pass before you can bring a legal action on a contract. These are called statutes of limitations. **A statute of limitations establishes a time limit for suing in a civil case, based on the date when the breach occurred or was discovered.** There are many special statutes of limitations in every state. To protect yourself fully in important business relationships, you should refer to the most recent statutes in your state. The statute of limitations for failure to perform contracts for the sale of goods is four years in most states. This means a legal action must be begun within four years after the contract is broken.

The parties may reduce the period of limitation to not less than one year by the original agreement. They may not, however, extend the period to more than the limit set by their state. However, a time-out is called when a creditor is a minor or is mentally ill. These situations stop the clock on the statute of limitations. In some states, people who are in prison suffer what is called civil death. They lose the right to vote, to make contracts, and to bring and defend against civil lawsuits. In these states, the statute of limitations on contracts often stops running while a person is in prison.

Reading Check

Analyze What are all the ways performance is looked at when determining if and how a contract may end?

Debt and Statutes of Limitations In some instances, the debt may be renewed. If a debtor makes a partial payment or admits that the debt exists after the time period has passed, the debt is renewed for another time period set by the state statute. In New York and some other states, such a new promise must be in writing.

Bankruptcy Congress has the authority to pass bankruptcy laws that set procedures for discharging a debtor's obligations. These obligations still exist, but the debtor cannot be imprisoned for failure to pay.

Certain debts cannot be discharged under bankruptcy laws. Education loans, for example, usually cannot be discharged during the first five years of the repayment period. In addition, debts for taxes, alimony, child support, and maintenance are not **affected** by a general discharge of debts in bankruptcy.

Breach of Contract

Suppose you advertise your aunt's Picasso painting online, and someone buys it immediately. Two months later the buyer discovers the painting is a fake. Was this fraud on your part?

A breach of contract is when a person fails to perform the duties spelled out by a contract. The effects of a breach vary depending on the case. When a breach of contract happens, one party is injured. The injuries are not physical, but that does not mean that they are not real. The injured party may demand justice.

The Transfer of Contractual Rights and Duties

If you signed a contract with a personal trainer, can you be assigned another trainer without a new contract?

When people establish contracts, they receive rights (benefits) and acquire duties (detriments). Most of the time, people manage their own rights and duties. Sometimes, these rights and duties are moved to someone new. For example, some people give another person their right to receive money because they owe that person money they cannot pay otherwise. Other people take on more work than they can handle and have to shift some of their duties to other qualified parties. The law permits this sort of transfer, with a few exceptions.

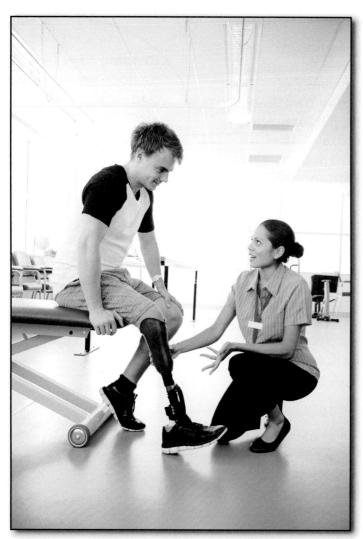

Transferring Duties Sometimes people have to shift some of their work to other qualified parties. *Can the duties of a physical trainer be transferred to another physical trainer?*

Assignment and Transfer of Rights

An assignment is the transfer of a right under a contract.
The general rule about assignments is that people can legally transfer contract rights as long as the contract does not specifically say they cannot. The party who transfers the rights is the assignor; the party who gets the rights is the assignee. The assignee is a third person who is not a party to the original contract.

> **Example** Anthony Cuomo entered into a contract with Cathy Michaud to rebuild the front steps of her house for $1,800. The carpenter was pleased to get the contract because he owed $1,800 to his landlord, David Brown. Before beginning work, Anthony assigned the right to receive payment for the work to his landlord. When payment was due, Cathy paid the $1,800 to David Brown directly.

How Rights May Be Assigned No consideration is necessary for an assignment to be valid. In most cases, the law does not even say how one party may assign a right to somebody else. However, it is best to put an assignment in writing because an oral assignment can be difficult to prove. Suppose that you owe money to a bank under a contract. Now suppose that the bank decides to assign the right to receive your money to another bank. Would you want to know about that change? Of course you would, and you would want the change in writing so that, when you send the money to the new bank, you know that you are doing the right thing.

What Rights May Be Assigned Most rights may be assigned unless the assignment changes the obligations of the other party to the contract in an important way. However, not all assignments are valid. For instance, the right to receive personal services usually cannot be assigned. An assignor can assign nothing more than the rights that he or she possesses. An assignee takes those rights, subject to other people's defenses.

> **Example** Suppose that when Anthony Cuomo, from the earlier example, assigned the right to receive the $1,800 to his landlord, Anthony then did a poor job. Cathy Michaud could raise the defense of a poor job if she were sued by the assignee, who wants to collect the $1,800.

Rights to the payment of money, such as wages, money owed on accounts, royalties on books, and rights to the delivery of goods are the most common types of rights that are assigned. After the assignment, the assignor no longer has an interest in the right that was assigned. This right now belongs exclusively to the assignee.

Generally, no special form is required to make an assignment. Any words that clearly indicate a person's intent are sufficient. This assignment may be made on a separate paper, or it may be written on the back of a written contract containing the rights to be assigned.

Third Parties The make-up artist is putting finishing touches on a television presenter before he goes in front of the cameras. Teachers, writers, and artists are selected to perform certain services because of their particular skills or talents. *In the context of rights, transfers of rights, and duties, do you think a chef you hired to oversee the catering of a dinner party could delegate the work to another cook?*

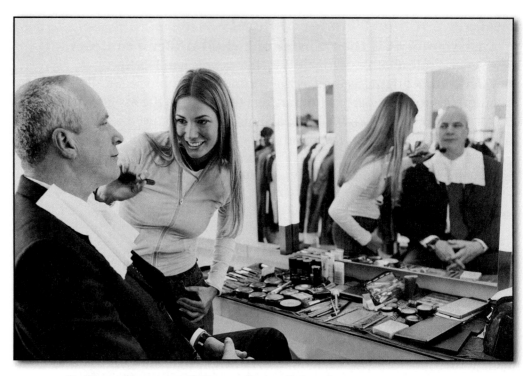

Delegation and Transfer of Duties

Delegation means transferring of a duty under a contract. A delegation should not be confused with an assignment. An assignment is a transfer of rights; a delegation is a transfer of duties. In a transfer of duties, a party to a contract trusts another person to do the job in his or her place.

> **Example** Ivan Remec, owner of the Eastern Print Shop, had overextended himself financially and could not meet all of his printing contracts. When the time came to print the monthly newsletter for the high school's Parent Teacher Association, he transferred his contract obligation to another printer who was not a party to the original contract. This was a legal form of subcontracting. However, if Ivan had told the PTA that he would personally do the printing, Ivan could not have delegated the task.

It is important to remember that the performance of an obligation may be delegated, but the responsibility for it may not. If both parties understand the situation, it is all right to hand over the duty of doing the work to someone else. This is a form of subcontracting that is common in business contracts. You may not delegate duties, however, in any of the following situations:

- A party agrees to perform the service personally.
- The contract calls for the exercise of personal skill and judgment.
- The contract itself prohibits delegation.

The offeror and the offeree may include in their contract a statement that the contract may not be assigned or delegated. In this case, both parties are restrained.

If you have the right to delegate a contractual obligation and decide to do so, choose your third party carefully. As explained, you retain responsibility for any job duties that you subcontract or assign to a third party.

Novation You do not need the permission of the other party to assign contract rights or to delegate duties to a third person. If you do receive permission, and the other party agrees to deal with the assignee, the resulting contract is called a novation. A novation is an agreement whereby an original party to a contract is replaced by a new party. The other terms of the new contract generally remain the same as those in the original contract. To be effective, the change requires the consent of all of the parties involved.

Third Parties A contract is a binding agreement that establishes a relationship between the parties to the contract. This relationship between the parties is termed privity of contract. It determines who can sue whom over a question of performance required by a contract. Usually the parties to a contract have standing to sue.

A third person may sometimes enforce a contract when it is made specifically for that person's benefit. A person who is not a party to a contract but still benefits from the contract is called a third party beneficiary.

After You Read

Summarize List ways you could get out of a contract to sing at your school's football game.

SECTION 6.1 ASSESSMENT

Self Check

1. How can contracts be discharged by performance?

2. What situations permit a contractual discharge by impossibility of performance?

3. What situations permit a contractual discharge by operation of law?

Academic Connection

Mathematics Last week, Cynthia used a credit card to purchase a snowboard for $277.89. This week, she saw the same snowboard on sale online for $250.43. The sales tax in Cynthia's state is 8%. The online store is not based in her state and charges only for shipping. Shipping charges are 2% of the item's price. How much would Cynthia save if she could return her snowboard for a refund and order the one she saw online?

CONCEPT **Numbers and Operations: Calculating Percentages and Comparing Prices** Calculate 8% of $277.89 by multiplying the price by 0.08. Add the result to the price of the snowboard. Calculate shipping charges by multiplying $250.43 by 0.02. Add the result to the price. Compare the two results to make a decision.

 For more math practice, go to the Math Appendix.

Critical Thinking

Discharged or Not? Debra agreed to work for Lupe for two years. At the end of two months, Debra went to Lupe and asked to be released from her contract. Lupe agreed. Was the contract discharged? Explain.

Voidable Contracts and Remedies

What You'll Learn

◆ Differentiate among the ways contracts can be undermined (fraud, non-disclosure, misrepresentation, mistake, duress, and undue influence).

◆ Explain what remedies are available when a contract is not fulfulled.

Why It's Important

Knowing the consequences of a breach of contract can help you prepare for the loss that follows and for deciding on possible recourse.

Before You Read

Connect Have you ever been pressured into agreeing to do something you did not really want to do? Do you think you should have been able to get out of it?

Focus on Ideas

A contract can be breached either intentionally or unintentionally.

Take Notes

Go to connectED. mcgraw-hill.com to download a graphic organizer you can use to take notes as you read this section.

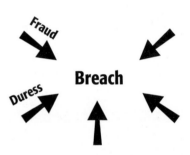

Key Terms

You will learn these legal words and expressions in this chapter. You can also find these terms in *Black's Law Dictionary* or in an online legal dictionary.

- fraud
- duress
- undue influence
- remedy

- damages
- punitive damages
- injunction

Academic Terms

You will find these words in your readings and in your tests. Look them up in a dictionary and familiarize yourself with them.

- intent
- exaggerate
- mutual

Defective Agreements

If a contract appears to meet the requirements of offer, acceptance, agreement, consideration, capacity, and legality, what could still prevent the contract?

Sometimes, what seems to be a valid contract turns out to be nothing of the kind. In these cases, the agreement is defective. Several circumstances might lead to this situation: fraud, misrepresentation, mistake, duress, and undue influence.

Fraud

Fraud is a deliberate deception intended to serve an unfair and unlawful gain. If you figure out that the seller lied, then you may be able to get your money back. That means you may have to sue for money damages. Lying weakens the entire world of contracts, therefore the law will let the injured party get punitive damages. To win a lawsuit based on fraud, five elements must be shown:

- There must be a false representation of fact (a lie).
- The person who lied must know it was a lie.
- The lie must be made with the **intent** that it be relied on.
- The innocent party must reasonably rely on the lie.
- The innocent party must experience a loss.

As You Read

Predict What are some reasons why a contract may be voidable?

Vocabulary You can find vocabulary definitions in the **Key Terms** glossary and Academic Vocabulary glossary in the back of this book.

Victims of Fraud Anybody can become a victim of fraud. *Why do unscrupulous telemarketers often target retired Americans for fraud?*

BellSouth Communications System, LLC v. West
902 So.2d 653 (Ala. 2004)

BellSouth is an Internet Service Provider in Alabama, where Thomas West resides. In 2002, Mr. West signed up with BellSouth for Internet service. The advertised price was $15.95 per month. When Mr. West received his bill from BellSouth, he discovered he had been charged $19.85 for one month's service and a $15.00 set-up fee. Mr. West sued for breach of contract. BellSouth countered, arguing that the membership agreement that Mr. West had signed said that BellSouth could change any terms of the agreement (including the monthly fee) by posting notice on the Internet. Mr. West said he never saw the posting.

Ruling and Resolution
The Alabama Supreme Court held that BellSouth could not provide proof of when it had posted the change in fees on its Web site. Neither could BellSouth prove that Mr. West had accessed the Web site after the alleged change. Therefore, Mr. West was able to recover damages against BellSouth.

Critical Thinking Should companies be allowed to notify customers of changes to their contracts by posting notices on Web sites?

False Representation of Fact The law requires that the lie be about a material fact that is really important. It cannot be a promise of something that will happen in the future, and it cannot be just an opinion. The law allows sales people to **exaggerate** their claims just as long as the exaggerations are obviously a statement of the seller's opinion.

In the context of fraud, a lie is not just something false that is written or spoken. It can also be actions that the seller uses to cover up a defect or to hide some factual piece of evidence. If your friend, Phil, tells you that he is going to turn back the odometer of his '65 Mustang so he can get a better price for it, you should let him know that he is about to commit fraud. Sometimes people lie by inaction. This happens when they do not say something that they are supposed to say. This is called passive fraud, concealment, or nondisclosure.

Knowledge of the Lie To be responsible for the lie, the person telling the lie must know that it is a lie. The innocent party has to show this by giving evidence in court that the other person had actual knowledge that he or she was lying. Short of this, the innocent party might succeed in the lawsuit by showing that the other party told the lie recklessly. This means that the defrauding party told the lie without regard for the true story.

Lie Intended to Be Relied Upon To prove fraud, the innocent person must show that the liar told the lie knowing that the other party, would hear it, believe it, and act on it. In other words, he or she told the lie to tempt the other party into the false contract.

Lie Actually Relied Upon To prove fraud, the innocent party has to show that he or she depended on the lie. Sometimes the defrauding party lies, but the other party pays no attention to the lie. If that happens, there are no grounds for a lawsuit.

Resulting Loss You can be enticed into a contract by a lie that the other party knows is a lie, and you still might not be able to recover damages in court. This happens if the last element is missing. If the innocent party does not lose anything in the deal, there is no loss, and with no loss, there is no fraud.

Innocent Misrepresentation

Misrepresentation occurs when a person who is involved in contract negotiations says something that he or she believes to be true that turns out to be false. The law gives the innocent party the right to get out of the contract in this situation.

Mistake, Duress, and Undue Influence

Sometimes a person enters a contract with a mistaken idea of what is at stake. Later, when the mistaken person realizes that an error has been made, he or she tries to get out of the agreement. Is this possible? Sometimes the answer is yes, but more often it is no.

Unilateral Mistake A unilateral mistake is an error on the part of one of the parties to the contract. Usually a person cannot get out of a contract just because of a mistake. The law wants people to pay attention to their business deals.

A mistake as to the nature of the agreement is one type of unilateral mistake. A unilateral mistake like this does not give anybody a way out of a contract. If you buy a DVD online and then find out that you have the exact same DVD on your shelf at home, you made a mistake. You will not be able to get out of the contract. People are bound to a contract even if they do not read it or are mistaken about what it says. Your signature shows that you agree to the terms whether you understood them or not. The rule applies even to those who cannot read English. People who cannot read English are expected to have someone who does understand the language read and explain the terms in the agreement.

A mistake as to value (about how much an object for sale is worth) is another type of unilateral mistake. It does not give anybody a way out of a contract.

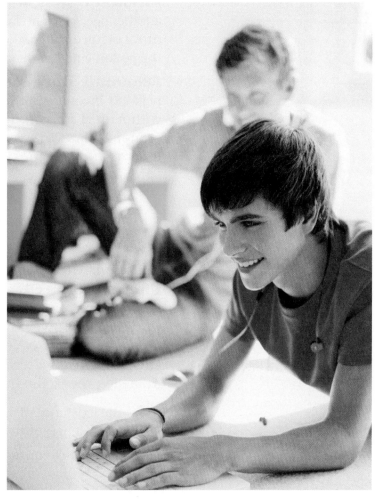

Unilateral Mistake If you mistakenly purchase a download of a game or movie you already own, you cannot simply negate the contract. *What can you do to avoid this situation?*

Duress: *n* Unlawful threat or coercion. From Latin *durus* = hard.

Punitive: *adj* Relating to punishment. From Latin *punitus* = punish.

Vocabulary Builder List three words that have a similar meaning to duress.

Bilateral Mistake A bilateral mistake is an error that is made on the part of both parties to the contract. This is also called **mutual** mistake. Often when the mistake is bilateral, either one of the parties can get out of the contract.

A bilateral mistake can be made as to the possibility of performance. This will get rid of the duty to perform. Suppose that you agree to pay your local bookstore owner $10 if he makes sure that you are the first person to buy the next Harry Potter novel. Now, suppose the author of the Harry Potter books says that she will never write another Harry Potter book—ever. Both you and the book dealer were mistaken as to the availability of a new Harry Potter book. The contract cannot be performed and the agreement is ended.

Suppose you believe you are buying the 2005 VHS version of *The Fantastic Four* feature film. When the tape arrives, you realize that the tape is actually the 1993 film. This is a bilateral mistake as to the subject matter. You were buying the 2005 version while the other party was selling the 1993 version. If the seller was selling one thing while the buyer was buying another, either party can void the contract.

Duress

Duress is the act of destroying somebody's free will by force, threat of force, or bodily harm. Agreements made under duress are either void or voidable.

Physical Duress When actual physical force is used to cause another person to enter a contract, the contract is void. When the threat of force is used, the contract is voidable. The threat can be against the person entering the contract or a family member of that person.

Economic Duress Economic duress is an act that threatens a person's income or business that makes that person enter a contract without real consent. To succeed in voiding a contract based on economic duress, the victim has to prove three things:

- The other party wrongfully placed them in a poor economic position.
- The victim had no choice other than to submit to the duress.
- Their submission to the duress was reasonable under the circumstances.

Undue Influence

Undue influence is an action or series of overly persuasive actions that make inappropriate use of one person's position of power over another person to create an agreement that is very favorable to the person with all the power. To succeed in voiding a contract based on undue influence, the victim has to prove three things:

- the existence of a caregiver-type relationship
- the use of excessive pressure by the caregiver
- a resulting contract that heavily favors the caregiver

Reading Check

Enumerate *What is necessary to prove that fraud has occurred?*

Remedies and Damages

What do you think you can do if someone has not fulfilled a contract you had agreed to?

When a contract is not fulfilled, the injured party has a choice of remedies. **A remedy is a legal means of enforcing a right or correcting a wrong.** If you are the injured party, you have three different options:

- You may accept the breach.
- You may sue for money damages.
- You may ask the court for an equitable remedy.

If one party breaches a contract, it is an excuse for the other party not to perform. For example, if someone failed to perform under a contract with you, you may simply accept the breach and consider the contract discharged. This is often the best choice, especially if no damages have been suffered.

Global Law

Remedies for Breach of Contract in Japan

The Japanese Civil Code was created in 1896. It was drafted by three private Japanese attorneys. Two of the drafters studied law in France, while the third had studied law in Germany. As a result, the Japanese Civil Code was influenced by both the French Code Napoléon and the German Civil Code. There are also traces of law from English and American sources. The drafters knew it would be almost impossible to base a system of laws on a Japanese common law created by judicial opinions since none existed.

Contract law was implemented in Japan for the first time under the Japanese Civil Code. The Japanese Civil Code includes some provisions that are unlike American contract law. Two major differences are the initial existence of the contract and remedies available for breach of contract.

Creation of Contract

In Japan, a contract comes into existence upon the sending of notice of acceptance. For example, if an offer is made via the mail and the recipient decides to accept the offer, the offer comes into existence the moment the acceptance is mailed. There is no chance to rescind the acceptance. Any rescission would constitute a breach.

Remedies for Breach

A remedy for breach of contract is only available if the contract was breached by the obligor, or the person required to perform under the contract. There are no remedies available if the obligee (the beneficiary of the contract) breaches.

> **Across Cultures: The Six Codes (六法 roppō)**
>
> In Japan, statutory law originates in the legislature, also called the National Diet of Japan. Under the current constitution, the Emperor may not veto or otherwise refuse to approve a law passed by the Diet.

Critical Thinking *Should the United States consider enacting statutory provisions similar to those in Japan?*

Figure 6.2 Damages

Type	Description
Actual Damages	An amount of money awarded for damages directly attributable to another party's breach of contract or tort; for example, physician's fees when one party wrongly injures another, and financial losses resulting from failure to deliver goods already contracted for.
Compensatory Damages	An award of an amount of money that compensates a plaintiff for the injuries suffered and nothing more.
Consequential Damages	Damage, loss, or injury (such as loss of profits) that does not flow directly and immediately from the act of the party but only from some of the consequences or results of the act.
Incidental Damages	Reasonable expenses that indirectly result from a breach of contract. They include expenses such as those incurred in stopping delivery of goods, transporting goods, and caring for goods that have been rightfully rejected by a buyer.
Liquidated Damages	An amount of anticipated damages, agreed to by both parties and contained in a contract, to be the basis of any award in the event of a breach of the contract.
Nominal Damages	Damages awarded by a court when a successful plaintiff has proven a legal injury but no actual resulting damages; six cents by common law, usually $1 today.
Punitive Damages	Damages in excess of losses suffered by the plaintiff awarded to the plaintiff as a measure of punishment for the defendant's wrongful act. Also called exemplary damages because they set an example of punishment awaiting other wrongdoers.
Speculative Damages	Damages not founded on fact but on the expectations that a party may have hoped for from a contract that has been breached; not allowed in any claim for money damages.

Suing for money damages is one remedy for breach of contract. *What is the objective of awarding damages to the injured party in a contract case?*

Damages

Damages are payment recovered in court by a person who has suffered an injury. (See **Figure 6.2.**) Damages awarded to recognize a breach of contract that did not cause loss often amount to less than one dollar. These damages are intended merely to recognize that a breach of contract has occurred. Your legal fees for pursuing and winning such a suit would likely far outweigh any damages you would receive.

Money Damages If you suffer a loss as the injured party, you may sue for money damages resulting from the breach of contract. The money damages should, by law, place you in the position you would have been in if the contract had been carried out. To recover damages, the injured party must make tender; that is, the injured party must offer to do what he or she agreed to do under the contract.

Punitive Damages or Rescission A plaintiff can also receive punitive damages in a lawsuit for fraud. **Punitive damages are money payments for damages that go beyond what the innocent party actually lost and that are designed to punish the wrongdoer.**

If the lawsuit is based on misrepresentation, the innocent party cannot receive punitive damages. The remedy available for innocent misrepresentation is rescission of the contract.

Equitable Remedies

The remedy of money damages is not always enough to repay an injured party for breach of contract. In these cases, the injured party may seek an equitable remedy. Two chief equitable remedies are specific performance and an injunction.

Specific Performance Specific performance asks the court to order the other party in a contract to do what he or she agreed to do. This remedy can only be used when money damages are not sufficient to give relief and when the subject matter of the contract is rare or unique. It would not be ordered in the case of contracts involving common goods or easily obtained services.

Injunction **An injunction is a court order that prevents a party from performing a specific act.** An injunction is only available in special circumstances, such as when money damages will be inadequate to compensate the injured party.

An injunction may be temporary or permanent. A temporary injunction is issued as a means of delaying further activity in any contested matter until the court determines whether a permanent injunction should be entered or the injunction should be removed entirely. One who disobeys an injunction does so under penalty of contempt of court.

After You Read

Summarize List all the possible remedies to a breach of contract.

SECTION 6.2 ASSESSMENT

Self Check

1. What are the elements of fraud?

2. What are the different remedies for fraud and misrepresentation?

3. What are the requirements of undue influence?

Academic Connection

Mathematics Veronica is considering a short-term commercial loan to expand her business. The amount of the loan would be $80,000 for sixty days at an interest rate of 10.5%. To see if this is a good deal, she will need to calculate the interest and the maturity value of her loan.

CONCEPT **Number and Operations: Calculating Interest** To solve this problem you will first need to calculate interest using the formula Interest = Principal × Rate × Time. Maturity value is calculated by adding the principal to the interest owed.

 Math

For more math practice, go to the Math Appendix.

Critical Thinking

Lying Is Never Worth the Trouble Suppose you advertised your old laptop computer for sale for $200. Suppose further that you said it could handle floppy disks when you knew it could not. Suppose further that Jim, the president of the computer club, buys the laptop, sight unseen, relying only on your ad. Have you defrauded Jim whether or not he needs the laptop to handle floppy disks? Explain.

Chapter 6 Review and Assessment

Summary

Section 6.1 Transferring and Ending Contracts

◆ When contracts end, they are said to be discharged. The parties to the contract may enforce their rights and must perform their duties up to the time of discharge.

◆ When people perform contractual services, the law requires that those services be done in a satisfactory manner.

◆ Substantial performance is a situation in which a party has, in good faith, completed the major requirements of a contract, leaving only a few minor details unfinished.

◆ Contracts can be discharged by performance, by agreement, by impossibility of performance, or by operation of law.

◆ An assignment is the transfer of a right under a contract.

◆ A delegation is the handing over of a duty.

Section 6.2 Voidable Contracts and Remedies

◆ When a contract is breached, the injured party has a choice of remedies. A remedy is a legal means of enforcing a right or correcting a wrong.

◆ Fraud is an unfair attempt to fool another person into buying something by lying to that person about a key characteristic of the thing that is up for sale.

◆ A unilateral mistake is an error on the part of one of the parties to the contract. A bilateral mistake is an error on the part of both parties to the contract.

◆ Duress is the act of destroying somebody's free will by force, threat of force, or bodily harm. Agreements made under duress are either void or voidable.

◆ Undue influence is an action or series of overly persuasive actions that make inappropriate use of one person's position of power over another person to create an agreement that is very favorable to the person with all the power.

Vocabulary Builder

❶ On a sheet of paper, use each of these terms in a sentence.

Key Terms

- substantial performance
- tender
- discharge by agreement
- impossibility of performance
- statute of limitations

- breach of contract
- assignment
- delegation
- fraud
- duress

- undue influence
- remedy
- damages
- punitive damages
- injunction

Academic Vocabulary

- substituted
- expire

- affected
- intent

- exaggerate
- mutual

Key Points Review

Answer the following questions. Refer to the chapter for additional reinforcement.

2 Why will the courts allow an innocent party to collect damages in the case of fraud?

3 What are punitive damages?

4 What types of statements are not fraudulent, even though they might not be 100% accurate?

5 Does fraud have to consist of words? Explain.

6 What remedy is available in the case of misrepresentation?

7 Is a person bound by the terms of an agreement that he or she failed to read? Explain.

Standardized Test Practice

8 Read the following information about the general rule of law in construction and complete questions 1 and 2.

The general rule of law is that strict performance of the duties of a contract is a condition precedent to recovery on the contract. If that rule were applied to construction, it would mean that owners could refuse to pay for work that did not meet minor quality standards of the contract. For reasons of fairness, building contracts are an exception to the general rule.

In construction, there is the substantial performance doctrine, which says that if the performance nearly equals what was bargained for by the parties, then payment must be made. If the owner can use the work for the purpose that was intended, then the work will be deemed substantially complete, and the owner is obligated to make payment. However, it should be remembered that an owner is permitted to make a reasonable deduction for the cost of achieving full performance.

1. As a general rule, when must strict performance occur to recover on a contract?

Ⓐ before final payment is made
Ⓑ at the start of the construction job
Ⓒ at the conclusion of the job
Ⓓ prior to the conclusion of the contract

2. Why is strict performance defined differently in contracts dealing with construction?

Ⓐ to be fair to contractors
Ⓑ less contracts would be written
Ⓒ cost of construction would rise
Ⓓ owners would not be obligated to pay

 Test-taking Strategies Read the stem of each question carefully, then read each of the possible answers all the way through.

Apply and Debate

Read the following scenarios. Get together with other students in pairs or groups of three and take a position on each scenario. Debate your position in class with students taking the opposite position or prepare a written argument justifying your position.

9 False Representation

Enola was in a collision that caused over $5,000 in damage to her car. After she had it repaired, she sold the car for $8,500. The buyer asked Enola if the car had ever been in a major car accident. Enola said no because it had been completely fixed.

You Debate   *Can Enola be accused of false representation?*

10 Implied Contract

While talking to a group of her friends at a picnic, Rosie said she would pay anything to get a tree cut down. The following day while she was at work, one of her friends cut the tree down and gave Rosie a $500 bill for doing the job.

You Debate   *Is Rosie required to pay the bill because of her statement the day before?*

11 Undue Influence

Jules advertised his motorcycle in the paper for $2,000. Two people arrived at the same time, and both decided they wanted to buy it. One of them offered $2,500 for the motorcycle. The other said he could not afford that much, so Jules took the $2,500 offer. The next day the buyer accused Jules of undue influence for causing him to pay $500 more for the motorcycle than advertised.

You Debate   *Did Jules use undue influence?*

12 Economic Duress

Mr. Sadri has had his lawn mowed by Ray's Landscaping for $25 a week for the past three years. Ray's Landscaping told Mr. Sadri that they were raising their fee to $30 a week. Mr. Sadri threatened Ray's Landscaping that if it did not keep the price at $25, he would tell his neighbors that Ray's had damaged his flower beds.

You Debate   *Can Mr. Sadri be accused of duress?*

13 Breach of Contract

Sally offered to sell Paco her CD player for $20. Paco told her he would think about it and let her know later that day. Later, Paco told Sally that he would buy her CD player, but Sally told him she had changed her mind.

You Debate   *Can Paco sue Sally for breach of contract?*

Case Study Practice – Parker v. Twentieth Century Fox Film Corp.

⑭ **What Is a Valid Offer?** Shirley MacLaine Parker and Twentieth Century Fox signed a contract in which Ms. Parker would star in a movie entitled *Bloomer Girl* and she would receive guaranteed compensation of $750,000 for her performance. The studio decided not to make the movie and notified Ms. Parker of its decision.

To prevent any monetary damage to Ms. Parker, the studio offered her another role in a movie entitled *Big Country, Big Man*. The compensation for the new film would be identical with the compensation offered in the first contract. *Bloomer Girl*, however, was a musical to be filmed in California while *Big Country* was a Western set to shoot in Australia. Ms. Parker was given one week to consider the new offer, which she rejected.

Ms. Parker then sued Twentieth Century Fox for her guaranteed compensation of $750,000. Twentieth Century Fox argued that Ms. Parker failed to mitigate her damages by refusing to accept the second contract.

Source: Parker v. Twentieth Century Fox Film Corp, 474 P.2d 689 (Cal. 1970)

Practice Was Ms. Parker required to mitigate by accepting the second offer?

⑮ Ethics ←?→ Application _____

Compensation or Not? Lukas had contracted Wilson's Roofing to replace the roof on his home. Before they finished the job, Lukas suffered water damage to his carpet from a leak in the roof. To make up for the inconvenience, he decided to claim that his sofa and recliner had also been damaged by water. The company agreed to replace the items immediately and apologized for the mishap.

◆ Should Lukas be entitled to any compensation for his inconvenience resulting from the water damage to his carpet?

⑯ Think back to the Legal Briefs feature you read at the beginning of the chapter. Then prepare a chart that shows who benefits from each kind of legal fees arrangement: American Rule, contingency fee, customer-pays-all, or loser pays. Then write one or more paragraphs to answer these questions: If you were a small business owner, how would you want your legal fees to be handled? Which way would benefit you most? Which way seems most fair to all parties? What if you're the attorney? Which arrangement might you prefer?

Careers in Law

Richard Stim

Editor and General Counsel, Nolo Press

What do you do at work?

"I review contracts, modify them, prepare contracts for other businesses to sign, and sometimes negotiate the terms. As an attorney for Nolo, I might get a contract for someone who wants to license materials from us, or a contract for a company that wants to distribute our software in some other configuration. Because we provide legal information, we have to be very careful that we're not violating any laws that restrict dissemination of legal advice. I deal with several different departments in the building. I might need to review the cover of a book, for instance, to make sure we're not making claims on the cover that might get us in trouble."

What skills are most important to you?

"Organization is really important. Perspective is important too—you have to be able to see the agreement through the client's eyes, not just from a legal perspective. The ability to predict problems is pretty important, and another one would be the ability to resolve an impasse."

What training do you recommend?

"For contracts, it really helps to have some business experience, because the biggest problems lawyers have when doing contracts for business clients is that they view all potential disasters as being of equal importance. And that is not the case with most businesses—there is usually one main possible disaster that they are primarily concerned about. Having some business experience is really, really important."

What is your key to success?

"Lawyers are often worried about malpractice, and because they're so worried about it, it drives them to over-prescribe. And letting go of that is key, wherever you can learn that—and usually you learn that by being in business yourself. Also, if I have any success it's because I get to know the people and their business. It really helps to understand it, because in the end, it's never about the paper—it's always about the people."

Resume Builder

Academic Skills

- Above average reading and writing skills
- Good speaking and debating skills

Education and Training

A bachelor's degree, a Juris Doctor degree, the bar exam in your state. The following high school and college courses will help develop the necessary background knowledge:

- English Language Arts
- Social Studies
- U.S. History
- U.S. Government
- Introduction to Law (in high school)
- Basic law courses (in college)
- Business, contracts, and consumer law

Critical Thinking

Why is it important for a lawyer to view a contract from the client's perspective, as well as from a legal perspective?

Persuasive Writing Practice

Is There a Contract? Carmen wants to sell her house. Dale contacts her after meeting her at a party and says she is looking for a house in Carmen's neighborhood. They discuss the matter over the phone. Then, Dale comes over and they reach an agreement on a price of $300,000. Carmen agrees to fence the yard and to replace the roof as part of the deal. They do not sign a contract. Carmen hires a contractor to do the work. Two days after the contractor has started working, Dale calls to say that she is backing out of the deal because she is being transferred to work in another city. Carmen has spent $2,000 on the repairs so far.

Assignments

Research Research which type of contract should be in writing in order to be enforceable by courts, and find out about a law called the Statute of Frauds.

Write Consider the situation above and write a persuasive essay about what a fair solution to the situation could be.

Writing Tips Before you start writing your essay, read through the following composition review tips:

- ✓ Generate two or three specific sentences that answer the question posed by the assignment.
- ✓ Decide how you will develop your argument.
- ✓ Create an outline.
- ✓ Create a topic sentence for each paragraph.
- ✓ Use transition words at the beginning of each paragraph.
- ✓ Reread, edit, correct, and rewrite as necessary.

Essay Test Strategies Preview the essay prompt. Spend five percent of your time reading through the prompt carefully, mark key terms, decide how to budget your time, and jot down brief notes for ideas.

UNIT 2

Thematic Project

Writing a Driving Contract

For this project, you will use what you have learned to prepare a written contract that lists issues and responsibilities associated with driving. You can work on this project alone or with a partner.

Here is a checklist of the skills that you will need to complete this project and that your teacher will consider when evaluating your work.

Evaluation Rubric

Academic Skills			
1.	Online and library research	1.	10 points
2.	Reading for information	2.	10 points
3.	Note-taking	3.	5 points
4.	Estimation and computation of your car-related expenses	4.	10 points
5.	English composition	5.	15 points
Legal Skills			
6.	Research of possible contract forms	6.	15 points
7.	Drafting the terms of the contract	7.	15 points
8.	Analysis of the essential elements of the contract	8.	15 points
9.	Use of technology	9.	5 points
		Total 100 points	

Step 1: Preparation

1. Write a contract between yourself and a parent or a family member.
2. Use all you have learned in this unit, at the library, or on the Internet as tools.
3. Complete this project in a format acceptable for a portfolio addition.

Step 2: Procedure

❶ Review the text in this unit and make a list of the essential elements of a contract.

❷ List all the contractual terms you might include in your document. What will your obligations be? What will the other party's obligations be? How will these obligations be enforced?

❸ Write the contract based on your knowledge and research. Use the Internet to download a form for an agreement, or create a contract by using word-processing software. Make enough copies so your classmates can review and annotate your contract.

❹ Describe the real-life scenario that is the basis for your contract (the amount of driving you need or want to do, the insurance contract, who the car belongs to, the rules governing teen driving in your state, etc.) and present your contract to the class.

Step 3: Create an Analysis Report

As a class, compare the contracts presented. Create a spreadsheet that describes the types of agreements created (for example, indicate whether the contracts are unilateral or bilateral) and the responsibilities involved. Make sure that you have also accounted for each of the elements required for a valid and enforceable contract. Look at the charts your classmates have created and answer the following questions:

❶ How many and what types of contracts were presented?

❷ Did all of the contracts presented include all the necessary elements?

❸ If not, how did the absence of the element(s) affect the contract(s)?

❹ How was your contract similar to and different from the other contracts presented?

Community Connection

Find statistics about teen driving offenses and accidents online. How do these facts relate to your contract project? Should teen driving offenses be handled in teen or youth courts? Prepare a brief research report to present in class.

Competitive Event Prep

Entering into Contracts

Situation Assume you are a sales associate for a cellular phone store. Besides selling cell phones, your store sells service contracts. You completed a sale to a teen-aged customer (event judge) for a phone and a contract. You checked the customer's identification and discovered that the customer is only 16 years old. Company policy states that any customer under 18 must have a parent or guardian sign the cell phone activation contract.

Activity Explain to your customer (event judge) that he or she is under the legal age to sign a contract and must bring a parent or guardian into the store to sign.

Mastrobuono v. Shearson Lehman Hutton, Inc.
United States Supreme Court 514 U.S. 52 (1995)

Read Critically As you read this case, ask yourself the following questions:

1. What type of contract is involved in this case?
2. Why did Shearson Lehman Hutton force the Mastrobuonos to participate in arbitration?
3. What does a court attempt to determine when it interprets a contract?

Assignment When you are done, write a short summary of the situation. Include the court's decision and a couple of sentences about why or how the court reached its decision.

Facts Terms of the Contract

Antonio Mastrobuono and his wife started an investment account at Shearson Lehman Hutton, Inc. When they opened their account, the Mastrobuonos signed a contract provided by Shearson Lehman Hutton. The contract required that the parties arbitrate any disputes that might arise. The contract also contained a provision stating that it would be governed by New York state law. In an arbitration proceeding, the parties present their dispute to an impartial third person or panel and agree to abide by the arbitrator's lawful decision. Because arbitration is considered less time consuming and less costly than litigation, many contracts contain a provision in which the parties agree that disputes be resolved through arbitration.

Arbitration or Court? For a variety of reasons, the Mastrobuonos became dissatisfied with the investment services they received from Shearson Lehman Hutton. They closed their account and sued Shearson

Lehman Hutton, alleging that their account had been mismanaged. Because of the contract's arbitration provision, Shearson Lehman Hutton suspended the litigation and forced the Mastrobuonos to go before a three-member panel of arbitrators. The panel awarded the Mastrobuonos compensatory damages of $159,327 and punitive damages of $400,000. Compensatory damages are awarded to compensate an injured party for actual losses. Punitive damages may be awarded in limited circumstances to punish a person or company for wrongful conduct. Punitive damages are also awarded to prevent other companies from behaving in a similar unlawful or unethical manner. In many cases, the threat of suffering financial loss by way of punitive damages will discourage a company or individual from engaging in unscrupulous behavior. Shearson Lehman Hutton paid the compensatory damages but obtained a court order vacating the award for punitive damages because New York law permits only courts to award punitive damages.

David Planchet

Opinion Different Interpretations

The Court observed that the contract between the parties in this case contained no express provision about punitive damages. Because the parties agreed to arbitrate a dispute, the Mastrobuonos claimed that the parties were bound by the arbitration panel's decision. Shearson Lehman Hutton argued that the contract limits the matters that may be arbitrated because the parties agreed that the contract would be governed by New York law, which only authorizes courts to award punitive damages. As a result of these differing views, the Court had to interpret the meaning of the contract.

Determining the Intent of the Parties

The Court said that when interpreting a contract, it must determine the intent of the parties at the time that they entered into the agreement. The original intent of the parties would be used to guide the court's decision. In this contract, the parties agreed that arbitration would be conducted in accordance with rules of the National Association of Security Dealers (NASD), which states that arbitrators may award "damages and other relief." The NASD manual further provides that "No agreement [between a member and a customer] shall include any condition which... limits the ability of a party to file any claim in arbitration or limits the ability of an arbitrator to make any award." However, the contract also states that it is governed by New York law, which permits only courts to award punitive damages. These conflicting provisions create an ambiguity in the contract.

Ambiguous Terms

Under common law, ambiguous terms in a contract are interpreted against the party that drafted the contract. Ambiguous terms can be understood in different ways. This view of ambiguity protects the party who did not prepare the contract. A party that

had no input in drafting a contract cannot be blamed for that contract's ambiguities. As stated in the Restatement (Second) of Contracts § 206, Comment a (1979):

"Where one party chooses the terms of a contract, he is likely to provide more carefully for the protection of his own interests than for those of the other party. He is also more likely than the other party to have reason to know of uncertainties of meaning. Indeed, he may leave meaning deliberately obscure, intending to decide at a later date what meaning to assert. In cases of doubt, therefore, so long as other factors are not decisive, there is substantial reason for preferring the meaning of the other party."

Because Shearson Lehman Hutton prepared the contract for the Mastrobuonos' signatures, any ambiguity must be interpreted in favor of the Mastrobuonos.

Holding The Court's Decision

The contract between the parties is ambiguous. Under well-established rules of common law, ambiguities in a contract are construed against the party who wrote the contract. As a result, the arbitration panel's award of punitive damages was upheld.

TRIAL PREP

The National High School Mock Trial Association organizes competitions at the local, regional, and national levels where teams of high school or college students prepare and argue fictional legal cases before practicing attorneys and judges. Mock Trial team members are each assigned a role as either an attorney or witness. Each team must develop a courtroom strategy, legal arguments, and a presentation style.

UNIT 3

Consumer Law

In This Unit You Will Find:

Consumers A consumer is anyone who buys or leases goods, real estate, or services. *Who are the consumers in this photo, and what goods and services are involved?*

Product Safety and Recalls

As you read this unit, use this checklist to prepare for the unit project:

- ✓ List federal agencies that protect consumers.
- ✓ Differentiate among the types of federal agencies and community protection agencies.
- ✓ Find consumer action information.
- ✓ Explain how consumers can file a consumer complaint.
- ✓ Determine the average time to process a consumer complaint.

Legal Portfolio When you complete the Unit Thematic Project, create an informational flyer to add to your portfolio.

Ask

AN EXPERT   Stocks and Bonds

Q: I keep hearing about investing in stocks and bonds. What is the difference between them?

A: When you buy stock in a company, you are buying a share of ownership in it. When you buy a bond from the government or from a company, you are lending it money. Just as any other loan, a bond usually pays a specified amount of interest over time. The amount of money you make investing in bonds is the amount you collect in interest. The amount of money you make investing in stocks, on the other hand, is based on how well the company does. The better the company does, the more the value of its stock increases and the more money you make. If a company does poorly, however, the value of its stock decreases, and you can lose money on your investment.

Consumer Law and Contracts

Legal Briefs

Consumer Identity Data and Privacy

Data breaches violate customer privacy and make businesses targets for lawsuits.

Consumers are uneasy about businesses collecting and using their personal information and about exposure to the theft of that information. They've had enough, and are fighting back through the courts.

Increasingly people are objecting to their personal data being used—and abused, some claim—for marketing purposes by businesses. They are demanding transparency from businesses as to how personal information is collected and shared.

Headlines are full of stories about cyberattacks and data hacking. Hackers breach firewalls and sophisticated intrusion-prevention security systems to steal consumers' financial and personal information. Businesses must be proactive in increasing the security of consumers' private information. At the same time, their legal teams must be ready with a plan to offset the lawsuits that come after a breach.

The courts will have the final word about what personal data can be collected and how they are used by businesses. The courts also will decide what lawsuits are valid against businesses whose data have been stolen by hackers, exposing the personal information of millions of consumers.

For attorneys this means there will be plenty of work to do.

Product Guaranteed Always read a product warranty carefully to find out what it covers. *What does a limited warranty usually cover?*

Sales Contracts

What You'll Learn

◆ Explain the Uniform Commercial Code.

◆ Compare and contrast service contracts and contracts for the sale of goods.

◆ Explain when title and risk of loss pass in a sale of goods.

◆ List the remedies of the buyer and seller when a sales contract is breached.

Why It's Important

The more you know about the law of sales, the more you can protect your legal rights and your money when buying or selling goods.

Reading Guide

Before You Read

Connect Some sales contracts you make are for goods, and some are for services. What are some examples of contracts you or someone you know made recently that included both goods and services?

Focus on Ideas

Sales contracts follow a special set of rules called the Uniform Commercial Code.

Take Notes

Go to connectED.mcgraw-hill.com to download a graphic organizer you can use to take notes as you read this section.

Special Rules for Sales Contracts → Good Faith

Key Terms

You will learn these legal words and expressions in this chapter. You can also find these terms in *Black's Law Dictionary* or in an online legal dictionary.

- Uniform Commercial Code (UCC)
- firm offer
- title

- bill of sale
- insurable interest
- voidable title
- risk of loss

Academic Vocabulary

You will find these words in your readings and in your tests. Look them up in a dictionary and familiarize yourself with them.

- uniform
- dominant
- revoke

Sales of Goods

At what point do you become the legal owner of something you purchased?

General contract law governs contracts for such things as real estate, employment, and services. A subset of contract law is sales law, which governs the sale of goods. It does not apply to sales of real property (houses and land) or services (work performed by someone else).

Sales law was established through the customs and practices of businesspeople, merchants, and mariners, and has gone through many changes. As interstate commerce (trade that crosses state lines) developed, the need arose to make **uniform** the many commercial laws in effect among the states. The result was the development of the Uniform Commercial Code, which includes the sale and lease of goods. **The Uniform Commercial Code (UCC) is a collection of laws that governs various types of business transactions.** You apply the law of sales under the UCC whenever you have a contract for the sale of goods.

Goods are all things (other than money, stocks, and bonds) that are movable. Examples are your clothing, books, cell phone, food, car, and even the gas you put in the car. A sale is a contract in which ownership of goods is transferred from the seller to the buyer for a price. Thus, every time you buy or sell goods and transfer ownership of them, a sale occurs.

Leasing Goods

The sale-of-goods rules also apply to the leasing of goods, with a few exceptions. Thus, rentals for items such as a DVD player, tuxedo, computer, or car are governed by the UCC.

Contracts for Both Goods and Services

When a contract includes both goods and services, the **dominant** element determines the law that will apply. For example, if a business buys three new computers and has them installed, the sale of the goods—the computers—is dominant and the laws of the UCC apply. However, if the business has the computers serviced and some new hardware is installed, the service is dominant, so the common law of contracts applies instead.

Special Rules for Sales Contracts

A sales contract must contain the same elements as other contracts, but the UCC has relaxed some of the strict rules of contract law. The performance obligations of both parties are similar to general contract law and set forth in the UCC. The following special rules apply to contracts for the sale of goods.

As You Read

Predict How is a sales contract different from any other kind of contract?

Vocabulary You can find vocabulary definitions in the **Key Terms** glossary and the Academic Vocabulary glossary in the back of this book.

Uniform Commercial Code The UCC governs contracts for the sales of goods. *Why was the UCC created?*

Methods of Dealing and Usage of Trade When you have dealt with another person before, the method you use to deal with them has special meaning. Similarly, any commonly used method of dealing in a particular area—or usage of trade—has special meaning. Unless you state otherwise, either an established method of dealing with someone or usage of trade may be used to supplement or qualify the terms of a sales contract.

Good Faith Parties to a sales contract must treat each other fairly.

Offer and Acceptance of a Sales Contract You may make a sales contract in any manner that shows the parties have reached an agreement. It may be oral (with some exceptions) or in writing. You may accept an offer by any means and in any reasonable manner. However, the party making the offer may request a particular method to be used for the acceptance. A contract comes into existence when the acceptance is sent in a reasonable manner.

Firm Offer The UCC holds merchants to a higher standard than nonmerchants. A merchant is a business or person who deals regularly in the sale of goods or who has a specialized knowledge of goods.

Case Study – Lohman v. Wagner

Critical Thinking *Should the UCC cover this transaction?*

 Your Reading **Note key facts in the text below and look up words you do not understand. Restate difficult ideas in your own words. Go back and reread the text quickly to make sure you did not miss any important detail. Now, you are ready to formulate an opinion.**

Service or Sales Contract? Prior to 1998, Charles Lohman ran a company that bred and raised young pigs. He raised the pigs from the time they were born until they reached 50 pounds. However, in 1998, Mr. Lohman decided that he only wanted to raise pigs until they were weaned from their mothers. Mr. Lohman contacted John Wagner, a buyer and seller of pigs, about selling only young pigs. Because Mr. Lohman decided to change the focus of his business, he needed to renovate his farming operation and sought financing for it. The bank required that Mr. Lohman provide a signed contract for the future sales of his pigs. Mr. Lohman called Mr. Wagner, who provided a signed copy of an unofficial contract to Mr. Lohman. The contract provided that Mr. Lohman would provide housing facilities, labor, utilities, and production supplies in producing and raising the young pigs, and that Mr. Wagner would buy the pigs for $28 each. The bank approved Mr. Lohman's loan and he began to raise the pigs. However, due to a sharp decline in the price of pork, Mr. Wagner told Mr. Lohman he could only pay $18 each for the pigs. Mr. Lohman was forced to end his business and sued Mr. Wagner for breach of contract. Mr. Lohman argued that it was a service contract. Mr. Wagner argued that the contract was for the sale of goods.

Lohman v. Wagner, 862 A.2d 1042 (Md. Ct. App. 2004)

Go to **ConnectED.mcgraw-hill.com** for more case study practice.

Although most rules under the UCC apply to both merchants and nonmerchants alike, some rules apply only to merchants. One such rule involves a firm offer.

A firm offer is a merchant's written promise to hold an offer open for the sale or lease of goods. No consideration is necessary when a merchant promises in writing to hold an offer open for the sale or lease of goods. A merchant cannot **revoke** a firm offer during the time stated in the offer or for a reasonable time if none is stated. However, no offer can stand for longer than three months.

Different or Additional Terms An acceptance may add different or additional terms. These terms are treated as proposals for additions to the contract if both parties are not merchants. If both parties are merchants, the changes become part of the contract unless they are major or the offeror objects. No consideration is necessary to modify—or change—a contract for the sale of goods. Modifications may be oral, unless the original agreement states that it must be modified in writing.

Statute of Limitations The statute of limitations for sales contracts is four years. However, the individual parties can reduce the time period to a minimum of one year, but may not extend it to longer than four years. The time limit begins to accrue when a breach occurs, regardless of whether the parties are aware the breach has occurred.

Form of Sales Contracts

If the price for goods is less than $500, an oral sales contract is enforceable. If the price is $500 or more, a sales contract must be in writing to be enforceable. This rule does not apply when:

- A written confirmation of an oral contract between two merchants is sent within a reasonable time, and no objection is made within ten days.
- The contract involves specially manufactured goods that cannot be resold easily.
- The buyer receives and accepts the goods or pays for them.
- The parties admit in court that they entered into an oral contract.

Title and Risk of Loss

When does right of ownership pass from seller to buyer?

The right of ownership to goods is known as title. People who own goods have title to them. **A bill of sale is formal evidence of ownership.** A bill of sale, however, only proves that you once had title, not that you still own the goods.

Insurable Interest

Insurable interest is a legal interest in the protection of property from injury, loss, or destruction. The buyer obtains an insurable interest when specific goods are identified as

Reading Check

Compare and Contrast
What is the longest an offer can stand on a sales contract?

Legal Talk

those in the contract. A seller retains insurable interest in goods when the seller retains title to the goods or has a security interest in the goods.

Voidable Title

Anyone who obtains property as a result of another's fraud, mistake, undue influence, or duress holds only voidable title to the goods. **Voidable title means title that may be voided (cancelled) if the injured party chooses to do so.** Voidable title is also received when goods are bought from or sold to a minor or a person who is mentally impaired. Anyone with voidable title to goods is able to transfer valid (good) title to others.

Passage of Title and Risk of Loss

Sometimes it is necessary to determine who has title to goods—the seller or the buyer. It is also necessary at times to determine who bears the risk of loss of goods. **Risk of loss is the responsibility for loss or damage to goods.** Title passes to the buyer when the seller does what is required under the contract to deliver the goods. No one can have title to goods that do not exist, such as crops that are not yet grown or items that are not yet made.

Shipment Contracts

A shipment contract is one in which the seller gives goods to a carrier for delivery to a buyer. A carrier is a transportation company. Both title and risk of loss pass to the buyer when the goods are given to the carrier.

Remedies for Breach of Sales Contract

What can you do if you receive damaged goods?

A breach of contract occurs when one party to a contract fails to perform the duties required by the contract. When this happens, there are things you can do as the buyer or the seller.

Seller's Remedies

Sometimes buyers refuse to accept goods that they ordered. They may also refuse to pay for them. When this happens, the seller may:

- Cancel the contract.
- Withhold delivery of goods.
- Stop delivery of any goods held by a carrier.
- Resell any goods that have been rightfully withheld, and bring a claim against the buyer for the difference between the agreed price and the resale price.
- If the goods cannot be resold, bring a claim against the buyer for the difference between the agreed price and the market price.
- Bring a claim against the buyer for the price of any goods that the buyer accepted.

Buyer's Remedies

Sometimes sellers fail to deliver goods after agreeing to do so. They may also send incorrect, damaged, or defective goods. In these cases the buyer may:

- Cancel the contract.
- Bring a claim against the seller for the return of money that was paid.
- Bring a claim against the seller for the difference between the agreed price and the market price.
- Refuse to accept the goods if something is wrong with them. The buyer must notify the seller about this and give the seller time to correct the problem.
- Buy similar goods from someone else and bring a claim against the seller for the difference between the agreed price and the cost of the purchase.
- Give notice to the seller that the goods have been accepted, but that there is something wrong with them. If no adjustment is made, the buyer may bring a claim against the seller for breach of contract or warranty.
- Revoke the acceptance and return the goods if a serious defect was undetectable, or if the buyer was led to believe that the seller would fix the defect.

After You Read

Summarize Name the special rules that apply to sales contracts under the UCC.

SECTION 7.1 ASSESSMENT

Self Check

1. To what kinds of transactions does the law of sales apply?

2. When must sales contracts be in writing? What are the exceptions?

3. When do title and risk of loss pass from the seller to the buyer in a delivery contract?

Academic Connection

Mathematics Jonathan Asbil wants to purchase a used Ford Mustang, which is advertised for $9,800. It has a CD player/radio, air conditioning, power windows and locks, and manual transmission. It has a total of 84,000 miles driven on it. The used car guide indicates that the average value of the car is $7,375–$9,725 with a $125 subtraction for no automatic transmission. What average retail price should Jonathan keep in mind when he makes an offer for the car?

CONCEPT **Number and Operations:** To calculate the average retail value, you would first find the mid-range value. Find the difference between the high and low value and divide by two, then add to the low value. Then, subtract the $125 from the price for not having an automatic transmission.

 For more math practice, go to the Math Appendix.

Critical Thinking

Goods or Services? Darlene bought a pair of jeans from a clothing store. The jeans did not fit perfectly, so the store agreed to alter them for her. How can you determine whether to apply the law of sales?

What You'll Learn

◆ Distinguish different types of consumer fraud.

◆ Describe laws and agencies that protect consumers.

◆ Identify various types of warranties.

◆ Describe how warranties may be excluded or modified.

◆ Determine where to get consumer protection assistance.

Why It's Important

Knowing about warranties and consumer protection laws will help you if you ever buy a faulty product.

Reading Guide

Before You Read

Connect What is the last thing you bought that has a warranty? How long is it for and what does it cover?

Focus on Ideas

A warranty is your personal guarantee that if a product does not work the way it should, you can get your money back or have it repaired or replaced.

Take Notes

Go to connectED. mcgraw-hill.com to download a graphic organizer you can use to take notes as you read this section.

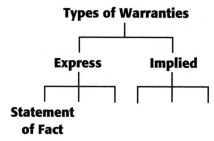

Types of Warranties

Key Terms

You will learn these legal words and expressions in this chapter. You can also find these terms in *Black's Law Dictionary* or in an online legal dictionary.

- warranty
- express warranty
- full warranty
- limited warranty

- implied warranty
- warranty of merchantability
- warranty of fitness for a particular purpose

Academic Vocabulary

You will find these words in your readings and in your tests. Look them up in a dictionary and familiarize yourself with them.

- disclose
- option
- exclude

Consumer Protection Laws

What is bait and switch?

Consumer protection laws apply to transactions between consumers and businesses. A consumer is someone who buys or leases goods, real estate, or services for personal, family, or household purposes. When you buy a new car from a car dealer, consumer protection laws can help you. When you buy a car from another consumer, however, you do not have the same protection. Nor do consumer protection laws protect you if you buy a product to use in your business.

The Federal Trade Commission (FTC) is the governmental agency that promotes free trade and fair competition. The Bureau of Consumer Protection safeguards consumers against unfair and deceptive practices.

Federal Consumer Protection Law

Both the federal and state governments have laws to protect the well-being of consumers in the marketplace.

Consumer Product Safety Act The federal Consumer Product Safety Act protects you from unreasonable risk of injury while using consumer products sold in interstate commerce. Manufacturers and sellers who place items on the market must test the quality and reliability (fitness) of all products before shipping. They must prove that the product has been tested and is safe.

Consumer Leasing Act The Consumer Leasing Act requires lease agreements to include certain terms of the lease, including the required number of lease payments and their dollar amounts. Leases must also include any penalties for not paying on time and whether there is a lump-sum payment due at the end of the lease.

State and Local Laws

The federal government has no control over intrastate commerce—the manufacturing and selling of goods within a state. For this reason many states have enacted their own product liability laws and have their own Department of Consumer Affairs.

Unfair and Deceptive Practices

An unfair and deceptive practice is an act that misleads consumers. Most states have enacted either the Uniform Deceptive Trade Practices Act or their own similar laws. In Texas, for example, the Texas Deceptive Trade Practices Act (DTPA) was enacted to protect consumers against false, misleading, and deceptive business and insurance practices, and breach of warranty.

Fraudulent Misrepresentation A fraudulent misrepresentation is any statement that deceives a buyer. A fraudulent misrepresentation occurs when a seller misstates or fails to **disclose** the facts about something that is important to the consumer. For example, it would be unlawful for a used car dealer to fail to inform a consumer that a car was damaged in a flood.

As You Read

Connect What experiences have you had with faulty products or false advertising?

Vocabulary You can find vocabulary definitions in the **Key Terms** glossary and the Academic Vocabulary glossary in the back of this book.

Reading Check

Analyze *How is a negative option negative?*

Bait and Switch Advertising In bait and switch advertising, a store advertises bargains that do not really exist to lure customers in hopes that they will buy something more expensive. This practice is illegal because the advertiser is trying to sell a different product than the one advertised.

FTC Trade Regulation Rules

The FTC has established trade regulation rules for interstate commerce to correct wrongdoing in the marketplace.

Negative Option Rule When you subscribe to a magazine, book club, CD club, or other plan that sends products regularly, the negative **option** rule applies. The business sends you a description of its current selection. If you do not want the selection, you must tell the seller not to send it. If you do not respond, the seller sends you the selection automatically. Under the negative option rule, sellers must legally tell you how many selections you must buy, if any, how to notify the seller when you do not want the selection, and when you can get credit for the return of a selection. They must also tell you how often you will receive announcements and forms, and how and when you can cancel your membership.

The Cooling-off Rule The cooling-off rule gives you three business days to cancel a transaction made away from a seller's regular place of business, such as a hotel, a restaurant, a fair, or your home. The rule applies to purchases of $25 or more. The seller must inform you of your right to cancel at the time the sale takes place. The seller must also give you a cancellation form and a copy of your contract or receipt. If you cancel, within 10 days the seller must cancel and return any papers you signed, refund your money, tell you whether any product left with you will be picked up, and return any trade-in. The cooling-off rule does not apply to contracts for real estate, insurance, securities, or emergency home repairs.

Telemarketing Sales Rule The Telemarketing Sales Rule protects you from abusive people who try to sell you products by phone. The Do Not Call Registry helps to reduce the number of unwanted calls you receive. Under the Telemarketing Sales Rule, it is illegal for telemarketers to call you if you have asked not to be called. Calling times are restricted to the hours between 8 a.m. and 9 p.m. Before beginning their sales pitch, telemarketers must inform you that they are making a sales call and identify the company that they represent. Telemarketers must tell you the total cost of the products or services offered and any restrictions that apply. It is also illegal for telemarketers to make false statements about their goods or services.

Shopping by Mail, Phone, Fax, or Internet The FTC has established rules to protect you when ordering goods by mail, telephone, fax, and the Internet. Sellers must ship goods within the time they promise in their catalogs or advertisements. If no time is stated, sellers must ship goods within 30 days after receiving an order. You have the right to cancel orders and get your money

Telemarketers It is illegal for telemarketers to call you without your permission. *Where should you report telemarketers who persist in calling you?*

back if time limits are not met. Sellers must notify you of any delay in shipment and give you a postcard or other free means of responding to the delay. When buyers are notified of a delay in a shipment of goods, they may either cancel the order and get their money back or agree to a new shipping date.

Warranties

What can you do if you buy something and it breaks down a month later?

A **warranty** **is a guarantee, usually by a seller to a buyer, that a product will perform as promised.** Warranty law gives consumers a great deal of protection. This protection is an important benefit in sales contracts.

Express Warranties

An **express warranty** **is an oral or a written statement, promise, or other representation about the quality of a product.** There are three ways an express warranty can be made: by a statement of fact or a promise by the seller; by a description of the goods; or by the use of a sample or model (see **Figure 7.1** on page 172).

Statement of Fact or Promise An express warranty is created when a private party or a merchant sells goods and makes a statement of fact or a promise about the goods to the buyer. The use of formal words, such as *warranty* or *guarantee*, is not necessary. Express warranties are often found in sales brochures, circulars, and advertisements.

To be useful, a warranty must be stated in precise and under-standable terms. Statements such as "This product is guaranteed" are not enough to give you protection. You need to know exactly what the seller will do for you in the event that a problem arises.

Figure 7.1 Express Warranties

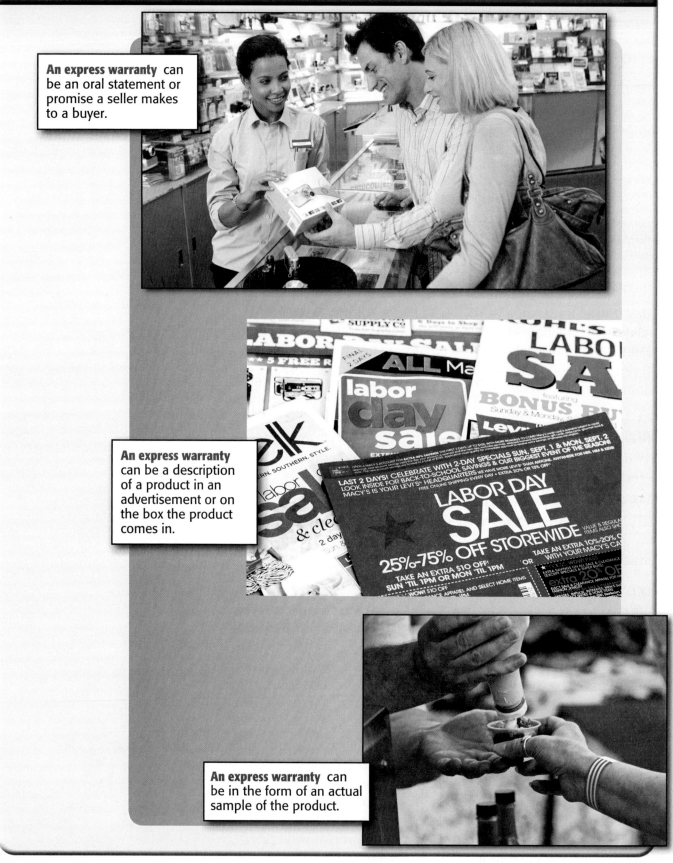

An express warranty can be an oral statement or promise a seller makes to a buyer.

An express warranty can be a description of a product in an advertisement or on the box the product comes in.

An express warranty can be in the form of an actual sample of the product.

Express warranties are oral or written guarantees about how a product will perform.
Is it necessary to include the word warranty *or* guarantee *in a warranty?*

Description or Sample of the Goods Any description or sample of the goods that is part of a transaction also creates an express warranty, such as in an advertisement or even the box the item comes in. The seller warrants that the goods will be the same as the description or sample.

Advertising Express Warranties Advertisements stating that a product is warranted must tell you how to get a copy of the warranty before you buy the product. Advertisers who warrant products for a lifetime must fully explain the terms of their promises.

Magnuson-Moss Warranty Act Under the Magnuson-Moss Warranty Act, a written warranty on goods in interstate commerce costing more than $10 must disclose whether it is full or limited. **A full warranty is an assurance that a defective product will be repaired or replaced without charge within a reasonable time. A limited warranty is any written warranty that does not meet the requirements of a full warranty.** Some limited warranties will cover parts, but not labor. Others cover a product only as long as it is owned by the original buyer.

Implied Warranties

An implied warranty is a guarantee of quality imposed by law. It comes automatically rather than verbally or in writing. There are three types of implied warranties: warranty of merchantability, warranty of fitness for a particular purpose, and usage of trade.

Merchantability A **warranty of merchantability is an implied warranty that goods are fit for the ordinary purpose for which the goods are sold.** Unless excluded, this warranty is given whenever a merchant sells goods. Retailers, wholesalers, and manufacturers imply this warranty in every sale. To be merchantable, goods must pass without objection in the trade under the contract description. They must be fit for the ordinary purposes for which the goods are used. They must also be adequately contained, packaged, and labeled, and conform to any promises or statements made on the container or label. Items that courts have held to be non-merchantable include a boat motor that produced excessive amounts of black smoke, applesauce that was inedible because of poor taste and smell, and food containing pieces of glass.

Fitness for a Particular Purpose A **warranty of fitness for a particular purpose is an implied warranty that goods will be fit for a specific use.** It comes about when the seller knows the purpose for which the goods are needed, such as a truck to haul heavy equipment. The seller warrants by implication that the goods will be fit for the purpose for which they are to be used. This warranty exists whether the seller is a merchant or a private party.

Global Law

Contracts and Warranties in South Korea

The South Korean legal system is very similar to the civil code systems found in Europe. However, after World War II, in 1948, South Korea adopted a constitution that was similar to the United States Constitution, although the civil code is still the primary source of law. Contract and warranty law stems from the South Korean Civil Code. There are some unique features in South Korean law.

There is no consideration for a contract. The concept of consideration is not present in South Korean contracting. Rather, there are 14 different types of contracts laid out in the Civil Code and the requirements for each type.

There is no Statute of Frauds. There is no law requiring specific contracts to be in writing, such as contracts for the sale of land. However, there is a definite preference in the courts for contracts to be done in writing.

In the case of breach, South Korea has a deposit clause. Any money that has been deposited in contemplation of a contract can be considered liquidated damages. That is, if a party puts down money to buy a house and then decides not to buy the house, that party can breach the contract by giving up the money. Alternatively, if the seller decides not to sell and breaches the contract, then that party must only pay twice the amount of the deposit.

There are specific warranty statutes. As in the U.S., sellers are liable for express warranties. The Korean Civil Code, again, is explicit on what qualifies as a warranty. However, a seller's liability depends upon whether the seller is aware of the defect. There are only limited situations where a seller is liable for unknown defects.

Across Cultures: Trials in South Korea

One major difference between U.S. and South Korean trials is that there is no jury in South Korea. Rather, a court comprised of one or three judges hears the case and makes a decision.

Critical Thinking: *Should manufacturers only be liable for known defects, as in South Korea, or should there be strict liability, as in the U.S.?*

Warranty of Title

In all sales, the seller warrants that the title being given to the buyer is good and that the transfer is lawful. This is called the warranty of title. It is a guarantee that the goods have no liens, or claims by others. If you buy stolen goods, the real owner has the right to the return of the goods. You may recover your loss from the seller, who breached the warranty of title.

Exclusion of Warranties

To **exclude** the warranty of merchantability, the word *merchantability* must be mentioned specifically. If the exclusion is in writing, the word must be written prominently. The warranty of title may not be excluded.

In some states, implied warranties can also be excluded or modified by the words *as is* and *with all faults*. Having buyers examine goods before the sale is another way to exclude or modify warranties. Under federal law, implied warranties cannot be excluded when an express warranty is given to a consumer.

Responsibilities of Consumers

Warranties are designed to protect you as a consumer. As a consumer, however, you also have certain responsibilities. You have a responsibility to use a product safely and as it is intended to be used. If a product comes with information, such as a warranty, you have a responsibility to read that information. To succeed in a claim for breach of warranty, you have a duty to notify the seller within a reasonable time after you discover the defect. Failure to do so will prevent you from recovering damages.

Consumer Protection Assistance

Where can you go if you feel you have been cheated by a business?

Many state and local governments have offices of consumer affairs to educate consumers and help protect them against fraud. The federal Consumer Product Safety Commission establishes safety standards for consumer products. It has the power to recall unsafe products and to impose fines on violators. The local business community also polices itself to protect consumers from questionable practices.

If a consumer feels wronged, the consumer should first try to contact the business involved. If that does not work, then the consumer can contact the Better Business Bureau (BBB). The BBB is a private agency that hears consumer complaints at the local and state levels. The BBB's mission is to promote highly ethical relationships between businesses and the public through voluntary self-regulation, consumer and business education, and service excellence. The BBB, however, does not have the power to enforce laws or recommend one business over another.

After You Read

Summarize Name the different types of warranties.

SECTION 7.2 ASSESSMENT

Self Check

1. What is the cooling-off rule?

2. What are the three ways an express warranty can be made?

3. What is the warranty of title?

Academic Connection

Social Studies In 1962, President John F. Kennedy presented to the American public what he called the Consumer Bill of Rights. The bill said that every person has four basic consumer rights. Over the years, three more rights were added. Look up these rights in the library or on the Internet and list them in your notebook.

English Language Arts Write a letter to your state's attorney general to find out what rights you have in your state when you purchase a defective car. Make sure to use proper business letter format.

Critical Thinking

Bait and Switch Bait and switch is an old gimmick unethical businesses use to lure people into a store and then get them to spend more money than they intended. Why do you think they call it bait and switch?

Chapter 7 Review and Assessment

Summary

Section 7.1 Sales Contracts

◆ The sale of goods is governed by sales law under the Uniform Commercial Code (UCC). The sale of services and real property is governed by general contract law.

◆ When a contract includes both goods and services, the dominant element of the contract determines whether it is a contract for goods or a contract for services.

◆ Title to goods is passed from a seller to a buyer when the seller does what is required under the contract to deliver the goods. The risk of loss is born by the party responsible for loss or damage to goods.

◆ Most contracts for the sale of goods of $500 or more must be in writing to be enforceable.

◆ There are several remedies both buyers and sellers may seek if a sales contract is breached.

Section 7.2 Consumer Protection

◆ The Federal Trade Commission (FTC) was created to promote free and fair trade competition. The Bureau of Consumer Protection safeguards consumers against unfair and deceptive practices. The Consumer Product Safety Act protects consumers from unsafe goods.

◆ An express warranty is an oral or written statement about the quality, ability, or performance of a product. An implied warranty is a guarantee of quality imposed by law.

◆ A full warranty promises to fix or replace a defective product at no extra charge within a reasonable time. A limited warranty covers only specific costs, such as parts but not labor.

◆ Consumer protection can be obtained from state and local consumer protection agencies, such as the Consumer Product Safety Commission and the Better Business Bureau.

Vocabulary Builder

1 On a sheet of paper, use each of these terms in a sentence.

Key Terms

- Uniform Commercial Code (UCC)
- firm offer
- title
- bill of sale

- insurable interest
- voidable title
- risk of loss
- warranty
- express warranty

- full warranty
- limited warranty
- implied warranty
- warranty of merchantability
- warranty of fitness for a particular purpose

Academic Vocabulary

- uniform
- dominant

- revoke
- disclose

- option
- exclude

Key Points Review

Answer the following questions. Refer to the chapter for additional reinforcement.

2 How are contracts for the sale of goods different from contracts for services or real property?

3 What are a seller's remedies when a buyer breaches a sales contract?

4 What are a buyer's remedies when a seller breaches a sales contract?

5 When do title and risk of loss pass from the seller to the buyer in a sale of goods?

6 What types of transactions do consumer protection laws cover and not cover?

7 What are the three types of implied warranties?

8 What are ways that implied warranties can be excluded or modified?

9 What organizations, businesses, and government agencies can consumers go to for assistance?

Standardized Test Practice

10 Read the following excerpt from a product warranty and complete questions 1 and 2.

The company will provide parts to replace defective parts without charge for one year from the date of the original retail purchase. Certain parts are excluded from this warranty. The company will provide the labor without charge for a period of one year from the date of the original retail purchase.

This warranty only covers failures due to defects in material or workmanship which occur during normal use. It does not cover damage which occurs in shipment, or failure or damage which results from accident, misuse, abuse, mishandling, misapplication, alteration, faulty installation, improper maintenance, commercial use such as for hotel or office use, or damage which results from fire, flood, or other natural disaster.

1. What does the warranty cover for the first year?

Ⓐ parts only
Ⓑ labor only
Ⓒ labor and all parts
Ⓓ labor and certain parts

2. Which type of damage is covered by the warranty?

Ⓐ damage due to a natural disaster
Ⓑ faulty installation
Ⓒ defects in workmanship
Ⓓ damage that occurs in shipment

Test-Taking Strategies Skip difficult questions until all other questions are answered. Keep a record of the unanswered items to return to, if time permits, on a scrap piece of paper.

Apply and Debate

Read the following scenarios. Get together with other students in pairs or groups of three and take a position on each scenario. Debate your position in class with students taking the opposite position or prepare a written argument justifying your position.

11 Firm Offer

Nathan's Burgers has bought its hamburger buns from a local bakery for a set price for the past five years based on an oral agreement. Recently, Nathan picked up his order and discovered that the cost for hamburger buns had increased ten percent.

You Debate | *Is the bakery required to notify Nathan prior to the price increase?*

12 Bulk Transfer

Mattie places an order with a moving company to deliver new fall fashions to her clothing shop in stages. The next day, she discovers that all of the merchandise has been delivered in bulk with a bill to be paid in full in ten days.

You Debate | *Is Mattie required to accept the merchandise and pay the bill in full?*

13 Express Warranty

You buy the floor model of a DVD player at half price. The sales clerk tells you it can be returned for a full refund if it is faulty. At home you discover it is missing the cables and remote, so you return to the store for a refund. Above the service desk is a sign stating, "All floor models are sold as is and cannot be returned."

You Debate | *Are you entitled to a refund?*

14 Full Warranty

Maria buys a set of tools at a trade show from a dealer who owns a store in the same town. When Maria uses the tools for the first time, one of them breaks. She goes to the merchant's local store for a refund. The merchant tells Maria she is not entitled to a refund since the sale was made at the trade show and not the store.

You Debate | *Does the Magnuson-Moss Warranty Act apply to this situation?*

15 Bait and Switch?

You find an ad for a great deal on a computer at a local store. When you get to the store, the clerk tells you they are out of stock and shows you another computer that is more expensive.

You Debate | *Is this a case of bait and switch?*

Case Study Practice – Princess Cruises, Inc. v. General Electric Co.

⑯ Which Type of Contract Applies? Princess Cruises (Princess) owns and operates the SS Sky Princess. In December of 1994, Princess requested that General Electric (GE) perform routine servicing and repair on the ship and provide any parts necessary.

GE noted rust on the rotor and removed it. However, good metal was also removed, which caused the rotor to become unbalanced. Even though GE attempted to correct the imbalance, the imbalance caused damage to the ship. Princess sued GE for damages. The case went to trial and the court instructed the jury on applying UCC protections, since repair parts were included in the contract. The jury awarded Princess $4,577,743 in damages. GE appealed the case, arguing that the trial court erroneously instructed the jury on principles from the UCC, since the contract was primarily for providing a service rather than for the sale of goods.

Source: Princess Cruises, Inc. v. General Electric Co., 143 F.3d 828 (4th Cir. 1998)

Practice Did the judge correctly use UCC principles, since the contract included the sale of repair parts?

⑰ Ethics
←?→ Application _____

Keep the Customer Satisfied You sell sprinkler systems to farmers. Your old customers have never signed a contract with you because most of your sprinkler systems sell for $400, and the UCC only requires written contracts for sales above $500. Your newest sprinkler system sells for $525. Some of your old customers want the new system, but want to keep the arrangement informal and not sign a contract.

◆ What can you do to keep your old customers happy?

⑱ Think back to the Legal Briefs feature you read at the beginning of the chapter. Then conduct research on one of the high-profile cyberattack cases on establishments such as Sony, Target, the U.S. Postal Service, Home Depot, and JPMorgan Chase. Summarize your research in a brief report that includes information on what data were stolen, what the organization did to protect itself and consumers (if consumer information was stolen), and other relevant information.

CHAPTER

8 Personal Property

Legal Briefs

Broken Engagements

Who gets the ring when the engagement is broken?

An engagement ring is a gift, with the promise of a wedding. It's that promise that makes the ring a *conditional* gift—the condition being that a marriage will take place. If that condition is not met, the ring belongs to the buyer, regardless of who broke the engagement. At least that's what most—but not all—state courts rule.

Kansas, New York, Pennsylvania, Tennessee, and Wisconsin, among others, take the approach that the ring belongs to the buyer if an engagement ends before marriage. These courts do not take into consideration who broke the engagement or why.

Laws in other states hold that the circumstances of the broken engagement do matter. In California, Texas, and Washington, if the buyer broke the engagement, the ring does not have to be returned.

Montana takes a third view. State law maintains that an engagement ring is an unconditional gift, which means once a gift is given and accepted, the gift is complete and irrevocable. The engagement ring becomes the property of the receiver, even if the engagement ends, regardless of who ended it.

Intellectual Property Patents, trademarks, and copyrights protect one's creative ideas from being stolen. *What are some examples of intellectual property?*

Types of Property

◆ Distinguish between real property, personal property, and fixtures.

◆ Describe the different types of co-ownership of personal property.

◆ Explain the concept of intellectual property.

◆ Give examples of intellectual property.

◆ Define the laws of patents, copyrights, and trademarks.

Why It's Important

Knowing the law about personal property will help you protect your possessions.

Reading Guide

Before You Read

Connect Intellectual property can be anything you created, discovered, or designed. Name some things you have done that could be considered intellectual property.

Focus on Ideas

There are different ways to protect the ownership rights to different types of intellectual property.

Take Notes

Go to connectED.mcgraw-hill.com to download a graphic organizer you can use to take notes as you read this section.

Patent	Copyright	Trademark
music player	novel	slogan

Examples

Intellectual Property Protection

Key Terms

You will learn these legal words and expressions in this chapter. You can also find these terms in *Black's Law Dictionary* or in an online legal dictionary.

- personal property
- intellectual property
- patent
- copyright
- trademark

Academic Vocabulary

You will find these words in your readings and in your tests. Look them up in a dictionary and familiarize yourself with them.

- tangible
- exclusive
- downloading

Personal Property

Can you keep something you find on the street?

Personal property is everything, other than real property, that can be owned. Real property is land and anything connected to it, including buildings, the earth below, and the air above. Items of property permanently attached to real property, such as built-in stoves and kitchen cabinets, are called fixtures and are considered real property. **Tangible** personal property is property that has substance and can be touched, such as CD players, vehicles, and food. Intangible personal property, is property that has no substance and cannot be touched, such as patents, copyrights, and trademarks. If someone owes you money, the right to receive the money is intangible personal property. It is necessary to distinguish between real and personal property because the law that applies to each may be different.

As You Read

Predict What is the difference between personal property and real property?

Vocabulary You can find vocabulary definitions in the **Key Terms** glossary and the Academic Vocabulary glossary in the back of this book.

Global Law

Inheritance Rights in Property for Women in Kenya

Women in the United States are granted the same rights in property as their male counterparts. However, that is not the case in the country of Kenya. Although the Kenyan Constitution outlaws discrimination on the basis of sex, there are numerous exemptions that provide for a system that seemingly discriminates against women.

The Kenyan Constitution permits discrimination in matters pertaining to adoption, marriage, divorce, burial, distribution of property upon death, or other matters of personal law.

One such act that discriminates against women is The Law of Succession Act of 1981, which affects the distribution of property after someone dies. The law states:

1 Both male and female inherit equally if there is no surviving spouse.

2 However, if a spouse survives, the spouse inherits all the movable property in the house but can only live in the house and does not own it. If the spouse chooses to sell the house, court permission must be granted. Further, if the

surviving spouse is a woman and she remarries, she loses all interest in the property when she remarries. If the surviving spouse is a man, he can remarry and his interest does not terminate.

3 If someone dies and does not have either a spouse or children, the estate passes first to the deceased's father and then, if the father is dead, to the mother.

4 Finally, the Act was amended in 1990 to exempt Muslim families from the provisions. Muslims in Kenya are subject only to Islamic laws, which provide that a son generally inherits double the share of a daughter. Also, if there are children and a wife, the wife only gets one-eighth of the estate.

Across Cultures: Source of Law in Kenya

Although Kenya has a constitution and statutory law, customary law (primarily unwritten) from each of the different regions is also valid law in those regions. The authorities must consider customary law to the extent it does not conflict with the constitution.

Critical Thinking: *Should different ethnic groups be able to follow their own laws, even though they are members of a larger country?*

Most property is acquired by:
- purchase
- gift
- inheritance

Co-ownership of Personal Property

When two or more people own personal property as tenants in common, each owner's share passes to his or her heirs upon death. If, instead, they own it as joint tenants, each owner's share passes to the surviving joint tenants upon death. Nine states recognize community property. This is property (except a gift or inheritance) that is acquired by the personal efforts of either spouse during marriage. It belongs to both spouses equally.

Lost, Misplaced, and Abandoned Property

If you find a watch, you have a legal duty to try to find the true owner. If you cannot find the owner, you may be able to keep the watch after following local requirements. Local laws may require you to advertise for the true owner or to deposit the article at the police station while the owner is being sought.

If property is found on the counter of a store, at a table in a restaurant, or on a chair in a washroom, it is considered misplaced rather than lost. The owner may recall where it was left and return for it. If you find an article in such a place, you should leave it with the proprietor. Abandoned property is property that has been discarded by the owner without the intent to reclaim it. With exceptions, anyone who finds abandoned property may keep it.

CYBERLAW

Venetian Casino Resort, LLC v. VenetianGold.com
380 F.Supp.2d 737 (E.D. Va. 2005)

The Venetian Casino Resort is a prominent Las Vegas casino known for its elaborate Venetian-style architecture. The Resort has trademarked numerous names, including, "Venetian," "The Venetian," and "The Venetian Resort Hotel Casino." After those names were trademarked, Vincent Coyle launched an international gambling Web site using the name VenetianGold.com. He also registered Web site names such as VenetianGoldCasino.com, VenetianCasinoVegas.com, and VeniceGoldCasino.com, all of which took users to the gambling Web site. The Venetian Casino Resort then sued VenetianGold.com under the Anti-Cybersquatting Consumer Protection Act.

Ruling and Resolution
The U.S. District Court in Virginia held that the Venetian Casino Resort in Las Vegas was a distinct trademark and that VenetianGold.com had tried to profit from using similar names on its Web sites. Therefore, Mr. Coyle's company must cease using Web site names that were similar and include the term "Venetian," along with similar-themed words.

Critical Thinking If users realize that the Web site is not actually the Las Vegas resort, then should Mr. Coyle be able to use similar names?

Stolen Personal Property

A person has no title to goods that are stolen and cannot give good title to anyone else. An innocent purchaser who acquires a stolen item in good faith is obliged to return it to the owner. Title to stolen goods never leaves the owner, who can always regain possession.

Gifts of Personal Property

A gift of personal property is completed when three requirements are met:

- The donor (gift-giver) must intend to make the gift.
- The gift must be delivered.
- The donee (gift-receiver) must accept the gift.

Once all three requirements are met, the gift cannot be taken back by the original owner.

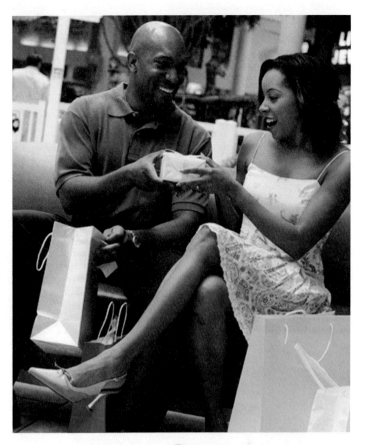

Gifts Like a contract, offer and acceptance are required for a gift to be complete. *How does a gift differ most from a contract?*

Intellectual Property

Can you patent a peanut butter and jelly sandwich?

Intellectual property is an original work fixed in a tangible medium of expression. Examples of intellectual property include inventions, works of art, software, and logos (see **Figure 8.1** on page 186). Intellectual property law has become even more important with the increase of computers and technology. Due to high research and development costs, technology companies want to ensure that their products are protected from other companies. Patents, copyrights, and trademarks assure that the rightful owners of intellectual property will have **exclusive** rights to their creations.

Patents

A patent is a grant giving an inventor the exclusive right to make, use, or sell an invention for a period set by Congress. The period is generally 20 years. To be patented, a device must be useful and consist of a new principle or idea. It also must not be obvious to people with ordinary skill in the field. For example, in 1999, the Smucker's Company obtained a patent on Uncrustables—frozen, crustless peanut butter and jelly pockets. Later, the company sought to expand its patent, arguing that the sealed edge was one of a kind. In 2005, the court held against the expansion, saying that the crimped edges on Uncrustables are similar to ravioli or pie crust. The patent office said it would reexamine the original patent given to Smucker's.

Reading Check

Explain *Can you keep something you bought that you later find out was stolen?*

Figure 8.1 Intellectual Property Rights

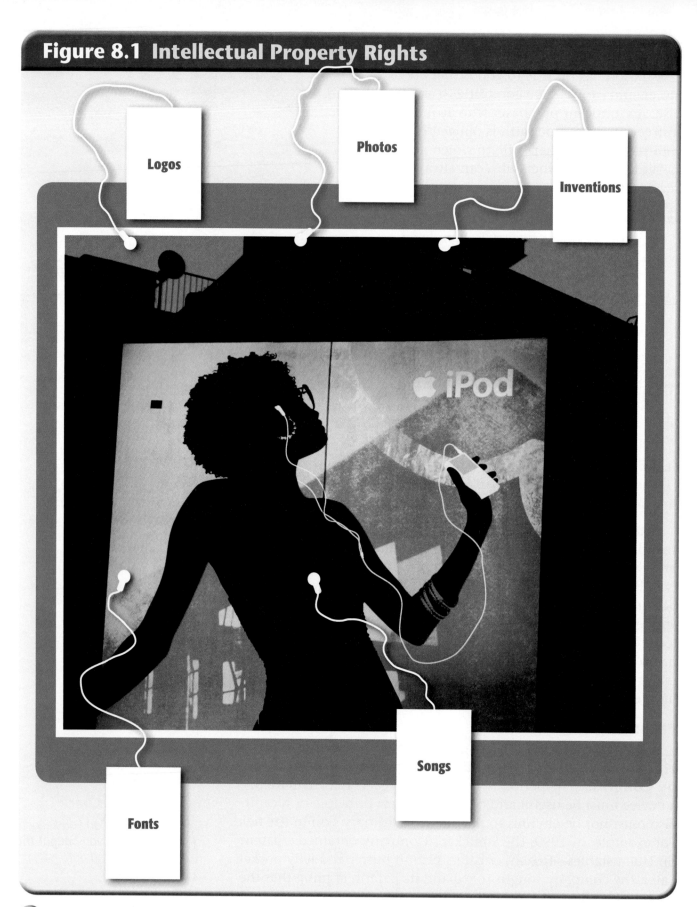

Logos

Photos

Inventions

Songs

Fonts

The Apple Computer Corporation owns numerous patent, copyright, and trademark rights. *What types of intellectual property protection are used to cover the different items in the figure?*

Copyrights

A copyright is a right granted to an author, composer, photographer, or artist to exclusively publish and sell an artistic or literary work. Copyrighted works are protected for the life of the author plus 70 years. In addition to printed items, computer software, graphic arts, architectural designs, motion pictures, and sound recording may be copyrighted. **Downloading** someone else's music from the Internet without paying a fee violates copyright law.

Under the fair use doctrine, copyrighted material may be reproduced without permission in certain cases. Copying is allowed for literary criticism, news reporting, teaching, school reports, and other research. The amount and use of the material must be reasonable and not harmful to the copyright owner.

Trademarks

A trademark is a distinctive mark, symbol, or slogan used by a business to identify and distinguish its goods from products sold by others. It may consist of a word, name, symbol, or other device. Owners of trademarks have the exclusive right to use the particular word, name, or symbol that they have adopted as their trademark. A trademark continues for ten years and may be renewed for additional ten-year periods. The ® symbol indicates that a trademark is legally registered.

After You Read

Summarize What are the three most common ways property is acquired?

SECTION 8.1 ASSESSMENT

Self Check

1. Give two examples of tangible personal property and one example of intangible personal property.

2. What are the three requirements of a completed gift?

3. When is copying allowed without permission?

Academic Connection

Social Studies Copyright law goes back to the invention of the printing press. The first copyright law enacted in the U.S. is the Copyright Act of 1790. Since then, there have been major and minor revisions to the act in 1831, 1865, 1870, 1909, 1912, and 1976. Go to the library or on the Internet to look up the Copyright Act and why it was changed each time. Create a time line describing the changes.

English Language Arts Suppose you lost or misplaced a valuable item of personal property. Write an ad to be posted in a newspaper and around your neighborhood describing the item and offering a reward for its return.

Be sure to use proper sentence structure and check your work for grammatical, punctuation, and spelling errors.

Critical Thinking

Give and Take When you admire your friend's portable CD player, your friend replies, "I've got another one just like it that you can have. I'll give it to you at school tomorrow." Two days later, you learn that your friend gave the player to someone else. Was the player a gift to you?

Bailments

What You'll Learn

- ◆ Define bailment.
- ◆ Explain the different types of bailments.
- ◆ Discuss the standard of care bailees must use.
- ◆ Define a hotel keeper's liability.
- ◆ Identify a common carrier's liability for loss or damaged goods.

Why It's Important

Knowing the law of bailment will help you understand your rights when you let someone hold your property for you.

Reading Guide

Before You Read

Connect A bailment is created whenever you let someone else keep something you own temporarily. Name some times when you had to do this in public.

Focus on Ideas

Different types of bailments require different standards of care.

Take Notes

Go to **connectED.mcgraw-hill.com** to download a graphic organizer you can use to take notes as you read this section.

Bailments		Standard of Care
Special	→	_____
	→	_____
	→	_____

Key Terms

You will learn these legal words and expressions in this chapter. You can also find these terms in *Black's Law Dictionary* or in an online legal dictionary.

- bailment
- special bailment
- gratuitous bailment
- mutual benefit bailment
- carrier
- common carrier

Academic Vocabulary

You will find these words in your readings and in your tests. Look them up in a dictionary and familiarize yourself with them.

- standard
- benefit
- register

Bailments

Is leaving your laptop at a repair shop considered a bailment?

You may have rented movies at a video store, left your car at a shop to be repaired, or dropped clothes off at the cleaners. These were all bailments. **A bailment is the transfer of possession and control of personal property to another with the intent that the same property will be returned later.** The person who transfers the property is the bailor. The person to whom the property is transferred is the bailee.

In a bailment, there is no intent to pass title to property. The bailee has an obligation to return the same property to the bailor. The bailee also has a responsibility to exercise a certain **standard** of care of the property. The standard of care depends on who receives the most **benefit** from the bailment. There are three types of bailments, each with a different standard of care.

Types of Bailments

A special bailment is a bailment for the sole benefit of the bailee. If you borrow a friend's laptop, with nothing offered in return, you alone benefit from bailment. This type of

As You Read

Predict What is a tortious bailee?

Vocabulary You can find vocabulary definitions in the **Key Terms** glossary and the **Academic Vocabulary** glossary in the back of this book.

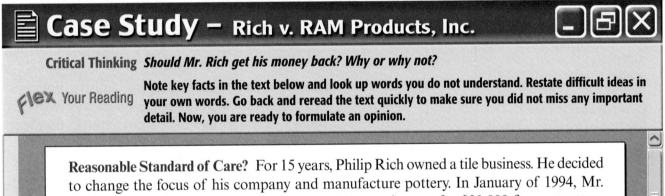

Case Study – Rich v. RAM Products, Inc.

Critical Thinking *Should Mr. Rich get his money back? Why or why not?*

Flex Your Reading Note key facts in the text below and look up words you do not understand. Restate difficult ideas in your own words. Go back and reread the text quickly to make sure you did not miss any important detail. Now, you are ready to formulate an opinion.

Reasonable Standard of Care? For 15 years, Philip Rich owned a tile business. He decided to change the focus of his company and manufacture pottery. In January of 1994, Mr. Rich purchased three pieces of pottery-making equipment for $30,000 from a pottery in Roseville, Ohio, that had been manufactured by RAM Products (RAM). Mr. Rich arranged to have the equipment transported from the pottery in Roseville to an enclosed, weatherproof storage building, where the equipment was stored on pallets.

In 1998, Mr. Rich decided to sell the three pieces of equipment and contacted RAM about selling the product for him. Mr. Rich was to transport the equipment to RAM's factory to be inspected and refurbished, if necessary. RAM would then try to sell the equipment. If RAM could not resell the equipment, it was to return the equipment to Mr. Rich.

RAM was unable to sell the equipment, so Mr. Rich traveled to RAM's factory to pick up the equipment. When he arrived at the factory, he discovered that the equipment had been stored in an open shed and that rain, snow, and other elements had ruined the equipment. Mr. Rich sued for the value of the equipment.

Rich v. RAM Products, Inc., 2005 WL 1491465 (Ohio Ct. App. 2005)

Go to **ConnectEd.mcgraw-hill.com** for more case study practice.

bailment requires great care. That means you, as the bailee, are liable for any kind of damage to the laptop while it is in your possession.

A gratuitous bailment is a bailment for the sole benefit of the bailor. This type of bailment might occur if a friend asks you to hold something, like a watch, while he or she goes swimming. Since your friend, as the bailor, receives the sole benefit of the bailment, you are required to use only slight care and can only be held liable for gross negligence. If the watch is scratched or stolen, you are not liable.

A mutual benefit bailment is a bailment in which both the bailor and the bailee receive benefits. This type of bailment might occur if you leave your car at a garage to be repaired. You, as the bailor, will have your car repaired, and the mechanic, as the bailee, will receive payment for the service. This type of bailment requires reasonable care, or the amount of care a reasonable person would use.

Sale-on-Consignment and Sale-on-Approval A consignment is a type of mutual benefit bailment. The consignor entrusts goods to the consignee for the purpose of selling them. If the goods are sold, the consignee, known as a factor, will forward the proceeds, minus a fee, to the consignor. If the goods are not sold, they are returned to the consignor. When goods are sold on approval, they remain the property of the seller until the buyer approves them.

Tortious Bailees Bailees have the right to use another person's property only for the purpose for which the bailment was created. Use for another purpose or for a longer time than agreed upon is a wrongful act.

A tortious bailee is someone who holds property wrongfully. This includes someone who keeps someone else's lost property or knowingly possesses stolen property. One who refuses to return property at the termination of a bailment is also a tortious bailee. Tortious bailees are responsible for all damage to property in their possession.

Burden of Proof Sometimes items are damaged, lost, or stolen when they are in the possession of a bailee. The bailor is not in a position to know what caused the loss. If a bailor brings suit for damages, courts shift the burden of proof to the one who is in the best position to know what happened—the bailee. As a result, the burden is on the bailee to prove a lack of negligence.

Special Bailments

What can you do if an airline loses your luggage?

Certain types of bailees have special obligations in addition to the duties imposed on all bailees. These include hotel keepers and common carriers.

Legal Talk

Consignment: *n* Giving goods to a dealer to sell for the owner. From Latin *com* = with + *sign* = mark or seal + *ment* = act of: to transfer authority to.

Lien: *n* A charge upon real or personal property for the satisfaction of some debt or duty. From Latin *ligare:* to bind.

Vocabulary Builder The root word *sign* means mark, seal, or symbol. Name words that contain *sign* and explain their meaning.

Hotel Keepers

A hotel keeper is the operator of a hotel, motel, or inn that regularly offers rooms to the public for a price. If rooms are available, a hotel keeper must accept all people who are not dangerous to the health, welfare, or safety of others and who are able to pay for their lodging. Moreover, the Civil Rights Act makes it a crime for hotel keepers to refuse a room to anyone on the grounds of race, creed, color, gender, or national origin.

Hotels and motels must provide a minimum standard of comfort, safety, and sanitation. Minimum standards include heat and ventilation, clean beds, and reasonably quiet surroundings. Guests are guaranteed the right of privacy.

With exceptions, hotel keepers are held by law to be insurers of their guests' property. In the event of loss, the hotel keeper may be held liable, regardless of the amount of care exercised.

Hotel keepers are not liable as insurers in the following cases:

- losses caused by a guest's own negligence
- losses to the guest's property due to acts of God (events such as earthquakes, floods, or cyclones) or due to acts of the public enemy (such as terrorists or wartime enemies)
- loss of property because of accidental fire in which no negligence may be attributed to the hotel keeper

Hotel Keepers Hotel keepers cannot turn away anyone who is not a danger to others if a room is available. *What can hotel keepers do to ensure guests pay their bills?*

Hotel Keeper's Lien and Credit Card Blocking Hotel keepers have a lien on their guests' property. If a guest cannot pay, the hotel keeper may hold the guest's property as security for payment at some later time.

Credit card blocking is a method used by hotels to secure payment for a room. Under this system, guests are asked for a credit card number when they **register**. The hotel contacts the card company with the estimated cost of the bill. If the card company approves the transaction, the guest's available line of credit is reduced by the estimated amount. This procedure is known as a block. The final actual charge for the room will replace the block within a day or two after the guest checks out.

Common Carriers

A **carrier** is a business that transports persons, goods, or both. A **common carrier** is a carrier that is compensated for providing transportation to the general public.

> **Reading Check**
>
> **Analyze** *Why is the burden of proof on the bailee rather than the bailor when property is damaged, lost, or stolen?*

Common Carriers Federal regulations require the screening of airline passengers and property. *What happens to passengers who do not consent to being screened?*

As with hotels, common carriers cannot turn away people who ask for their services.

Common Carriers of Goods Common carriers are liable for damages to all goods they ship, regardless of whether they are negligent. However, carriers are not liable when damages occur as a result of acts of God, the public enemy, public authorities, the shipper, and the **inherent** nature of the goods.

With these exceptions, common carriers must accept all goods offered to them for shipment. However, common carriers:

- are not required to accept goods they are not equipped to carry
- may refuse goods that are inherently dangerous
- may refuse goods that they do not haul
- may refuse goods that are improperly packaged
- may refuse goods that are not delivered at the proper place and time

Common carriers will not be excused from liability for losses because of strikes, mob violence, fire, and similar causes. Labor unions are required to give notice of impending strikes weeks in advance of the strike dates to allow carriers to reject shipments that might be damaged by delays during a strike.

Carriers have a lien on all goods shipped for the amount of the shipping charges due. Should the shipper and the party receiving the goods fail to pay the charges, the carrier may sell the goods at public sale.

Common Carriers of Passengers Carriers are responsible for protecting passengers. They are not responsible, however, if injuries are unforeseeable or unpreventable. Federal regulations require the screening of airline passengers and property. Passengers who do not consent to the screening must be refused transportation.

Bumped Airline Passengers When an airline flight is overbooked, the airline is responsible for accommodating passengers. The airline must ask for volunteers to give up their seats for seats on the next available flight. If there are not enough volunteers, other passengers may be denied a seat. Passengers who are bumped may be entitled to compensation plus the money back for their tickets.

Baggage Carriers are obligated to accept a reasonable amount of passengers' baggage. Luggage kept at one's seat does not count toward the weight limits permitted each passenger. You may ship excess baggage by paying additional fees. Dangerous weapons, explosives, destructive items, and those that are a potential threat are not allowed.

Federal rules place limits on the liability of airlines for lost luggage. Within the U.S., the maximum liability is $2,500 per passenger. Excess valuation may be declared on certain types of articles. Some carriers assume no liability for fragile, valuable, or perishable articles.

After You Read

Summarize What are the different standards of care required by bailees for the different types of bailments?

SECTION 8.2 ASSESSMENT

Self Check

1. What is the difference between a bailor and a bailee?

2. What is credit card blocking?

3. What do federal regulations require when passengers do not consent to a screening?

Academic Connection

Mathematics Duo Corporation manufactures home security monitors. It needs to rent storage space to warehouse its monitors. Each monitor is packaged in a carton measuring 2 feet long, 1.5 feet wide, and 2 feet high. How many cubic feet of space does Duo Corporation need to store 800 monitors?

CONCEPT **Number and Operations: Using Fractions, Decimals, and Rounding** To solve this problem you will need to find the volume per item first. This is done by doing the following: length × width × height = volume per item. Next you will need to find the storage space, which is calculated by volume per item × number of items.

 For more math practice, go to the Math Appendix.

Critical Thinking

Living Bailments The agricultural class at your school raises small animals, such as hamsters and rabbits. Every weekend several students take the animals home to feed them. Is this a bailment? If so, what kind?

Summary

Section 8.1 Types of Property

◆ Personal property is everything, other than real property, that can be owned.

◆ Real property is land and anything connected to it, including buildings.

◆ Most property is acquired by purchase, as a gift, or by inheritance.

◆ Forms of co-ownership of personal property include tenants in common, joint tenants, and community property.

◆ A gift of personal property is completed when the donor intends to give the gift, it is delivered, and the donee accepts the gift.

◆ Intellectual property is an original work fixed in a tangible medium of expression, such as an invention, a work of art, or a logo.

◆ Intellectual property is protected by patents, copyrights, and trademarks.

Section 8.2 Bailments

◆ A bailment is the transfer of possession and control of personal property to another with the intent that the property will be returned later.

◆ The main types of bailments are: special bailment for the sole benefit of the bailee; gratuitous bailment for the sole benefit of the bailor; and mutual benefit bailment in which both the bailor and the bailee receive benefits.

◆ Hotel keepers are held by law to be insurers of their guests' property. In the event of loss, a hotel keeper may be held liable, regardless of the amount of care exercised.

◆ Common carriers are liable for damages to all goods they ship, regardless of whether they are negligent.

◆ Common carriers are responsible for protecting passengers.

Vocabulary Builder

① **On a sheet of paper, use each of these terms in a sentence.**

Key Terms

- personal property
- intellectual property
- patent
- copyright
- trademark
- bailment
- special bailment
- gratuitous bailment
- mutual benefit bailment
- carrier
- common carrier

Academic Vocabulary

- tangible
- exclusive
- downloading
- standard
- benefit
- register

Key Points Review

Answer the following questions. Refer to the chapter for additional reinforcement.

2 What is the difference between personal property, real property, and fixtures?

3 What are some of the types of personal property?

4 What are some methods of acquiring ownership of personal property?

5 What are the different forms of co-ownership of personal property?

6 What is intellectual property and what are some types of intellectual property?

7 How is a bailment created?

8 What are the principal types of bailments?

9 What are some of the responsibilities of common carriers?

Standardized Test Practice

10 Read the following information about the use of bailment law to transfer technology and then answer questions 1 and 2.

In the 1980s, biotechnology companies solved the problem of transferring tangible material through use of the ancient legal tool of bailment, where possession, but not title, of tangible personal property is transferred for a limited purpose and duration. Then universities started utilizing bailment to transfer new technology as well. Bailment is a useful technology transfer tool in two particular situations. One case arises out of the explosive growth of biotechnology over the last two decades, and the other case is a mechanism to accomplish technology transfer through the use of tangible research products generally. In many instances over the past two decades, the traditional patent system has not been able to provide practical or cost-effective protection for a biotechnology invention, if any protection was available.

1. How did biotechnology companies solve the problem of material transfer?

Ⓐ Stopped new technology transfer

Ⓑ Transferred for limited purpose or duration

Ⓒ Required formal licensing

Ⓓ Utilized bailment laws

2. What have traditional patent systems not been able to provide?

Ⓐ Laws that have evolved in patents

Ⓑ National laboratories run by universities

Ⓒ Practical or cost-effective protection

Ⓓ Tangible research products

Test-Taking Strategies If you find yourself taking too long to answer a question, skip it and go back to it later.

Apply and Debate

Read the following scenarios. Get together with other students in pairs or groups of three and take a position on each scenario. Debate your position in class with students taking the opposite position or prepare a written argument justifying your position.

11 **Trademarks**

Jana is a junior in high school. She designed a Web site to promote her small business and purchased a domain name and logo, but did not trademark them.

You Debate   *Is Jana's business protected from another company using her domain name and logo?*

12 **Copyrights**

The Myers High School literary club wants to sell a book of students' poems for $12. It will include quotes from famous authors and a credit line for each quote.

You Debate   *Can the literary club legally use copyrighted material without the owner's permission or paying a royalty fee?*

13 **Nonprofit**

The Ellis High School Business Club plans to sell buttons featuring players' photos. To create the photos, the club members used video clips from previous games without asking the players' permission. The Business Club is a nonprofit club and the video clips were created by the school to use for promoting school sports.

You Debate   *Is the club in violation of intellectual property laws since it did not create or own the video clips and did not receive permission?*

14 **Bailment**

Joycelyn's friend agreed to keep Jocelyn's iPod in her purse since it was beginning to rain. When she gave the iPod back to Joycelyn, they discovered a pen had leaked ink all over the iPod and damaged it. Joycelyn said her friend did not take proper care of the iPod and should replace it.

You Debate   *Was there a bailment between Joycelyn and her friend and, if so, is the friend liable for the damages?*

15 **Mutual-Benefit Bailments**

Jonathan rented a key-locker for $3.00 at a waterpark. When he went back to the locker, he found it open and his things were missing.

You Debate   *Was there a mutual-benefit bailment present? If so, what did the water park owe Jonathan?*

Case Study Practice – Vigil v. Walt Disney Co.

16 **Who Owns the Trademark?** In 1992, the Walt Disney Company (Disney) released the movie *The Mighty Ducks,* the story of a fictional hockey team. Disney later acquired the rights to a real hockey team, naming it the Mighty Ducks. The logo for both consists of a hockey mask shaped like a duck's bill and crossed hockey sticks.

Mark Vigil argued that he created the logo Disney used and that he owned the intellectual property rights to it. Disney introduced evidence to the court that it had applied to register the logo as a trademark with the U.S. Patent and Trademark Office (PTO) on June 7, 1993. The logo was officially registered on April 26, 1994.

Mr. Vigil argued that Disney did not enter its logo until September 18, 1993, and that he had filed disclosure documents with the PTO on June 8, 1993. Disclosure documents are not applications for a trademark or patent, but rather give notice to the PTO that a specific design or invention may later be trademarked or patented.

Source: Vigil v. Walt Disney Co., 1995 WL 621832 (N.D. Cal. 1995)

Practice Does Mr. Vigil have a right to the Mighty Ducks logo?

17 **Ethics** ←?→ **Application**

Duty of Care? Fernando asked Nikki to store his computer at her house while he was away for the summer. Fernando never made any comments about whether Nikki could use it. Nikki used the computer every day to do her schoolwork. She was very careful with the computer, but eventually the keyboard stopped working properly.

◆ Should Nikki have to replace the keyboard?

18 Think back to the Legal Briefs feature you read at the beginning of the chapter. Then ponder the following scenario and write one or more paragraphs to answer these questions: During their senior year in college, Joe and Jane get engaged. Jane and her family plan—and pay for—the upcoming wedding including invitations, a banquet hall, Jane's dress, the DJ, flowers, caterer, and so on. Two weeks before the wedding, Joe breaks off the engagement. Joe and Jane live in your state. Should Jane return the one-carat engagement ring Joe gave her? Why or why not?

CHAPTER 9 Renting or Owning a Home

Legal Briefs

Groundwater and Property Rights

Laws differ from state to state.

Groundwater is the water table (or aquifer) that exists in gravel beds underground. Groundwater comes mostly from rain, snowmelt, and rivers. People can use groundwater by building a well to access it. Who owns groundwater and who can use it? That depends on where you live.

California enacted a controversial law that lets the state decide who can use groundwater, as well as how much and for what. The state now has the right to put meters on wells on private land. Property owners who do not follow regulations on water use are subject to fines, or even closure of the wells. Supporters say California's extreme drought, need for irrigation, and large cities make this necessary. Farmers and others say the state has become the "water police."

In the eastern United States, the situation is different. Plentiful aquifers mean that groundwater is a shared resource and property owners can use as much as they want, for any purpose—even selling it. The Midwest and Plains states are beginning to suffer from decreasing water tables and starting to go the way of California and its regulations.

Renting an Apartment Tenants and landlords have different responsibilities. *Who is responsible for making repairs to an apartment?*

Reading Guide

Before You Read

Connect You may want to rent your own apartment some day. What would your responsibilities as a tenant be?

Focus on Ideas

Rental agreements are contracts about real property that create rights and responsibilities.

Take Notes

Go to connectED. mcgraw-hill.com to download a graphic organizer you can use to take notes as you read this section.

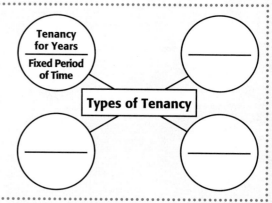

Tenancy for Years — Fixed Period of Time

Types of Tenancy

Key Terms

You will learn these legal words and expressions in this chapter. You can also find these terms in *Black's Law Dictionary* or in an online legal dictionary.

- lease
- lessee
- lessor
- tenancy

- sublease
- fixtures
- eviction

Academic Vocabulary

You will find these words in your readings and in your tests. Look them up in a dictionary and familiarize yourself with them.

- vacate
- assign
- provision

The Landlord-Tenant Relationship

How do you become a landlord or tenant?

If you rent real property, such as an apartment or house, you are a tenant. If you own real property and rent it to someone else, you are a landlord. **A lease is the contract between a tenant and a landlord. In a lease, the lessee is the tenant, and the lessor is the landlord.**

Types of Tenancies

Tenants own an interest in the real estate they lease called a leasehold estate or tenancy. The types of tenancies are tenancy for years, periodic tenancy, tenancy at will, and tenancy at sufferance.

Tenancy for Years A tenancy for years is the right to occupy property for a definite or fixed period of time. It may be for one week, six months, one year, five years, 99 years, or any other period of time, as long as the time period is definite. A tenancy for 100 years or more has the effect of transferring absolute ownership to the tenant. Some states require every tenancy for years to be in writing. Others require it to be in writing only if it exceeds a year.

Periodic Tenancy A periodic tenancy is a tenancy that continues for successive, fixed periods of time. A periodic tenancy may be from year to year, month to month, or week to week.

As You Read

Predict How far in advance do you have to notify a landlord if you plan to move?

Discrimination Landlords cannot legally refuse to rent to anyone because of their race, color, or national origin. *What laws require landlords to refrain from discrimination?*

Legal Talk

Either party may terminate this tenancy by giving advance notice to the other party. If such notice is not given, the tenancy continues for the same period of time. State laws establish the required notice.

Tenancy at Will A tenancy at will is an interest in real property that continues for an indefinite period of time. No writing is necessary to create this tenancy. It ends when the landlord or tenant gives the notice required by law. In most states, the required notice is 30 days.

Tenancy at Sufferance A tenancy at sufferance occurs when a tenant does not leave the premises when the tenancy expires. Tenants at sufferance, also called holdover tenants, are wrongdoers. They no longer have legal rights in the property. They are not entitled to notice to **vacate** and must pay rent for the illegal occupancy.

The Lease Agreement

A written agreement between a lessor and a lessee is called a lease. The lease creates the landlord-tenant relationship. It provides the tenant with exclusive possession and control of the real property of the landlord. The general rules of contract law apply to this form of agreement.

Terms in a Lease The terms of a lease, known as covenants, set forth the rights and duties of the landlord and the tenant. Tenants' basic rights are possession and continued occupancy, free from intrusion or annoyance. Landlords' basic rights are rent and possession of the property in good condition at the term's end.

Security Deposit In addition to the first month's rent, landlords often require a security deposit and the last month's rent at the beginning of a tenancy. The security deposit often equals one month's rent. Some states limit the amount of a security deposit and require interest to be paid on it.

Assignment and Subletting An assignment of a lease occurs when you transfer the remaining period of time in a lease to someone else. **A sublease is the transfer of part of the term of a lease, but not the remainder of it, to someone else.** If a landlord does not want a tenant to **assign** or sublet the property, a covenant in the lease must say that. Otherwise, a tenant may either assign or sublet the property to someone else. Nevertheless, the original tenant is responsible to the landlord for the rent.

Option to Renew Many leases contain a **provision** allowing renters the option to renew the lease for one or more additional periods. This provision gives renters the right to a new lease, under the same terms, for an additional period. To exercise an option, a lessee must notify the lessor on or before the date set forth in the lease.

Responsibilities of Landlord and Tenant

What are your duties as a tenant or as a landlord of a rental property?

Reading Check

State *What can you do if your landlord fails to maintain the premises properly?*

Both landlords and tenants have legal obligations when property is rented.

The Landlord's Duties and Obligations

Landlords have specific responsibilities imposed by law, in addition to those found in a lease. These duties include refraining from discrimination in renting property, maintaining the premises, and providing peaceful possession.

Refrain from Discrimination The federal Civil Rights Act and various state laws place special emphasis on human rights. It is against the law to refuse to rent property to any person because of race, religion, color, national origin, gender, age, ancestry, or marital status.

Maintain the Premises Rental property offered for dwelling purposes must be fit for human habitation. This means that it must be relatively clean, properly heated, furnished with utilities, and safe. In some states, if the landlord does not maintain the premises, you can pay rent to the court instead of the landlord until problems are resolved. In other states, after notifying the landlord, you can correct problems at your own expense and deduct the amount you spent from the rent.

Transfer Peaceful Possession Tenants are entitled to the exclusive peaceful possession and quiet enjoyment of the premises. Quiet enjoyment is the right to use and enjoy property without interference.

Business ETHICS

Trade Fixtures

You own a jewelry business that is looking at leasing a new storefront on Main Street. The current occupier of the property, Ace Company, runs a pawn shop. When Ace originally moved into the property, there were no enclosed glass cases on the premises, so Ace purchased a number of glass cases to house its products. You know that Ace can remove the cases, but you also know that it will be expensive to install new cases, if Ace takes them. You are pretty sure that Ace believes the trade fixtures must remain after it vacates the property.

Critical Thinking: Should you tell Ace that it can legally remove the cases?

Fixtures Fixtures become part of the property and belong to the landlord, even when installed by the tenant. *What are some examples of fixtures?*

The Tenant's Duties and Obligations

Tenants have the duties of paying rent, abiding by the terms of the lease, avoiding waste, and returning fixtures.

Abide by the Terms of the Lease As a tenant, you have the duty to pay rent to the landlord when it is due. You must also observe the valid restrictions contained in the lease. Failure to abide by the restrictions gives the landlord the right to seek eviction.

Avoid Waste Tenants have a duty to avoid waste; that is, damaging or destroying the property. Waste is damage to premises that significantly decreases a property's value. You must return the premises to the landlord in as good a condition as when you moved in, except for reasonable wear and tear.

Return Fixtures The tenant must turn over to the landlord all fixtures in the premises at the end of the tenancy. **Fixtures are items of personal property attached in such a way that they become real property.** They include built-in stoves, kitchen cabinets, and ceiling light fixtures. Unless otherwise agreed, fixtures are part of the real property and belong to the landlord, even when installed by the tenant.

In determining whether an item is a fixture, courts consider the following questions:

- Has there been a temporary or permanent installation of the personal property?
- Can the fixture be removed without damaging the building?
- What was the intent of the parties at the time the attachment was made?

Trade fixtures are fixtures attached to business property that are needed to carry on the business. For example, if you leased a storefront for a small mending business, you might install sewing machines, shelves, and special lights. When you leave, you could take these items with you. Contrary to the general rule, trade fixtures remain the property of the tenant.

Eviction

Can a landlord force you to move out of your apartment?

An eviction occurs when a landlord deprives a tenant of the possession of the premises. You can be evicted for not paying rent, staying after the lease expires, damaging the premises, and violating provisions in the lease.

It is illegal in every state for landlords to use force to evict tenants. Landlords must first obtain a court order. The court appoints an officer to carry out the eviction.

A constructive eviction occurs when a landlord breaches a duty under a lease. This may occur if the landlord deprives you of heat, electricity, or some other service called for by the lease. When a constructive eviction occurs, you may consider the lease terminated, leave the premises, and stop paying rent.

Tort Liability

When someone is injured on rented or leased property, both the landlord and the tenant may be liable. Whoever is in control of the area where the injury occurs determines liability. Landlords can be held liable for injuries caused by defects in common areas, such as hallways or stairways. Tenants can be held liable for injuries caused by defects in private areas within the leased property.

After You Read

Summarize What are the most basic rights of landlords and tenants?

SECTION 9.1 ASSESSMENT

Self Check

1. What is a lease?
2. What is the difference between a tenancy for years and a tenancy at will?
3. How must an eviction be carried out?

Academic Connection

Social Studies Most laws that affect the tenant-landlord relationship are governed by state and federal statutes. Go on the Internet, visit the local library, or get a copy of a rental agreement to find out what the rights of renters are in your area. In class, discuss what you think are the most important things renters should know.

English Language Arts Put yourself in the place of a landlord. You own an apartment building with units you want to rent. Write up a list of basic conditions you expect your tenants to meet.

Critical Thinking

Injury Liability You rent an apartment in a building that has a swimming pool. You have a group of friends over for a swimming party. One of them slips on the wet pavement next to the pool and is injured. Who is liable for the injury? Why?

Buying a Home

What You'll Learn

- Explain the ways real property can be co-owned.
- Describe how title to real property can be transferred.
- Explain the function of warranty and quitclaim deeds.
- Define and compare liens, licenses, and easements.

Why It's Important

You need to know your rights and responsibilities as a homeowner when you buy real property.

Reading Guide

Before You Read

Connect You might want to buy your own home some day. What are the advantages and disadvantages of owning a home?

Focus on Ideas

Ownership of a home or other real property is shown through legal documents called title and deed.

Take Notes

Go to connectED.mcgraw-hill.com to download a graphic organizer you can use to take notes as you read this section.

Types of Deeds			
General Warranties	**Special Warranties**	**Bargain and sale**	**Quitclaim**
Contains express warranties that title to property is good			

Key Terms

You will learn these legal words and expressions in this chapter. You can also find these terms in *Black's Law Dictionary* or in an online legal dictionary.

- real property
- estate
- deed
- eminent domain
- lien
- license
- easement

Academic Vocabulary

You will find these words in your readings and in your tests. Look them up in a dictionary and familiarize yourself with them.

- permission
- spouse
- consent

The Nature of Real Property

What do you really own when you own real property?

Real property is the ground and everything permanently attached to it. It includes buildings, fences, and trees on the surface; and soil, rocks, and minerals under the surface. Landowners own the airspace as high as they can effectively use. Some courts have applied the same rule to how deep one owns property underground. The federal government owns the navigable airspace, where air traffic occurs.

Estate is the interest or right that a person has in real property. A leasehold estate consists of one of the tenancies discussed in the previous section and is evidenced by a lease. A freehold estate is an estate in which the holder owns the land for life or forever. Anyone having a freehold estate may transfer the interest to another by sale, gift, will, or by dying without a will. There are two types of freehold estates. A fee simple estate is an estate in which the owner owns the property outright with the exclusive right to use it or dispose of it freely. Most real property is owned this way. A life estate is an estate in which the owner owns real property for the length of the owner's life or for the life of another.

As You Read

Predict If you cannot repay someone to whom you owe a lot of money, can that person take your home away from you?

Taking Ownership

How can you show or prove that you own a piece of property?

Ownership of property comes about by deed, inheritance, or law. Title can be taken in your name alone or with someone else as a co-owner.

Co-ownership

The principal forms of co-ownership are tenancy in common, joint tenancy, community property, tenancy by the entirety, and tenancy in partnership. All co-owners, or co-tenants, own an undivided interest in the entire property.

Tenancy in common is a type of co-ownership with each owner's share going to his or her heirs upon death. An owner may deed away his or her interest without **permission** of the other owners.

Joint tenancy is a type of co-ownership with each owner's share going to the surviving co-owners upon death. An owner may deed away ownership interest without permission of the other owners.

Community property is property acquired by the efforts of either **spouse** during marriage. By law, it belongs to both spouses equally. A gift or an inheritance does not become part of community property. Only nine states recognize community property.

Tenancy by the entirety is property held by a husband and wife, who have an equal right to the property. Each spouse owns the entire property, which neither can transfer without the other's **consent**. When one spouse dies, the survivor owns the property outright.

Vocabulary You can find vocabulary definitions in the **Key Terms** glossary and the Academic Vocabulary glossary in the back of this book.

Ownership of real property by partners is called a tenancy in partnership. Partners have the right to use the property only for partnership purposes. When a partner dies, the heirs inherit an interest in the partnership but not the specific real property.

Transfer of Ownership

Most real property is transferred by a written deed. A deed is not the same as a lease. **A deed is a written instrument that transfers title of ownership of property.** A lease transfers only possession of property. The person transferring ownership is the grantor. The person given ownership is the grantee. Title is transferred when the deed is signed and delivered. The are four main types of deeds.

A general warranty deed contains express warranties that title to the property is good. The warranties are the personal promises of the grantor that if title is discovered to be faulty, the grantor will make up for any loss suffered by the grantee. This is the most desirable form of deed because it gives the grantee the most protection.

A special warranty deed contains express warranties that no defect arose in the title during the time that the grantor owned the property. Unlike a general warranty deed, no warranties are made as to defects arising before the grantor owned the property.

A bargain and sale deed transfers title to property without giving warranties. A bargain and sale deed requires consideration to be valid. As a result, it cannot be used to make a gift of real property.

Global Law

Property Ownership in Cuba

Cuba became an independent sovereign nation in 1898. Since then property ownership rights in that country have changed.

Agricultural Reform

In 1959, Fidel Castro became the nation's leader and undertook property reform. One of the first reforms limited land ownership to about 165 acres per person or corporation. The Cuban government recognized 66 acres as the bare minimum amount of land a person needed to live on, so every rural person was guaranteed that amount, for free. This meant that 229,000 people became landowners.

Urban Reform

In Cuba's cities, property ownership was also reformed. The government took control of all rental property and set up a payment plan so that the inhabitants would eventually own their homes. Following further reforms, by 2004, 90% of all Cuban adults held title to their homes.

Across Cultures: Trade Embargo

The United States has had an embargo, which is a ban on trade, against Cuba since 1962. It is illegal to buy Cuban products in the U.S., and travel between the U.S. and Cuba is restricted.

Critical Thinking: *Are there benefits to a system of property ownership such as Cuba's?*

Critical Thinking *Can a government use eminent domain to give property to private interests?*

Flex Your Reading | Note key facts in the text below and look up words you do not understand. Restate difficult ideas in your own words. Go back and reread the text quickly to make sure you did not miss any important detail. Now, you are ready to formulate an opinion.

In the Interests of the Public? In 2000, the city of New London, Connecticut, approved a plan to revive the city's economy. In contrast to the rest of the state, New London was economically depressed. The city of New London had the New London Development Corporation (NLDC) devise a plan for economic development.

The NLDC chose an area of the city known as Fort Trumbull for the revival. The land comprised 115 acres of privately owned land as well as 32 acres of public land.

The city of New London was able to purchase most of the privately owned land. However, a few owners declined to sell their land. The city then exercised its power of eminent domain, claiming that the land was needed to create jobs, bring in tax money, and help build downtown New London.

The Plaintiffs argued that, since the city was going to turn the land over to private developers, the eminent domain action was a "taking," contrary to the Fifth Amendment of the United States Constitution, and was not for a "public use."

Kelo v. City of New London, Connecticut, 545 U.S. ___ , 125 S.Ct. 2655 (2005)

➤ Go to **ConnectEd.mcgraw-hill.com** for more case study practice.

A quitclaim deed transfers whatever interest the grantor has in the property, but it does not warrant that the grantor has any interest. It merely releases the grantor's rights to the property.

Limitations on Property Use

There are limitations on property use you should know about when you become a homeowner. These limits may affect how you build on your land, and how you can use your property. (See **Figure 9.1** on page 210.)

Communities have zoning laws that limit the way property may be used in specified areas. One area, for example, might be zoned for single-family houses only, another for multifamily dwellings, and another for business, industry, or farming. Zoning laws might also regulate how tall or how large a building may be.

Eminent domain is the right of the government to take private land for a public purpose. Usually, governments take private land for such things as public buildings, highways, and schools. In 2005, the Supreme Court held that the government could take private property to promote private economic development.

> **Reading Check**
> **Infer** Why would communities want to create different zones for different types of property use?

Figure 9.1 Limitations on Property Use

Zoning laws restrict how property can be used in specified areas. For example, an area might be zoned for single-family houses or for business properties only.

Adverse possession occurs when someone has had open possession of a property for so long, usually over 20 years, that they have a right to claim ownership of it.

Eminent domain is the right of the government to take land from a private owner to use for the public good. The private owner, however, must be paid a fair amount for the property.

Homeowners face some limitations on how they can use their property. *Under eminent domain, can the government take private property to use for private development? Why or why not?*

Ownership of real property can be lost by adverse possession. This occurs when someone who does not own a property occupies it for a period set by state law—often 20 years. The possession must be open, not secretive, with a claim that is done rightfully.

Property use can also be limited by liens, licenses, or easements. To finance the cost of buying a house or other real property, the buyer will usually take out a mortgage. A mortgage is a type of loan in which the borrower pledges the property to the lender in the form of a lien. **A lien is a legal claim against another person's property as security for a debt or loan to ensure it will be repaid.** The lien is released when the debt is repaid. If the debt is not repaid, the lender has the right to take the property (or foreclose on it) and sell it to collect the amount owed.

Property that is foreclosed may have more than one lien on it. In that case, the lienholder with a perfected lien has priority over one with an unperfected lien. A lien is perfected when the lienholder files an official statement with a government office or actually possesses the property. If none of the lienholders has a perfected lien, whoever filed the first lien has priority. If all of the lienholders have a perfected lien, whoever files to collect first has priority.

A license is a temporary, revocable right to the limited use of another's land. The right to use the land can be taken away at any time by the owner of the land.

An easement is an irrevocable right to the limited use of another's land. It might be a right to cross someone else's property at a particular place, such as a driveway, or the right to use it for a particular purpose, such as extending wires or laying pipes. Once established, an easement cannot be terminated without the consent of the owner of the right.

After You Read

Summarize What are the different types of limitations on the use of property?

SECTION 9.2 ASSESSMENT

Self Check

1. What is an estate?
2. What is the major difference between co-owning property as tenants in common and as joint tenants?
3. What is a lien?

Academic Connection

Mathematics Samantha and Fernando are buying a new home for $175,000. A 15% down payment is required. What is the amount of the mortgage loan needed to finance the purchase?

CONCEPT **Number and Operations:** To find the down payment, multiply the cost of the house by the percent of the down payment. To find the mortgage loan amount, subtract the down payment from the selling price.

 For more math practice, go to the Math Appendix.

Critical Thinking

Lending Criteria If you were planning to borrow money to buy a home, why would your employment history be important to a lender?

Chapter 9 Review and Assessment

Summary

Section 9.1 Rental Agreements

◆ The tenant is the lessee; the landlord is the lessor.

◆ The types of tenancies are tenancy for years, periodic tenancy, tenancy at will, and tenancy at sufferance.

◆ Landlords must avoid discrimination, transfer peaceful possession, and maintain the premises. Tenants must pay rent on time, observe lease restrictions, avoid waste, and return fixtures.

◆ A landlord can evict a tenant for not paying rent, damaging the premises, or violating provisions in the lease. A constructive eviction occurs when a landlord breaches a duty under a lease.

◆ Landlords are liable for injuries that occur in common areas. Tenants can be held liable for injuries that occur in private areas.

Section 9.2 Buying a Home

◆ The two major types of estates are leasehold estates and freehold estates. The two types of freehold estates are fee simple estates and life estates.

◆ The principal forms of co-ownership are tenancy in common, joint tenancy, community property, tenancy by the entirety, and tenancy in partnership.

◆ Property may be transferred by sale, gift, will, or by dying without a will.

◆ The four main types of deeds are general warranty deed, special warranty deed, bargain and sale deed, and quitclaim deed.

◆ Property use can be limited by liens, licenses, or easements.

Vocabulary Builder

❶ On a sheet of paper, use each of these terms in a sentence.

Key Terms

- lease
- lessee
- lessor
- tenancy
- sublease
- fixtures
- eviction
- real property
- estate
- deed
- eminent domain
- lien
- license
- easement

Academic Vocabulary

- vacate
- assign
- provision
- permission
- spouse
- consent

Key Points Review

Answer the following questions. Refer to the chapter for additional reinforcement.

2 What is the difference between a lease and a deed?

3 What are the different types of tenancy for rental property?

4 What are the rights and responsibilities of landlords and tenants toward each other?

5 What are the rights of landlords regarding eviction?

6 What is the difference between a fee simple estate and a life estate?

7 What are the different forms of co-ownership of real property?

8 What are the different ways real property can be transferred, or deeded?

9 What are the differences between a lien, a license, and an easement?

Standardized Test Practice

10 Read the following information about the Department of Housing and Urban Development and complete questions 1 and 2.

The Department of Housing and Urban Development (HUD) enforces the Fair Housing Act and the other federal laws that prohibit discrimination and the intimidation of people in their homes, apartment buildings, and condominium developments—and nearly all housing transactions, including the rental and sale of housing and the provision of mortgage loans.

Equal access to rental-housing and home-ownership opportunities is the cornerstone of this nation's federal housing policy. Landlords who refuse to rent or sell homes to people based on race, color, national origin, religion, sex, familial status, or disability are violating federal law, and HUD will vigorously pursue them.

1. Landlords can refuse to rent or sell homes based on:

A race, color, or national origin

B familial status, disability, or education

C work history, religion, or familial status

D none of the above

2. The above passage can best be summarized as:

A rights under the Department of Housing and Urban Development

B how to rent or purchase a home in the United States

C landlords can't refuse to rent or sell their properties

D housing discrimination is only illegal if you get caught

 Test-Taking Strategies Do not cram the night before a test. Plan to get a full eight hours of sleep.

Apply and Debate

Read the following scenarios. Get together with other students in pairs or groups of three and take a position on each scenario. Debate your position in class with students taking the opposite position or prepare a written argument justifying your position.

11 Air-Space Ownership

Jacques purchased a house 15 years ago in a large development. A local airport is proposing an alternative flight path directly over his house. Jacques is petitioning the rezoning court for an injunction to prevent the change.

You Debate *Can property owners restrict the use of air-space above their property?*

12 Discrimination

The Butlers are in their thirties with two young girls. They apply for an apartment. Two weeks later, they have heard nothing, but continue to see it advertised. The Butlers discover that most of the residents are over 50, with no children.

You Debate *If the Butlers met all requirements for rental, could their application be rejected on an unwritten rule of no children or pets?*

13 Lease Agreement

Sally rents a condo. Her lease does not expire for six months. A two-month notice is required for any change to the terms of the lease. The owners inform Sally that she must vacate the condo in two months, before her lease is up.

You Debate *Does the two month clause regarding changes of "terms" in the lease allow the condo owner to force Sally to vacate before her current lease is up?*

14 Apartment Complex Liability

Chen and Emilo share a third-floor apartment. Chen notices one of the stair treads is loose and reports this to the management office. Later, Emilo falls on the stairs and breaks his leg.

You Debate *Who is responsible for Emilo's medical bills and lost wages? Could punitive damages be awarded?*

15 Rental Rates

Paolo signed a lease two months ago for $700 a month. Now the apartment complex rents the same-size apartment for $350–$600 a month.

You Debate *Can an apartment complex charge such a varying amount under the clause of rental specials or could this be a way to discriminate?*

Case Study Practice – Reeves v. Rodgers

16 What Is a Tenant at Sufferance? Roy and Mary Reeves, along with their daughter, Sandra Jean Rodgers, bought a number of residential properties in Oregon and Arizona over a period of fifteen years. In 1994, Mr. and Mrs. Reeves bought a home in Hillsboro, Oregon. Although Ms. Rodgers had helped to buy other properties, she did not contribute any money to buy the Hillsboro home.

In the fall of 2001, Ms. Rodgers moved into the Hillsboro home. The Reeves alleged that Ms. Rodgers had an oral agreement with them that she would pay $895.00 per month in rent to help cover the expenses of the property. After moving in, however, Ms. Rodgers failed to make monthly rent payments. Mr. and Mrs. Reeves then sued Ms. Rodgers, alleging that Ms. Rodgers was a tenant at sufferance of the property and that upon giving notice, the Reeves could evict Ms. Rodgers.

Ms. Rodgers alleged that there was no rental agreement between the parties. She claimed that she had some ownership in the property because she had transferred some of her ownership rights to her parents from the other houses that they owned together.

Source: Reeves v. Rodgers, 129 P.3d 721 (Ore. Ct. App. 2006)

Practice Can Mr. and Mrs. Reeves evict their daughter, Ms. Rodgers?

17 Ethics
←?→ Application

Cat and Mouse Raul lives in an apartment building with a lease that forbids owning pets. The apartment building had a mouse problem until a stray cat showed up and scared the mice away. To keep the cat around so the mice will not come back, Raul started feeding the cat.

◆ Does Raul have an ethical obligation to report the cat to the landlord as a pet?

18 Think back to the Legal Briefs feature you read at the beginning of the chapter. Research arguments for each side of the groundwater debate. Then write two or more paragraphs to explain each side of the debate.

Careers in Law

Dino Tsibouris
Attorney, Mallory & Tsibouris Co., LPA

What do you do at work?

"I am responsible for negotiating software licenses and data processing agreements when a company hires another company to host Web sites, perform data processing services, or perform electronic payments.

I also help companies comply with all of the laws and regulations that require personal and financial information to be held and processed privately and securely.

We represent banks, insurance companies, and government agencies as they offer new services over the Internet.**"**

What skills are most important to you?

"My writing skills. A lawyer must be able to draft documents and agreements in a concise and understandable style. I try to draft my agreements in a manner that allows the reader to understand the terms of a transaction using a minimum of legal jargon if possible. Clearly written agreements are more enforceable in court. I also have to be able to communicate clearly with my clients. Communication isn't just about talking to the client or opposing party; it's about listening carefully.**"**

What kind of training do you recommend?

"I majored in business administration, with an emphasis in finance. I represent a number of financial institutions, so my undergraduate training has helped me better understand how to create solutions for their business-specific needs. Developing a work-related network through social contacts is important. If you have the opportunity to obtain a clerkship or internship in your desired area of practice before graduation, you can gain practical experience and professional relationships—as well as a possible job.**"**

What is your key to success?

"I have to stay current on changing legal trends and new laws that may affect my clients. I also participate in presentations through the bar associations and professional organizations.**"**

Resume Builder

Academic Skills

- Strong writing skills
- Good communication skills (attentive listener)

Education and Training

A bachelor's degree of business administration, finance, accounting, or other areas specific to the attorney's specific industry. The following high school and collegiate courses will help develop the necessary background knowledge:

- Business, contracts, and consumer law
- Business law courses
- Communication courses
- E-commerce
- English Language Arts (composition and rhetoric in particular)
- Mathematics for business
- U.S. government

Critical Thinking

List the benefits of social contacts, clerkships, and internships.

The Writing Connection

Persuasive Writing Practice

Who Pays? Four college friends, all 20, rent a three-bedroom apartment on the top floor of a small building. Everyone has her own bedroom except Amie and Caitlin, who share a bedroom; hence they each pay about $260 less than Claire and Jasmine. One night water started leaking from the light fixture in Amie and Caitlin's bedroom. Soon the leak turned into a gush, pouring water into their bedroom. Within minutes the ceiling fell in their bedroom and practically everything in the room was soaked and covered in wet drywall. Firemen shut off the water and investigated the leak. The landlord arrived and said to the girls, "Wow, I hope one of you has renter's insurance." For one month after the incident, Amie and Caitlin lived in a hotel since their portion of the apartment was uninhabitable.

Assignments

Research Research what a renter's rights are in such a situation. Also research who pays for the damages if the tenants do not have renter's insurance but are still considered dependents under their parents' homeowners' insurance policy.

Write Consider the situation above and write a persuasive essay about what a fair solution could be.

Writing Tips Before you start writing your essay, read through the following writing tips:

✓ Organize logical arguments to support your position and support them with evidence.

✓ Make sure the evidence you use is up-to-date, unbiased, and verifiable.

✓ Use different types of evidence: firsthand observation, informed opinions (double-check your sources), facts, or statistics.

✓ Avoid generalizations and oversimplification.

Essay Test Strategies Beyond describing the issue and stating of your opinion, be sure to convince others of your viewpoint. Review your outline to detect flaws in logic.

Thematic Project

Product Safety and Recalls

For this project, you will use what you have learned about the types of federal agencies that offer support, guidance, and help to consumers regarding product safety and recalls. You can work on this project alone or with a partner.

Here is a checklist of the skills that you will need to complete this project. Your teacher will consider these skills when evaluating your work.

Evaluation Rubric		
Academic Skills		
1. Online and library research	**1.**	10 points
2. Reading for information	**2.**	10 points
3. Note-taking	**3.**	5 points
4. Estimation and computation of facts/figures you discover	**4.**	10 points
5. English composition to summarize findings	**5.**	15 points
Legal Skills		
6. Research of governmental consumer protection agencies	**6.**	15 points
7. Ability to translate code enforcement in a method to explain concept	**7.**	15 points
8. Analysis of essential statistical information	**8.**	15 points
9. Use of technology	**9.**	5 points
	Total 100 Points	

Step 1: Preparation

❶ Create a vocabulary reference guide of terminology consumers will need to know in understanding procedures used for recalls.

❷ Use all you have learned in this unit, at the library, or on the Internet as tools.

❸ Complete this project in a format acceptable for a portfolio addition.

Step 2: Procedure

1 **Review** the text in this unit and make a list of consumer protection agencies that are sponsored by the government.

2 **List** all the terms a consumer might see in understanding their rights and that you will include in your informational flyer. What information is important to include in your flyer? How will you organize your research to present a concise product? Where can consumers go for additional guidance and help?

3 **Write** an outline based on your knowledge and research to use in creating your informational flyer. Use the Internet to download frequently asked questions for the area you will be covering. Make enough copies of your outline, so your classmates can review and annotate the information you plan on presenting for completeness and understanding.

4 **Describe** a real-life scenario that a consumer could resolve by using the information you have created, and present your flyer to the class.

Step 3: Create an Analysis Report

As a class, compare the informational flyers presented. List the governmental agencies available to consumers and explain their span of control. Look at the outlines your classmates have created and answer the following questions:

1 How many and what types of agencies were presented?

2 Did all of the outlines presented include all the necessary elements to give guidance to a consumer in search of help?

3 If not, how does the absence of the element(s) affect the ability for a consumer to solve his or her problem/situation?

4 How was your outline similar to and different from the other outlines presented?

Community Connection

Find recall statistics for a product that you used in your project. How would researching product recalls help your purchase decisions? Does a manufacturer recall when problems occur? Prepare a brief report on how to request a product recall.

Competitive Event Prep

Understanding Consumer Law

Situation Assume the role of a high school business law student. Your friend is ready to buy first car. The salesperson recommends buying an extended warranty that would take effect after the manufacturer's warranty expires. Your friend is unclear about what warranties do and do not offer. Your friend also has a specific budget for this purchase. Your friend asks you for advice about the extended warranty.

Activity Explain the pros and cons of warranties. Make a recommendation about purchasing an extended warranty.

Landmark Case

Hyundai Motor America, Inc. v. Goodin
Indiana Supreme Court 822 N.E.2d 947 (2005)

Read Critically As you read this case, ask yourself the following questions:

1. Was Ms. Goodin's car still under warranty when she sued?
2. Why could Ms. Goodin not sue the dealer she bought the car from?
3. Why did the Indiana Court of Appeals overturn the jury verdict?
4. What are the current privity requirements in Indiana?

Assignment When you are done, write a short summary of the situation. Include the court's decision and a couple of sentences about why or how the court reached its decision.

Facts **Automobile Purchase** On November 18, 2000, Sandra Goodin test drove a Hyundai Sonata at AutoChoice Hyundai in Evansville, Indiana. The car only had 19 miles on the odometer, but when Ms. Goodin drove the car and applied the brakes, she experienced a "shimmy, shake, pulsating type feel." The dealer told Ms. Goodin that it was caused by flat spots on the tires due to extended inactivity and offered to have the tires rotated and inspected. After that, Ms. Goodin purchased the vehicle for $22,710.00.

Automobile Warranty The vehicle that Ms. Goodin purchased came with 3 limited warranties from Hyundai Motor America: 1 year/12,000 miles on "wear items"; 5 years/ 60,000 miles "bumper to bumper"; and 10 years/100,000 miles on the powertrain. The brakes were covered under the 5 years/ 60,000 mile warranty; however, only if the repair work, or replacement, was done by an authorized Hyundai dealer. Further, separate

from Hyundai's warranty papers, the dealer, AutoChoice, included wording on its own sale papers that stated:

All warranties, if any, by a manufacturer or supplier other than dealer are theirs, not dealer's and only such manufacturer or other supplier shall be liable for performance under such warranties, unless dealer furnishes buyer with a separate written warranty made by dealer on its own behalf. Dealer hereby disclaims all warranties, express or implied, including any implied warranties of merchantability or fitness for a particular purpose, on all goods and services sold by dealer.

Jury Verdict In the year following Ms. Goodin's purchase, she took the car to a Hyundai dealer at least seven times to have the brakes looked at. During those visits, numerous repairs were done, but the brakes continued to sound and act improperly. Ms. Goodin said that she experienced problems with her brakes about 70 percent of the time.

Ms. Goodin had driven the car for two years and put 77,600 miles on it. Ms. Goodin was still frustrated by the brakes and decided to sue Hyundai and request a refund for breach of an express warranty, or breach of an implied warranty of merchantability. After a jury trial, the jury returned a verdict for Hyundai on the claim for breach of express warranty, but for Ms. Goodin on the breach of an implied warranty of merchantability. Hyundai appealed.

Opinion Indiana Court of Appeals

Proceedings Hyundai appealed the verdict of the jury on the grounds that Ms. Goodin lacked vertical privity with Hyundai and could not bring a claim for breach of an implied warranty against them. Hyundai argued that Ms. Goodin could sue the dealer that she purchased the vehicle from, AutoChoice, but could not sue the actual car manufacturer. The Indiana Court of Appeals agreed with Hyundai and reversed the jury verdict for Ms. Goodin. Ms. Goodin then appealed to the Indiana Supreme Court.

Federal Warranty Law Ms. Goodin's original case was brought under the Federal Magnuson-Moss Warranty Act. Although it is a federal law, the act looks to state law to determine the source of any express or implied warranty. The Indiana Court of Appeals held that Indiana case law required vertical privity between Ms. Goodin and Hyundai, that is, there must be a contract between Hyundai and Ms. Goodin. In this case, there was a contract between Ms. Goodin and AutoChoice, but not between Ms. Goodin and Hyundai.

Origin of Privity Privity of contract is a concept American courts adopted from England. It limits the tort relief for breach of warranties by requiring parties to have some sort of contractual relationship. Ms. Goodin argued that traditional vertical privity was not required between herself and Hyundai because Hyundai provided an express warranty under the Magnuson-Moss Warranty Act, and as such, an implied warranty can also exist without any requisite vertical privity.

Further, Ms. Goodin argued that AutoChoice's disclaimer did not allow her to sue them, and she could only sue Hyundai.

Privity in Indiana The state of privity requirements evolved over the years in most states. Originally, privity requirements were quite stringent, but as consumer protection issues have become more developed, courts have lessened the privity requirements. In Indiana, the state legislature passed a Product Liability Act in 1999 that no longer required vertical privity in order to assert a product's liability claim against a manufacturer.

Before the passage of the act, the Uniform Commercial Code allowed breach of warranty claims to be initiated by family members or guests of persons who actually purchased the product. They do not have to have privity with the manufacturer. However, neither of these provisions applied directly to Ms. Goodin's situation.

Holding The Court's Decision

The Court held that vertical privity was no longer required in breaches of implied warranties of merchantability in the state of Indiana. Consumer expectations are such that when they buy a car and are told it is under warranty by the manufacturer, consumers believe they can obtain recourse from the manufacturer, not the dealer.

TRIAL PREP

The National High School Mock Trial Association organizes competitions at the local, regional, and national levels where teams of high school or college students prepare and argue fictional legal cases before practicing attorneys and judges. Mock Trial team members are each assigned a role as either an attorney or witness. Each team must develop a courtroom strategy, legal arguments, and presentation style.

Your Money and the Law

● ● ● ● ● ● ● ● ● ● ● ● ● ● ● ●

Methods of Payment
In the age of e-commerce
virtually all purchase and
credit transactions can now
be done electronically. *What
are some types of cards you
can use to make a purchase?*

Thematic Project Preview

Correcting a Credit Report Error

As you read this unit, use this checklist to prepare for the unit project:

- ✓ List the three major credit reporting bureaus.
- ✓ Define the five main components used to calculate credit rating.
- ✓ Explain ways of repairing a low credit rating.
- ✓ Explain what information is needed to resolve a credit dispute.
- ✓ Determine the appropriate tone and style for a credit report dispute letter.

Legal Portfolio When you complete the Unit Thematic project, you will have a sample letter for reporting a credit dispute to add to your portfolio.

Ask AN EXPERT   Paying for a College Education

Q: I cannot pay for college on my own and will need to apply for financial aid. What is the best way to go about this?

A: To apply for financial aid from almost every public and private college and university in the U.S., you need to fill out the Free Application for Federal Student Aid (FAFSA). You can get the application from your guidance counselor at school or online. At many colleges and universities, the FAFSA is the only form you need to fill out. After you submit the form, the Department of Education determines your expected family contribution (EFC), which is based on your family's income and assets. Once you have been accepted to a school, you might be offered a financial aid package. This often includes a combination of loans and scholarships and possibly work-study arrangements.

Banking and Negotiable Instruments

Legal Briefs

The End of the Float
Using technology to speed the check-clearing process.

What is "float"? It's the time it takes from when a check is deposited until it clears. Once you write a check for a product or service, you have a brief period of time—typically a few days—to use the funds before they are deducted from your account.

Some people take advantage of the float time to commit financial crimes by spending money that is not in the account, but "in transit" to the seller's bank. This is a dangerous practice. If you write a check for more money than is in your account and the float time expires, the check will not clear. The merchant then faces a loss and the bank customer may incur fees for insufficient funds.

Thanks to modern technology, online banking and e-money reduce float time by at least 40 percent. Banks are using check-clearing services that allow merchants to scan checks and have the funds quickly deducted from your account.

With online banking and e-money, there is less time for your money to "float" from your bank to the vender's.

For Deposit Only If your check is lost or stolen, it could be cashed by someone else. *What can you do to make sure your check can only be used to deposit in your bank account?*

Using Negotiable Instruments

Reading Guide

Before You Read

Connect Have you ever received a paper that could be exchanged for cash? If so, you have some idea of what a negotiable instrument is.

Focus on Ideas

A negotiable instrument is a written promise or order by one person to pay another.

Take Notes

Go to **connectED.mcgraw-hill.com** to download a graphic organizer you can use to take notes as you read this section.

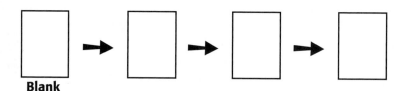

Blank

Types of Indorsements

Key Terms

You will learn these legal words and expressions in this chapter. You can also find these terms in *Black's Law Dictionary* or in an online legal dictionary.

- negotiable instrument
- note
- maker
- payee

- draft
- drawer
- drawee
- negotiation
- holder

- assignment
- indorsement
- holder in due course

Academic Vocabulary

You will find these words in your readings and in your tests. Look them up in a dictionary and familiarize yourself with them.

- advantage
- signature
- unconditional

Types of Negotiable Instruments

*How can you guarantee payment when you have
no cash or credit card?*

People often need to conduct business without carrying around
large sums of money or to buy items they can pay for later.
Negotiable instruments were created to meet these needs.

**A negotiable instrument, also known as commercial
paper, is a written document giving legal rights that may
be passed to others by indorsement or delivery.** A negotiable
instrument is a type of contract. However, the laws of negotiable
instruments are governed by the Uniform Commercial Code (see
Chapter 7) rather than general contract law. There are two basic
kinds of negotiable instruments: notes (including certificates of
deposit, stocks, and bonds) and drafts (including checks and bills of
sale). Negotiable instruments can be obtained from places such as
banks, credit unions, and other types of financial institutions.

Notes

**A note (often called a promissory note) is a written
promise to pay money. A maker is a person who promises
to pay money in a note. A payee is a person in a note to
whom the promise to pay is made.** Two or more persons who
sign a note are known as comakers. An **advantage** of using a note
is that it can be negotiated (transferred) to other people easily.

A demand note is a note that is payable at the time the payee
demands payment. In contrast, a time note is a note that is payable
at a future date. An installment note is a note that is paid in a series
of payments. People often sign this type of note when they borrow
money to buy a car or a house.

A certificate of deposit (CD) is a note issued by a bank that earns
interest over time. CDs are written for specific time periods, such as
six months, one year, two years, and five years. The interest on a
CD is higher than the interest on a savings account because the
depositor cannot withdraw the money before the due date. Banks
pay higher interest for longer-term CDs.

Drafts

A note is a promise to pay money. **A draft is an order to
a third party to pay money. A drawer is a person who
orders money to be paid in a draft. A drawee is the person
to whom an order is given to pay money in a draft.**

Although ordered to pay money, drawees are not required
to do so unless they agree. Drawees agree to pay a draft by writing
the word *accepted* on the document and signing their name. A
drawee that has done this is called an acceptor and must pay the
draft. The person to whom the draft is paid is called the payee.

A sight draft is a draft that is payable when it is given to the
drawee for payment. A time draft is a draft that is not payable until
a particular period of time has passed.

As You Read

Predict How many types
of negotiable instruments
can you list?

Vocabulary You can find
vocabulary definitions in the **Key
Terms** glossary and the Academic
Vocabulary glossary in the back of
this book.

Letters of credit are a special type of draft used in international business. Banks issue letters of credit on behalf of buyers, agreeing to pay sellers money when specific conditions are met. The bank accepts liability for the payment of the money involved in the transaction. The seller is guaranteed payment even if the buyer changes his or her mind. However, if the bank pays, the buyer is still liable for payments to the bank.

Drafting Instruments

What makes an instrument negotiable?

To be negotiable, negotiable instruments must have several elements.

Written Instrument

The promise, or order, to pay must be in writing. It can be printed, typed, or handwritten in pen or pencil. A negotiable instrument written in pencil is, however, an invitation for forgery or alteration.

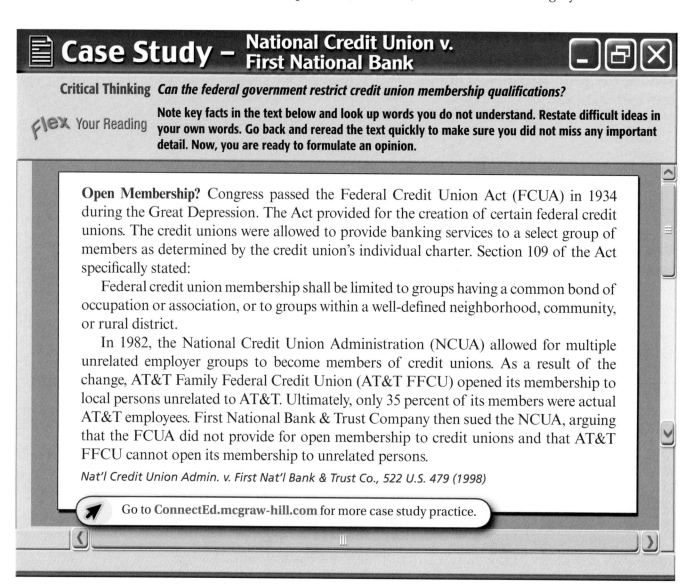

Case Study – National Credit Union v. First National Bank

Critical Thinking *Can the federal government restrict credit union membership qualifications?*

Flex Your Reading Note key facts in the text below and look up words you do not understand. Restate difficult ideas in your own words. Go back and reread the text quickly to make sure you did not miss any important detail. Now, you are ready to formulate an opinion.

Open Membership? Congress passed the Federal Credit Union Act (FCUA) in 1934 during the Great Depression. The Act provided for the creation of certain federal credit unions. The credit unions were allowed to provide banking services to a select group of members as determined by the credit union's individual charter. Section 109 of the Act specifically stated:

Federal credit union membership shall be limited to groups having a common bond of occupation or association, or to groups within a well-defined neighborhood, community, or rural district.

In 1982, the National Credit Union Administration (NCUA) allowed for multiple unrelated employer groups to become members of credit unions. As a result of the change, AT&T Family Federal Credit Union (AT&T FFCU) opened its membership to local persons unrelated to AT&T. Ultimately, only 35 percent of its members were actual AT&T employees. First National Bank & Trust Company then sued the NCUA, arguing that the FCUA did not provide for open membership to credit unions and that AT&T FFCU cannot open its membership to unrelated persons.

Nat'l Credit Union Admin. v. First Nat'l Bank & Trust Co., 522 U.S. 479 (1998)

Go to **ConnectEd.mcgraw-hill.com** for more case study practice.

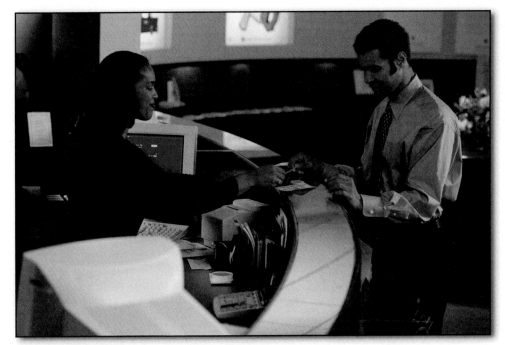

Signature of Maker or Drawer Banks keep signature cards on file to verify the signature on a check. *What are other ways a signature can be verified?*

Signature of Maker or Drawer

A negotiable instrument must be signed. The maker must sign a note, and the drawer must sign a draft. A **signature** may be any mark placed on the instrument with the intent to be a signature. The signature on a check, however, should match the signature card on file with the bank. The signature card is a record of an account holder's signature that the bank uses to verify it.

Unconditional Promise or Order

The promise in a note, or the order in a draft, must be **unconditional**. If either is qualified in any way, the instrument is not negotiable.

Fixed Sum of Money

A negotiable instrument must be payable in a fixed sum of money. This can be in U.S. dollars or the currency of a foreign country.

Payable on Demand or at a Definite Time

Negotiable instruments must be payable on demand. Instruments that state they are payable "on demand" or "on sight" are called demand paper. Instruments must also be payable at a definite time. For instance, a check payable when a person marries or reaches a certain age is not negotiable because the time of payment is not definite.

Payable to Order or Bearer

Except for checks, negotiable instruments must be payable to order or to bearer. The words *to the order of* and *to bearer* are called the words of negotiability. The maker or drawer may write "Pay to the order of Jane Doe," "Pay to Jane Doe or order," or "Pay to Jane Doe or her assigns."

Dates and Controlling Words

When the date is omitted, the date on which the instrument is received is considered the date of issue. A check can also be postdated, or written with a later date on it than the date it is signed.

Sometimes, due to an error or alteration, the words or figures on a negotiable instrument do not match each other. In that case, words control, or win out, over figures. Terms that are typed control terms that are printed, and terms that are handwritten control typed and printed terms.

Transferring Negotiable Instruments

What is the right way to sign a negotiable instrument?

When an instrument is signed by the maker or drawer and given to another person, the instrument is issued. When that person gives it to a third party, the instrument is transferred. The transfer can be done by assignment or by negotiation. **Negotiation is the transfer of an agreement in such a way that the transferee becomes a holder. A holder is a person who possesses a negotiable instrument payable to "the order of" the person holding it or to "bearer."** You are a holder when you receive a check made out in your name. Negotiability is the ability of an instrument to be transferred in a way that the transferee becomes a holder.

Reading Check

Enumerate *What are the main characteristics of negotiable instruments?*

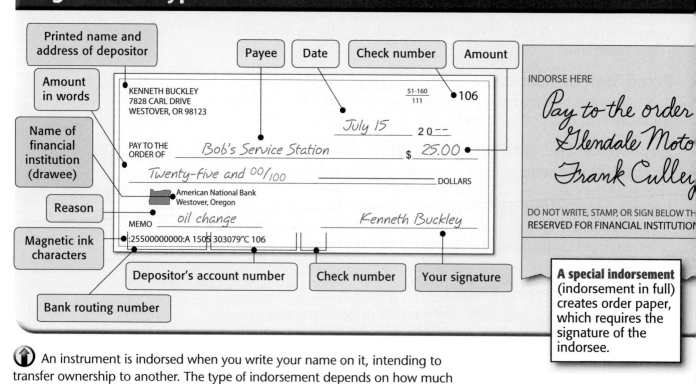

Figure 10.1 Types of Indorsements

An instrument is indorsed when you write your name on it, intending to transfer ownership to another. The type of indorsement depends on how much information you include. *Why should you avoid using a blank indorsement?*

Instruments that do not meet the requirements of negotiability cannot be negotiated, but they can be assigned. **An assignment is the transfer of your rights under a contract to someone else.** Assignability is the ability of an instrument to be transferred to someone else without the transferee becoming a holder.

The person who assigns an instrument is the assignor. The person who receives the assignment is the assignee. Instruments are assigned when a person whose indorsement is required transfers the instrument without indorsing it.

Indorsements

An indorsement is the act of placing one's signature on an instrument, usually on the back, to transfer it to another. The person who writes the indorsement is called the indorser, and the person to whom the instrument is transferred is the indorsee. Indorsements may be written in ink, typed, or stamped with a rubber stamp. They are usually placed on the back of the instrument. There are four types of indorsements (see **Figure 10.1**).

Blank Indorsement A blank indorsement consists of a signature alone on the instrument. By signing an instrument in this way, you are saying in effect, "This instrument may be paid to anyone." An instrument indorsed in blank becomes bearer paper and may be transferred by delivery alone. If it is lost or stolen, someone else can cash it.

NDORSE HERE

or deposit only
udson Trust Company

Frederick Herberts

NOT WRITE, STAMP, OR SIGN BELOW THIS LINE
SERVED FOR FINANCIAL INSTITUTION USE*

A restrictive indorsement limits the subsequent use of the instrument.

INDORSE HERE

Pay to the order of
James Ingram when he
becomes eighteen years old
George Gallo

DO NOT WRITE, STAMP, OR SIGN BELOW THIS LINE
RESERVED FOR FINANCIAL INSTITUTION USE*

A conditional indorsement makes the rights of the indorsee subject to a certain event or condition.

INDORSE HERE

Pay to the order of
George Rose without
recourse
Samuel Brock

DO NOT WRITE, STAMP, OR SIGN BELOW THIS LINE
RESERVED FOR FINANCIAL INSTITUTION USE*

A qualified indorsement limits the contractual liability of the indorser.

Special Indorsement A special indorsement is an indorsement with the words *pay to* or *pay to the order of.* This is followed by the name of the transferee and signed by the indorser. It is also called an indorsement in full. When indorsed this way, the instrument remains an order instrument and must be indorsed by the indorsee before negotiating it further.

Restrictive Indorsement A restrictive indorsement is an indorsement in which words have been added that limit the use of an instrument. Before it can be further transferred, an instrument must be used as stated in the indorsement. For example, when a check is indorsed "for deposit only," that amount of money must be added to the indorser's bank account before it can be negotiated further. Retail stores often stamp checks "for deposit only" when they are received. This provides protection in the event the checks are stolen.

Qualified Indorsement A qualified indorsement is an indorsement that limits the liability of the indorser. The words *without recourse,* for example, mean the indorser is not liable if the maker or drawer does not pay.

Holder in Due Course

A holder in due course is a holder who takes an instrument for value, in good faith, and without notice that the instrument is defective. To be a holder in due course, you must first be a holder. You must also give value for an instrument, which means you give the consideration that was agreed upon, such as payment of a debt. You must take the instrument in good faith, which means to do it fairly and honestly. You must also be unaware of anything wrong with the instrument, such as a claim to the instrument by someone else, evidence of alteration or forgery, or the instrument being overdue.

Defenses to Negotiable Instruments Holders in due course take instruments free from all claims to them by anyone. They also take instruments free from all personal defenses of anyone with whom they have not dealt. They are only subject to real defenses.

Personal, or limited, defenses are defenses that can be used against a holder, but not a holder in due course. The most common personal defenses are breach of contract, lack of consideration, fraud in the inducement, lack of delivery, and payment.

Multiple Payees If an instrument is payable to either of two payees, only one of them needs to indorse it. *What is required if an instrument is payble to both of two payees?*

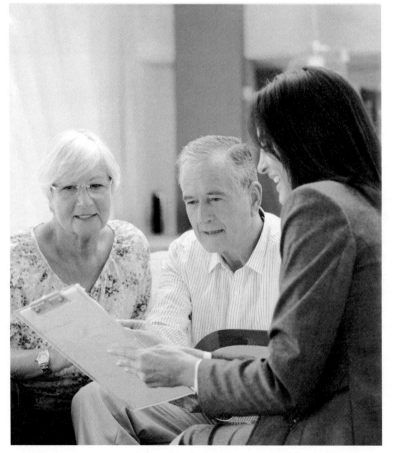

Real, or universal, defenses are defenses that can be used against everyone, even holders in due course. No one is required to pay an instrument when there is a real defense. Real defenses include mental incompetence, illegality, duress, bankruptcy, unauthorized signature, and alteration.

Liability

No person is liable on an instrument unless that person's signature appears on it. A signature can be written by an authorized agent. Parties to negotiable instruments have different liability.

The following (formerly known as primary parties) are absolutely liable to pay:

- the maker of a note
- the issuer of a cashier's check or other draft in which the drawer and drawee are the same person
- the acceptor of a draft

When there are two or more makers on a note, all have absolute liability. Very often, one of the comakers is the person who borrowed the money. The other serves as a surety—a person who promises to pay another's debt whether or not the other defaults.

Discharge of Negotiable Instruments

Obligations of parties to pay negotiable instruments are discharged by payment, by agreement, by the debtor becoming the holder after maturity, and by the intentional cancellation of the instrument by the holder. Indorsers are discharged when anyone entitled to enforcement extends the due date, or agrees to modify the instrument.

After You Read

Summarize How can you transfer negotiable instruments?

SECTION **10.1** ASSESSMENT

Self Check

1. What is the difference between a note and a draft?
2. What qualifies as a signature on a note or draft?
3. What is an indorsement?

Academic Connection

Social Studies The use of metal for money can be traced back over 4,000 years. The first coins were made of electrum, a natural mixture of silver and gold. They were crude lumps of metal bearing a primitive mark that certified its weight or fineness. Beads, shells, and even leather were also used to create money. Go on the Internet or to the library to look up what other cultures have used as a form of money or currency and make a short list of them.

English Language Arts Get together in teams with other students in your class. Using props, drawings, or other visual means of communication, describe what each of the key terms in this section refer to and how they relate to each other.

Critical Thinking

Negotiable Instruments Why do you think a person who writes a negotiable instrument in pencil would be responsible for any loss due to negligence?

SECTION 10.2 Banking Basics

What You'll Learn

◆ Explain the contractual relationship between a bank and its customers.

◆ Distinguish stop-payment orders, forgeries, and material alterations.

◆ Differentiate between types of checks.

◆ Define electronic fund transfer.

Why It's Important

You need to know what your legal rights and duties are when you open a checking account.

Reading Guide

Before You Read

Connect Take a note card or cut out a piece of paper and sign your name on it. Now give it to the teacher. You have just created a signature card.

Focus on Ideas

Checks are the most common type of negotiable instrument.

Take Notes

Go to connectED.mcgraw-hill.com to download a graphic organizer you can use to take notes as you read this section.

Key Terms

You will learn these legal words and expressions in this chapter. You can also find these terms in *Black's Law Dictionary* or in an online legal dictionary.

- forgery
- electronic fund transfer (EFT)

Academic Vocabulary

You will find these words in your readings and in your tests. Look them up in a dictionary and familiarize yourself with them.

- schedule
- reconcile
- substitute

Checking Accounts

How does a checking account work?

The check is the most common type of negotiable instrument. The parties to a check are the same as the parties to a draft. The person who writes the check is the drawer. The bank that is ordered to pay the money is the drawee. The one to whom the check is payable is the payee.

To open a checking account, you deposit money in a bank and sign a signature card. A signature card is a record of your signature the banks uses to verify your identity.

A checking account creates a contractual relationship between a bank and a customer. When you write a check, you order your bank to pay someone money from your checking account. The bank agrees to pay money out, up to the amount you have deposited when you write a check. People to whom you write checks can cash them or deposit them in their own bank. Their bank then collects the money from your bank, which takes it out of your account. If your bank refuses to cash your check when sufficient funds are on deposit, it would be a breach of the bank's contract.

A bank may refuse to pay a stale check, which is a check that is more than six months old. A bank may also refuse to pay a check if it is submitted ten days after the death of the drawer.

CYBERLAW

Hospicomm, Inc. v. Fleet Bank, N.A.
338 F.Supp.2d 578 (E.D. Penn. 2004)

Hospicomm, Inc. provides data processing and other management services to health care providers. In 2002, Hospicomm began to provide services to Hamilton Continuing Care Center. On Hamilton's behalf, Hospicomm opened several bank accounts with Fleet Bank. Access to those bank accounts was limited to those persons who were authorized signatories on the account. In 2003, Hospicomm ended the employment of Guillermo Martinez. It was discovered that Mr. Martinez, without authorization, had obtained an ATM card for the Fleet Bank accounts over the Internet and had withdrawn $148,000 from the accounts. Hospicomm sued Fleet Bank for negligence in giving Mr. Martinez an unauthorized ATM card and allowing the unauthorized ATM withdrawals.

Ruling and Resolution
The Federal District Court held that Hospicomm could not sue Fleet for negligence since the relationship between Hospicomm and Fleet was based in contract. Further, the Court held that the UCC does not apply because ATM transactions are not considered banking deposits or collections.

Critical Thinking Should the UCC be updated to cover electronic transactions such as ATM usage?

Legal Talk

Forge: *v* To imitate falsely with intent to defraud. From Latin *fabrica* = workshop.

Certified: *adj* Officially endorsed or attested to. From Latin *certus* = certain + *facere* = to do: to make certain.

Vocabulary Builder The Latin root *facere* means to do, to make, or to form. List and define three words that have *facere* as a root.

Vocabulary You can find vocabulary definitions in the **Key Terms** glossary and the Academic Vocabulary glossary in the back of this book.

Reading Check

Interpret *Why do you think a bad check is also called a bounced or rubber check?*

Availability of Funds

Under federal law, banks must make funds available to you according to a set **schedule**. Exceptions are made for new accounts, accounts that are often overdrawn, and suspicious deposits. Some state laws require even shorter time periods for banks to make funds available.

Balancing Your Checkbook

Whenever you write a check, you should record it in your check register, a checkbook log of all your checking transactions. Every month you should receive a statement of the bank's record of all your transactions, called a bank statement. You should balance—or **reconcile**—your bank statement soon after receiving it. Carefully compare the check register balance with the bank statement balance to be sure they agree. Do not forget to account for outstanding checks. Outstanding checks are checks you have written that have not yet been returned to the bank for payment.

The Check 21 Act

Physically moving paper checks throughout the country can take time and increase the possibility of checks getting lost or mishandled. Congress enacted the Check 21 Act (named after the 21st Century) which allows electronic processing to clear checks quickly and safely. An instrument called a **substitute** check is used. A substitute check is a paper copy of both sides of an original check. Check 21 also allows for an electronic signature to replace an original signature on the substitute check. It is processed just like the original check. Bank customers no longer have the right to have their original canceled checks returned to them.

Writing Checks

You should take care to write checks so they cannot be changed easily. You are responsible for altered checks only if your negligence contributed to the alteration. Sign your name in ink. Sign it the same way it appears on the bank signature card, such as with a middle initial. Never sign a blank check. Never cross out or change a check once it has been written. If you make a mistake when writing a check, shred it and write a new one.

Stopping Payment of a Check

Sometimes you want to cancel a check you have already written but has not yet been paid. You can put a stop on the check by requesting a stop-payment order from your bank. An oral stop-payment order is binding on the bank for 14 calendar days, unless the order is confirmed in writing within that period. A written stop-payment order is effective for six months, unless it is renewed in writing. If the bank pays the check anyway, it is liable for any loss you suffer as a result. If you stop payment on a check given in payment of an amount actually owed, you still owe the amount of the debt.

Bad Checks

A bad check, also called a bounced check or rubber check, is a check you draw on an account in which you do not have enough funds. Unless it is accidental, writing a check on an account with insufficient funds is a crime.

Forgeries and Material Alterations

Suppose a large amount of money disappears from your checking account. You discover someone has stolen one of your checks and faked your signature on it or changed the amount on a check you wrote to a much larger amount. This is called forgery. **Forgery is the fraudulent making or material alteration of a writing.** A forged check is one that is signed by someone other than the drawer without authority. A material alteration occurs when someone changes a check you wrote, such as adding an extra "0" to the amount. Forgery is a crime subject to a fine and imprisonment. It is the bank's duty to know the signatures of its depositors.

Global Law

Banking in Switzerland

Since 1685, Swiss banks have provided services to their clients that range from ordinary checking accounts to large numbered accounts. Swiss banks also provide services such as offering stocks and bonds for sale.

Secrecy

One of the most famous aspects of Swiss banks is their attention to secrecy.

As in most countries around the world, banks are prohibited from giving out any information about their clients. Swiss banking law was amended in 1934, one year after Adolph Hitler became Chancellor of Germany, to create criminal penalties for any bank employee who divulges information about a client's account.

The penalties include six months in jail and/or a fine of 50,000 Swiss Francs (approximately $39,000). There are only four reasons why a bank may give secret information about a client to another party:

1. a criminal investigation (national or international)
2. an investigation by financial market authorities
3. bankruptcy proceedings
4. some civil proceedings (such as inheritance and divorce cases)

Secret numbered accounts enjoy the same protections as named accounts. The main distinction is that only a few select people in the bank know the names associated with the accounts. In other words, there are really no anonymous bank accounts in Switzerland. Someone always knows who owns the money.

Across Cultures: Lingua Franca

Switzerland has four official languages: French, German, Italian, and the native language of Romansh. However, the language used to conduct business internationally, or the lingua franca, is English.

Critical Thinking *Why do you think Switzerland passed such strict banking laws when it did?*

Electronic Banking With electronic banking, you can withdraw or deposit money, or check your account balance 24 hours a day. *Can a debit card be used the same as a credit card?*

If a bank pays a forged check and the drawer was not negligent, the bank must bear the loss. The bank must also bear the loss if a check is changed from its original amount to a higher amount.

Knowingly giving a forged instrument to someone else is a criminal offense called uttering. You are guilty of this crime even if you did not personally commit the act of forgery. If one of your checks is forged, you must notify your bank within a reasonable time. Otherwise, the bank is relieved of liability.

Other Types of Checks

If you do not have a regular checking account or need to use a check for a special purpose, such as a gift or to write checks in a foreign country, you can purchase other types of checks from banks and other financial institutions. These other types of checks include:

- certified checks, which are checks guaranteed by a bank
- cashier's checks, which are checks drawn by a bank upon itself
- bank drafts, which are drawn by a bank against funds the bank has on deposit with another bank
- money orders, which are drafts that substitute for checks and may be purchased from places such as banks and post offices
- traveler's checks, which are like cashier's checks in that the financial institution that issues them is both the drawer and the drawee

Electronic Banking

Can you pay for things using your checking account without writing a check?

Computer technology and the Internet have greatly reduced the need to use paper and increased the speed of banking transactions. **Electronic fund transfer (EFT) is a computerized system for transferring funds electronically rather than by writing checks.** With electronic banking, or e-banking, you can access your bank account on a computer or by using a debit card. A debit card, also called an ATM card or a check card, is a bank card that takes money from your own bank account, as if writing a check.

EFT is safe, secure, and less expensive than paper check payments. When you purchase a product online using EFT, you can pay for it by having money transferred from your checking account to the checking account of the seller. You can also use EFT to pay routine bills online.

To regulate this means of banking, the federal government enacted the Electronic Fund Transfer Act (EFTA). Under the EFTA you can:

- purchase merchandise at a store with your debit card
- withdraw money from your bank at an automated teller machine (ATM) 24 hours a day
- authorize your employer to deposit your earnings directly into your bank account
- authorize direct withdrawals from your account to pay bills automatically
- make payments from your bank by telephone
- use your computer to view your account balances and pay bills electronically
- have your paper check changed to an e-check (electronic check) so that it can be processed instantly

If your debit card is lost or stolen, you must notify the bank within two business days after learning that the card is missing. You will then lose no more than $50 if someone else uses your card. If you do not notify the bank within two business days and your card is used, you can lose as much as $500, or even more if 60 days have passed.

After You Read

Summarize Who are the different parties to a check?

SECTION 10.2 ASSESSMENT

Self Check

1. How do you open a checking account?
2. Summarize the process of balancing your checkbook.
3. What should you take care to do when writing a check?

Academic Connection

Mathematics Aisha Brewer's checking account has a balance of $523.45. She has a check for $435.62 and a check for $65.98. She would like to receive $40 in cash and deposit the rest of the money in her checking account. What is Aisha's total deposit and what will her new checking account balance be?

CONCEPT **Number and Operations:** To calculate the amount of the deposit, first add the total amount of the items to be deposited and then subtract the amount of cash to be received. Next, to obtain the new checking account balance, take the current balance and add the amount of the net deposit.

 For more math practice, go to the Math Appendix.

Critical Thinking

Stop-payment Order Why might you want to stop payment on a check?

Chapter 10 Review and Assessment

Summary

Section 10.1 Using Negotiable Instruments

◆ There are two basic kinds of negotiable instruments—notes and drafts. A note is a promise to pay money. A draft is an order to a third party to pay money.

◆ To be negotiable, an instrument must be in writing, signed by the maker or drawer, and contain an unconditional promise or order to pay.

◆ An instrument must be made out for a fixed amount of money, payable on demand or at a definite time.

◆ The four types of indorsements are blank indorsements, special indorsements, restrictive indorsements, and qualified indorsements.

◆ A holder in due course must take an instrument for value, in good faith, and without notice that the instrument is defective.

Section 10.2 Banking Basics

◆ The check is the most common type of negotiable instrument. The parties to a check are the same as the parties to a draft.

◆ When you write a check, you order your bank to pay someone money from your checking account. If your bank refuses to cash your check when sufficient funds are on deposit, it would be a breach of the bank's contract.

◆ You can put a stop on the check by requesting a stop-payment order from your bank.

◆ A forged check is one that is signed by someone other than the drawer without authority. A material alteration occurs when someone changes a check you wrote.

◆ Electronic fund transfer (EFT) is a computerized system for transferring funds electronically rather than by writing checks.

Vocabulary Builder

❶ On a sheet of paper, use each of these terms in a sentence.

Key Terms

- negotiable instrument
- note
- maker
- payee
- draft

- drawer
- drawee
- negotiation
- holder
- assignment

- indorsement
- holder in due course
- forgery
- electronic fund transfer (EFT)

Academic Vocabulary

- advantage
- signature

- unconditional
- schedule

- reconcile
- substitute

Key Points Review

Answer the following questions. Refer to the chapter for additional reinforcement.

2 What are the different types of negotiable instruments?

3 Who are the parties to each kind of negotiable instrument?

4 What are the elements of negotiable instruments?

5 What are the different types of indorsements?

6 What are the requirements to be a holder in due course?

7 What is a stop-payment order, and what are the different types?

8 What are the legal responsibilities for forgeries and material alterations?

9 What are electronic fund transfers?

Standardized Test Practice

10 Read the following excerpt from the Uniform Commercial Code (UCC) and complete problems 1 and 2.

§ 3-104. NEGOTIABLE INSTRUMENT.

(e) An instrument is a "note" if it is a promise and is a "draft" if it is an order. If an instrument could be a note or a draft, a person may treat it as either.

(f) "Check" means (i) a draft, other than a documentary draft, payable on demand and drawn on a bank or (ii) a cashier's check or teller's check.

(g) "Cashier's check" means a draft with respect to which the drawer and drawee are the same bank or branches of the same bank.

(h) "Teller's check" means a draft drawn by a bank (i) on another bank, or (ii) payable at or through a bank.

(i) "Traveler's check" means an instrument that (i) is payable on demand, (ii) is drawn on or payable at or through a bank, (iii) is designated by the term "traveler's check" or by a substantially similar term, and (iv) requires, as a condition to payment, a countersignature by a person whose specimen signature appears on the instrument.

1. If an instrument could be a note or a draft

Ⓐ it must be treated as a note
Ⓑ it must be treated as a draft
Ⓒ it may be treated as either
Ⓓ it must be treated as neither

2. Which of the following is *not* true about a traveler's check?

Ⓐ It is payable on demand.
Ⓑ It is drawn on or payable at or through a bank.
Ⓒ It is a type of draft.
Ⓓ It is a type of note.

 Test-Taking Strategies Before a test or exam, break study sessions into manageable time segments and meaningful units.

Apply and Debate

Read the following scenarios. Get together with other students in pairs or groups of three and take a position on each scenario. Debate your position in class with students taking the opposite position or prepare a written argument justifying your position.

⑪ Checks

Alan filled out a check in red ink to pay for a new suit. The cashier said the bank would not cash the check and refused to accept it. Alan disagreed.

You Debate   *Who is correct, Alan or the cashier?*

⑫ Check Dispute

Smita paid $100 for textbooks at the college bookstore by check. She incorrectly wrote the number $1,000.00 on the check rather than $100.00. She correctly wrote the words "one hundred and no cents." When Smita received her bank statement, she saw the check had been cashed for $1,000 and not $100. She notified the bookstore of the error, but the bookstore refused to refund the $900 over-payment.

You Debate   *Can Smita require the bank to credit her account for $900?*

⑬ Overdrawn

Harriet post-dated a check to Xander and asked him not to cash it until Friday. That same day Xander took the check to the bank, which cashed it. When Harriet looked at her account balance a couple days later, she discovered she was overdrawn.

You Debate   *Is the bank responsible for not checking the date, and should it have refused the check?*

⑭ Negotiability

Macy took her car in for repairs. When she arrived at the garage to pick it up, she realized she did not have her checkbook. Macy drew a picture of a check made out to the mechanic with the name of her bank, account number, date, and signature for payment.

You Debate   *Is Macy's drawing of a check a negotiable instrument?*

⑮ Forged Checks

Robin hired a cleaning company to shampoo her carpets. A couple days later, she discovered some of her checks were missing. When she notified the bank, she learned that several checks had been forged and cashed.

You Debate   *Is Robin liable for the amount of the money taken from her account?*

Case Study Practice – Leavings v. Mills

16 **What Is a Negotiable Instrument?** In 1984, John and Evelyn Leavings contracted with Solar Marketing to have a heating system installed in their home. The Leavings signed a note with Solar Marketing to make 120 monthly payments in the amount of $146.82 each. Solar Marketing then placed a lien on the Leavings's property.

Solar Marketing assigned the note and lien to Briercroft Service Corporation (BSC). BSC, in turn, assigned the note and lien to Briercroft Savings Association (BSA). After numerous problems with the system, the Leavings stopped making payments. BSC sent a letter in 1989 advising the Leavings that their note was in default. The Leavings's attorney responded to BSC. BSC did not pursue demands for payment any further.

In 1997, after Mr. Leavings had died, Mrs. Leavings received a letter from a Mr. James Mills. The letter stated that Mrs. Leavings's installment contract had fully matured and she must pay $21,196 immediately or Mr. Mills would foreclose on her property. Mrs. Leavings argued that Mr. Mills could not foreclose on the property because the contract was not payable "to bearer" or "to order" and thus was not a negotiable instrument.

Source: Leavings v. Mills, 175 S.W.3d 301 (Tx. Ct. App. 2004)

Practice Is the retail installment contract a negotiable instrument?

17 Ethics
←?→ Application _____

Who Is Responsible? Deborah goes to the bank to cash her payroll check for $160. At the bank, the teller accidentally gives Deborah $180. Deborah instantly notices the error but puts the money into her wallet and leaves the bank.

◆ Is not telling the bank teller that she gave you too much money the same as stealing?

18 Think back to the Legal Briefs feature you read at the beginning of the chapter. Some forms of payment cause money to immediately be deducted from the customer's bank account. What problems might this cause the customer or a business? Write a paragraph from the point of view of either the customer or the store.

Credit and Debt

Legal Briefs

Avoid Student Loan Debt

Think creatively, search for value, and borrow smart.

College is expensive. There's no denying that. But there are ways you can keep the costs down. Here are four strategies to keep student loan debt under control:

- Before taking out a student loan, consider other options including scholarships and grants, paid internships, work study or part-time work, working for a year and saving money, or receiving help from your parents or other family members.

- Choose the right school. Weigh the tuition costs against the academic program. Look at state schools, not just private ones, which tend to be more costly.

- Think creatively. Do you need to start at a four-year university? Can you take your first two years at a local junior college and live at home to save on room and board? What about other types of higher education such as technical schools? Look into online courses offered by many colleges.

- Go federal before considering a private loan. Generally, federal loans have lower interest, but do investigate the different types of student loans: Direct Subsidized and Direct Unsubsidized Loans; Direct PLUS Loans; and Federal Perkins Loans. Choose the one that best suits you and your budget.

Buying on Credit Some purchases are too expensive to pay for in cash and you need to use credit. *What is the maximum percentage of your monthly income that should go to making credit payments, according to financial experts?*

What You'll Learn

◆ Define the main types of credit.

◆ Explain what a secured transaction is.

◆ Describe how a security interest is created.

◆ Identify the main types of collateral.

Why It's Important

You need to know what your legal obligations are when you borrow money or obtain credit.

Reading Guide

Before You Read

Connect Have you ever used a credit card or borrowed money to buy something you could not afford?

Focus on Ideas

To borrow money or buy on credit, you need to own something of value.

Take Notes

Go to connectED. mcgraw-hill.com to download a graphic organizer you can use to take notes as you read this section.

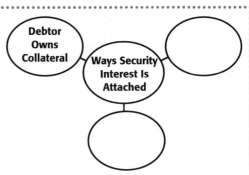

Key Terms

You will learn these legal words and expressions in this chapter. You can also find these terms in *Black's Law Dictionary* or in an online legal dictionary.

- credit
- creditor
- debtor
- interest

- secured loan
- collateral
- security interest
- default

Academic Vocabulary

You will find these words in your readings and in your tests. Look them up in a dictionary and familiarize yourself with them.

- assets
- acquired
- effective

Credit

What is a possible financial solution if you really need to buy something and you do not have enough money?

Credit is an arrangement in which you receive cash, goods, or services now and pay in the future. The creditor is the party who sells the goods on credit or lends the money. The debtor is the party who buys the goods on credit or borrows the money. Interest is a fee creditors charge for lending money or extending credit.

The amount of interest you pay depends on the amount of the loan or purchase, the length of time it takes to pay back the money, and the interest rate. The longer you take to pay off a loan and the larger the amount of the loan, the more you have to pay in interest.

Open-End Credit

Open-end credit is credit that can be increased by the debtor by continuing to purchase goods or services on credit, up to a certain limit. You are given a line of credit—a maximum amount of money available to you. Credit cards issued by a bank, such as Visa and MasterCard, and charge cards for a particular store, such as Macy's and Target, are examples of open-end credit.

Closed-End Credit

Closed-end credit is credit given for a specific amount of money, which cannot be increased by making additional purchases. Buying a vehicle, a house, a refrigerator, or a couch for a fixed amount and paying for it in monthly installments is an example of closed-end credit.

As You Read

Predict What can happen if you are unable to repay a loan?

Business ETHICS

Necessary Guarantors and Sureties

You are the owner of a local major appliance store that sits on the border of two states. As normal practice, you allow your customers to buy items on credit, while retaining a security interest in the appliance. However, through your personal experience, you feel that residents from your neighboring state are more likely to default on their loans than the residents in your own state. After talking to fellow business owners, you discover that one option would be to require buyers from the neighboring state to have a guarantor or a surety when they sign a credit agreement with you.

Critical Thinking: Should you require buyers from a neighboring state to have a guarantor or surety?

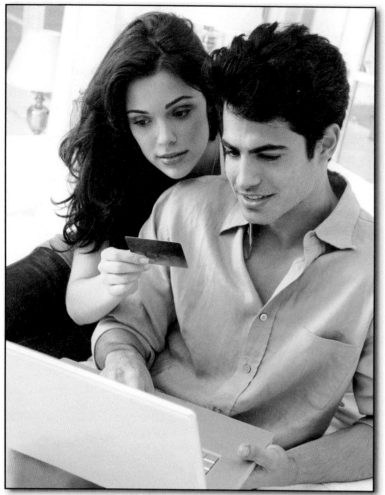

Credit Score Once you start using credit cards, paying bills, and borrowing money, credit reporting agencies collect financial information on you and assign you a credit score. *Why is your credit score important?*

Vocabulary You can find vocabulary definitions in the **Key Terms** glossary and Academic Vocabulary glossary in the back of this book.

Obtaining Credit

If you borrow money, how can the creditor be sure the money is not lost?

To obtain credit or a loan, you need to fill out an application from a store, bank, or other financial institution. Lenders will usually check into your credit history, your income, and your **assets**, to determine if you are a good credit risk. Lenders also need security—a way of getting their money back in case the borrower does not pay.

Secured Transactions

A secured loan is a loan which is backed up by property that the creditor can take if the loan is not repaid. Collateral is the property that is offered as a security interest. A security interest is a creditor's right to use collateral to recover a debt. Main types of collateral are consumer goods, fixtures, equipment, inventory, and farm products.

A security can be created by the creditor possessing the collateral. It can also be created by the debtor signing a security agreement that identifies the collateral. The lender who holds the security interest is called the secured party.

If a debtor defaults, the secured party may take the collateral and sell it at a public auction or private sale. **Default is failure to make timely payments on a loan.** Different types of collateral have different laws with regard to default. There are more conditions when a debtor defaults on something as major as a home loan than when a debtor defaults on a car loan.

An unsecured loan does not require any collateral. However, because the risk is much greater to the creditor, the interest on an unsecured is usually much higher than on a secured loan. Unsecured loans are usually available only to well-established businesses or customers.

Attachment of Security Interest A security interest is said to attach when it is legally enforceable by the secured party. Attachment occurs when:

- The debtor owns the collateral.
- The secured party transfers something of value, such as money or goods, to the debtor.
- The secured party either takes possession of the collateral or signs a security agreement.

Security agreements may contain provisions that include future advances of credit. Future advances of credit allow the debtor to get additional credit in the future that is secured by the same collateral, such as a house.

In a transaction for the sale of goods, the security interest attaches to the actual individual goods. In contrast, when the security interest is on inventory, which are all the things you own, the security interest attaches to the inventory as a whole, including new inventory that comes and goes from a business. The inventory is what is called after-acquired property, since the property was **acquired** after the credit agreement was entered into.

Reading Check

Interpret *What is secure about a secured loan?*

Example Good Health Grocers bought ten cases of a special health food from a wholesaler on credit. The security agreement signed by the grocer contained a clause covering all future goods the grocer bought. In this way, all replacement goods were covered by the original security agreement as the grocer's inventory was continuously sold and restocked.

📄 Case Study – Fifth Third Bank/Visa v. Gilbert   ⊟ ⧉ ☒

Critical Thinking *Can an unemancipated minor be liable for unauthorized charges she made on her father's credit card?*

Flex Your Reading Note key facts in the text below and look up words you do not understand. Restate difficult ideas in your own words. Go back and reread the text quickly to make sure you did not miss any important detail. Now, you are ready to formulate an opinion.

Necessary Expenses? John Gilbert was having domestic problems and no longer wanted to have a joint credit card account with other members of his family. On May 9, 1983, he canceled his Visa credit card, and on June 6, 1983 he applied for a new one from Fifth Third Bank. The credit card application included a space for additional authorized users. Mr. Gilbert left it blank.

The application was approved and fifteen days later, one credit card was issued with Mr. Gilbert's name on the front. The card was sent to Mr. Gilbert's business address. During the next month, approximately $1,300 in charges were made on the card. When Mr. Gilbert got his statement in the mail, he notified Visa that all $1,300 were unauthorized charges.

Visa then conducted an investigation and determined that the charges were made by three people. Mr. Gilbert admitted to charging $90. His married daughter, Christine, charged $85. His unemancipated daughter, Ann (who lived separately with her mother), charged the remaining $1,125. Visa then sued to recover the amount from Ann.

Fifth Third Bank v. Gilbert, 478 N.E.2d 1324 (Ohio Mun. Ct. 1984)

➤ Go to **ConnectEd.mcgraw-hill.com** for more case study practice.

Perfection of Security Interest When a security interest attaches, it is **effective** only between the debtor and creditor. To be effective against the claims of any other creditors, a creditor must perfect the interest. A security interest is perfected when the secured party has done everything that the law requires to give the secured party a greater claim than anyone else has.

A security interest can be perfected in three ways:

- attachment alone for consumer goods bought in a store
- filing a financial statement in a public office for most other items
- possession of the collateral (such as with a pawn shop)

> **Example** When Jane bought a truck, the dealer took a security interest in the vehicle. To protect the dealer's rights in the vehicle, notice of the security interest would be written on the back of Jane's certificate of title to the truck.

Guarantors and Sureties

A loan can be protected by having another party stand behind the loan to guarantee it will be repaid. There are two types of parties who can guarantee a loan: guarantors and sureties. A guarantor, sometimes referred to as a secondary party, agrees to pay off a debt only if the debtor defaults. A surety, sometimes called a primary party, agrees to pay off a debt outright, just as the debtor would have.

There are certain defenses guarantors and sureties can use when called upon to pay back a loan. These include that the debtor has already paid back or released the debt, their own minority, insanity, or bankruptcy.

After You Read

Summarize Who are the various parties to credit?

SECTION 11.1 ASSESSMENT

Self Check

1. Give some examples of open-end credit and closed-end credit.
2. What are the main types of collateral?
3. What are future advances of credit?

Academic Connection

English Language Arts The history of credit and banking goes back at least 4,000 years to ancient Egypt. The Egyptians used a type of banking called the giro system, in which grain was deposited in state-run storehouses and could be used to pay off debts. In medieval Italy, loans and other banking transactions were conducted in large open areas where each merchant would work from a bench, or *banco*, which is where we get the word *bank* from.

Go on the Internet or to a library and look up how these first banks worked and write a brief description of them.

Critical Thinking

Credit and Debit How is a credit card different from a debit card?

Credit and You

Reading Guide

Before You Read

Connect Do you have a department store charge card? If so, you are familiar with having credit.

Focus on Ideas

Credit cards, charge cards, car loans, and student loans are types of credit.

Take Notes

Go to connectED. mcgraw-hill.com to download a graphic organizer you can use to take notes as you read this section.

Advantages of Credit	Disadvantages of Credit
Finance Large Purchases	_____
_____	_____
_____	_____
_____	_____
_____	_____

Key Terms

You will learn these legal words and expressions in this chapter. You can also find these terms in *Black's Law Dictionary* or in an online legal dictionary.

- finance charge
- annual percentage rate (APR)

Academic Vocabulary

You will find these words in your readings and in your tests. Look them up in a dictionary and familiarize yourself with them.

- involved
- unauthorized
- subsidized

What You'll Learn

- ◆ Define finance charge and annual percentage rate.
- ◆ Describe the advantages of using a credit card.
- ◆ Determine how to obtain student loans.
- ◆ Recognize the warning signs of debt problems.

Why It's Important

There are things you need to know if you want to finance a car, get a credit card, or take out a student loan.

Financing Your Future

What are some things you might need and that might cause you to borrow a large amount of money?

You will need to use credit to finance many things from short-term goals, such as buying a computer, to long-term goals, such as buying a house (see **Figure 11.1**). To build up credit for long-term goals, you need to set priorities, start with small purchases, and stay within your credit limit and income.

Buying a Vehicle

What can you do if you cannot afford to buy a car with cash?

You will probably buy many automobiles in your life. The law that applies to these purchases comes from several different sources. Because cars are considered goods, the Uniform Commercial Code (UCC) applies to their sale. If you buy a car for personal purposes, both federal and state consumer protection laws apply. In addition, if you finance the car, special laws regulate credit.

If you want to buy a car, you should first find out how much you can afford. This depends on your savings, monthly earnings, living expenses, and the amount of your debt.

Financing a Vehicle

When buying a car, you can save money by paying cash because car loans require you to pay interest. Offering to pay cash also puts you in a better position to negotiate a lower price. If you need to borrow money, you can save by shopping around. Federal law requires lenders to disclose the finance charge and annual percentage rate (APR) to borrowers. **The finance charge is the cost of the loan in dollars and cents. The annual percentage rate (APR) is the true interest rate of the loan.**

Before you sign any documents, you should know the following information:

- the exact price you are paying for the vehicle
- the amount you are financing
- the finance charge
- the APR
- the number and amount of payments
- the total sales price (the sum of the monthly payments plus the down payment)

Dealers sometimes offer very low financing rates for specific models but may not negotiate. They also may require a large down payment. As a result, it is sometimes better to pay higher financing charges on a car with a lower price or to buy a car that requires a smaller down payment.

Figure 11.1 Financing Future Goals

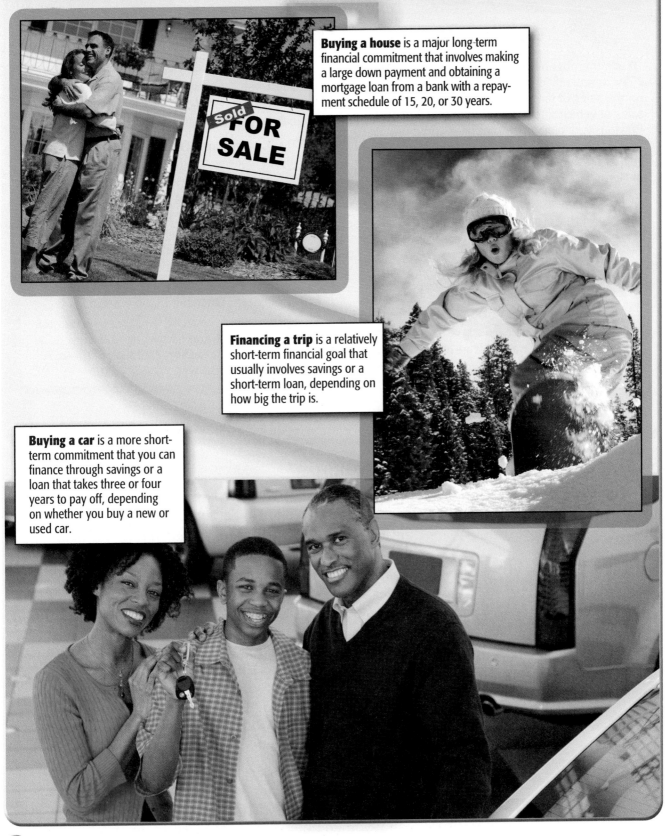

Buying a house is a major long-term financial commitment that involves making a large down payment and obtaining a mortgage loan from a bank with a repayment schedule of 15, 20, or 30 years.

Financing a trip is a relatively short-term financial goal that usually involves savings or a short-term loan, depending on how big the trip is.

Buying a car is a more short-term commitment that you can finance through savings or a loan that takes three or four years to pay off, depending on whether you buy a new or used car.

Your future goals might involve long-term or short-term financial commitments. *What are some immediate financial goals you have?*

Global Law

German Lemon Law

As a member of the European Union, Germany was recently directed to change its laws on the sales of tangible property, including the sales of vehicles, to better protect the consumer. Previously, dealers of automobiles could provide little or no warranty as to the condition of used vehicles it sold. Now the consumer has the benefit of Germany's own lemon law.

1 All German dealers must warrant used cars for a minimum of one year. Unfortunately, this applies only to dealerships and does not apply to private sales of used cars.

2 The dealer is responsible for any defect determined to have been present at the time of sale. There is no protection for damage done during normal wear and tear on a vehicle. For example, worn brake pads are probably not warranted. The determination is normally done by an independent third-party appraiser.

3 The claim must be filed within one year of the purchase of the vehicle. There is no additional time period for the filing of claims. Claims can only be filed during the one-year period.

4 The European Union directive applies to all mobile property. A European Union directive that required member states to pass statutes providing for consumer protection also applies to other sales of goods. Therefore, not only is there a one-year warranty on cars, but on other items such as televisions and motor homes.

Across Cultures: European Union Protections

Although this example details the German law, the European Union directive applies to all member countries of the European Union. Those countries must also pass similar warranty laws for their citizens.

Critical Thinking: *What are the benefits and detriments of having a mandatory one-year warranty on all goods?*

Defective Vehicles

Some cars continually have mechanical problems. The seller may be liable on any of the following grounds:

- breach of an express warranty, if a guarantee was made and not kept
- breach of warranty of merchantability, if the seller was a dealer and the car was not fit to drive
- fraud or breach of an express warranty, if the seller made any statements about the car that were not true
- breach of the state consumer protection law, if the vehicle was for non-business use

Using Credit Cards

What are some of the costs of using credit?

When you use a credit card, you are borrowing money. The interest rate and late-payment fees can be very high unless you pay your bill by the due date. You can go deeply into debt, even bankrupt, if you do not use your credit card carefully. In order to make a wise decision when purchasing on credit, you must consider all the fees and costs **involved**.

Example Tim charged many items on his credit card, up to its $2,000 limit. Each month he pays $40 on the account, the minimum required by the card issuer. The interest rate is 19 percent. If Tim maintains the same payment rate, it will take him 33 years to erase the debt. He will pay $7,000 in interest on the $2,000 that he borrowed to make his purchases. Tim could save a lot of money by doubling his monthly payments and making every effort to bring the account balance down to zero as soon as possible.

Reading Check

Explain *Is it better to pay cash for electronic goods or buy them on credit?*

There is an advantage to using a credit card if you have a dispute involving a purchase. You do not have to pay the bill for the disputed item. Instead, notify the credit card issuer by telephone immediately. The issuer must put the disputed amount on hold and send you a form to fill out explaining the dispute. The card issuer will attempt to resolve the dispute and inform you of the results. If the problem is not corrected and the credit card issuer brings suit, you may use as a defense the fact that unsatisfactory goods or services were received.

Another advantage of using a credit card arises if the card is stolen. You may have to pay up to $50 of **unauthorized** charges made before you notify the credit card issuer of the loss. You are not, however, responsible for charges made after the issuer has been notified.

Example Tara lost her credit card but did not notify the card issuer for a week. Meanwhile, someone who found the card had charged a purchase of $175 with it. Tara will have to pay $50 toward this unauthorized purchase. If she had notified the card issuer before the illegal purchase happened, however, she would not have had to pay anything.

Student Loans

What can you do if you cannot afford to pay for college?

Education costs are on the rise and do not seem to be slowing down. For most people, going to college requires careful planning in order to pay the costs of tuition and basic living expenses.

A common way of financing your education is through student loans. There are two types of student loans, government loans and private loans.

Government Student Loans

The federal government is an enormous student loan lender. Under the Direct Loan Program, money is lent to students based on need. When a student applies to college, he or she fills out a FAFSA, or Free Application for Federal Student Aid. This application asks detailed information about the student and his or her family. The government then makes a determination about how much money it can loan the student. The figure is also based on the amount necessary to attend a specific college.

Legal Talk

Dispute: *v* To question the truth and validity. From Latin *disputare* = to examine.

Resolve: *v* To find a solution; to solve. From Latin *resolvere* = to untie.

Vocabulary Builder Look up the words *dispute* and *resolve* in the dictionary. Break them down into and define their root words.

RTimages/Alamy

Figure 11.2 Ways to Build and Protect Your Credit

☑ Open a checking or savings account, or both.
☑ Apply for a local department store credit card.
☑ Take out a small loan from your bank.
☑ Make payments on time.

Be aware that a creditor must:

1. Evaluate all applicants on the same basis.
2. Consider income from part-time employment.
3. Consider the payment history of all joint accounts, if this accurately reflects your credit history.
4. Disregard information on accounts if you can prove that it does not affect your ability or willingness to repay.

Be aware that a creditor cannot:

1. Refuse you individual credit in your own name if you are creditworthy.
2. Require your spouse to cosign a loan. Any creditworthy person can be your cosigner if one is required.
3. Ask about your family plans or assume that your income will be interrupted to have children.
4. Consider whether you have a telephone listing in your name.

Firm Foundation If you want a good credit rating, you must prove you can use credit wisely. *Why is it a good idea to apply for a local department store credit card or a small loan from your bank?*

Within the Direct Loan Program, there are two types of government loans, **subsidized** and unsubsidized. If you receive a subsidized loan, the government pays the interest on the loan while you are in school. However, with an unsubsidized loan, the student remains responsible for the interest that accrues on the loan while in school. Under both loans, the student will pay interest on the loan after graduation. For more information visit the U.S. Department of Education Web site.

Private Student Loans

Private student loans are similar to other consumer loans. They are offered by banks across the country. The amount of money offered is based on the cost of tuition at your specific school. The interest rate on private loans is usually higher than on government loans, and students are responsible for the interest that accrues, even while the student is in school. Private education loans are also available to parents who want to take out loans to pay for their children's education.

Student Loan Repayment

Student loans in most circumstances must be repaid. There are a few exceptions. Student loans can be discharged in bankruptcy, but only in cases of extreme hardship. The government will discharge some or all of a student loan debt for students who enter special job programs after they graduate. These programs, such as AmeriCorps and the Peace Corps, usually require students to work in the health, education, or public safety field in an underdeveloped community for a certain period of time.

Warning Signs of Debt Problems

How can you tell if you have credit problems?

It is important to use credit wisely to build a good credit rating and to avoid getting heavily into debt early in life (see **Figure 11.2**). Here are some of the warning signs that you may be in financial trouble:

- You make only the minimum monthly payment on credit cards or have trouble paying even that much. The total balance on your credit cards increases every month.
- You miss loan payments or often pay late.
- You receive second or third payment due notices from creditors.
- You borrow money to pay off old debts.
- You exceed the credit limits on your credit cards.
- You have been denied credit because of a bad credit rating.

If you experience two or more of these warning signs, it is time to rethink your financial priorities.

After You Read

Summarize Identify the advantages and disadvantages of using credit.

SECTION 11.2 ASSESSMENT

Self Check

1. On what grounds can a seller be liable for selling a defective vehicle?

2. What can you do if you have a dispute involving a purchase on a credit card?

3. What is the difference between a subsidized and an unsubsidized student loan?

Academic Connection

Mathematics You want to buy a used car from a dealer for $8,400. The dealer requires a 20% down payment and you will have

to finance the rest with a car loan. Use two different methods to figure out how much you will have to finance.

CONCEPT **Problem Solving: Use a Variety of Appropriate Strategies to Solve Problems** One method is to multiply the percent of the down payment by the total cost to find out the amount of the down payment. Then subtract the amount of the down payment from the total cost. Another method is to subtract the percent of the down payment from 100% to find out the

percent of the amount you will have to finance, then multiply that by the total cost of the car.

 For more math practice, go to the Math Appendix.

Critical Thinking

Disadvantages of Credit Advantages of using credit are that it is convenient, you can pay for expensive items over time, and it contributes to the growth of the economy. What are some of the disadvantages of using credit?

Chapter 11 Review and Assessment

Summary

Section 11.1 Understanding Credit

◆ Open-end credit is credit that can be increased by continuing to purchase goods or services on credit. Closed-end credit is credit given for a specific amount of money.

◆ A secured loan is a loan which is backed up by property, called collateral, that the creditor can take if the loan is not repaid.

◆ A security interest is created by the creditor possessing the collateral for a loan, or by the debtor signing a security agreement that identifies the collateral.

◆ The main types of collateral are consumer goods, fixtures, equipment, inventory, and farm products.

Section 11.2 Credit and You

◆ Before you sign any documents to buy a vehicle, you should know the exact price you are paying, the amount you are financing, the finance charge, the APR, the number and amount of payments, and the total sales price.

◆ When you use a credit card, you are borrowing money. You can go deeply into debt, even bankrupt, if you do not use your credit card carefully.

◆ There are both government and private loans available to students. To apply for government student loans, students fill out a FAFSA, or Free Application for Federal Student Aid.

Vocabulary Builder

1 On a sheet of paper, use each of these terms in a sentence.

Key Terms

- credit
- creditor
- debtor
- interest

- secured loan
- collateral
- security interest

- default
- finance charge
- annual percentage rate (APR)

Academic Vocabulary

- assets
- acquired

- effective
- involved

- unauthorized
- subsidized

Key Points Review

Answer the following questions. Refer to the chapter for additional reinforcement.

2 What is the difference between open-end credit and closed-end credit?

3 What is a secured loan?

4 What are the three ways a security interest is attached?

5 What is the difference between a guarantor and a surety?

6 What are the six things you need to know before you sign a document to buy a vehicle?

7 What are a finance charge and an APR?

8 What are some advantages to using a credit card?

9 What are the different types of government loans available to students?

Standardized Test Practice

10 Read the following excerpt from the Federal Reserve Board on how to use your credit card and complete questions 1 and 2.

The first step in choosing a credit card is thinking about how you will use it.

- If you expect to always pay your monthly bill in full (and other features such as frequent flyer miles don't interest you) your best choice may be a card that has no annual fee and offers a longer grace period.
- If you sometimes carry over a balance from month to month, you may be more interested in a card that carries a lower interest rate (stated as an annual percentage rate, or APR).
- If you expect to use your card to get cash advances, you'll want to look for a card that carries a lower APR and lower fees on cash advances. Some cards charge a higher APR for cash advances than for purchases.

1. When you choose a credit card, you should be more concerned about

Ⓐ the credit card features
Ⓑ who the credit card issuer is
Ⓒ what the credit limit is
Ⓓ what the interest rate is

2. If you expect to pay your credit card bill in full every month, you should choose a credit card that offers a

Ⓐ lower fee for purchases
Ⓑ lower cash advance fee
Ⓒ longer grace period
Ⓓ lower interest rate

 Test-Taking Strategies Formulate your own answer before reading the options when answering multiple-choice questions.

Apply and Debate

Read the following scenarios. Get together with other students in pairs or groups of three and take a position on each scenario. Debate your position in class with students taking the opposite position or prepare a written argument justifying your position.

11 Collateral

Wilson purchased a used computer from Jana for $400. He did not know that Jana had purchased the computer through a loan company and had not been making her payments on time. The loan company decided to repossess the computer.

You Debate *Can the loan company repossess the computer from Wilson?*

12 Lemon Laws

Tomas purchased a new car from a local dealer. Within two months he began to have several minor mechanical problems. Although the repairs were not major, Tomas felt that since there were so many of them, the car fell under the lemon law.

You Debate *Is Tomas entitled to get his money back for the car?*

13 Credit Cards

Quinton, a seventeen-year-old college freshman, was offered a credit card and accepted. He quickly ran up charges until he was unable to afford the payments. Just prior to his eighteenth birthday he attempted to get out of his contract with the credit card company because he was a minor when he received the credit card.

You Debate *Can Quinton get out of his debt with the credit card company?*

14 Credit Limit

Travis has reached the limit on his credit card and cannot make the monthly payments. He receives an offer in the mail for another credit card and is considering getting the other card to pay off some of the debt on his current card.

You Debate *Should Travis use the second card to pay off some of the first card?*

15 Student Loans

Levar was accepted to the college of his choice but did not qualify for a grant or scholarship. He makes money working a part-time job, but not enough to pay for all his expenses. He can cover the rest by taking out a student loan, which he will have to pay back later, or by using his credit card, which he can pay off on a monthly basis.

You Debate *Is Levar better off taking out a student loan or using his credit card?*

Case Study Practice – Patzka v. Viterbo College

16 The Price of Credit Mariann Patzka was enrolled at Viterbo College in Wisconsin. She incurred debt in the amount of $3,530.16 during her first semester. At that time, Ms. Patzka was not informed of any fees she could be charged if she did not pay in full by the first day of classes. Interest charges came to $2,253.55, making the total amount due $5,783.71. Ms. Patzka paid $1,509.55 to Viterbo College, but still owed $4,274.16.

Viterbo College assigned the debt to a collection agency, Security Credit. Prior to doing so, the College assessed Ms. Patzka a collection fee of 33% ($1,410.47), making the total amount due $5,684.63. Ms. Patzka made payments to Security Credit in the amount of $4,284.63. Ms. Patzka now argues that she does not owe the remaining $1,400 because her account was an open-end credit account and she was never informed of the potential charges and fees when credit was extended as required under the Federal Fair Debt Collection Practices Act.

Source: Patzka v. Viterbo College, 917 F.Supp.654 (W.D. Wis. 1996)

Practice Does Ms. Patzka need to pay the remaining $1,400?

17 Ethics ←?→ Application

Breach of Trust? Arjang's parents gave him a credit card to use for textbooks, supplies, and in case of an emergency. When he was short of cash, he used the credit card to buy a new computer game at the campus bookstore. Since the purchase would show up as computer software, his parents would assume the purchase was a required school supply and he would not have to ask their permission.

◆ Was Arjang's purchase of the computer game without his parent's permission ethical? Why or why not?

18 Think back to the Legal Briefs feature you read at the beginning of the chapter. Then conduct research to investigate these types of federal loans: direct subsidized and direct unsubsidized Loans. Write a brief explanation that explains the difference.

Credit Protection and Bankruptcy

Legal Briefs

Getting Your Finances in Order

What you can learn from credit counseling.

Most Americans owe some kind of debt—for student loans, credit cards, doctor bills, and more. Sometimes they find themselves owing more than they can pay. Where can they turn?

Enter the credit counseling service. A professional credit counselor can:

- Collaborate to create a debt management plan.
- Negotiate to lower interest rates or waive late fees.
- Accept a monthly payment and distribute the funds to creditors.
- Counsel clients about creating a budget.
- Show how saving small amounts can add up.

Not all companies that call themselves debt-settlement services are trustworthy, however. The federal Consumer Financial Protection Bureau advises:

- Beware of promises that the counselor can reduce the balance you owe.
- The counselor's services should be free or low-cost.
- The firm should offer a number of services, such as budget advice, counseling on student loans, and training on financial issues.
- Check with your state Attorney General's office to make sure there have been no complaints about the service.

You can find credit counseling at universities, credit unions, military bases, and local consumer protection agencies. Help is available for anyone who needs it.

Running up Bills Americans have a big problem managing debt. *What is the average amount of credit card debt per household in the United States?*

What You'll Learn

- ◆ Define repossession and garnishment.
- ◆ Describe the federal laws that regulate consumer credit.
- ◆ Discuss your rights under the Consumer Credit Protection Act, the Fair Credit Reporting Act, and the Fair Credit Billing Act.
- ◆ Explain the purpose of the Equal Credit Opportunity Act and the Fair Debt Collection Practices Act.

Why It's Important

You need to know the laws that protect you from creditors when you borrow money or use credit.

Reading Guide

Before You Read

Connect Have you ever borrowed money from someone who tried to profit from your situation?

Focus on Ideas

The federal and state legal systems protect your rights as a credit user.

Take Notes

Go to connectED.mcgraw-hill.com to download a graphic organizer you can use to take notes as you read this section.

Federal Laws Protecting Debtors

Consumer Credit Protection Act				

Key Terms

You will learn these legal words and expressions in this chapter. You can also find these terms in *Black's Law Dictionary* or in an online legal dictionary.

- repossession
- garnishment
- usury law
- Consumer Credit Protection Act
- Fair Credit Reporting Act
- Equal Credit Opportunity Act (ECOA)
- Fair Debt Collection Practices Act (FDCPA)
- Fair Credit Billing Act

Academic Vocabulary

You will find these words in your readings and in your tests. Look them up in a dictionary and familiarize yourself with them.

- dominant
- exceed
- impersonate

Laws Protecting Creditors

What can creditors do if you owe them money?

Historically, creditors have not needed special laws to protect them. They lend money or extend credit, and have the right to be paid back with interest. In their relations with debtors, creditors are the **dominant** parties. They are in a better position to control the terms of a transaction.

Repossession

When a debtor borrows money or uses credit to buy property such as a car or refrigerator, the creditor places a legal claim on the property called a lien. **Repossession is when a creditor reclaims property on which it has a lien if the debtor does not make payment.** Repossession must be done without causing a disturbance. If the debtor refuses to surrender the goods, legal process must be used to obtain them.

After repossessing goods, secured parties may keep them (with exceptions) or sell them. Sales may be public auctions or private sales. If the goods are consumer goods for which the debtor has paid 60 percent or more of the price, the secured party cannot keep them—they must be sold. The debtor must be notified and is entitled to receive any surplus of the sale after debts and expenses have been paid.

Garnishment of Wages

If a debtor defaults on a loan, creditors also have the right to garnish their wages. **Garnishment is the legal procedure through which a worker's earnings are withheld for payment of a debt.** Garnishment of a worker's wages cannot **exceed** 25 percent of weekly take-home pay, except for certain amounts of support payments and taxes.

As You Read

Predict Can a finance company take your car away from you for not making the monthly payments?

Vocabulary You can find vocabulary definitions in the **Key Terms** glossary and Academic Vocabulary glossary in the back of this book.

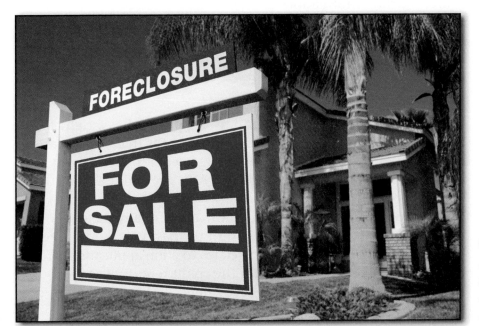

Repossession Creditors have a right to repossess property when a debtor defaults on a loan. *What does a creditor need in order to claim property?*

Legal Talk

Entitle: *v* To furnish with a right or claim to something. From Latin *intitulare; in* = provide with + *titulus* = title: to give a name or title to.

Discriminate: *v* To make distinctions on the basis of class or category without regard to individual merit; show preference or prejudice. From Latin *discriminare* = to distinguish between.

Vocabulary Builder List and define five words that begin with the prefix *en*, where *en* has the meaning of "to be in something."

Laws Protecting Debtors

What rights do you have when you borrow money or use credit?

To protect consumers, both the federal and state governments regulate the credit industry. Most states, for example, have set a maximum amount that can be charged for interest. **A usury law is a law restricting the amount of interest that can be charged.** Other laws created by the federal government to protect debtors include the Consumer Credit Protection Act, the Fair Credit Reporting Act, the Equal Credit Opportunity Act, the Fair Debt Collection Practices Act, and the Fair Credit Billing Act.

Consumer Credit Protection Act

The Consumer Credit Protection Act, also known as the Truth in Lending Law, is a federal law that requires creditors to inform consumers of the costs and terms of credit. Creditors must tell you both the finance charge and the annual percentage rate (APR) of a loan. With this information you can compare the costs of loans from different lenders.

> **Example** When shopping for a truck, Carmen asked each dealer she visited what the APR would be to finance the purchase. The first dealer said 7.9 percent, another dealer quoted 8.2 percent, and her bank said that it would be 12 percent. Carmen went back to the first dealer, confident that she had found the best deal when shopping around for credit.

Fair Credit Reporting Act

The Fair Credit Reporting Act is a federal law that grants people the right to know what is contained in their credit reports. You have the right to know all personal information that is in a credit reporting agency's files and the sources of that information.

The three national credit reporting agencies in the United States are:

- Equifax
- Trans Union
- Experian

Under recent federal legislation, every person has a right to receive one copy of his or her credit report for free every year from each of the three credit reporting agencies. To find out more, visit the government's official Web site about annual credit reports.

You also have the right to be told the name of anyone who received a copy of your credit report in the past year (and in the past two years if the credit report relates to a job application). You may correct errors in the report. If the credit reporting agency retains information that you believe is inaccurate, your version of the facts must be inserted in the file.

Reading Check

Analyze *Why is it important to find out what is in your credit report?*

In re MasterCard International, Inc., et al.

132 F.Supp.2d 468 (E.D. La. 2001)

Larry Thompson and Lawrence Bradley filed a class action lawsuit against various banking companies and Internet gambling sites. They argued that the companies had entered into agreements that were illegal under the Racketeer Influenced and Corrupt Organizations Act (RICO) and the Federal Wire Act. Thompson and Bradley argued that Internet gambling is illegal in the United States and that because credit card companies such as MasterCard and Visa allowed customers to use their credit cards to buy gambling chips on foreign Internet gambling Web sites, the American banks were committing illegal racketeering activities. The foreign Web sites included graphics of the MasterCard and Visa logos on their sites. Thompson and Bradley argued that they were charged outrageous fees by MasterCard and Visa when they used their credit cards on these gambling sites.

Ruling and Resolution

The Federal District Court in Louisiana held that the RICO Act did not apply to this case. Although Internet gambling may be illegal in the U.S., the Web sites were all foreign and the Federal Wire Act only prohibits Internet gambling on sporting events, not on other types of gambling. Therefore, the banks could not be sued under the RICO Act.

Critical Thinking Should the Federal Wire Act be amended to prohibit all Internet gambling?

Equal Credit Opportunity Act

The Equal Credit Opportunity Act (ECOA) makes it illegal for banks and businesses to discriminate against credit applicants on the basis of their gender, race, marital status, national origin, religion, age, or because they get public assistance income. There are only three reasons a creditor may deny credit: low income; large current debts; and a poor record of making payments in the past. If you are denied credit, under the ECOA you have the right to know why (see **Figure 12.1** on page 268). If it is due to information in your credit report, you have a right to receive a copy of the report for free. If you find inaccurate or incomplete information in the report, you have the right to dispute it and have it corrected.

Fair Debt Collection Practices Act

The Fair Debt Collection Practices Act (FDCPA) prohibits certain practices by debt collectors. The FDCPA makes it illegal for debt collectors to threaten debtors with violence, use obscene language, or contact consumers by telephone at inconvenient times or places. Debt collectors are not allowed to **impersonate** government officials or attorneys, obtain information under false pretenses, or collect more than is legally owed. They must identify themselves, tell why they are calling you, and cannot tell anyone else about the debt.

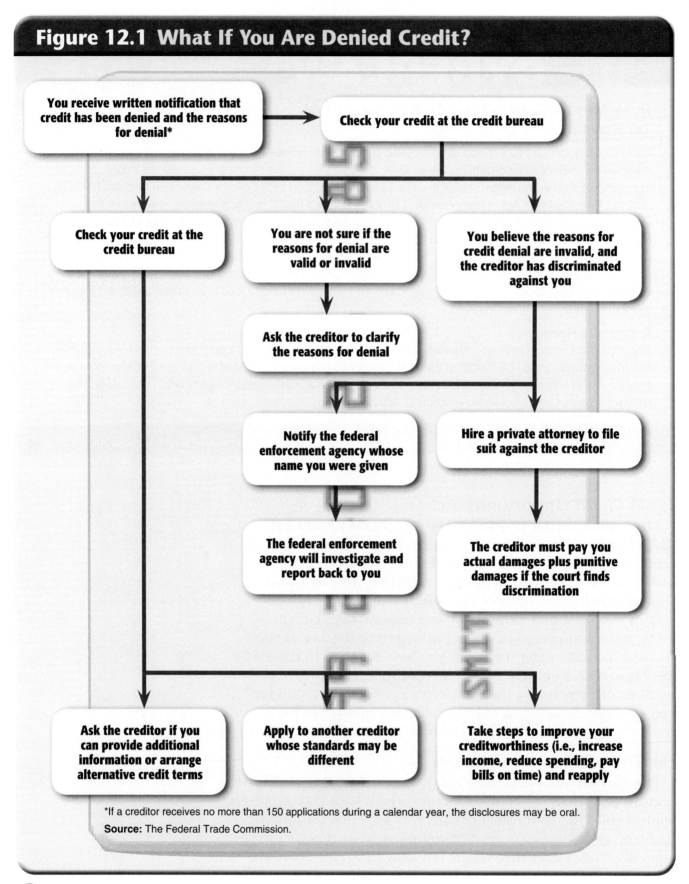

Figure 12.1 What If You Are Denied Credit?

You receive written notification that credit has been denied and the reasons for denial*

Check your credit at the credit bureau

Check your credit at the credit bureau

You are not sure if the reasons for denial are valid or invalid

You believe the reasons for credit denial are invalid, and the creditor has discriminated against you

Ask the creditor to clarify the reasons for denial

Notify the federal enforcement agency whose name you were given

Hire a private attorney to file suit against the creditor

The federal enforcement agency will investigate and report back to you

The creditor must pay you actual damages plus punitive damages if the court finds discrimination

Ask the creditor if you can provide additional information or arrange alternative credit terms

Apply to another creditor whose standards may be different

Take steps to improve your creditworthiness (i.e., increase income, reduce spending, pay bills on time) and reapply

*If a creditor receives no more than 150 applications during a calendar year, the disclosures may be oral.
Source: The Federal Trade Commission.

Sometimes you can be denied credit because of information from a credit report. The law requires credit card companies to correct inaccurate or incomplete information in your credit report. *Why would it be better to request changes of incorrect information by letter rather than by phone?*

Fair Credit Billing Act

The Fair Credit Billing Act requires creditors to correct billing errors brought to their attention. When errors are made in bills sent by credit card companies and businesses that give credit, this law can help you. If you believe an error has been made, notify the creditor in writing within 60 days of the date of the statement. State your name, account number, the charge in question, and why you believe there is an error. The creditor must acknowledge your letter within 30 days. Also, the creditor must investigate and explain why the charge is correct or fix the mistake within 90 days. You do not have to pay the amount in dispute while waiting for an answer from the creditor, but you must pay all charges not in dispute. Creditors may not report you as being delinquent because of the disputed charge.

Credit Repair Organizations

Credit repair companies that promise they will fix your credit are not allowed to charge you until their services have been performed. They also must tell you about your legal rights. They must provide a written contract that details what services are to be performed, how long it will take, the total cost of the service, and any guarantees that are offered. The contract must also tell you that you have a three-day grace period to cancel the service at no charge.

After You Read

Summarize Name the federal laws that regulate consumer credit.

SECTION 12.1 ASSESSMENT

Self Check

1. What are two things creditors can do if a debtor defaults on a debt?

2. Under the Consumer Credit Protection Act, what must creditors tell consumers?

3. What are debt collectors prohibited from doing under the FDCPA?

Academic Connection

Social Studies Usury is lending money at an outrageous rate of interest. The practice of usury goes back at least four thousand years and originally meant simply charging interest. Even then, charging interest of any kind was considered immoral. It was prohibited by Chinese and Hindu law and frowned upon by the ancient Greeks. As the need to use credit to conduct business increased, however, the meaning of the word changed. It became acceptable for lenders to charge a reasonable rate of interest on loans so they could make a profit. In 1545, the British government set a maximum rate of interest that could be legally charged, and anything over that was considered usury. This practice was followed by most of the other European countries and later, the United States.

Research and write an outline on the historical development of usury or the attitude toward usury in different cultures.

Critical Thinking

Credit Protection Why do you think debtors need laws to protect them from creditors?

What You'll Learn

◆ Identify and discuss alternatives to bankruptcy.

◆ Distinguish between the different types of bankruptcy.

◆ Explain the difference between voluntary and involuntary bankruptcy.

◆ Identify debts which cannot be discharged by bankruptcy.

Why It's Important

You will need to know the laws about bankruptcy if you ever find yourself unable to pay off your debts.

Reading Guide

Before You Read

Connect Have you ever owed money and had no way of paying it back?

Focus on Ideas

Federal law provides the process for erasing your debts and restoring your credit.

Take Notes

Go to connectED.mcgraw-hill.com to download a graphic organizer you can use to take notes as you read this section.

Key Terms

You will learn these legal words and expressions in this chapter. You can also find these terms in *Black's Law Dictionary* or in an online legal dictionary.

- bankruptcy
- voluntary bankruptcy
- involuntary bankruptcy
- Chapter 7 bankruptcy
- Chapter 11 bankruptcy
- Chapter 12 bankruptcy
- Chapter 13 bankruptcy

Academic Vocabulary

You will find these words in your readings and in your tests. Look them up in a dictionary and familiarize yourself with them.

- alternative
- petition
- discharge

Bankruptcy

What can you do to avoid bankruptcy?

Sometimes people and businesses accumulate so much debt through no fault of their own that they can no longer afford to repay it. A business might suffer from a slump in the economy or be hit by a natural disaster. An individual might run up huge credit card debts because of a catastrophic illness and lack of medical insurance or simply by losing his or her job.

In the past, under old English law, people who could not pay their debts were put into debtor's prisons. The drafters of the U.S. Constitution opposed this treatment of debtors and gave Congress the authority to help people in this situation by enacting the bankruptcy law.

Bankruptcy is the legal process by which a debtor can make a fresh start through the sale of assets to pay off creditors. Certain bankruptcy proceedings allow a debtor to stay in business and use the revenue collected to pay his or her debt. Another purpose of bankruptcy law is to allow some debtors to free themselves from the debt they have accumulated, after their assets are distributed, even if their debts have not been paid in full.

As You Read

Predict Can you keep your business if you go bankrupt?

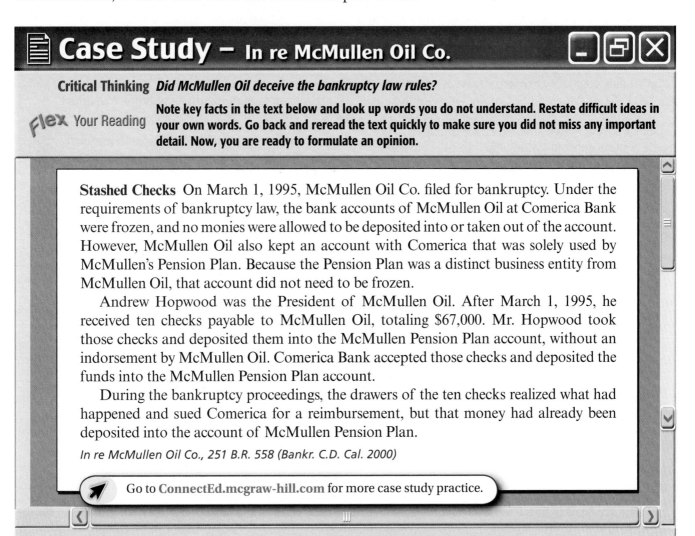

Case Study – In re McMullen Oil Co.

Critical Thinking *Did McMullen Oil deceive the bankruptcy law rules?*

Flex Your Reading Note key facts in the text below and look up words you do not understand. Restate difficult ideas in your own words. Go back and reread the text quickly to make sure you did not miss any important detail. Now, you are ready to formulate an opinion.

Stashed Checks On March 1, 1995, McMullen Oil Co. filed for bankruptcy. Under the requirements of bankruptcy law, the bank accounts of McMullen Oil at Comerica Bank were frozen, and no monies were allowed to be deposited into or taken out of the account. However, McMullen Oil also kept an account with Comerica that was solely used by McMullen's Pension Plan. Because the Pension Plan was a distinct business entity from McMullen Oil, that account did not need to be frozen.

Andrew Hopwood was the President of McMullen Oil. After March 1, 1995, he received ten checks payable to McMullen Oil, totaling $67,000. Mr. Hopwood took those checks and deposited them into the McMullen Pension Plan account, without an indorsement by McMullen Oil. Comerica Bank accepted those checks and deposited the funds into the McMullen Pension Plan account.

During the bankruptcy proceedings, the drawers of the ten checks realized what had happened and sued Comerica for a reimbursement, but that money had already been deposited into the account of McMullen Pension Plan.

In re McMullen Oil Co., 251 B.R. 558 (Bankr. C.D. Cal. 2000)

Go to **ConnectEd.mcgraw-hill.com** for more case study practice.

Avoiding Bankruptcy

If you are having trouble paying your bills, you should immediately stop using a credit card and switch to a debit card. As an **alternative** to bankruptcy, you can contact your creditors and work out an adjusted repayment plan. Another possible solution is to get a consolidation loan, which combines all your debts into one loan with lower payments. For example, you can combine monthly payments on credit cards, student loans, and a car into one lower monthly payment.

You can also contact a nonprofit financial counseling program. The Consumer Credit Counseling Service (CCCS) is a nonprofit organization affiliated with the National Foundation for Consumer Credit. Local branches of the CCCS provide debt-counseling services. Check the white pages of your telephone directory, the Internet, or call 1-800-388-2227. All information is kept confidential.

Vocabulary You can find vocabulary definitions in the **Key Terms** glossary and Academic Vocabulary glossary in the back of this book.

Global Law

Chilean Bankruptcy Law

Chile's original bankruptcy law was passed in 1931 and served the country for more than 50 years. In the 1980s the country decided to reform its bankruptcy laws. Chilean Law Number 18,175 of the Commercial Code went into effect in 1982.

The Chilean legal system follows the French civil system when it comes to bankruptcy. The bankruptcy laws apply to both businesses and individual persons. There are three specific conditions under which a debtor can be declared bankrupt.

1. Default: a qualified debtor is no longer making payments to its creditor

2. Pending Executions (Titulo Ejecutivo): a debtor has three or more outstanding contracts and cannot pay at least two of them

3. Fugitive Debtor: a debtor leaves Chile as a fugitive

There are also two types of debtors in Chile: qualified and not qualified. A qualified debtor only applies to those debtors engaged in commercial, manufacturing, mining, or agricultural activities. Qualified debtors are allowed to begin bankruptcy proceedings on their own behalf. Not qualified debtors can only have bankruptcy proceedings brought against them by their creditors. Individual persons are not qualified debtors.

Qualified debtors may also be subject to criminal proceedings to determine whether the debtor is claiming bankruptcy because of criminal or negligent acts. A qualified debtor has only 15 days to file for bankruptcy, once it becomes clear that it is bankrupt. Failure to file within 15 days is a criminal offense and the debtor is held criminally liable for the bankruptcy.

Once bankruptcy is determined, the debtor's assets are immediately liquidated so that creditors may be paid. However, some qualified debtors are allowed to continue to operate so that the entire business may be sold, rather than breaking up the business.

Across Cultures: Receipts

Whenever you buy something in Chile, you will always get a receipt. It is against the law in Chile to sell something and not give a receipt.

Critical Thinking *Is it fair that you can be declared bankrupt if you just stop paying your bills?*

Filing for Bankruptcy

The moment a **petition** for bankruptcy is filed, an automatic stay goes into effect. An automatic stay is a postponement of collection proceedings against the debtor. Further efforts by creditors against the debtor to collect debts must stop immediately. Creditors, such as credit card companies and lenders of unsecured revolving loans, cannot bring suit for what is owed them. Debit cards can no longer be used because any money in the debtor's bank belongs automatically to the bankruptcy trustee. However, lawsuits involving evictions, divorces, and child custody and support proceedings may continue.

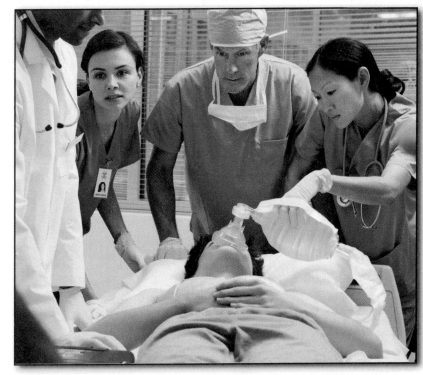

Personal Bankruptcy An individual might need to declare personal bankruptcy because of running up huge medical bills with no medical insurance. *What kinds of bankruptcy can an individual petition for?*

Types of Bankruptcy

What property are you allowed to keep if you declare bankruptcy?

Bankruptcy can be voluntary or involuntary. **Voluntary bankruptcy is when the debtor files for bankruptcy to eliminate or reduce the burden of debt. Involuntary bankruptcy is when creditors begin the proceeding instead of the debtor.** Three creditors must file the petition for bankruptcy if the debtor has 12 or more creditors. The combined debt owed to the three must exceed $11,625. A single creditor who is owed a debt of more than $11,625 can also file if the debtor has fewer than 12 creditors.

Bankruptcy law is federal statutory law contained in Title 11 of the United States Code. There are four main kinds of bankruptcy proceedings. They are named for the chapter of the federal Bankruptcy Code that describes them.

Chapter 7 Bankruptcy (Liquidation)

Chapter 7 bankruptcy, also called ordinary bankruptcy, is a type of bankruptcy which allows individual debtors to discharge all their debts and get a fresh start. With this form of bankruptcy, debtors must sell most of their property and pay their creditors from the proceeds. Debtors must also do the following:

- Get credit counseling from a nonprofit agency before filing for bankruptcy.
- Have a family income below the state's average family income. (If the income is greater, a debtor may be able to file Chapter 13 bankruptcy.)

Business Bankruptcy
A business might need to declare bankruptcy due to a natural disaster. *What should businesses do to avoid such problems?*

- Provide a federal tax return for the most recent tax year.
- Complete a course in financial management after filing for bankruptcy.

As part of the fresh start policy of the Bankruptcy Act, some assets can be kept by the debtor. These so-called exemptions can be doubled for married couples filing jointly. Depending on your state law, you use either your own state exemptions or the federal ones.

Chapter 11 Bankruptcy (Reorganization)

Chapter 11 bankruptcy is a type of bankruptcy that allows businesses to reorganize their financial affairs and still remain in business. When a petition is filed, a reorganization plan for the business is developed. Once the plan is approved by a certain number of creditors and the court, it will go into operation. If the plan is successful, the business will continue. If not, it will be forced to close.

Chapter 12 Bankruptcy (Family Farmers)

Chapter 12 bankruptcy is a form of bankruptcy that lets family farmers, and fishing businesses, create a plan for debt repayment that allows them to keep their operations running. They must receive more than one-half of their total income from farming or fishing. Also, 50 percent of the debt must result from farm or fishing expenses.

Chapter 13 Bankruptcy (Repayment Plan)

Chapter 13 bankruptcy is a form of bankruptcy that permits individual debtors to reorganize their debts and develop repayment plans. During the period of repayment (three to five years) creditors may not continue collection activities. People who have too much income to file for Chapter 7 bankruptcy may file for Chapter 13. This can be done only if they can make debt repayments of $100 a month for five years. Debtors who wish to keep their car must pay the full loan amount on car loans.

Exceptions to Discharge

Some debts cannot be **discharged** by bankruptcy. That means you still have to pay them even if you qualify for bankruptcy.

Reading Check

Analyze *Which types of bankruptcy apply to individuals and which types apply to businesses?*

These include debts caused by the debtor's fraud, back taxes, and student loans that do not impose a hardship on the debtor.

Administration of the Debtor's Estate

Following a court hearing, a trustee will be appointed to sell the debtor's property, or estate, to obtain cash. The trustee then distributes the cash among the debtor's creditors according to a priority list. Secured debts are paid first, followed by administrative costs, wages, benefit plans, alimony and support, taxes, and unsecured debts.

Restoring Credit after Bankruptcy

Can you still get credit after you have declared bankruptcy?

A bankruptcy filing remains on a debtor's credit report for ten years and has a bad effect on obtaining a line of credit. However, most debtors who file bankruptcy already have a poor credit rating anyway, and bankruptcy gives them a chance to begin anew. Many of their debts become discharged, which improves their debt-to-income ratio—a factor that creditors look at carefully. The more time that elapses after the bankruptcy filing, the easier it is to reestablish credit.

After a bankruptcy, debtors must educate themselves on developing a budget, managing their money, and using credit and debit cards wisely to avoid accumulating debt again that they cannot resolve.

After You Read

Summarize What are the four main types of bankruptcy?

SECTION 12.2 ASSESSMENT

Self Check

1. What are some alternatives to bankruptcy?

2. What are the differences between voluntary and involuntary bankruptcy?

3. What is the difference between declaring Chapter 7 and Chapter 13 bankruptcy?

Academic Connection

Mathematics You applied for a loan. The lender tells you that you will get a better rate if your debt payments-to-income ratio is low. If your monthly income is $1,200 and your monthly debt payments total $180, what is your debt-payments-to-income ratio (DPR)?

CONCEPT **Number and Operations:** To figure out a ratio, you need to use a fraction. To calculate the DPR ratio, divide the total debts by the total income. Convert the decimal outcome to a percentage by moving the decimal point two places to the right and adding a percent sign (%).

 For more math practice, go to the Math Appendix.

Critical Thinking

Debt Burden How much money do you think someone should owe before declaring bankruptcy?

Chapter (12) Review and Assessment

Summary

Section 12.1 Credit Protection Laws

◆ If a debtor fails to make payments, the creditor has a right to repossess property or garnish the person's wages.

◆ The Consumer Credit Protection Act requires creditors to inform consumers of the costs and terms of credit.

◆ The Fair Credit Reporting Act grants people the right to know what is contained in their credit reports.

◆ The Equal Credit Opportunity Act (ECOA) makes it illegal to discriminate against credit applicants.

◆ The Fair Debt Collection Practices Act (FDCPA) prohibits certain practices by debt collectors.

◆ The Fair Credit Billing Act requires creditors to correct billing errors brought to their attention.

Section 12.2 Bankruptcy Laws

◆ Bankruptcy can be voluntary or involuntary.

◆ Chapter 7 bankruptcy allows individual debtors to discharge all their debts and get a fresh start.

◆ Chapter 11 bankruptcy allows businesses to reorganize their financial affairs and still remain in business.

◆ Chapter 12 bankruptcy allows family farmers and fishing businesses to repay debts and still keep their operations running.

◆ Chapter 13 bankruptcy is a form of bankruptcy that permits individual debtors to develop repayment plans.

◆ Debts that cannot be discharged by bankruptcy include debts caused by fraud, back taxes, and student loans.

Vocabulary Builder

❶ On a sheet of paper, use each of these terms in a sentence.

Key Terms

- repossession
- garnishment
- usury law
- Consumer Credit Protection Act
- Fair Credit Reporting Act

- Equal Credit Opportunity Act (ECOA)
- Fair Debt Collection Practices Act (FDCPA)
- Fair Credit Billing Act
- bankruptcy

- voluntary bankruptcy
- involuntary bankruptcy
- Chapter 7 bankruptcy
- Chapter 11 bankruptcy
- Chapter 12 bankruptcy
- Chapter 13 bankruptcy

Academic Vocabulary

- dominant
- exceed

- impersonate
- alternative

- petition
- discharge

Key Points Review

Answer the following questions. Refer to the chapter for additional reinforcement.

2 What is garnishment and what is the most a creditor can garnish?

3 What rights does the Fair Credit Reporting Act give people?

4 What are the only three reasons a creditor may deny credit?

5 According to the Fair Credit Billing Act, what should you do if you believe an error has been made on a bill?

6 What are the differences between Chapters 7, 11, 12, and 13 bankruptcies?

7 Which types of bankruptcy are personal and which are business bankruptcies?

8 How is a debtor's property distributed upon bankruptcy?

9 Which debts are not extinguished by bankruptcy?

Standardized Test Practice

10 Read the following excerpt from the terms and conditions of a credit card and do problems 1 and 2.

Default Rate: All your APRs may increase if you default under any card agreement, if you fail to make a payment when due, you exceed your credit line, or you make a payment that is not honored. In these circumstances, we may automatically increase your interest rate on all balances to the default APR, which is equal to the prime rate plus 23.99% or up to 28.99%, whichever is greater.

Late Fee: We add a late fee to each billing period if you fail to pay by the due date. This fee is based on your account balance as of the payment due date. The late fee is: $15 on a balance up to $100, $29 on balances of $100 to $250, and $39 on balances over $250.

1. If you default under a card agreement, your interest rate can be automatically increased to:

Ⓐ the prime rate
Ⓑ 23.99%
Ⓒ the prime rate plus 23.99% or up to 28.99%, whichever is greater
Ⓓ the prime rate plus 23.99% or up to 28.99%, whichever is lower

2. You make a late payment on a balance of $234. You will be charged a late fee of:

Ⓐ $15
Ⓑ $29
Ⓒ $100
Ⓓ $39

Test-Taking Strategies When trying to answer difficult questions, first eliminate answers you know are incorrect, then analyze the remaining answers.

Apply and Debate

Read the following scenarios. Get together with other students in pairs or groups of three and take a position on each scenario. Debate your position in class with students taking the opposite position or prepare a written argument justifying your position.

11 Repossession

Tamara purchased a car for $5,000 down and a four-year loan with payments of $400 per month. During the last year of her loan, she lost her job and fell behind in her payments. The bank repossessed her car, leaving Tamara with nothing.

You Debate *Can the bank sell Tamara's car for below-market value to settle her loan?*

12 Consumer Credit Protection Act

Jason was reviewing the loan documents he had just signed with a lender, who had quoted him the lowest interest rate. He noticed that his loan was increased by $2,000, which is the cost of points he had to pay for the low interest rate. The lender had not explained this to him.

You Debate *Is the lender violating the Consumer Credit Protection Act by not disclosing the additional costs to Jason?*

13 Fair Credit Billing Act

When Ned received his credit card bill, he noticed a charge he had not made. He notified his credit card company by phone, then in writing. After an investigation, the company determined that Ned would be held responsible for the complete charge.

You Debate *If Ned did not make this charge, should he be required to pay for it even after the investigation?*

14 Credit Repair Organizations

Maria contacted a credit repair company to help her with her credit. At the end of her meeting, Maria was asked to pay $450 in administrative costs.

You Debate *Is Maria required by law to pay the fee to the credit repair company?*

15 Chapter 7 Bankruptcy

The Mundy family has not been able to pay their debts since Hurricane Katrina struck their home and business. They decided to file for Chapter 7 bankruptcy to get relief from their creditors.

You Debate *Is bankruptcy the best option for the Mundy's considering the circumstances?*

Case Study Practice – Ardis v. Educational Management Corp.

16 Can Student Loans Be Discharged in Bankruptcy? In July 1991 Robert Ardis consolidated his student loans into one loan totaling $23,756. He made 14 payments totaling approximately $2,700 until August, 1994, when he stopped paying the loan. In April of 1995, his account went into default. Ten years later, in 2005, the amount, with interest, had increased to $70,600.

In 2005, Mr. Ardis sought to have his student loan debt discharged in bankruptcy. He had previously filed for bankruptcy in 1995 and 2003. Both times, the bankruptcy court declined to discharge his student loans. Mr. Ardis, a single father, worked as a teacher at an annual salary of $40,000 and did not anticipate any salary increases in the near future. His offer to pay a lump sum of $8,000 was rejected.

Student loan debt is not normally dischargeable in bankruptcy, but can be if the debtor demonstrates three things: 1) that the debtor could not maintain a minimal standard of living if forced to repay the loans; 2) that the debtor's financial situation is likely to persist into the future; and 3) the debtor has made good faith efforts to repay the loan.

Source: Ardis v. Educational Management Corp., 2006 WL 931563(D.S.C. 2006)

Practice Should Mr. Ardis's student loan debt be discharged?

17 Ethics
←?→ Application _____

Student Loans Paul graduated from college with a business degree owing $20,000 in credit cards and personal loans. Two years after graduating, he is not making enough money to keep up with his debts and is considering filing for bankruptcy.

◆ Would it be unethical for Paul to declare bankruptcy under these circumstances?

18 Think back to the Legal Briefs feature you read at the beginning of the chapter. Then prepare a chart. On the left side, list the qualities a consumer wants in a credit counseling service. Go online to find credit counseling and debt-settlement services in your area. Put their names across the top of your chart. Check off the services or qualities that each offers. Then compile a class list of the various services you might contact in order of trustworthiness and services offered.

Ira A. Finkelstein

Attorney, Harnik & Finkelstein

What do you do at work?

"My primary area of legal practice entails representing sports organizations, leagues, teams, and athletes who are involved in legal disputes of many kinds. Sometimes the disputes involve disagreements over contracts such as athlete employment agreements, or contracts involving athletes' endorsements of products. Sometimes the disputes involve much more serious legal problems such as when someone is accused of violating an important rule of a sport, like not obeying a referee's decision, or cheating, or using prohibited substances to improve athletic performance."

What skills are most important to you?

"My ability to conduct a trial or hearing and, perhaps even more important, my ability to negotiate a settlement. Most sports disputes result in out-of-court settlements. It is also very important to me that I learn everything I can about the sport I am working with and the people who are involved in it."

What training do you recommend?

"Any good lawyer can become a good sports lawyer, because the basic legal skills and learning experiences are the same. However, lawyers who want to represent athletes or clubs in salary contract negotiations should have good training in employment negotiations. Since in so many sports the athletes are organized similar to labor unions, previous experience in labor relations law is a plus. I recommend that if you really love a particular sport, get involved at the local level of the sport initially to meet as many people as possible, and learn about all of the particular legal issues that the sport may involve."

What is your key to success?

"I believe in having a very close relationship of trust with my client. A lawyer's duty of confidentiality to a client is essential to establish trust and protect the client's interests."

Resume Builder

Academic Skills

• Above average critical-thinking skills
• Good speaking and debating skills

Education and Training

A bachelor's degree in business administration, finance, sports and leisure science, or a basic legal background augmented with specific study of chosen industry or sport. The following high school and college courses will help develop the necessary background knowledge:

• Athletic administration (college)
• Athletic management (college)
• Business, contracts, and consumer law
• Business management
• English language arts (rhetoric and composition)
• Sports management (college)
• Sports marketing

Critical Thinking

Why does it benefit a negotiator to remain cool and calm while working on a deal?

The Writing Connection

Persuasive Writing Practice

Is It Legal Even in a Changed World? After the events of September 11, 2001, Congress enacted the Uniting and Strengthening America by Providing Appropriate Tools Required to Intercept and Obstruct Terrorism Act of 2001, also known as the U.S. Patriot Act. The new crimes of domestic terrorism became credible threats to the Homeland Security. The White House states that the Act "has been vital to winning the War on Terror and protecting the American people." President George W. Bush stated in a speech that the Act allows intelligence and law enforcement officials to continue to share information by using tools against terrorists; the intent is to ensure the nation's security while safeguarding the civil liberties of the people.

Assignments

Research Research what makes the U.S. Patriot Act controversial legislation.

Write After considering the situation above and conducting research, write a persuasive essay about your stance on the constitutionality of the Act.

Writing Tips Before you start writing your essay, read through the following prewriting techniques:

✓ Read newspaper archives on your specific subject. Pay attention to the different angles of the editorials. How do you respond to the different issues raised?

✓ Reading editorials may give you ideas for developing evidence towards your position in the essay.

✓ Create a graphic organizer to help you organize and visually show the plan for your argument.

Essay Test Strategies Keep your audience and purpose in mind:

✓ Audience: peers, classmates, and teacher

✓ Purpose: present an opinion, acknowledge alternative viewpoints, and provide reasons for your opinion

Thematic Project

Correcting a Credit Report Error

For this project, you will use what you have learned to prepare a business letter disputing an error you have discovered on your credit report. For this project, you will work individually.

Here is a checklist of the skills that you will need to complete this project. Your teacher will consider these skills when evaluating your work.

Evaluation Rubric		
Academic Skills		
1.	Online and library research	1.	10 points
2.	Reading for information	2.	10 points
3.	Note-taking	3.	5 points
4.	Estimation and computation of facts/figures	4.	10 points
5.	English composition to summarize findings	5.	15 points
Legal Skills		
6.	Research of consumer reporting and credit rights	6.	15 points
7.	Methods of comparing the three main credit bureaus' reports	7.	15 points
8.	Analysis of the essential statistical information	8.	15 points
9.	Use of technology	9.	5 points
		Total 100 Points	

Step 1: Preparation

❶ Write an outline of a business letter to dispute an error you have discovered on your credit report.

❷ Use all you have learned in this unit, at the library, or on the Internet as tools.

❸ Complete this project in a format acceptable for an addition to your portfolio.

Step 2: Procedure

1 **Review** the text in this unit and make a list of essential tools to protect or repair your credit report.

2 **List** all the credit terms you might use in your business letter. What are you disputing in the report? What remedy are you expecting from the reporting bureau? What proof can you offer that the information is incorrect? How long will you allow the agency to rectify the error?

3 **Write** a standard business format letter, based on your knowledge and research, to one of the three credit report bureaus regarding a dispute on your credit report. Use the Internet to download a sample dispute letter, or create an original letter using word-processing software. Make enough copies of your letter to allow classmates to review and annotate.

4 **Describe** the scenario that is the basis for your dispute business letter and present your letter to the class.

Step 3: Create an Analysis Report

As a class, compare the letters presented. Generate a list of common areas that all letters included and what information could make it easier to resolve the conflict.

1 What formats of business letters were used to compose this assignment?

2 Did the letters include all the necessary elements to resolve the conflict?

3 If not, how does the absence of the element(s) affect the resolution?

4 How was your letter similar to or different from the other business letters presented?

Community Connection

Find the information on the number of judicial courts, judgeships, and number of districts in the United States. What steps are required in filing a bankruptcy? How are jurors selected to stand on bankruptcy hearings? Are there any special requirements to being a juror in a judicial court?

Competitive Event Prep

Establishing Credit

Situation: Assume the role of a high school business law student who recently turned 18. Since turning 18, you have received a great many offers from several credit card com-panies. The offers vary in the interest rates charged and incentives such as airline frequent flier miles and points for free hotel stays. You have learned the importance of establishing credit and main-taining a good credit rating. You would like to begin to establish credit in your name by opening a credit card account.

Activity: You are to discuss with your parents your credit card options. Your discussion should include some selection criteria and other factors to consider when choosing a credit card.

Landmark Case

Household Credit Services, Inc. v. Pfennig
United States Supreme Court 541 U.S. 232 (2004)

Read Critically As you read this case, ask yourself the following questions:

1. Why did Ms. Pfennig have to pay over-limit fees?
2. Does the Truth in Lending Act include a clear definition of finance charge?
3. Who is responsible for creating regulations under the Truth in Lending Act?
4. What does Regulation Z define?

Assignment When you are done, write a short summary of the situation. Include the court's decision and a couple of sentences about why or how the court reached its decision.

Facts Consumer's Credit Card

Sharon Pfennig had a credit card with a limit of $2,000. She originally had the card issued by Household Credit Services, Inc. However, after she received the card, Household Credit Services, Inc. sold its credit card business to MBNA America Bank, N.A. Although she had a credit limit of $2,000, Ms. Pfennig was able to make charges on her credit card that caused her to exceed the limit. For every month that Ms. Pfennig exceeded her credit limit, she was charged an over-limit fee of $29.

Class Action Suit On August 24, 1999, Ms. Pfennig filed a class action lawsuit against MBNA alleged on behalf of all consumers nationwide that they were charged or assessed over-limit fees on cards issued by MBNA. Ms. Pfennig alleged that MBNA allowed its customers to exceed its stated credit limits, thereby subjecting the customers to the over-limit fees. Ms. Pfennig further argued that the over-limit fees were "interest charges" under

the Truth in Lending Act (TILA) and that MBNA, therefore, misrepresented "the true cost of credit" to its customers.

The Truth in Lending Act Congress passed the TILA as a means to encourage the "informed use of credit" by American consumers. In order to achieve those ends, the TILA requires that creditors include adequate disclosure in their documentation to ensure that all the relevant credit terms are meaningfully disclosed. Congress also gave expansive power to the Federal Reserve Board to enact appropriate and extensive regulations to ensure that Congress's intent in passing the TILA was followed by creditors.

Under the specific legislation, TILA requires that:

The credit card statement must include the account's outstanding balance at the end of the billing period and the amount of any finance charge added to the account during the period, itemized to show the amounts, if any due to the application of percentage rates and the amount, if any imposed as a minimum or fixed charge. *15 U.S.C. §1637(b)*

A finance charge is an amount payable directly or indirectly by the person to whom the credit is extended, and imposed directly or indirectly by the creditor as an incident to the extension of credit. 15 U.S.C. §1605(a)

Regulation Z Under the TILA, Congress gave the Federal Reserve power to enact regulations that include "classifications, differentiations, or other provisions, and [to] provide for such adjustments and exceptions for any class of transactions, as in the judgment of the [Federal Reserve] are necessary or proper to effectuate the purposes of [the TILA], to prevent circumvention or evasion thereof, or to facilitate compliance therewith." Regulation Z is one of those more specific regulations that seeks to further define finance charge. Regulation Z specifically excludes some fees from the definition of finance charge.

Regulation Z excludes, among other things, the following:

1. *Application fees charged to all applicants for credit, whether or not credit is actually extended.*
2. *Charges for actual unanticipated late payment, for exceeding a credit limit, or for delinquency, default, or similar occurrence.*
3. *Charges imposed by a financial institution for paying items that overdraw an account, unless the payment of such items and the imposition of the charge were previously agreed upon in writing.*
4. *Fees charged for participation in a credit plan, whether assessed on an annual or other periodic basis.*
5. *Seller's points.*
6. *Interest forfeited as a result of an interest reduction required by law on a time deposit used as security for an extension of credit.*
7. *Certain fees related to real estate.*
8. *Discounts offered to induce payment for a purchase by cash, check, or other means, as provided in section 167(b) of the Act.*

Opinion Court of Appeals

The Sixth Circuit Court of Appeals found that the TILA was ambiguous in its definition of finance charge. The Court reasoned that Ms. Pfennig only had to pay the over-limit fee because MBNA had chosen to extend her additional credit, thus allowing her to exceed her credit limit for a limited time. Therefore, the Court of Appeals held the MBNA might have violated the TILA and remanded the case to the Federal District Court.

Ambiguity Under the TILA, the definition of finance charge is ambiguous. Therefore, the Federal Reserve's regulation is binding on the courts, unless the regulation is "procedurally defective, arbitrary or capricious in substance, or manifestly contrary to the statute." The Supreme Court, thus, must determine whether Regulation Z falls under any of the above exclusions.

Holding The Court's Decision

The Supreme Court held that the Federal Reserve's Regulation Z is not defective, arbitrary, capricious, or contrary to the statute. Therefore, because Regulation Z specifically excludes over-limit fees from the definition of finance charge, MBNA is not liable to Ms. Pfennig for failing to meaningfully disclose all finance charges under the TILA.

TRIAL PREP

The National High School Mock Trial Association organizes competitions at the local, regional, and national levels where teams of high school or college students prepare and argue fictional legal cases before practicing attorneys and judges. Mock Trial team members are each assigned a role as either an attorney or witness. Each team must develop a courtroom strategy, legal arguments, and a presentation style.

The Law and the Workplace

In This Unit You Will Find:

On the Job The federal government has passed a number of laws to protect employees. *What kinds of protection are workers guaranteed?*

Thematic Project Preview

Employment Guide

As you read this unit, use this checklist to prepare for the unit project:

✓ List the laws, legislation, and acts governing employers and employees.

✓ Differentiate between federal and state labor laws.

✓ Compare advantages and disadvantages of each.

✓ Explain how laws protect employees as well as employers from possible litigation.

✓ Determine appropriate employment forms needed for employees to sign.

Legal Portfolio When you complete the Unit Thematic project, you will have created a guide of federal and your state's employment laws to add to your portfolio.

Ask

AN EXPERT

Saving for Your Retirement

Q: I am still in high school. Why should I think about saving for retirement now?

A: The fact is, retirement always seems far off and many people never start saving for it, even when they get close to retirement. The amount most people receive in Social Security benefits when they retire is usually not enough to live on comfortably. Many companies do not offer pension plans. So, it is wise to save money in a retirement account. The sooner you start, the better. Suppose that at the age of 35 you start putting $150 per month into a retirement account that pays an annual interest rate of 8 percent. By the time you retire at age 65, you will have about $225,000 in your account. Now suppose you start putting the same amount of money into the same account at age 25, ten years sooner. By the time you retire at age 65, you will have over $525,000 in the account, or more than $300,000 extra.

Legal Briefs

Vacation Laws of Other Countries

Should the government require employers to provide paid vacation?

Nearly one in four workers in the United States does not receive pay for vacation time or holidays. This puts the country at the low end of the scale for 21 of the richest countries in the world, according to a recent study on international labor laws. Other advanced economies, including 16 European nations, Australia, Canada, Japan, and New Zealand are ahead of the U.S.

Workers in Ireland enjoy three weeks paid vacation and an additional nine paid holidays. The Luxembourg government mandates employees receive 25 days of vacation and 10 paid public holidays. Swedish law provides workers five weeks of vacation time, with 10 weeks after five years of employment. In Denmark workers receive five weeks, while Spain's law provides employees 30 vacation days and 14 holidays. The United Kingdom, like the United States, does not mandate paid vacation time for workers.

Proponents for government-backed paid vacation days argue that it is a matter of equality and that workers are more productive if given time away from the stress of the job. Non-supporters claim government mandated paid vacation days hurt businesses.

Types of Agents A store manager is a general agent, and a salesperson is a special agent. *What is general rather than special about a general agent?*

SECTION 13.1 The Agency Relationship

Reading Guide

Before You Read

Connect Name some situations in which you were paid to do specific tasks, such as running errands, in place of someone else.

Focus on Ideas

An agent is a person who represents someone else in business.

Take Notes

Go to connectED.mcgraw-hill.com to download a graphic organizer you can use to take notes as you read this section.

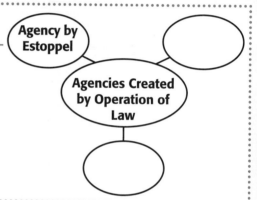

Agency by Estoppel

Agencies Created by Operation of Law

Key Terms

You will learn these legal words and expressions in this chapter. You can also find these terms in *Black's Law Dictionary* or in an online legal dictionary.

- agency
- principal
- agent
- third party
- independent contractor
- agency by estoppel

Academic Vocabulary

You will find these words in your readings and in your tests. Look them up in a dictionary and familiarize yourself with them.

- genuine
- conduct
- gratuitous

Understanding the Agency Relationship

How many people are involved in a work relationship?

The concept of agency is an important legal foundation in the work world. You can be in an agency relationship whether you work for a company or for yourself. **Agency refers to a type of working relationship in which one person represents another person in a business transaction with a third party.** The agency relationship involves three parties:

- **The principal is the person who authorizes someone to represent his or her interests.**
- **The agent is the person who has been authorized to do the work.**
- **The third party is the person with whom the agent does business on behalf of the principal.**

Agents can sign business deals, make contracts, and perform many other business tasks for the principal. An agency relationship underlies many employer-employee situations. The cashiers at a supermarket are agents for their store. Salespeople in a department store are agents. So is a literary agent representing an author to a publishing company. Whether a worker is actually called an agent does not matter. What counts in deciding if there is an agency relationship are the functions people play as principals, agents, or third parties.

As You Read

Predict What does an agent do?

Types of Work Relationships

Is a lawyer a type of agent?

Principal-Agent Relationship

The principal-agent relationship is a **genuine** agency relationship. The party who needs help is the principal; the party who provides help is the agent. Legally, agents are different from other types of representatives because agents can **conduct** business on behalf of a principal. When an agent acts for a principal, it is as if the principal has acted. Some agents, but not all, are employees. A real estate broker is an agent who represents a party in a contract involving the transfer of real property. Real estate brokers are agents, but they are not generally considered employees.

Not every job involves an agency relationship. There are other types of work relationships recognized by the law. The legal differences between these are especially important in determining which party has liability when there are errors, accidents, or contract disputes.

Proprietor-Independent Contractor Relationship

A proprietor is a person who hires someone to perform a task. **An independent contractor works for a proprietor to perform a particular task using his or her own tools and deciding the best way to do the job.** Proprietors and

Vocabulary You can find vocabulary definitions in the **Key Terms** glossary and Academic Vocabulary glossary in the back of this book.

Legal Talk

independent contractors can be either a single individual or an entire company. Plumbers, gardeners, electricians, accountants, lawyers, designers, architects, and personal trainers are often independent contractors.

The proprietor-independent contractor relationship is not legally the same as a principal-agent relationship. The proprietor has no control over the independent contractor. The independent contractor also cannot sign contracts or handle business transactions for the proprietor unless expressly authorized to do so, in which case the independent contractor can also be an agent for the proprietor.

Master-Servant Relationship

The terms *master* and *servant* are legal terms used to describe a type of work relationship. A master is a person who has the right to control the conduct of another person. The person who is performing the task for the master is a servant. Many employer-employee relationships are legally considered to be master-servant relationships when the employer has a high degree of control over the employee's time, place of work, tools and methods used, and output results. However, if a servant has authority to conduct business for the master, the servant can also be considered an agent for those tasks.

Bailees and Trustees

These are two special types of relationships that are discussed in depth elsewhere in this book. A bailee is a person who holds the personal property of another for a certain purpose (see Section 8.2). A trustee is an individual who manages a trust (see Section 21.2).

➡️ **Independent Contractors**
An independent contractor works for but is not an agent for a principal. *What makes an independent contractor independent, as opposed to an agent?*

Creating an Agency Relationship

Can a minor be a principal or an agent?

Agency relationships are usually formed when a principal and an agent agree to the arrangement. Agreement makes the relationship consensual, meaning either party is free to terminate it at any time. However, if the arrangement involves the principal paying the agent, the agreement is contractual. Having a contract may prevent or limit one of the parties from terminating early, despite the consensual nature of the agreement.

The agency agreement can be oral or written. However, under the Equal Dignity Rule, if contracts made by the agent to third parties must be in writing, then the contract that creates the agency relationship must also be in writing.

Reading Check

Explain *When must a contract creating an agency relationship be in writing?*

Agreements Requiring Licensed Agents

Sometimes an agent represents a principal for free. This is called a **gratuitous** agent. The consensual arrangement in this case is not a contract and the agent can terminate at any time. While nearly anyone can act as a principal, all states regulate certain professions of agents. Lawyers, stock brokers, insurance agents, auctioneers, and real estate brokers must pass an examination and be licensed in their state before they can serve as agents.

Agreements Involving Minors

Even a minor can be a principal or an agent in a contractual agency agreement. However, because minors do not have contractual capacity, two situations can arise:

- A minor principal who has an adult agent—The agent may be liable if an injury, error, or breach of contract results unless the third party has been informed that the principal is a minor and the party still agrees to the contract.

- A minor agent representing an adult principal—A principal must uphold a contract made by a minor, unless it can be shown that the minor lacked capacity to understand the transaction.

Example Jason Bently, a 17-year old, invented a software game and hired Sam Lacey to represent him. Lacey sold the game to a small publisher but neglected to tell them that Bently was a minor. Bently did not like the contract and refused to accept it. Lacey is now liable for the $1,000 the company already spent in designing the packaging for the game.

Agencies Created by Operation of Law

In certain situations, an agency relationship may be created automatically by law even though the principal and agent did not consensually agree in advance.

Commercial Agents in the United Arab Emirates

When foreign companies wish to conduct business in the United Arab Emirates (UAE), there are two possible ways they can do this. First, the company can incorporate a new company in the UAE or open an office in the UAE. The second way to conduct business is by using a commercial agent.

If the foreign company chooses to use a commercial agent, it must follow the law as set forth in the UAE Commercial Agencies Law. There are six main requirements under the law:

1 The agents must be nationals (citizens) of the UAE or companies that are wholly-owned by UAE nationals.

2 Both the agent and the agency agreement must be registered with the UAE Ministry of Economy and Commerce.

3 An agent must be given its own territory that consists of at least one emirate (state) within the country.

4 Agents are normally paid for any sales that occur in their territory whether or not they made the sales themselves.

5 An agent can bar the products of the company with which he has a distribution agreement from being imported if the agent is not the exclusive importer and distributor for that company.

6 If the agent and agency agreement are properly registered, the agency relationship cannot be ended without just cause.

In the case that an agency relationship is ended without just cause, or if the foreign company fails to renew the agency relationship, then the agent is entitled to compensation. Further, the foreign company may not be able to appoint a replacement agent.

> **Across Cultures: UAE Courts**
> The UAE comprise seven independent emirates under a federal government. There is a federal court system, but it only has jurisdiction over five of the seven emirates. In each emirate there is a unique system of secular and Islamic courts.

Critical Thinking: *Does the UAE law benefit the agent in the UAE too much?*

Agency by Estoppel Sometimes a principal, through words or actions, may unintentionally lead a third party to believe that someone has authority to act as an agent on his or her behalf, when the person does not. **Agency by estoppel is when the principal's actions lead the third party to believe that the agent is working for the principal.** When estoppel occurs, the law prevents the principal from denying that the person was a nonagent. The principal is still liable for the agent's actions.

> **Example** Phil Tumbry told Terry Jankura to come to his jewelry store at 8 p.m. where someone would help her buy a ring on sale. However, Phil left his store early for a family emergency. He asked his acquaintance, Axel, to keep an eye on the store. Terry arrived at 8 p.m. and assumed that Axel was an employee. She picked out a ring and paid Axel $1,000. The next day, Phil called Terry and said her ring was not on sale and cost $500 more. Terry refused to pay it. She is within her rights because Phil created an agency by estoppel with Axel.

Agency by Ratification Sometimes a person performs a task he or she was not authorized by the principal to do, such as a stock clerk signing for a delivery. Sometimes an agent who has the authority to negotiate one type of contract oversteps that authority and negotiates another type of contract. In such cases, the principal for whom the agent claimed to act may either ignore the action or ratify it. An act is said to be ratified when a principal approves or accepts an agent's unauthorized act after the fact. The principal becomes bound as though the agent had authority to act. If the principal does not ratify the act, however, the would-be agent could be held liable to the third party.

To ratify the act, the principal must meet certain conditions. First, the principal must have the capacity to ratify and know all the facts. Second, the act to be ratified must be legal and done on behalf of the principal. Finally, the ratification must apply to the entire act of the agent, and ratification must occur before the third party withdraws.

Agency by Statute Sometimes a state legislature decides that certain situations justify automatic creation of an agency relationship by statute. For example, in many states the law requires corporations to appoint an agent within the state who can be served with a complaint and summons in case the corporation is sued. If the corporation's appointed agent leaves the state, the secretary of state automatically becomes its statutory agent of process. The state has a special interest to protect in this case: making certain that its citizens have a way to sue a corporation that has injured them.

After You Read

Summarize Name the ways in which an agency relationship can be created.

SECTION 13.1 ASSESSMENT

Self Check

1. What is agency and who are the parties in an agency relationship?
2. What is the difference between an agent and an independent contractor?
3. What is agency by ratification?

Academic Connection

English Language Arts
An independent contractor is a self-employed person who provides a service to someone, but who is not controlled, supervised, or directed by that person. If you use the services of an independent contractor, you do not have to worry about collecting and paying that person's payroll taxes as you would an employee. Although the IRS has established 20 separate criteria to help employers distinguish between independent contractors and employees, the distinctions between one type of worker and another can still be a puzzle. Go on the Internet or to the library and look up IRS Publication 937. Read the section called Employee or Independent Contractor?. Write a brief summary of your findings.

Critical Thinking

Representation What are some reasons why you might want to hire an agent to represent you?

Types of Authority and Agents

What You'll Learn

◆ Identify the different types of agency authority.

◆ Explain the difference between actual and apparent authority.

◆ Distinguish between the different types of agents.

Why It's Important

If you ever work as an agent, you need to know the extent of your authority and responsibility.

Reading Guide

Before You Read

Connect Have you ever worked at a job where you were only allowed to perform specific tasks?

Focus on Ideas

Agents must act within the authority they receive from the principal.

Take Notes

Go to connectED.mcgraw-hill.com to download a graphic organizer you can use to take notes as you read this section.

Types of Agency Authority — Actual

Key Terms

You will learn these legal words and expressions in this chapter. You can also find these terms in *Black's Law Dictionary* or in an online legal dictionary.

- actual authority
- express authority
- power of attorney
- implied authority
- apparent authority

- general agent
- special agent
- subagent
- agent's agent

Academic Vocabulary

You will find these words in your readings and in your tests. Look them up in a dictionary and familiarize yourself with them.

- apparent
- incidental
- extent

Types of Agent Authority

If you are an agent, how much authority do you have to make decisions on you own?

Agents conduct business and make contracts on behalf of their principals. In order to know what they are allowed to do, agents must have authority from their principals. There are two types of authority: actual authority and **apparent** authority.

Actual Authority

Actual authority is the real power a principal gives to an agent. Actual authority may be specifically expressed in words or implied from the agreement.

Express Authority **Express authority comes from the orders, commands, or instructions a principal explicitly gives an agent.** The instructions may be oral or in writing. The wording of the instructions may be very general or very specific.

> **Example** Guinevere Kellogg was going away on a long business trip. She asked her friend Allen Eton to be her agent in selling her DVD collection. In a written document, Kellogg instructed Eton to accept no less than $2,000 in cash and to sell the collection to a person over the age of 18. These instructions made up Eton's express authority as the agent for Kellogg.

A **power of attorney is any writing granting someone authority to act as an agent.** The authority granted by a power of attorney comes in three forms:

- A general power of attorney gives the agent authority to act for the principal in a wide range of activities.
- A limited power of attorney gives the agent authority to deal only with the tasks named in the agreement.
- A durable power of attorney gives the agent the power to make health care decisions when the principal becomes incapacitated.

Powers of attorney end when the principal withdraws the authority or dies.

Implied Authority Writing down every single act that an agent is allowed to perform would make an agency agreement long and complicated. The law thus allows actual authority to be understood from the expressly stated terms of the principal. This is called implied authority.

As You Read

Predict What is the difference between actual and apparent authority?

Vocabulary You can find vocabulary definitions in the **Key Terms** glossary and Academic Vocabulary glossary in the back of this book.

Implied Authority Authority may be implied that reasonably comes from the express authority. *What kind of authority might be reasonably implied this cashier does or does not have?*

Critical Thinking *Why did the court rule in Mr. Nielson's favor even though he acted beyond his authority?*

 Your Reading Note key facts in the text below and look up words you do not understand. Restate difficult ideas in your own words. Go back and reread the text quickly to make sure you did not miss any important detail. Now, you are ready to formulate an opinion.

Scope of Authority Nielson was an agent of Hauser Packing. He had the authority to buy cattle from various suppliers. That authority, however, was severely limited. Christensen was a supplier who knew that Nielson was exceeding his authority. Christensen ignored this and sold the cattle to Nielson anyway. Hauser refused to ratify the deal and Christensen sued Nielson. The court ruled that Nielson could not be made responsible for the deal with Christensen, despite the fact that he had acted on his own when he exceeded his authority.

Christensen v. Nielson, 276 P. 645 (Utah)

Go to **ConnectEd.mcgraw-hill.com** for more case study practice.

Implied authority is additional authority that allows an agent to perform reasonable acts necessary to carry out the express authority. In some states, implied authority is known as **incidental** authority.

> **Example** From the express authority Kellogg granted Eton in the previous example, it would be reasonably understood that Eton has the authority to allow potential buyers to inspect the collection and to play some of the DVDs. These instructions are not written down but are understood as reasonable actions the agent may take.

Sometimes an agent and a principal end up disagreeing about what powers can be implied from the express authority in an agreement. To resolve a dispute, the court says that implied authority must reasonably come from the express authority. In general, a court determines reasonableness by looking at the actions that other agents carry out in similar cases.

Apparent Authority

Apparent authority is actually not authority that an agent has. **Apparent authority is authority that a third party believes an agent has while acting on behalf of the principal.** This belief can arise from the third party's previous dealings with the principal and agent in similar prior transactions. When apparent authority is based on previous dealings, it is known as customary authority. Apparent authority can also be created by law under agency by estoppel. If a principal gives the appearance

Reading Check

Infer *For what reason do you think the law recognizes apparent authority?*

to a third party that an agent has authority on his or her behalf, while in reality the agent does not, the principal can be required to uphold the contract.

Types of Agents

Can an agent hire another agent?

Agents can be distinguished from each other in two ways: on the **extent** of their authority to perform tasks for the principal or on their relationship to other agents (see **Figure 13.1** on page 300).

General Agent

A general agent is an agent who has authority to perform any act within the scope of a business. The manager of a department store, for instance, is a general agent. General agents are also called discretionary agents because they have the right to use their discretion, or judgment, in all matters involving the agency. General agents may decide to hire or fire employees, decide on salaries, purchase supplies, and add or dispose of stock.

Special Agent

A special agent, also called a limited agent, is an agent whose authority is restricted to accomplishing only a specific job or purpose. Many types of employees are considered limited agents. For example, the counter people at fast-food restaurants can take orders and collect money, but they cannot make purchases, sign for deliveries, or hire other employees.

Agents Who Relate to Other Agents

These terms are used to classify agents based on their relationship to other agents rather than to the principal.

Business ETHICS

Contract Negotiations

You are a new attorney at the firm Smith, Jones, & Miller. On your second day of work, your boss tells you that you need to go to a negotiation meeting that your client, Large Corp., is having with another company, Small, Inc. When you arrive at the meeting, you realize that Small, Inc. is selling 400 cars to Large Corp. and that Small, Inc. wants $15,000 per car. You think that this is reasonable and agree to the contract. After you return to the office, you realize that Large Corp. only wanted to pay $14,000 per car and that you made a mistake.

Critical Thinking: Did you have apparent authority?

Figure 13.1 Types of Agents

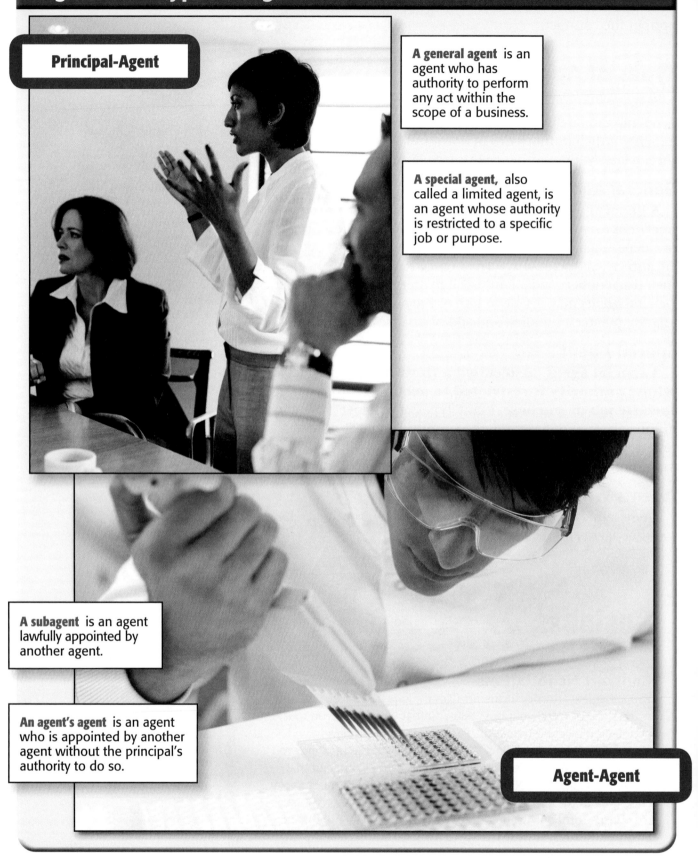

Principal-Agent

A general agent is an agent who has authority to perform any act within the scope of a business.

A special agent, also called a limited agent, is an agent whose authority is restricted to a specific job or purpose.

A subagent is an agent lawfully appointed by another agent.

An agent's agent is an agent who is appointed by another agent without the principal's authority to do so.

Agent-Agent

An agent can be appointed by a principal or another agent. *How does an agent's agent relate to an agent in terms of the principal-agent relationship?*

Subagents **A subagent is an agent lawfully appointed by another agent.** For example, a principal may authorize an agent to appoint a subagent if the agent is too busy or faced with an emergency and needs someone to help or take over.

Agent's Agents **An agent's agent is an agent who is appointed by another agent without the principal's authority to do so.** The principal cannot be held liable for anything done by the agent's agent. In legal terms, the agent actually becomes the principal in relation to the agent's agent.

Coagents If the principal hires two or more agents, they are coagents. Coagents are subject to the authority of the principal unless the principal has authorized one agent to have power over others.

Agency Relationships and International Law

Are agency agreements made in the United States valid in other countries?

Agency law in this country is based on U.S. statutes and appellate decisions. However, agency law can differ in other countries. If you want to do business in other countries, it is therefore important to consult with a local attorney. Some countries may limit who may be an agent to citizens of those countries. The concepts of implied and apparent authority may also be different.

After You Read

Summarize Identify the different types of agents.

SECTION 13.2 ASSESSMENT

Self Check

1. What is the difference between express and implied authority?

2. What is a power of attorney?

3. What is the difference between a subagent and an agent's agent?

Academic Connection

Mathematics Marcus bought a house for $180,000. The real estate broker received a total fee of $8,100 on the amount of sale. According to the brokerage agreement, the real estate broker pays 2.5% out of the total fee to the real estate agent making the sale, and the broker keeps the remainder. What is the net broker fee in percentage form?

CONCEPT **Problem Solving:** To figure out the net broker fee, you need to subtract the agent fee from the total broker fee. To figure out what percentage is the total broker fee, divide the total fee by the sales amount. To write the decimal as a percentage, move the decimal point two places to the right and add a percent sign.

 For more math practice, go to the Math Appendix.

Critical Thinking

Agency and the Responsibilities of an Agent If you have ever worked for someone as a sales clerk, then you were involved in an agency relationship even if you did not know it at the time. What are some concerns that might face a person who has been given the responsibility to do business for somebody else?

Chapter **13** Review and Assessment

Summary

- Agency is a relationship in which one person represents another person in a business transaction with a third party.
- A person hired to represent another person is the agent. The person who hires the agent is the principal. The person the principal and agent do business with is the third party.
- Agents can sign business deals, make contracts, and perform other business tasks for a principal.
- A proprietor-independent contractor relationship is different from a principal-agent relationship in that an independent contractor works for but is not under the control of a proprietor.
- Agency relationships are created by agreement or by operation of law.
- The law can create an agency relationship by estoppel, by ratification, or by statute.

- Actual authority is the real power a principal gives to an agent.
- Apparent authority is authority that a third party believes an agent has while acting on behalf of the principal.
- Express authority comes from the orders, commands, or instructions a principal explicitly gives an agent.
- Implied authority is additional authority that allows an agent to perform reasonable acts necessary to carry out the express authority.
- Power of attorney is a formal writing granting someone authority to act as an agent. Power of attorney can be general, limited, or durable.
- Different types of agents include general agents, special agents, subagents, agents' agents, and coagents.

Vocabulary Builder

1 On a sheet of paper, use each of these terms in a sentence.

Key Terms

- agency
- principal
- agent
- third party
- independent contractor

- agency by estoppel
- actual authority
- express authority
- power of attorney
- implied authority

- apparent authority
- general agent
- special agent
- subagent
- agent's agent

Academic Vocabulary

- genuine
- conduct

- gratuitous
- apparent

- incidental
- extent

Key Points Review

Answer the following questions. Refer to the chapter for additional reinforcement.

2 How are agents different from other types of representatives?

3 What is the difference between the master-servant and proprietor-independent contractor relationship?

4 What is the difference between an agency created by agreement and one created by law?

5 What is agency by estoppel?

6 What is the difference between actual and apparent authority?

7 Distinguish the types of power of attorney.

8 What are the two ways agents can be distinguished from one another?

Standardized Test Practice

9 Read the following excerpts from IRS Publication 937 on the differences between employees and independent contractors, then complete problems 1 and 2.

Training. An employee may be trained to perform services in a particular manner. Independent contractors ordinarily use their own methods and receive no training from the purchasers of their services.

Set hours of work. An employee usually has set hours of work established by an employer. An independent contractor generally can set his or her own work hours.

Full time required. An employee may be required to work or be available full time. An independent contractor can work when, how, and for whom he or she chooses.

Payments. An employee is generally paid by the hour, week, or month. An independent contractor is usually paid by the job or on a straight commission.

Right to fire. An employee can be fired by an employer. An independent contractor cannot be fired so long as he or she meets the specifications of the contract.

1. What hours is an independent contractor required to work?

Ⓐ full time

Ⓑ hours established by an employer

Ⓒ hours he or she chooses

Ⓓ part time

2. Employees are generally paid

Ⓐ whatever they want

Ⓑ by the job

Ⓒ on a straight commission

Ⓓ by the hour, week, or month

 Test-Taking Strategies Read test directions carefully and pay attention to details.

Apply and Debate

Read the following scenarios. Get together with other students in pairs or groups of three and take a position on each scenario. Debate your position in class with students taking the opposite position or prepare a written argument justifying your position.

⑩ Snowmobile Sale

Sheila hired her friend Michael to sell her snowmobile, and to do "whatever it takes" to sell it for $1,000. He sold it, allowing the buyer to pay in three months.

You Debate *Did Michael have authority to let the buyer delay the payment?*

⑪ When Is a Clerk Not a Clerk?

Kyle went to a hardware store to purchase a saw. The clerk at the counter said he was a friend of the owner, who had gone to lunch, and asked Kyle to wait for the owner to return. But Kyle was in a hurry, so he paid and left. He tried to return the tool the next day, but the owner told him it was non-returnable.

You Debate *Should Kyle be able to return the saw?*

⑫ Carpenter Signs for Package

Ansar, an independent carpenter, was building a cabinet at the Williams's home. Mrs. Williams left to pick up her child. The doorbell rang, so Ansar opened it and signed for a package delivery. Mrs. Williams returned and told him that she had cancelled that order and did not want the package.

You Debate *Is Ansar responsible for paying for the goods?*

⑬ Independent Contractor

Uma hired an independent plumber to repair her dishwasher. The plumber repaired the motor and did not check any of the other parts. Uma felt the plumber should have checked all of the mechanical parts as a part of the repair service.

You Debate *Does Uma have a right to tell the plumber how to repair the dishwasher?*

⑭ Sales Mistake

Mark was a new salesperson in an electronics store. He sold a TV to a customer and accidentally gave a 35% discount. His manager told him to be careful next time, but did not contact the customer to correct the sale. The next day, a friend of the original customer came in and wanted to buy the same TV with the same 35% discount.

You Debate *Should the second customer be allowed to receive the same discount?*

Case Study Practice– Amedas, Inc. v. Brown

15 **Independent Contractor or Agent?** During the early 1980s, Craig Allen and his wife formed Amedas, Inc. to sell medical goods manufactured by Designs for Vision, Inc. (DVI). Mr. Allen contacted a former coworker, Edward Brown, about selling DVI goods for Amedas. Mr. Brown entered into a sales representative agreement with Amedas.

The agreement provided that Mr. Brown was to devote full time and to promote the best interests of Amedas. The agreement also stated that Mr. Brown was not allowed to represent any other company during the life of the agreement and that Mr. Brown would receive a ten percent commission for his sales.

In 1985, DVI told Mr. Allen that Amedas would no longer be able to sell DVI products. Mr. Brown had secretly been meeting with DVI about selling DVI on his own, and DVI decided to give him the exclusive sales contract. Amedas then sued Mr. Brown, claiming he violated his sales agreement. At issue before the court was whether Mr. Brown was an independent contractor or agent of Amedas.

Source: Amedas, Inc. v. Brown, 505 So.2d 1091 (Fla. Ct. App. 1987)

Practice Was Mr. Brown an agent of Amedas?

16 **Ethics**
←?→ Application _____

Customer Freebies You work in a camera store. Your manager allows you to entice customers with two free add-ons to help make a sale. A customer of yours is ready to buy an expensive camera on which you will get a big commission. You offer a one-year warranty and batteries for free. The customer asks for a free carrying bag and you agree, just to make the sale.

◆ Is it ethical for you to offer more free items than you are allowed to make in order to make the sale? Explain.

17 Think back to the Legal Briefs feature you read at the beginning of the chapter. Then write a brief argument either for or against government mandated paid vacation days. Cite a research study to support your argument. For example, if you argue for paid vacation days, you might cite a study that shows time off improves employee health, which cuts costs for health insurance. Or, if you're against government backed paid vacation days for employees, you might cite statistics that show the cost to small business. Cite the study you used to support your position.

Legal Briefs

Employment Agreements
The implications of non-compete clauses.

If you're a business owner, you don't want valuable employees quitting and taking their expertise to a competitor. Enter the non-compete clause in employment contracts.

Non-compete clauses can be worthwhile for both management and workers. Businesses with non-compete clauses tend to invest more in training and benefits, such as higher pay, to retain talented employees. Employees reap the benefits and businesses keep the valuable employees.

Like many good ideas, though, non-compete agreements have proved troublesome. One restaurant, with multiple franchises in different states, made every worker, even minimum-wage employees, agree that for two years after leaving, they would not work for a restaurant that sold even a small number of similar items. Nor could they work in food service within three miles of the restaurant's many locations.

Different states have different opinions about non-compete clauses. Texas, Georgia, and New Jersey courts are suspicious of non-compete clauses. Connecticut, Florida, Indiana, and New York tend to look on non-competes as legitimate business tools. Many other states are looking at the issue and considering legislation to add clarity to the issue.

The Agency Relationship Principals trust their agents to be loyal to them, and agents trust their principals to compensate them fairly. *What is a relationship based on trust called?*

Duties and Liability in Agency Relationships

What You'll Learn

◆ Identify the duties of agents to principals.

◆ Identify the duties of principals to agents.

◆ Describe the nature of contract liability in agency law.

◆ Explain the doctrine of *respondeat superior* in relation to tort liability.

Why It's Important

Understanding the duties and liability of agents and principals will help you in the world of work.

Reading Guide

Before You Read

Connect Have you ever had to pay money out of your own pocket while running an errand for someone?

Focus on Ideas

Agency relationships are based on trust.

Take Notes

Go to connectED. mcgraw-hill.com to download a graphic organizer you can use to take notes as you read this section.

Duties in Agency Relationships

Principal's Duties to Agent	Agent's Duties to Principal
	Obedience

Key Terms

You will learn these legal words and expressions in this chapter. You can also find these terms in *Black's Law Dictionary* or in an online legal dictionary.

- fiduciary relationship
- double representation
- self-dealing
- compensation
- reimbursement
- indemnification
- respondeat superior
- nondelegable duty

Academic Vocabulary

You will find these words in your readings and in your tests. Look them up in a dictionary and familiarize yourself with them.

- loyal
- adhere
- cooperation

Agent's Duties to the Principal

Suppose you are an employee in charge of a project. What are your duties?

Principals trust their agents with their business, property, money, and reputation. This is why an agency relationship is considered a fiduciary relationship. **A fiduciary relationship is a relationship based on trust.** The word comes from the Latin word for faith. A good way to remember this term is to think of the name people often give a faithful dog: Fido.

The law imposes five fiduciary duties that an agent owes a principal: obedience, good faith, loyalty, an accounting, and good judgment. If the agent does not uphold these duties or goes beyond them, the agent, not the principal, is liable for any resulting injury such as a lawsuit from a third party.

Obedience

Obedience means that the agent must obey all reasonable commands that lie within the scope of the agency agreement.

As You Read

Predict Does a principal have to pay you for any expenses or losses you incur while working as an agent?

Global Law

Doing Business in Israel

If a foreign company wants to market products in Israel, it can set up one of two different types of relationships with a party in Israel. Which one to choose depends on how much control the foreign company wants over its representative in Israel and how much liability it is willing to accept.

Commercial Agent

The first option is for the company to contract for a commercial agent in Israel. In Israel, an agent has the authority to act in the foreign company's name and bind the company to any contract the agent feels is proper. However, the agent is also required to follow any directives given by the foreign company.

Under Israel's Agency Act, the agent's obligations include:

1 Loyalty

2 Promotion of the interests of the foreign company

3 Not acting as an agent for competing companies

In return, the foreign company agrees to:

1 Provide just compensation to the agent

2 Insure the agent for any liabilities

Distributor

The second option is to contract with a distributor in Israel to market the products. A distributor is a lot like an independent contractor. The distributor in Israel buys the product from the foreign company and then resells the product in Israel under the distributor's own name. A distributor is responsible for promoting the product and getting liability insurance, but is not barred from selling competing products.

Across Cultures: Becoming a Citizen

The Israeli government has passed the Law of Return in Israel. The law allows any Jew, anywhere in the world, to become a citizen of Israel simply by moving there. Citizenship is automatically granted upon arrival in Israel.

Critical Thinking *Is the situation in Israel much different from the United States?*

Even a gratuitous agent must follow instructions. If an agent disobeys instructions, he or she becomes liable to the principal for any resulting loss. However, an agent is not obligated to follow a principal's instructions to do anything illegal or immoral. For example, if a manager tells a salesperson to lie about a product's features, the agent may refuse to do so.

Good Faith

The duty of good faith means that the agent must deal honestly with other parties and have no intent to seek personal advantage. The agent must not commit fraud. Good faith also requires the agent to notify the principal of all matters that involve the agency.

Loyalty

Agents must be **loyal** to their principal. They must not work at the same time for one of their principal's competitors or for their own personal benefit. **Double representation is when an agent works simultaneously for two competing principals. Self-dealing is when agents make deals that benefit themselves rather than their principals.**

Duty to Account

An agent who handles money for the principal must keep a record and account for every cent. The agent must also keep the principal's money safe and separate from other people's money, including his or her own. This is done using trust accounts, which are separate banking accounts from the agent's personal or office accounts. If the agent mixes personal money with the principal's money and cannot figure out whose money is whose, the entire amount of money belongs to the principal.

Judgment

Agents must be skillful and use good judgment when working for the principal. However, agents are not perfect. Even the most well-informed agents make mistakes from time to time. For this reason, agents are not held liable for honest mistakes if they have performed to the best of their abilities.

Principal's Duties to the Agent

If you are an agent, what can you do if your principal does not pay you?

Principals also have obligations in dealing with their agents. These duties are compensation, reimbursement, indemnification, and cooperation. If a principal does not **adhere** to these duties, he or she may be liable to the agent or the third party.

Compensation

An agent has the right to receive compensation from a principal. **Compensation is fair payment for the job performed.** The principal must pay the compensation agreed to in the contract.

If no amount is stated, the principal must pay a reasonable amount, determined by checking the usual amount paid to other agents in the same line of work. The duty of compensation does not apply if the agent is a gratuitous agent who works for free.

Reimbursement and Indemnification

Agents have the right to reimbursement. **Reimbursement is payment for money spent by an agent on behalf of a principal.** Agents also have the right to indemnification. **Indemnification is payment for losses suffered by an agent because of a principal's instructions.**

Cooperation

The principal gives an agent the duty to perform certain tasks. The principal must not interfere with the performance of those tasks. This is called **cooperation**. If the principal makes the agent's job difficult or impossible, he or she has breached the duty of cooperation.

Reimbursement Agents have the right to be repaid for spending their own money on a principal's behalf. *What factors should be considered regarding whether the person in the photo should be reimbursed for gas money?*

Example Pam Phillips hired Jason Abrams and told him that he had exclusive rights to sell her company's video games online to all customers. But she said that to keep his job he had to sell $100,000 of product per quarter. Later, Abrams learned that Phillips had hired 15 other agents to sell the same video games online. This competition made it nearly impossible for Abrams to meet his quota. Abrams could argue successfully that Phillips had violated her duty to cooperate.

Who Has Liability?

If you are a third party and something goes wrong with a deal you made, who do you take to court, the agent or the principal?

In business, mistakes happen, people disagree, and sometimes people are hurt in accidents. When such things happen, one party may experience a monetary, physical, or other loss and want compensation for the injury. Injury is any loss that a person experiences, not just physical harm. Who is liable for an injury depends on two questions:

- Are the parties in a principal-agent or proprietor-independent contractor relationship?
- Does the liability concern a contractual matter or a tort?

The answer to the first question is important. However, the labels the parties use to describe themselves do not matter. Instead, the court considers numerous questions to determine the actual status of the relationship:

- Does the hiring person make available the tools for the worker?
- Is the worker paid hourly?
- Does the principal set the worker's hours?
- Is the worker employed only by the hiring person?
- Is the business of the worker the same as the business of the hiring person?
- Does the hiring person have the authority to hire or fire other workers?
- Does the hiring person supervise the tasks of the worker?
- Is little skill needed to do the worker's job?

The more questions with "yes" answers, the more likely it is a principal-agent relationship. If so, liability follows the rules that apply to principals and agents for contracts and torts. The more "no" answers, the more likely a proprietor-independent contractor relationship exists and liability follows the rules for this type of relationship.

Contractual Liability of Principals

When an agent makes a contract on behalf of a principal, it is just as if the principal had acted directly. The agent is said to "stand in the shoes of the principal." The law thus usually holds principals liable for proven injuries in contractual disputes.

Contractual Liability of Agents

Three situations can occur in which an agent becomes liable for an injury to a third party.

- The agent has made an agreement or performed tasks beyond his or her authority to do so.
- The principal is a minor or does not have the capacity to sign a contract, yet the agent has not disclosed this fact to the third party.
- The principal is undisclosed, and the third party cannot identify the principal.

The third situation often arises when a principal does not want to be identified, such as a celebrity principal. If a breach of contract occurs, the third party has no choice but to hold the agent liable or attempt to identify the principal to hold liable. However, the third party may not hold both of them liable.

Contractual Liability of Independent Contractors

In general, independent contractors are not agents because they are not authorized to make agreements or conduct business for the proprietor. However, if the contractor makes an agreement without the proprietor's authority, the contractor is liable. If the proprietor has authorized the contractor to act as his or her agent, the same contractual liability rules apply as in an agency relationship.

Reading Check

Analyze Why is the principal usually responsible for contractual and tort liability?

Example Mister P., a famous rock star, hired a real estate agent to find him a home without revealing his identity. The agent found a house and told the seller that the buyer wanted to conceal his identity. After the contract was signed, however, Mister P. refused to buy the house. The seller can attempt to discover the identity of Mr. P. to sue him, or the seller can sue the agent. However, Mr. P. must indemnify the agent for any money paid out to satisfy the judgment since the agent acted on Mr. P.'s behalf.

Tort Liability of Principals

All people are responsible for their own torts. However, in legal terms, the law holds a person who hires another person responsible for the torts of the hired person if the torts are committed on the job. This is called vicarious liability. Vicarious liability is based on the principle of respondeat superior (see **Figure 14.1** on page 314). **Respondeat superior is a legal doctrine that holds that the master is responsible for the torts of his or her servants.** The law extends the master-servant relationship to the agent-principal relationship because the agent is acting on behalf of the principal. For example, a department store may be liable if a security guard falsely imprisons a suspected shoplifter.

CYBERLAW

Iceland Telecom, Ltd. v. Information Systems & Networks Corp.
268 F.Supp.2d 585 (D. Md. 2003)

Iceland Telecom entered into a contract with ISN Global Communications (Global) for Internet telecommunication services. Global ceased to exist as a company in 2001. Iceland Telecom then tried to sue Global's parent company, Information Systems & Networks Corp. (ISN), for breach of contract. A parent company is a company that owns or controls another company (called a subsidiary). Iceland Telecom argued that Global was an agent of ISN and that ISN could be held liable for Global's breach of contract. Iceland Telecom argued there was apparent authority between the two because Global had sent documents with ISN listed at the top and had told Iceland Telecom to contact ISN if there was a problem when Global's offices were closed.

Ruling and Resolution
The United States District Court in Maryland held that Global was not an agent of ISN. For apparent authority to exist, Iceland Telecom must prove that ISN, not Global, misled Iceland Telecom into believing that Global was its agent. This was not present in the facts of the case.

Critical Thinking Should parent companies be liable for the actions of their subsidiaries?

Figure 14.1 Respondeat Superior

Master-Servant Relationship An employer (master) who has control over an employee (servant) has entered a legal situation that may make the employer liable for the torts of the employee.

Scope of Employment As long as the employee is acting within the scope of employment, the employer is liable for the actions of the employee.

Liability If an employee commits a tort, such as negligence, while on the job, the employer would be held liable.

According to the doctrine of respondeat superior, a master is responsible for the torts of his or her servants. *What is the reasoning behind this?*

A principal may escape vicarious liability if it can be shown that the agent was not acting within the scope of employment. For instance, the principal is not responsible for a delivery agent who has an accident while driving on personal business.

Tort Liability of Proprietors

A proprietor can sometimes be liable for the torts of an independent contractor. This is true if the proprietor's own actions lead to the injury. For example, a proprietor is liable if he or she is negligent when checking qualifications and hires someone who is incompetent. This is called negligent hiring. Another doctrine is called negligent retention. This arises when a proprietor fails to fire a contractor after learning that he or she is incompetent. In the meantime, the contractor injures someone. In these cases, the proprietor is held liable for his or her own negligence, not the actions of the independent contractor.

A proprietor can also be open to liability if a contractor has been hired to perform a task that involves a nondelegable duty. **A nondelegable duty is a duty that cannot be delegated, or transferred, to another party.** For example, a landlord has a nondelegable duty to maintain a building. The landlord can hire an independent contractor to do repairs, but cannot pass on the duty and is thus still liable if someone is injured due to poor maintenance.

After You Read

Summarize List the principal's duties to the agent.

SECTION 14.1 ASSESSMENT

Self Check

1. What is a fiduciary relationship?

2. What is the difference between reimbursement and indemnification?

3. What is the difference between negligent hiring and negligent retention?

Academic Connection

Mathematics Ann Finke is a real estate agent who sells real estate at a 7½% straight commission. Last week her sales totaled $180,000. What would her commission be? How much would it be if she earned 8%, and what is the difference between the two rates?

CONCEPT **Number and Operations:** To find the amount of the commission you would use the following formula:

Total Sales × Commission Rate (remember to change the percent to a fraction) = Commission

 Math For more math practice, go to the Math Appendix.

Critical Thinking

When Do You Give In? Suppose that your boss gave you $1,200 in cash and told you to buy a plasma screen television for his office.

Now, suppose that you found a discount plasma screen television at a store for $1,100. Can you keep the difference and use the extra $100 as your own pocket money? Why or why not?

Termination of Agency Relationships

What You'll Learn

◆ Determine when an agency relationship is terminated by operation of law.

◆ Explain when an agency relationship is terminated by act of the parties.

◆ Identify the individuals who are entitled to notice that an agency relationship has ended.

Why It's Important

You need to know when an agency relationship ends so you know when your rights and duties end.

Reading Guide

Before You Read

Connect Suppose you are a writer, musician, or actor with an agent who has not found you work in months. How can you get out of your contract with the agent?

Focus on Ideas

Agency relationships come to an end because the parties end them on their own or because the law ends them.

Take Notes

Go to connectED. mcgraw-hill.com to download a graphic organizer you can use to take notes as you read this section.

Ways to Terminate an Agency — Operation of Law

Key Terms

You will learn these legal words and expressions in this chapter. You can also find these terms in *Black's Law Dictionary* or in an online legal dictionary.

- actual notice
- notice by publication

Academic Vocabulary

You will find these words in your readings and in your tests. Look them up in a dictionary and familiarize yourself with them.

- benefit
- mutual
- irrevocable

Ways to Terminate an Agency Relationship

If you were unhappy with an agent, how could you terminate your agreement?

If an agency is contractual, the usual rules that apply to ending contracts apply to ending agency relationships. Agency relationships can be terminated either by operation of law or by the acts of the parties.

Termination by Operation of Law

A major change can affect the parties involved in an agency relationship or alter its operation. When this happens, a court may say that the agency relationship has ended by operation of law.

The death of the agent or the principal will end the agency relationship.

The bankruptcy of the principal ends an agency. This is because it closes down all the principal's ordinary contracts. Bankruptcy also gives a trustee title to the principal's property for the **benefit** of creditors.

Bankruptcy of the agent sometimes ends the agency. This is true if the agent has used his or her own funds to do the principal's business. If not, there is no reason to terminate the agency because the agent may be able to continue doing business.

An agency can also end due to impossibility of performance. This happens if the necessary subject matter is destroyed. For example, if an agent is authorized to sell a boat for the principal, but the boat sinks in a storm, the loss of the boat terminates the agency. Performance can also become impossible if the agent or principal becomes incapacitated or ill.

As You Read

Predict Do agencies always end by agreement?

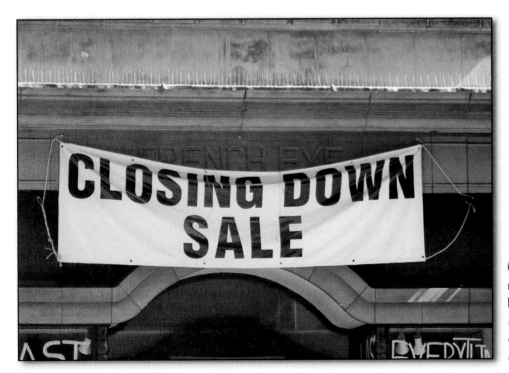

Bankruptcy An agency relationship is terminated by bankruptcy of the principal. *Does bankruptcy of the agent terminate an agency relationship?*

Reading Check

Discuss *Why might a principal and agent agree to end an agency before a task is completed?*

The agency is ended if the agent's objective becomes illegal. If only part of the agent's activities becomes illegal, then only that part of the authority ends. The authority to perform the legal activities is still in effect.

Termination by Acts of the Parties

Most agency relationships end when the parties have fully carried out their duties. The relationship can also end by **mutual** consent. Certain acts by either party can also end the relationship.

An agency relationship ends through completion of performance if an agent accomplishes the specific result that the principal desired.

The principal and the agent may end the agency by mutual agreement at a certain time. It could be a specific date or at any time they want. This can be binding even if the task is not done, as long as it is mutual.

The agent's withdrawal ends an agency. An agent may withdraw from the agency at any time. However, if the agency is terminated by the agent before the specified time in the agreement or causes a breach of contract, the principal can sue the agent for damages.

📄 Case Study – Morgan Associates, Inc. v. Midwest Mutual Insurance Co.

Critical Thinking *Does restricting an agent's business terminate an agency relationship?*

Flex Your Reading **Note key facts in the text below and look up words you do not understand. Restate difficult ideas in your own words. Go back and reread the text quickly to make sure you did not miss any important detail. Now, you are ready to formulate an opinion.**

Unfair Restrictions? Morgan Associates, Inc. (Morgan) was an insurance agency specializing in motorcycle and high-risk automobile insurance. It sold insurance on behalf of two companies, Colonial Insurance Co. of California (Colonial) and Midwest Mutual Insurance Co. (Midwest).

For years Morgan sold insurance for both companies without any problems. However, in early 1992, Colonial told Morgan that Morgan would no longer be able to write any new policies for Colonial until further notice. Colonial said that Morgan's clients were filing too many claims. Colonial told Morgan it could renew policies and Colonial would review the situation on a monthly basis.

In late 1992, Midwest also restricted Morgan's ability to write new policies for the same reason: its clients were filing too many claims. Morgan could renew current policies, and Midwest would continue the agency relationship in hopes that Morgan could improve its numbers.

Morgan then sued Colonial and Midwest, arguing that the two companies had constructively terminated the agency relationship contrary to Minnesota law by restricting Morgan's ability to write new policies.

Morgan Associates, Inc. v. Midwest Mutual Insurance Co., 519 N.W.2d 499 (Minn. Ct. App. 1994)

 Go to **ConnectEd.mcgraw-hill.com** for more case study practice.

The agent's discharge can also end the agency. The principal may end the agency at any time by discharging, or firing, the agent. However, the principal may not be able to fire the agent if the agent has an interest in the subject matter of the agency. This is called **irrevocable** agency, meaning that the agency cannot be revoked until the agent is paid in full.

Giving Notice to Third Parties

If a third party has never heard of the agency relationship, the principal does not need to give notice. Otherwise, a principal must give notice to all third parties who have done business with the principal through the agent or who know of the agency relationship. A principal who does not notify third parties may be liable for future acts of the agent. The type of notice given to a third party depends on how business relations have been carried out. There are two types of notices:

- **Actual notice is formal notice given directly to a party, usually using certified mail with a receipt.** Actual notice is required when the third party has given credit to the principal through the agent.

- **Notice by publication is notice usually given by publishing a notice in a local newspaper.** When the third party has never given credit but has done a cash business with the agent, or knows that other persons have dealt with the principal only on a cash basis through the agent, notice by publication is sufficient.

After You Read

Summarize List the ways an agency relationship can be terminated by operation of law.

SECTION 14.2 ASSESSMENT

Self Check

1. What are the two ways an agency relationship can be terminated?

2. When is an agency relationship terminated by an act of the parties?

3. What parties are entitled to notice that an agency has ended?

Academic Connection

English Language Arts Writers, musicians, actors, and athletes often hire talent agents to find jobs and negotiate contracts for them. Assume you are an artist or athlete contracting an agent to represent you. Write up a set of conditions the agent has to meet or you can terminate the contract. For example, the agent has to find you work within a particular period of time.

Critical Thinking

Notice of Termination Suppose you have just ended the agency relationship with your boss. Your job had been to buy stock on credit from a wide variety of suppliers, including Freshwater Industries, Oppenheimer, Inc., and Harrisburg Supplies. You have also done a consistent cash business with Thompson Inc. and with Kennedy Industries. You also intended to call on Georgetown Ltd. the next day to buy some stock. Nobody at Georgetown has ever laid eyes on you. Who is entitled to actual notice, who is entitled to notice by publication, and who is not entitled to any notice?

Summary

Section 14.1 Duties and Liability in Agency Relationships

◆ An agent's duties to a principal include obedience, good faith, loyalty, an accounting, and good judgment and skill.

◆ Agents are liable for fulfilling fiduciary duties.

◆ Principal's duties to an agent include compensation, reimbursement, indemnification, and cooperation.

◆ Respondeat superior is a legal doctrine that holds that a master is responsible for the torts of his or her servants.

◆ Negligent hiring occurs when a proprietor hires a person who is incompetent.

◆ Negligent retention occurs when a proprietor fails to fire a contractor after learning that he or she is incompetent.

◆ A nondelegable duty is a duty that cannot be delegated, or transferred, to another party.

Section 14.2 Termination of Agency Relationships

◆ Agency relationships can be terminated by operation of law or by the acts of the parties.

◆ Agency relationships can be ended by operation of law in the following circumstances: the death of the principal or the agent, bankruptcy, impossibility of performance, and illegality.

◆ Agency relationships can be ended by the acts of the parties in the following circumstances: completion of performance, mutual agreement, the agent's withdrawal, and the agent's discharge.

◆ Third parties who have done business with the principal through an agent or who knew of the agency relationship should receive a notice that it has ended.

◆ Actual notice is required when the third party has given credit to the principal through the agent.

◆ Notice by publication is sufficient when business has been done only by cash (not credit) between third parties and agents or principals.

Vocabulary Builder

❶ On a sheet of paper, use each of these terms in a sentence.

Key Terms

- fiduciary relationship
- double representation
- self-dealing
- compensation
- reimbursement
- indemnification
- respondeat superior
- nondelegable duty
- actual notice
- notice by publication

Academic Vocabulary

- loyal
- adhere
- cooperation
- benefit
- mutual
- irrevocable

Key Points Review

Answer the following questions. Refer to the chapter for additional reinforcement.

2 What duties does an agent owe to the principal?

3 What are the three situations in which an agent becomes liable for an injury to a third party.

4 What is the doctrine of respondeat superior?

5 What is a nondelegable duty?

6 When is an agency relationship terminated by operation of law?

7 Does bankruptcy of the agent or the principal always end the agency relationship?

8 What might happen if the agency is terminated by the agent before the specified time in the agreement?

9 What two types of notices can a principal send a third party that an agency has ended?

Standardized Test Practice

10 Read the following excerpt from Carter v. Gugliuzzi (Vt. 1998) on an agent's duties to a principal and complete questions 1 and 2.

Ana Barreto and Flavia Gugliuzzi asked Ruth Bennett, a real estate agent who worked for Smith Bell Real Estate, to sell their house in Underhill, Vermont. Diana Carter, a California resident, visited the house as a potential buyer. Bennett worked under the supervision of David Crane, an officer of Smith Bell. Crane knew, but did not disclose to Bennett or Carter, the house was subject to frequent and severe winds, that a window had blown in years earlier, and that other houses in the area had suffered wind damage. Crane knew of this because he lived in the area. Carter bought the house. Several months later, high winds blew in a number of windows and damaged the property. Carter filed a suit in a Vermont state court against Smith Bell and others, alleging fraud. She argued in part that Crane's knowledge of the winds was imputable to Smith Bell. Smith Bell responded that Crane's knowledge was obtained outside the scope of employment.

1. Who is the injured party in this case?

Ⓐ Smith Bell Real Estate

Ⓑ Ruth Bennett

Ⓒ Diana Carter

Ⓓ David Crane

2. What is Smith Bell Real Estate's defense in this case?

Ⓐ Smith Bell did not know about the weather conditions in the area.

Ⓑ Smith Bell was not asked about the weather conditions.

Ⓒ Smith Bell did not have a legal obligation to disclose knowledge about the weather conditions.

Ⓓ The employee's knowledge about weather conditions was obtained outside the scope of employment.

 Test-Taking Strategies When an essay question tells you to contrast, it is telling you to point out the differences between two or more things.

Apply and Debate

Read the following scenarios. Get together with other students in pairs or groups of three and take a position on each scenario. Debate your position in class with students taking the opposite position or prepare a written argument justifying your position.

⑪ Sharing Unexpected Expenses

Jackie, a jewelry artist, was attending a one-day fair in another city. She told two other jewelry makers that she would sell their work at the fair in exchange for a commission, but she wanted them to share her gas and travel expenses too. After the fair was over, Jackie was tired and decided to stay in a motel for $109.

You Debate   *Can Jackie ask the other artists to share in the cost of the hotel?*

⑫ Multiple Clients

Isaiah hired a public relations company to promote his new business venture. Unknown to Isaiah, the company already represented one of his competitors, who asked not to be revealed.

You Debate   *Is the public relations company obligated to tell Isaiah that it also represents his competitor?*

⑬ Tennis Pro with a Broken Arm

Shinea hired Franklin, a right-handed tennis pro, to teach at her tennis camp. Unfortunately, Franklin broke his right arm before the camp started. Frank insisted to Shinea that he could still teach tennis using his left arm.

You Debate   *Can Shinea discharge Frank because of his incapacitation to teach tennis?*

⑭ Delivery Accident

Jorge is a senior in high school. He also works delivering pizzas using his personal car. While delivering a pizza one day, Jorge visited at a friend's house. While parking, he hit another car and damaged it. He continued to deliver the pizza.

You Debate   *Is the employer responsible for the damage Jorge caused the other car?*

⑮ Stock Market Crash

Rena Pellas transferred $100,000 to her stockbroker, Bill Andrews. With Pellas's permission, Andrews invested the money in risky stocks. The portfolio soon rose to $140,000. However, the stock suddenly fell, and Andrews could not react fast enough to prevent his client from losing $50,000.

You Debate   *Can Andrews be held liable for Pellas's loss?*

Case Study Practice – Nationwide Mutual Insurance Co. v. Prioleau

16 What Is Implied Agency? On April 25, 1997, Julius Prioleau applied for auto insurance with Nationwide Mutual Insurance Company for himself and his wife, Paula. Ms. Prioleau was not with Mr. Prioleau at the time. While at the insurance agent's office, Mr. Prioleau declined to purchase additional uninsured and underinsured automobile coverage and signed a form stating his decision.

On February 3, 1998, Ms. Prioleau was involved in an automobile accident. She suffered bodily injuries in the accident and made a claim against the other driver. The other insurance company paid Ms. Prioleau the amount allowed under that driver's policy, but it did not cover all of her medical expenses. Ms. Prioleau then made a claim with Nationwide for underinsured motorist insurance. Nationwide claimed that she did not have underinsured coverage because her husband, acting as her agent, had declined it. Ms. Prioleau argued that she did not decline the coverage, and her husband could not make that decision for her.

Source: National Mutual Insurance Co. v. Prioleau, 597 S.E.2d 165 (S.C. Ct. App. 2004)

Practice Was Julius Prioleau the agent of Paula Prioleau?

17 Ethics Application

Hiring a Friend You are the manager of a clothing store. You must hire a new buyer who gets to go to New York and Paris to select inventory for your store. There are five candidates, including your friend. She has less experience than the others. However, since you know her, you believe she can learn the business quickly.

◆ Would it be ethical for you to hire your friend? Explain your reasons.

18 Think back to the Legal Briefs feature you read at the beginning of the chapter. Imagine you are a minimum-wage employee at a large company with locations in many states. Write a letter to the fictitious company's president expressing your opinion of non-compete agreements. In your correspondence, explain the problems that non-compete agreements cause in industries such as food service that have high worker turnover. Then write a reply that the business owner might make to the employee.

15 Employment Law

Legal Briefs

A Social Media Policy Is a Business Necessity

Don't be careless with social media.

Social media is trending with the business community. Social media helps businesses communicate with customers and suppliers. Using social media also has risks, though. It could be used to disclose trade secrets and other business information that should be kept private, for example. This is why every business must have a Social Media Policy (SMP). An SMP is a legal document written by the employer for employees that spells out what they can and cannot do when using electronic communication devices, formats, websites, and other electronic messaging techniques, such as blogs, text messaging, tweeting, Skype transmission, and email.

An SMP lets employees know what is and is not acceptable online behavior. Not acceptable, for example, is using social media to write about private business matters or to gossip about another employee. An SMP must be written clearly in language that is precise, exact, plain, and explicit. Employees must be able to read and comprehend the policy. Employers also must inform employees their online activity will be monitored.

Equal Opportunity It is against the law to discriminate against someone on the basis of race or gender. *What other forms of discrimination are illegal?*

What You'll Learn

◆ Discuss the employer-employee relationship.

◆ Define employment-at-will.

◆ Name the exceptions to employment-at-will.

◆ Explain the collective bargaining process.

◆ Describe the laws that regulate labor unions.

Why It's Important

Understanding employment-at-will and wrongful discharge will help you protect your rights as an employee.

Reading Guide

Before You Read

Connect Has anyone in your family ever belonged to or dealt with a labor union?

Focus on Ideas

Employers and employees are free to end the employment relationship any time they choose.

Take Notes

Go to **connectED.mcgraw-hill.com** to download a graphic organizer you can use to take notes as you read this section.

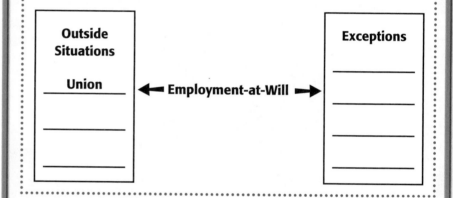

Key Terms

You will learn these legal words and expressions in this chapter. You can also find these terms in *Black's Law Dictionary* or in an online legal dictionary.

- employment-at-will
- union
- implied contract
- public policy tort
- implied covenant
- collective bargaining

Academic Vocabulary

You will find these words in your readings and in your tests. Look them up in a dictionary and familiarize yourself with them.

- exception
- corruption
- solicit

Employment-at-Will

Can you be fired from a job for no reason?

Most employees in the United States work in states that follow a rule called employment-at-will. **Employment-at-will means that an employer or employee can end an employment relationship at any time, for any reason or for no reason, with or without notice.** The doctrine is based on the principle that each party should be free to end employment at any time without penalty. Still, some employees fall outside of this rule. Some also benefit from certain **exceptions** that the courts have created recently.

Situations outside Employment-at-Will

Certain situations fall outside the rule of employment-at-will. These situations include unionized employees, employees with individual employment contracts, and protected classes of employees.

Unionized Employees **A union is an organization of employees formed to promote the welfare of its members.** Employers cannot hire or fire union members at will, because employees who are members of labor unions have specific procedures built into their employment agreements. Union members are guaranteed certain wages, conditions, and benefits, but they are not free to negotiate their own contracts.

Employees with Individual Employment Contracts Some employees, such as sports stars and entertainment figures, negotiate their own individual employment contracts.

Some businesses and educational institutions also establish contracts for certain classes for employees, such as senior officers in a company or faculty members at a college.

Employment contracts can benefit employees, but they can also prevent people from leaving a job when they want and working for whomever they want.

Situations Outside Employment-at-Will Employment-at-will does not apply to entertainers, sports figures, and executives who negotiate their own individual employment contracts. *What other types of employees are not subject to employment-at-will?*

As You Read
Predict Can you be fired from a job for no reason?

Vocabulary You can find vocabulary definitions in the **Key Terms** glossary and Academic Vocabulary glossary in the back of this book.

Protected Classes of Employees Groups such as women, racial minorities, people with disabilities, and veterans are often referred to as protected classes. Protected classes of employees cannot be fired for a reason based on their race, color, creed, national origin, or gender. The law also protects workers from being fired based solely on their age.

Exceptions to Employment-at-Will

Despite the protections noted above, many workers remain at-will employees in most situations. Ending employment relationships under employment-at-will can lead to injustice. As a result, many courts now challenge employment-at-will by ruling against the company or the firm which has discharged an employee. However, to challenge a firing in an at-will state, an employee must base his or her argument on one of the following grounds: promissory estoppel, implied contract, public policy tort, or implied covenant. Lawsuits that challenge employment-at-will are called wrongful discharge or unjust dismissal suits.

Promissory Estoppel Promissory estoppel bars an employer from taking back certain types of promises. To build a solid case on promissory estoppel, a terminated employee must show four elements:

- The employer made a promise that the employee reasonably expected to rely on.
- The employee actually relied on the promise and changed his or her position as a result.
- The employee would not have acted as he or she did, if the employer had not made the promise.
- The employee was harmed (usually in a financial way) by the employer's refusal to honor the promise.

If all of these elements exist, then the court may prevent the employer from denying responsibility for the loss suffered by the employee as a result of that reliance.

Implied Contract Another exception to employment-at-will is when an implied contract exists. **An implied contract is a contract that exists when an employer has said, written, or done something to lead an employee to reasonably believe that he or she is not an at-will employee.** When determining whether an employer has created an implied contract, the court can look at all of the facts involving the employment relationship, not just the oral promises made by the employer.

Public Policy Tort Public policy holds that no one should be allowed to do anything that harms the public. **Public policy tort is a legal theory that permits a discharged employee to bring a wrongful discharge lawsuit against a former employer based on the argument that the firing somehow hurts the public at large.** Many states now permit a fired employee to recover compensatory and punitive damages in public policy tort if he or she can prove that the firing violated public policy.

Reading Check

Discuss *How might firing an employee violate public policy?*

Implied Covenant **Implied covenant** is a legal argument that holds that any employment relationship is based on an implied promise that the employer and the employee will be fair and honest with one another. Unlike an implied contract, an implied covenant exists simply because the employment relationship exists. If a state has adopted the implied covenant rule, then both the employer and the employee have the duty to treat one another with honesty and fair play.

Unionized Employees

What laws protect you if you are a member of a labor union?

In the past, employees were at the will of their employers on an individual basis. During the Industrial Revolution, workers banded together into labor unions to demand better working conditions.

Global Law

Collective Bargaining in Poland

Poland is an ex-communist country in Central Europe. During the 1980s, there was labor turmoil in the country that led to the establishment of Solidarity, an independent trade union. Solidarity eventually gained political force and caused a change in the Polish government. Following the fall of communism in Poland, many new laws were passed, including a law governing the resolution of collective bargaining disputes.

The law was passed on May 23, 1991, and then later amended after the passage of Poland's new constitution in 1997. Following are some important points of the law.

Article 1 Employees' collective disputes with an employer or employers can concern working conditions, wages, or social benefits.

Article 3 In a place of work in which more than one union organization is active, any of them can represent the employees' interests in the collective dispute.
  In a place of work in which no trade union is active, a union organization that the employees ask to represent their collective interests can conduct a collective dispute in the name of the employees.

Article 7 A collective dispute exists from the date it is announced by the unit representing the employees' interests to the employer.
  The employer has not less than three days to remedy the situation.

Article 10 If the employer does not adequately respond to the employees' demands, the issue goes into mediation.

Article 15 If mediation fails, the employees have the right to strike as a means of last resort.

Article 18 Participation in a strike is by choice.

Article 23 During a strike, employees are entitled to all benefits from their jobs, except wages.

Across Cultures: Lech Walesa

Lech Walesa was an instrumental leader in the Solidarity movement. In the 1970s and 1980s he worked for creating and maintaining rights for workers in Poland. Eventually, after Solidarity gained power in the Polish Congress, Lech Walesa was elected President of Poland.

Critical Thinking *Who benefits from collective bargaining agreements?*

Collective Bargaining
Unionized employees negotiate their employment contracts with company lawyers in collective bargaining sessions. *What kinds of employment issues are worked out in these sessions?*

Governments felt unions were destructive to the economic system and banned most of them as illegal conspiracies. During the Great Depression in the 1930s, however, the government began to recognize unions and allow them to negotiate their own contracts through collective bargaining. **Collective bargaining is a process in which union and management representatives get together to work out issues such as wages, working conditions, and hiring and firing policies.**

The Norris-LaGuardia Act (1932)

This act is one of the first federal laws in support of employees joining unions. It outlaws yellow dog contracts, which are contracts workers are forced to sign in which they agree not to join a union as a condition of employment. The act also bars the federal courts from issuing orders preventing labor strikes. Strikes are organized work stoppages.

The Wagner Act (1935)

This Wagner Act requires employers to negotiate wages, hours, and conditions of employment with unions. It created the National Labor Relations Board (NLRB) to hear complaints about unfair labor practices. However, the courts have ruled that, despite the act, executives still have the ability to control decisions that are not considered true conditions of employment such as plant closures.

The Taft-Hartley Act (1947)

As the unions grew more powerful in the 1930s and 1940s, this act amended the Wagner Act. Officially known as the Labor-Management Relations Act, it requires unions to give a 60-day notice before calling a strike. It prohibits strikes that endanger the nation's health or safety, such as air traffic controllers, and allows the president to go to court to stop a strike for 80 days. The act also prohibits labor unions from featherbedding, or requiring employers to hire more employees to a job than are actually needed.

The Landrum-Griffin Act (1959)

The Landrum-Griffin Act also amended the Wagner Act and is aimed at halting **corruption** in unions. Unions must have a constitution and bylaws which they must register with the Secretary of Labor. They must also submit yearly reports on their financial condition, including sources of revenue and loans to union members. Unions must also have a members' bill of rights.

Forming or Dissolving a Union

Employees today may still create unions. The usual process is to contact one of the large national unions, such as the AFL/CIO. The organizers must then try to **solicit** workers within the company. At least 30 percent of the workers must agree to contact the National Labor Relationshions Board (NLRB) to organize a full vote to form a union. In a secret ballot, a majority of the workers must approve the union. The NLRB will then certify it as an official union which the employer must recognize. A similar process must be followed if employees want to dissolve an existing labor union.

After You Read

Summarize What are the situations outside employment-at-will?

SECTION 15.1 ASSESSMENT

Self Check

1. What is employment-at-will?
2. What are the exceptions to employment-at-will?
3. What is collective bargaining?

Academic Connection

Social Studies The history of labor unions can be traced back to Medieval Europe, when artisans and craftsmen formed guilds to protect their interests, set working standards, and help each other get jobs. The modern labor movement begins with the Industrial Revolution in the late 18th and early 19th centuries, when thousands of people went to work in factories that offered extremely poor pay and working conditions. Workers organized into unions to demand conditions such as fair pay and working hours.

Go on the Internet or to the library and do some research on the history of labor. Create a time line showing some of the milestones in labor history.

Critical Thinking

Pros and Cons Is it better to be an employee-at-will or a member of a labor union? What are the advantages and disadvantages of each?

SECTION 15.2 Employee Rights

What You'll Learn

- ◆ Explain how the law protects employee health and safety.
- ◆ Describe the laws that guarantee fair wages and benefits.
- ◆ Identify the laws that prohibit different forms of discrimination.
- ◆ Define disparate treatment and disparate impact.

Why It's Important

Understanding employment law will help you to protect your rights to safety, privacy, and fair pay as a worker.

Reading Guide

Before You Read

Connect Maybe you have family members who had to leave a job because they were laid off, injured, or retired. If so, were they entitled to any benefits?

Focus on Ideas

Once you have a basic understanding of the rights and benefits that are due to workers on the job today, you will be better equipped to deal with problems in the workplace.

Take Notes

Go to connectED.mcgraw-hill.com to download a graphic organizer you can use to take notes as you read this section.

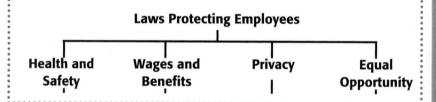

Laws Protecting Employees

| Health and Safety | Wages and Benefits | Privacy | Equal Opportunity |

Key Terms

You will learn these legal words and expressions in this chapter. You can also find these terms in *Black's Law Dictionary* or in an online legal dictionary.

- Occupational Safety and Health Administration (OSHA)
- equal pay rule
- pension plan
- Social Security
- unemployment compensation
- workers' compensation
- discrimination
- disparate treatment
- disparate impact

Academic Vocabulary

You will find these words in your readings and in your tests. Look them up in a dictionary and familiarize yourself with them.

- voluntary
- random
- waiver

Health and Safety

What laws protect your health and safety on the job?

In the beginning of the Industrial Revolution, employers had little regard for their workers' safety and quality of life. Since then, the government has passed numerous laws to regulate employment conditions and to protect employees. Employee rights can be divided into four areas:

- right to health and safety protections
- right to fair wages and benefits
- right to privacy
- right to equal opportunity in the workplace

Two major federal government acts protect the health and safety of workers.

The Occupational Safety and Health Act

This act set up the Occupational Safety and Health Administration (OSHA), the federal government agency that regulates health and safety standards for companies in the United States. To make sure employers follow the rules, OSHA does the following:

- inspects workplaces at random
- investigates written employee complaints, workplace deaths, and disasters
- protects employees from being fired for filing complaints
- levies fines for rule violations

The Environmental Policy Act

In 1969, Congress passed the National Environmental Policy Act, which established the Environmental Protection Agency (EPA). The purpose of the EPA is to set up a national policy for fighting pollution, and to protect the environment and human health from exposure to hazardous chemicals and waste. The EPA encourages **voluntary** compliance by businesses. It also supports the efforts of state and local governments to carry out enforcement actions in their own territory. When such efforts do not work, the EPA can act against companies that pollute the environment.

Fair Wages and Benefits

What wages and benefits are you guaranteed when you work?

The government has long been concerned about the conditions under which employees perform their jobs. The government responded

Vocabulary You can find vocabulary definitions in the **Key Terms** glossary and **Academic Vocabulary** glossary in the back of this book.

Employee Benefits
Employee benefits include Social Security and disability insurance, but can also include health and life insurance. *What other kinds of benefits may be available to employees?*

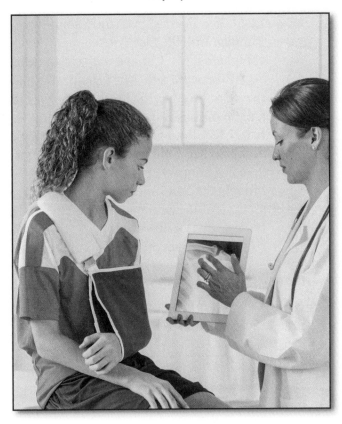

to many of the hardships suffered by workers during the Great Depression by passing several laws to regulate wages, hours, and benefits.

The Fair Labor Standards Act

The Fair Labor Standards Act, also known as the Wage and Hour Law, requires certain employers, such as hospitals, retail businesses, restaurants, and schools, to pay their workers a minimum hourly wage and time-and-a-half for all work over 40 hours per week. The Fair Labor Standards Act also regulates the employment of minors. The act covers employees who produce goods for interstate commerce. Professional employees, administrators, and executives are not covered by this act.

Equal Pay Act

The Equal Pay Act is an amendment to the Fair Labor Standards Act. It established the equal pay rule. **The equal pay rule is a standard that states that employers working in interstate commerce must pay women the same rate of pay as men**

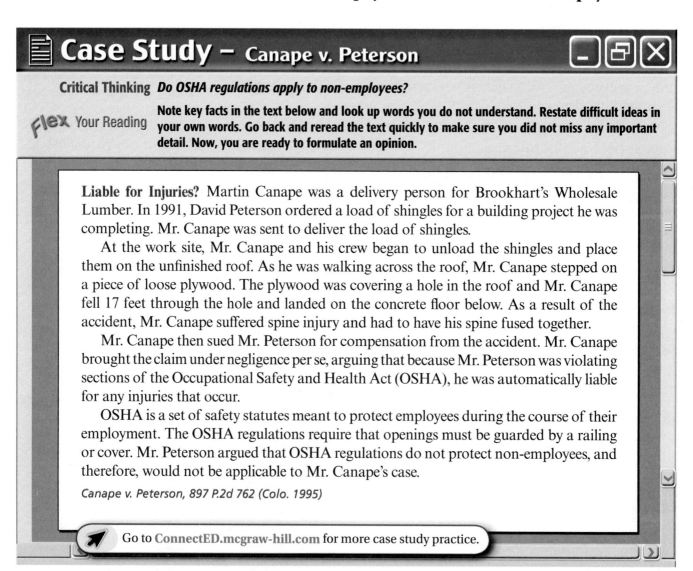

Case Study – Canape v. Peterson

Critical Thinking *Do OSHA regulations apply to non-employees?*

Flex Your Reading — **Note key facts in the text below and look up words you do not understand. Restate difficult ideas in your own words. Go back and reread the text quickly to make sure you did not miss any important detail. Now, you are ready to formulate an opinion.**

Liable for Injuries? Martin Canape was a delivery person for Brookhart's Wholesale Lumber. In 1991, David Peterson ordered a load of shingles for a building project he was completing. Mr. Canape was sent to deliver the load of shingles.

At the work site, Mr. Canape and his crew began to unload the shingles and place them on the unfinished roof. As he was walking across the roof, Mr. Canape stepped on a piece of loose plywood. The plywood was covering a hole in the roof and Mr. Canape fell 17 feet through the hole and landed on the concrete floor below. As a result of the accident, Mr. Canape suffered spine injury and had to have his spine fused together.

Mr. Canape then sued Mr. Peterson for compensation from the accident. Mr. Canape brought the claim under negligence per se, arguing that because Mr. Peterson was violating sections of the Occupational Safety and Health Act (OSHA), he was automatically liable for any injuries that occur.

OSHA is a set of safety statutes meant to protect employees during the course of their employment. The OSHA regulations require that openings must be guarded by a railing or cover. Mr. Peterson argued that OSHA regulations do not protect non-employees, and therefore, would not be applicable to Mr. Canape's case.

Canape v. Peterson, 897 P.2d 762 (Colo. 1995)

Go to **ConnectED.mcgraw-hill.com** for more case study practice.

holding the same type of job. The equal pay rule covers hourly workers, executives, administrators, professional employees, and outside salespeople who receive a salary and/or a commission.

The Employment Retirement Income Security Act

The Employment Retirement Income Security Act (ERISA) prevents the abuse of employee pension plans. **A pension plan is a program established by an employer or a union to provide income to employees after they retire.** Pensions are typically based on an employee's salary and length of service. ERISA came about because some employers failed to invest the employee retirement funds wisely or used the money for their own business expenses. The act thus requires employers to place employee pension contributions in a trust fund outside of the employer's control. It also imposes a duty of good faith on pension fund managers. Employees must receive regular reports about their retirement benefits.

The Family and Medical Leave Act

Under the Family and Medical Leave Act, an employee of a company with at least 50 employees is entitled to 12 weeks of unpaid leave during any 12-month period to care for a new child or a relative with a serious medical condition. The employee is entitled to return to his or her previous job or an equivalent job with the same pay and benefits. To be eligible, the employee must have at least one year of service with the company.

The Social Security Act

Social Security is a government program that provides continuing income to workers and their dependents when their earnings stop or are reduced because of retirement, disability, or death. The Social Security Act and its amendments set up a social insurance program funded by contributions from both employers and employees. People become eligible to receive Social Security benefits by working for a certain time period or by being a dependent of a person who meets that requirement.

Unemployment Compensation

Unemployment compensation is a system of government payments to people who are out of work and looking for a job. The program is funded by having employers pay payroll taxes or insurance premiums. Under the Federal Unemployment Tax Act, each state operates its own system, subject to conditions imposed by the federal government. Each state determines the tax rate employers must pay and the amount an unemployed worker can receive. Unemployed workers must apply at state employment offices. They may be disqualified if they refuse to accept a suitable job, if their unemployment is due to a labor strike, if they were discharged for misconduct, or if they voluntarily quit a job without good cause.

Workers' Compensation

Workers' compensation is an insurance program that provides income for workers who are injured on the job or develop a disability or disease as a result of their job. Loss of income due to accidents, illness, or death on the job became a serious problem with the introduction of machines to industry. Faced with this situation, several state legislatures passed laws in the early 1900s creating workers' compensation programs. By 1959 all 50 states had programs in place.

Workers' compensation laws vary by state. In many states, employers pay into a state's workers' compensation fund through payroll taxes. In Texas, workers' compensation law was first enacted in 1913, and the Texas Workers' Compensation Program evolved over time to address a variety of workplace needs. The Texas Workers' Compensation Act of 1989 was adopted to consolidate and strengthen workplace health and safety programs, improve benefits and benefits delivery, assist in resolving claim disputes, ensure compliance with workers' compensation laws, and develop medical fee and treatment guidelines to help control medical costs. Texas has also established the Texas Workforce Commission (TWC), the state agency that provides workforce development services to employers and job seekers in Texas. Employers are offered recruiting, retention, training, and outplacement services, as well as labor market statistics. Job seekers are provided with access to job search tools, training programs, and career development information, among other job-related resources. For a general review of basic employee rights, see **Figure 15.1.**

Employee Privacy Rights

Do you have a right to privacy in the workplace?

Three areas of privacy law have become important in recent years:
- guaranteeing privacy for governmental employees
- testing employees for drug use
- using polygraph (lie detector) tests in the hiring and firing of employees

The Federal Privacy Act

The Federal Privacy Act protects the privacy of government workers, but not workers in the private sector. It gives government employees the right to know what is in their employment files, to restrict access to their files, and to fix any mistake they might find in their files.

The Drug-Free Workplace Act

The Drug-Free Workplace Act, which applies to companies that have contracts with the federal government, aims to create a drug-free work environment. Drug testing is not required, but if a drug test is given improperly, it can violate the Fourth Amendment to the United States Constitution, which prohibits unreasonable

Figure 15.1 Employee Rights

Under Title VII of the Civil Rights Act of 1964, an employer cannot ask a job applicant about his or her religion, race, or marital status during a job interview.

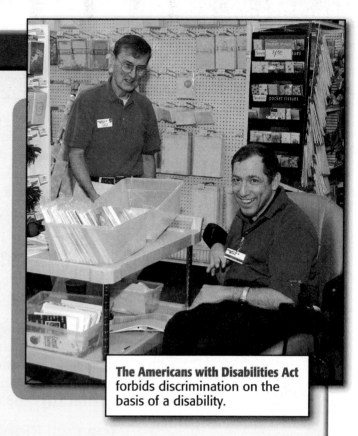

The Americans with Disabilities Act forbids discrimination on the basis of a disability.

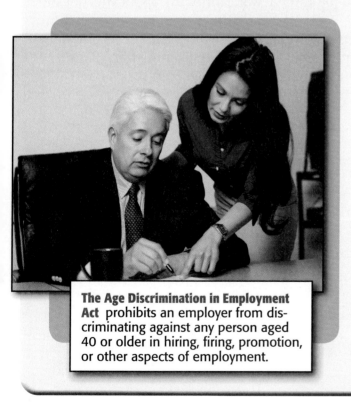

The Age Discrimination in Employment Act prohibits an employer from discriminating against any person aged 40 or older in hiring, firing, promotion, or other aspects of employment.

The Equal Pay Act requires employers to pay women the same rate of pay as men for doing the same type of job.

The federal government has passed laws guaranteeing employees certain rights. *Can employers make employees take a polygraph test?*

search and seizure. Some states have passed statutes that regulate drug testing in the private sector.

The Employee Polygraph Protection Act

The Employee Polygraph Protection Act bars employers from using lie detector tests for the screening of employment applicants. It also prohibits the **random** testing of employees. There are, however, several exceptions. It does not apply to businesses involved in security or the handling of controlled substances. Drug firms and private investigation companies are also permitted to use polygraph tests.

Equal Employment Opportunity

What can you do if you think you have been discriminated against?

Since the 1960s, the federal government has passed six major acts to ensure fairness and ethical behavior in employment and to prevent discrimination. **Discrimination is the unequal treatment of individuals based on sex, age, race, nationality, or religion.**

The Civil Rights Act of 1964

Title VII of the Civil Rights Act of 1964 prohibits discrimination in employment based on race, color, religion, sex, or national origin. The attempt to recruit, hire, and promote workers based on these characteristics is referred to as affirmative action.

Under Title VII, a job interviewer cannot ask applicants questions about their religion, race, age, or marital status. Employees who believe they have been discriminated against can file a complaint with the Equal Employment Opportunity Commission (EEOC) or seek a private remedy in court. The EEOC can seek a court injunction or sue the employer for damages.

Disparate Treatment Disparate treatment **is when an employer intentionally discriminates against an individual or a group of individuals belonging to a protected class.** For instance, an employer who holds a general policy against hiring female engineers or male nurses would be practicing this type of discrimination.

A defense employers can use against the charge of disparate treatment is a *bona fide* occupational qualification, or BFOQ. A *bona fide* occupational qualification is a job requirement that might seem discriminatory but which is actually a good faith requirement to perform a particular job. For example, requiring that applicants for a job modeling women's clothing be female is a *bona fide* occupational qualification. The BFOQ defense can never be used to justify discrimination based on race.

Disparate Impact Disparate impact **is when an employer has an employment policy that appears neutral on the surface but has an unfair impact on members of a protected class.** For example, an employer who requires applicants to be over six feet tall is discriminating by disparate impact. The height requirement seems neutral on the surface, but has an unfair impact on women.

A defense against disparate impact is business necessity. Business necessity is a job requirement based on actual skills needed by an employee to perform a specific job. For example, it is acceptable for a hospital to require that all applicants for a job as a surgeon have a medical degree.

The Civil Rights Act of 1991

The Civil Rights Act of 1991 was enacted by Congress to strengthen the doctrine of disparate impact. The law requires employers to prove business necessity in disparate impact cases. It requires employers to prove that the qualifications for hiring or promoting employees are directly related to the specific job involved in a court case. It also allows plaintiffs who have been discriminated against to recover not only back pay owed to them, but compensatory and punitive damages.

The Pregnancy Discrimination Act

The Pregnancy Discrimination Act makes it unlawful to discriminate against a woman because of pregnancy or childbirth. An employer cannot create an employee benefits package that discriminates against women who are pregnant.

The Immigration Reform Act

The Immigration Reform Act makes employers responsible for verifying the identity and employment eligibility of all employees. It applies to U.S. citizens, permanent residents, and nonimmigrant visa holders. All job applicants must present original documents and, if hired, they must sign an employment eligibility verification form in front of a supervisor or human resources officer.

Reading Check

Explain *Why did the government think it was necessary to create protected classes of workers?*

Legal Talk

Bona fide: *adj* Latin for *good faith.*

Quid pro quo: *n* Latin for *something for something.*

Vocabulary Builder Many European languages are romance languages, or languages based on the Roman language of Latin. In Latin, *bonus* means good and *fides* mean faith. In class, name words in other languages you know that mean good or faith.

Business ETHICS

Contract Negotiations

You are an attorney for a nationwide chain of weight-loss clinics for men. Your company provides counseling to men and encourages them to eat in a healthier manner and to exercise regularly. Clients visit your clinics weekly where they are weighed and undergo personal counseling for 30 minutes. After performing a random survey of 1,000 men, you determine that men are more comfortable with male workers and counselors in your clinics, and that more men would become clients if they were assured that a male would assist them in their weight loss. Right now your company has approximately 45% female workers.

Critical Thinking: *Can you replace the women with men?*

The Age Discrimination in Employment Act

The Age Discrimination in Employment Act (ADEA) applies only to employment agencies, employers with 20 or more employees, and labor unions with more than 25 members. The act forbids discriminating against any person aged 40 or older in hiring, firing, or other employment decisions. The law does not apply if age is a true job qualification, such as modeling children's clothing. The ADEA was amended by Congress in 1990 to forbid discrimination against older employees with regard to their retirement and pension plans. The amendment, known as the Older Workers' Benefit Protection Plan Act (OWBPPA), gives workers a legal way to remedy a situation in which they have been cheated or coerced into surrendering their ADEA rights by signing a **waiver**.

Americans with Disabilities Act

The Americans with Disabilities Act of 1990 (ADA) forbids discrimination on the basis of a disability if the disabled individual can do the essential functions of a job. Employers cannot discriminate against those with disabilities when screening or hiring, granting promotions, offering pay raises, or offering on-the-job-training opportunities. Both direct and indirect forms of discrimination are outlawed. Indirect discrimination occurs when an employer makes a hiring decision based on a qualification that is not related to job performance but has the effect of eliminating disabled individuals.

Sexual Harassment

There are also laws covering sexual harassment in the workplace. Sexual harassment can occur either through a quid pro quo activity or through the creation of a hostile working environment. Quid pro quo sexual discrimination occurs when one worker demands sexual favors from another worker in exchange for something employment related, such as a raise or a promotion. A hostile working environment exists when a pattern of severe and pervasive sexually demeaning behavior has altered the workplace, making it a distressing, humiliating, or hostile place. Such demeaning behavior could include sexually explicit comments, jokes, photographs, cartoons, posters, or gestures.

International Employment Law

What rights do you have when you work in another country?

Most U.S. employment laws do not apply to employment in other countries, even if you work for an American company overseas. For example, minimum wage laws will be different. Protections against discrimination may not exist in other countries. Some countries, however, have better pension and compensation programs, and more legal guarantees of job security. In Europe, for example, it can be extremely difficult to fire a employee.

After You Read

Summarize What wage and benefit rights are held by workers?

SECTION 15.2 ASSESSMENT

Self Check

1. What four areas can employment conditions be divided into?

2. For what reasons can you be disqualified from receiving unemployment compensation?

3. What are the objectives of the Civil Rights Act?

Academic Connection

English Language Arts
Businesses that violate the law are subject to fines, lawsuits, and additional government regulations. To avoid such problems, many companies have created their own code of ethics to set standards of conduct for both employers and employees in the workplace. Assume the classroom is a business, with the teacher as employer and students as employees. Get together in a group with other students and write a code of ethics for the classroom. Issues can range from classroom conditions to the behavior of students and teacher. For assistance, go online and look up the code of ethics for a well-known company such as Ben and Jerry's or Microsoft.

Critical Thinking

Meet the New Boss
Suppose you learn that your friend, June (aged 42), was passed up for a promotion where you work in favor of a younger (aged 27) and much less qualified male candidate who also happens to be the boss's nephew. Do you have any advice to give June under these circumstances? Explain.

Summary

Section 15.1 Employment Agreements

◆ According to the doctrine of employment-at-will, employers and employees are free to end the employment relationship at any time without penalty.

◆ Situations that fall outside employment-at-will include unionized employees, employees with individual employment contracts, and protected classes of employees.

◆ Wrongful discharge exceptions to employment-at-will include implied contract, promissory estoppel, and public policy tort.

◆ Implied covenant is a legal argument that holds that any employment relationship is based on an implied promise that the employer and the employee will be fair and honest with one another.

◆ Legislation that regulates union activities includes the Norris-LaGuardia Act, the Wagner Act, the Taft-Hartley Act, and the Landrum-Griffin Act.

Section 15.2 Employee Rights

◆ Legislation that regulates employment conditions includes the Occupational Safety and Health Act, the Fair Labor Standards Act, the Equal Pay Act, and the Immigration Reform and Control Act.

◆ Worker benefits include Social Security, unemployment compensation, workers' compensation, and pension protection.

◆ Legislation that regulates employee rights includes Title VII of the Civil Rights Act, the Americans with Disabilities Act, the Age Discrimination in Employment Act, and the Family and Medical Leave Act.

◆ Disparate treatment is when an employer intentionally discriminates against an individual or a group.

◆ Disparate impact is when an employer has an employment policy that appears neutral on the surface but has an unfair impact on the members of one or more of the protected classes.

Vocabulary Builder

1 On a sheet of paper, use each of these terms in a sentence.

Key Terms

- employment-at-will
- union
- implied contract
- public policy tort
- implied covenant

- collective bargaining
- Occupational Safety and Health Administration (OSHA)
- equal pay rule
- pension plan

- Social Security
- unemployment compensation
- workers' compensation
- discrimination
- disparate treatment
- disparate impact

Academic Vocabulary

- exception
- corruption

- solicit
- voluntary

- random
- waiver

Key Points Review

Answer the following questions. Refer to the chapter for additional reinforcement.

2 What is the general rule of employment that guides hiring and firing in the U.S. today?

3 What types of employees can negotiate their own individual employment contracts?

4 What are the major provisions of the Wagner Act?

5 What classes of employees are protected by the Civil Rights Act?

6 What law bans discrimination based on age?

7 What requirements were instituted by the Fair Labor Standards Act?

8 What is the equal pay rule?

9 What is the difference between disparate treatment and disparate impact?

Standardized Test Practice

10 Read the following information about the Occupational Safety and Health Act and complete questions 1 and 2.

The Occupational Safety and Health Act of 1970 assigns OSHA two functions: setting standards and conducting inspections to ensure that employers provide safe and healthful workplaces. OSHA standards may require that employers adopt certain practices, means, methods, or processes reasonably necessary and appropriate to protect workers on the job. Employers must become familiar with the applicable standards and eliminate hazards.

Compliance may include ensuring that employees have been provided with, have been effectively trained on, and use personal protective equipment when required for safety or health. Where specific standards do not exist, employers must comply with the Act's "general duty" clause [Section 5(a)(1)], which requires each employer to "furnish . . . a place of employment which is free from recognized hazards that are causing or are likely to cause death or serious physical harm to his employees."

1. The Occupational Safety and Health Act of 1970 requires employers:

A to furnish employees with information about their jobs

B to ensure employees are provided and trained to use protective equipment

C give general employee training sessions to keep trends and policies current

D fire any employees who do not comply with OSHA regulations

2. OSHA ensures employer compliance by:

A providing posters, training, and informational sessions for employers and employees

B having three regulatory functions to set standards and oversee guidelines of employers

C requiring a place of employment free from recognized hazards that could harm employees

D providing safety equipment and training to employees to meet regulations

Test-Taking Strategies Rely on your first impression. The first answer that comes to mind is often correct.

Apply and Debate

Read the following scenarios. Get together with other students in pairs or groups of three and take a position on each scenario. Debate your position in class with students taking the opposite position or prepare a written argument justifying your position.

11 Promises, Promises

Rose's company sent her to London to open a new store. They promised her a position as manager of their Boston store if she spent two years in London. When Rose moved to Boston after two years, the company was having financial problems. They closed the Boston store within three weeks of her arrival and Rose was terminated.

You Debate   *Can Rose sue for wrongful discharge based on the promise made to her?*

12 Personal vs. Company Time

Johnson Manufacturing had a strict company policy forbidding personnel to use office computers for personal business. They dismissed Eliot Menson, a 3-year employee, after discovering that he used his computer to trade stocks during his lunch hour.

You Debate   *Was Eliot wrongfully terminated? What if Eliot had been writing a novel?*

13 Men's Fitness Center

Archer & Bower Architects received a contract to design two fitness centers—a men's and a women's—in a new housing tract. The company insists that it must hire a male architect to work on the men's center and a female to work on the women's center.

You Debate   *Can the company make a case for bona fide job qualifications?*

14 Roofer Accident

Franco works as a roofer. His employer normally supplies safety harnesses to all roofers. One day, Franco and his co-worker Mario could find only one harness in the truck. The boss asked Franco to wait on the ground until one was obtained. Mario needed help, so Franco went up on the roof. He slipped and fell, breaking his leg.

You Debate   *Can Franco sue his company for negligence in addition to workers' comp?*

15 Young and Hip

Ashley, age 44, an advertising executive with 12 years experience, applied to become Senior Director at her firm's new office in Seattle. The job was given to a flashy 33-year old woman who had seven years experience. The firm claimed their clients wanted someone "young and hip."

You Debate   *Should Ashley sue for age discrimination?*

Case Study Practice – Bearley v. Friendly Ice Cream Corp.

16 Fair Offer? Dorothy Bearley worked 22 hours a week as a bookkeeper for Friendly Ice Cream Corporation (Friendly's) in Dunmore, PA, and 18 hours a week for the Friendly's district that covered Dunmore. This amounted to full-time employment. She also worked a few hours a week as a hostess in the Dunmore restaurant. On July 5, 2000, Ms. Bearley informed her boss that she needed to undergo toe surgery. Her boss granted her medical leave, but informed her that while she was gone, Friendly's bookkeeping functions were going to be automated.

Upon returning to work in August, Ms. Bearley discovered that much of her job had been automated and her bookkeeping hours reduced. Friendly's offered Ms. Bearley 22 hours bookkeeping, 13 hours food preparation, and three hours hostessing. Ms. Bearley rejected the offer and sued Friendly's, claiming it had violated the Family Medical Leave Act by not reinstating her to a position equal to her previous one.

Source: Bearley v. Friendly Ice Cream Corp., 322 F.Supp.2d 563 (M.D. Pa. 2004)

Practice Was Friendly's offer acceptable under the law?

17 Ethics
←?→ Application

Safety Standards Serena works in the stockroom of a sports clothing company. Her co-worker, Kim, has decided to take the forklift for a ride. Serena knows that heat, noise, and intoxication can lead to work-related accidents, but is not sure Kim is violating safety standards.

◆ Does Kim have a careless attitude toward workplace safety? Should Serena report Kim to their supervisor?

18 Think back to the Legal Briefs feature you read at the beginning of the chapter. Then write a social media policy for high school students. Write your policy clearly in language that is precise, exact, plain, and explicit. Include information on what is and is not acceptable to put online. For example, bullying another student online is unacceptable.

Careers in Law

Judith Silver
CEO, CoolLawyer.com Legal Forms

What do you do at work?
"I look at the online marketplace to identify what makes CoolLawyer.com unique compared to other legal forms companies, figure out how to best sell my product, and understand my customer base. I also spend time doing search engine marketing, writing articles that are posted on the Web to help my search engine standing (to reach more customers), monitoring my marketing efforts and updating them, and conducting interviews for publicity to enhance my Web site."

What skills are most important to you?
"The most important is the ability to follow through and solve problems in the way I believe to be best, regardless of what others might say is the most important thing in being a successful entrepreneur. This doesn't mean you don't ask and listen to advice from others, but ultimately, you are the key to understanding your business and you are your business."

What training do you recommend?
"Get as much experience as possible in regards to problem solving in the area in which you want to work. I understand my business and other aspects of my career well because I have handled every aspect of the business at one time or another. It's important to learn a position and a career from the ground level and up. Learning from others is just never the same as learning from your own hands-on experience."

What is your key to success?
"There are so many—persistence, creativity, curiosity, common sense. This profession requires that you constantly learn new technology and gain business information to move your business forward. It's amazing what you can learn from simple things like talking to customers and helping them. Often you'll discover entirely new lines of business or ways that you never thought of to improve your business."

Resume Builder

Academic Skills
- Manage numerous sets of information at one time
- Ability to shift focus while staying on task

Education and Training
A bachelor's degree in business administration, finance, and marketing, plus the following high school and college courses:
- Business, contracts, and consumer law
- English language arts (rhetoric and composition)

- E-commerce
- International business
- Marketing
- Technology/media arts
- U.S. government
- Social Studies

Critical Thinking
Why is technology essential for small business owners? What are some software programs entrepreneurs might use to manage their companies?

Expository Writing Practice

The Price of a Dream Marcus meets Jackie, a talent agent for Hackman & Broad Agents, who tells him he could be a model. Jackie says he could probably make $1,000 an hour. A few days later, Marcus pays her a $500 consultation fee to discuss his career and the agency's offerings. At this point, Marcus still has not signed a contract. Marcus also needs to pay an additional $1,500 for a portfolio of photographs to show prospective clients. A few weeks later, Jackie calls to tell Marcus his portfolio is ready for pick-up, but that unfortunately the agency has closed due to bankruptcy.

Assignments

Research Research employee rights in the modeling and talent industry.

Write Consider the situation above and write an expository essay about laws that protect employees. Describe how and why Marcus should have investigated the talent agency before acting on a verbal agreement. Include a list of warning signs of a non-reputable talent manager or agent, and the factors for choosing the right representative.

Writing Tips Authors organize their writing in a specific way for a specific purpose. These patterns of organization are called text structures. When writing an expository essay, it is important to address these common types of text structures:

- ✓ Comparison and contrast shows how things are the same and different.
- ✓ Cause and effect shows how events are related.

- ✓ Problem and solution describes a problem and offers solutions.
- ✓ Chronological order presents events in time order.

Essay Test Strategies Preview the test question by slowly reading through all its parts and pieces. In the directions, underline the questions that your essay needs to answer. In the paper's margin, create a rough outline of the information you want to be sure to include in the essay. Use the outline as a checklist while working your way through the writing.

Thematic Project

Employment Guide

For this project, you will use what you have learned to prepare an employment guide of federal and state employment laws to add to your portfolio. This project is to be done individually.

Here is a checklist of skills that you will need to complete this project. Your teacher will consider these skills when evaluating your work.

Evaluation Rubric

Academic Skills		
1. Online and library research	1.	10 points
2. Reading for information	2.	10 points
3. Note-taking	3.	5 points
4. Estimation and computation of facts/figures you discover	4.	10 points
5. English composition to summarize findings	5.	15 points
Legal Skills		
6. Researching employment laws	6.	15 points
7. Knowledge of federal versus state labor laws	7.	15 points
8. Analysis of essential legislative acts governing employers and employees	8.	15 points
9. Use of technology	9.	5 points
	Total 100 Points	

Step 1: Preparation

❶ Write a proposal for the area of employment law you plan to research.

❷ Use all you have learned in this unit, at the library, or on the Internet as tools.

❸ Complete this project in a format acceptable for portfolio addition.

Step 2: Procedure

1 **Review** the text in this unit and make a list of the laws that relate to your area of interest, such as discrimination or unions. Ask anyone you know who is employed or employees in your community how they have been affected by this legislation.

2 **List** all the employment terms you might include in your document that pertain to your area of research.

3 **Write** an informational guide about the legal terms and documents that an employer and employee must abide by for employment placement. Use the Internet to research and download labor forms (e.g., work permit) and other important documents. Make enough copies so your classmates can review and annotate your guide.

4 **Describe** an advertisement for an employment opportunity. Present your guide and see if your classmates can use it as a primer to apply for the job.

Step 3: Create an Analysis Report

As a class, compare the employment guides presented. Compare and contrast the information presented in each and look for common themes or areas covered. See if any of the guides stand out and if so what makes the information presented easier to understand. After comparing the guides, answer the following questions:

1 How many and what areas of laws were presented?

2 Did the guides presented include all the necessary information needed to apply for a job?

3 If not, what should have been added to make the information easier to use?

4 How was your guide similar to and different from the other guides presented?

Community Connection

Select a business you are interested in learning more about. Look up statistics on employment opportunities, salary range, and future expectations for that business. How do these statistics affect your chosen career path? Summarize your findings for the class.

Competitive Event Prep

Equal Employment

Situation Your aunt (event judge) owns a maid service called Maid for You. She has owned the service, which specializes in house cleaning, for over ten years. During the entire company history all of the cleaners have been female. Your aunt recently advertised for new cleaners to fill vacancies. For the first time, a well-qualified man has applied for a position. Your aunt wonders if her clients will accept a man as a cleaner. She is unsure about how to handle the situation and asks you for your advice.

Activity You are to explain to your aunt the legal aspects of equal employment legislation and the impact it could have on her business.

Jackson v. Birmingham Board of Education

U.S. Supreme Court 544 U.S. 167 ____ (2005)

Read Critically As you read the case, ask yourself the following questions:

1. Who did Mr. Jackson file a sex discrimination claim for?
2. Under what law did Mr. Jackson bring his claim?
3. Why did the Eleventh Circuit rule against Mr. Jackson?
4. What did the U.S. Supreme Court hold about retaliation?

Assignment When you are done, write a short summary of the situation. Include the court's decision and a couple of sentences about why or how the court reached its decision.

Facts **New Coaching Job** Roderick Jackson was an employee of the Birmingham Alabama School District for more than 10 years. He was hired in 1993 to be a physical education teacher and girls' basketball coach. In 1999, Mr. Jackson transferred within the district to Ensley High School. When he started, he discovered that the girls' teams at Ensley were not receiving equal funding and equal access to the athletic equipment and facilities. Because of the inequalities, Mr. Jackson discovered he was unable to do his job as the girls' basketball team's coach.

Sex Discrimination Complaint In December of 2000, Mr. Jackson began to complain to his supervisors about the unequal treatment of the girls' basketball team. However, his supervisors did not respond to his claims and the school district failed to remedy the situation. Instead, Mr. Jackson began to receive negative work evaluations and ultimately was removed as the girls' basketball coach in May 2001.

Mr. Jackson was retained as a teacher, but was no longer a coach and did not receive the supplemental pay he did as a coach.

Lawsuit Commencement After the Birmingham School District terminated Mr. Jackson's coaching duties, he filed a lawsuit in U.S. District Court against the school district. Mr. Jackson alleged that the Birmingham School District had violated Title IX of the Education Amendments by retaliating against him for protesting the discrimination against the girls' basketball team.

Opinion **U.S. Eleventh Circuit Court of Appeal Proceedings** The U.S. Court of Appeals for the Eleventh Circuit held that Title IX does not include a provision where Mr. Jackson could bring a claim for retaliation, since there is no private cause of retaliation available under Title IX. The Court also held that even if Title IX prohibited retaliation, Mr. Jackson would not be entitled to relief because he is not within the class of persons protected by the statute, nor is he an actual victim of sex discrimination himself.

Title IX Title IX was passed in 1972 as part of the Education Amendments. It states as follows:

20 U.S.C. §1681 (Title IX)
   (a) Prohibition against discrimination; exceptions
   No person in the United States shall, on the basis of sex, be excluded from participation in, be denied the benefits of, or be subjected to discrimination under any education program or activity receiving Federal financial assistance.
   (c) "Educational institution" defined

An educational institution means any public or private preschool, elementary, or secondary school, or any institution of vocational, professional, or higher education, except that in an educational institution composed of more than one school, college, or department which are administratively separate units, such term means each such school, college, or department.

In 1979, in Cannon v. University of Chicago, the Supreme Court held that Title IX includes a private right of action. Private citizens have the right to bring a claim against the offending party, to enforce the prohibition on intentional sex discrimination. Later, in 1992, in Franklin v. Gwinnett County Public Schools, the Supreme Court held private parties can seek monetary damages for intentional violations of Title IX. In all the cases, the Court relied on the text of Title IX, which except for a few narrow exceptions prohibits discrimination on the basis of sex.

Retaliation The court then looked at retaliation. Like private causes of action, Title IX does not speak directly to the issue of retaliation. In previous cases, the Supreme Court has held that retaliation is, by definition, an intentional act. It is also a form of discrimination, since the complaining person is subjected to differential treatment. Further, retaliation is discrimination on the basis of sex when it is an intentional response to a sex discrimination complaint.

School District's Argument The Birmingham School Board argued that if Congress wished to include retaliation in Title IX, then it would have included it as it did in the Civil Rights Acts. However, the causes of action under the Civil Rights Acts are explicit, whereas the courts have inferred all the causes of action under Title IX. Under Title IX Congress prohibited all forms of discrimination in education and the courts have, therefore, allowed that broad prohibition to apply to a broad number of actions. Discrimination is a term that covers a wide range of intentional unequal treatment and the Court will ensure that the action is not allowed in the educational system by allowing a broad number of causes of action.

Holding **The Court's Decision** The Supreme Court held that retaliation is an actionable cause under Title IX. Further, retaliation can occur not only against persons bringing sex discrimination claims for themselves, but also for people who bring sex discrimination claims on behalf of third parties. The actions of the Birmingham School District could amount to retaliation and Mr. Jackson is permitted to bring his cause of action before a jury to make that determination.

TRIAL PREP

The National High School Mock Trial Association organizes competitions at the local, regional, and national levels where teams of high school or college students prepare and argue fictional legal cases before practicing attorneys and judges. Mock Trial team members are each assigned a role as either an attorney or witness. Each team must develop a courtroom strategy, legal arguments, and a presentation style.

UNIT 6

Starting a Business

In This Unit You Will Find:

• • • • • • • • • • • • • • • •

Be Your Own Boss An alternative to going to work for someone else is starting your own business. *What are the three main forms of business ownership?*

Protecting Social and Environmental Concerns

As you read this unit, use this checklist to prepare for the unit project:

- ✓ List the environmental laws the government requires businesses to obey.
- ✓ Differentiate between safe and unsafe business practices as they relate to environmental laws.
- ✓ Explain how laws protect the environment and society in general.
- ✓ Determine the impact environmental laws have on business and society.

Legal Portfolio When you complete the Unit Thematic project, you will have a guide of environmental protection law for your portfolio.

Ask

AN EXPERT — Get Listed on a Stock Market

Q: How do shares of a company get traded on the New York Stock Exchange?

A: Suppose you run a successful company and want to start selling shares on the New York Stock Exchange (NYSE). The first thing you need to do is hire an investment banker to arrange an initial public offering (IPO), which is a company's first sale of stock to the public. After the government approves the sale, the stock is made available to investors. Then, the stock can be traded on a stock market. For your company's stock to be traded or listed on the NYSE, you must apply with the NYSE, which will review your company to determine if it meets certain requirements (such as having a minimum number of shareholders, a minimum market value, follows basic reporting procedures, has a board of directors, and has in place appropriate corporate governance rules). The NYSE's listing application and requirements are available online.

Legal Briefs

Partnerships in Japan

Giri influences business relationships.

Giri, a central aspect of Japanese culture, is living in a way that serves the greater good and not just your own self-interests. *Giri* requires that your life demonstrates the highest regard for human relationships. To have business partners in Japan, you must practice *giri*.

Unlike in the United States, where business and personal relationships are often kept separate, Japanese business partnerships are molded by the personal relationships of the partners. *Giri* creates a loyalty among partners that necessitates performing your best for someone else—and you must perform selflessly. For *giri* to be present, you must put aside your wants for the benefit of others.

Americans often have a difficult time with the concept of *giri*, because the United States is an individualist society that celebrates individual accomplishment. Japan, on the other hand, is a collective society that exchanges individual needs for those of all members of the society. The Japanese people believe that acting for the greater good of all will benefit the individual.

When working cross-culturally you must respect the beliefs and values of other cultures to obtain business success.

Paying Your Dues Running a business comes with responsibilities. *Who pays the taxes, and who is liable for debts in a partnership?*

Sole Proprietorships and Partnerships

What You'll Learn

- Describe how to form and run a sole proprietorship.
- List the advantages and disadvantages of a sole proprietorship.
- Explain the rights and responsibilities of partners.
- Identify the different types of partners.
- Explain how a partnership can be terminated.

Why It's Important

Knowing the differences between sole proprietorships and partnerships will help you decide which form of business is best for you.

Reading Guide

Before You Read

Connect Have you ever tried to start your own business on the Internet or at school?

Focus on Ideas

Sole proprietorships and partnerships both have advantages and disadvantages.

Take Notes

Go to **connectED.mcgraw-hill.com** to download a graphic organizer you can use to take notes as you read this section.

	Sole Proprietorships	Partnerships
Advantages		
Disadvantages		

Key Terms

You will learn these legal words and expressions in this chapter. You can also find these terms in *Black's Law Dictionary* or in an online legal dictionary.

- sole proprietorship
- unlimited liability
- partnership
- joint liability
- dissolution
- dissociation
- limited partnership
- limited liability partnership (LLP)

Academic Vocabulary

You will find these words in your readings and in your tests. Look them up in a dictionary and familiarize yourself with them.

- perpetual
- dormant
- incompetence

Sole Proprietorships

If you start a babysitting service, what kind of business is it?

A sole proprietorship is a form of business that is owned and operated by one person. A sole proprietorship is the most common way to do business. It is also the easiest type of business to form. Common sole proprietorships are repair shops, small retail stores, and service organizations.

Advantages of a Sole Proprietorship

Sole proprietorships offer specific advantages. These advantages include ease of creation, total control, retention of profits, and one-time taxation of profits.

Ease of Formation There are only a few requirements to meet in forming a sole proprietorship. Some businesses, such as restaurants and motels, must get licenses to operate legally. Other businesses, such as barbers or plumbers, must have occupational licenses and liability insurance. Zoning ordinances which forbid the operation of businesses in residential neighborhoods can restrict the location of a sole proprietorship. If an owner plans to hire employees, he or she must obtain an employer identification number (EIN) from the Internal Revenue Service for tax purposes.

Total Control and Retention of Profits In a sole proprietorship, the owner has complete control of the business and makes all of the decisions. The proprietor also gets to keep all of the profits from the business. Proprietors, however, must still pay taxes on the profits that they make.

One-Time Taxation of Profits Sole proprietorships do not pay taxes as a business. The sole proprietor pays taxes based on his or her income. A full-time sole proprietor will pay income

As You Read

Predict Who pays taxes in a business partnership?

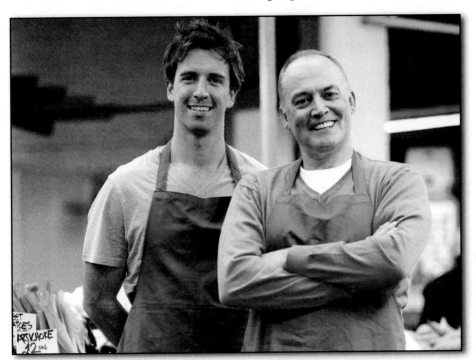

Family Business Many sole proprietorships are family-owned businesses passed down from one generation to the next. *About what percentage of businesses in the U.S. are sole proprietorships?*

taxes on all profits made in a year. If the business is a part-time venture, those profits plus all other income made by the sole proprietor are taxed.

Disadvantages of a Sole Proprietorship

Sole proprietorships have several disadvantages. These disadvantages include limited capital, unlimited liability, and limited lifetime.

Limited Capital An obvious shortcoming of a sole proprietorship is the fact that the business owner has limited access to capital. All money used to finance the business must come from the proprietor's savings or income, or from loans obtained by the proprietor.

Unlimited Liability Perhaps the biggest disadvantage of a sole proprietorship is unlimited liability. **Unlimited liability is a legal duty placed on a business owner that requires the owner to be responsible for all losses experienced by the business.** Even the personal property of a sole proprietor may be used to satisfy the debts of the business.

Limited Lifetime Unlike a corporation, which has **perpetual** existence, a sole proprietorship lasts only as long as the proprietor. When the proprietor dies or chooses to sell or close the business, the business ceases to exist.

Vocabulary You can find vocabulary definitions in the **Key Terms** glossary and Academic Vocabulary glossary in the back of this book.

General Partnerships

How can you start a business with some friends?

Partnership law is in a developmental stage. A new law called the Revised Uniform Partnership Act (RUPA) has been adopted by many states. However, many states still operate under the traditional Uniform Partnership Act (UPA). This chapter will discuss both laws and point out where the two acts are the same and where they differ. You will need to find out which partnership act your state follows.

Elements of a Partnership

A **partnership, according to the RUPA, is an association of two or more persons to carry on as co-owners of a business for profit.** This definition differs slightly from the definition in UPA, but both emphasize two essential elements:
- A partnership must involve at least two persons.
- A partnership must carry on a business for profit.

Advantages and Disadvantages of a Partnership

Partnerships have several advantages over sole proprietorships. More capital and credit is usually available to a partnership. The burden of all the work does not fall on one person. A partner does not have sole responsibility for any losses suffered.

A disadvantage to a partnership is that the partners must share the profits. Also, because all partners have a voice in running the business, bickering can cause problems. The biggest disadvantage is that the partners share in the liability. Each partner is responsible for the other partners' actions taken within the scope of the partnership. Partners share in two types of liability.

Contract Liability Partners have joint liability when a contract is made for the partnership. **Joint liability is liability shared by two or more people.** Every partner must be included in a breach of contract case against the partnership.

Tort Liability In a tort case against the partnership, partners have joint and several liability. Joint and several liability means that a tort case can be brought against all of the partners, one of the partners, or any combination of the partners. The partners named in the tort case must pay if they lose in court. If one partner settles the case on his or her own behalf, the rest of the partners are not released from the lawsuit. However, the partner who is actually responsible for the tort may be forced to pay the other partners back.

Forming a General Partnership

A general partnership can be formed in one of two ways: by agreement and by proof of existence.

Partnership by Agreement Forming a general partnership by agreement requires the valid assent of all parties. Such an agreement is usually express and may be written or oral. However, under the Statute of Frauds, if a partnership is to last more than a year, it must be in writing. A partnership formed to sell, buy, or lease real property must also be in writing. The partnership agreement is called the Articles of Partnership.

A partnership that is set to last for a certain period of time or to do a certain job is a term partnership. Partners cannot leave a term partnership until the time has passed or the job is done. A partnership at will means that the partners are free to leave the partnership any time that they want to. No liability follows a partner who leaves such a partnership.

Partnership by Proof of Existence A partnership can also be formed by the way two or more people conduct business together, regardless of what they label the business. For example, if two or more people share the profits of a business venture, it is likely that a partnership exists. This is called a partnership by proof of existence. Both the RUPA and the UPA provide a list of characteristics to show whether a partnership actually exists.

Partnerships An advantage a partnership has over a sole proprietorship is the burden of all the work does not fall on one person. *What is the main disadvantage of a partnership?*

Types of Partners

The law recognizes five types of partners who may be involved in a partnership: general, secret, silent, dormant, and limited. They differ according to how active a role they play in the partnership, whether their role is known to the public, and the amount of liability they have.

General Partner A general partner plays an active role in the management of the partnership and is known to the public. Every partnership must have at least one general partner. A general partner has unlimited liability.

Secret Partner A secret partner is a general partner who has an active role in the management of the partnership, but whose connection with the partnership is kept a secret. A secret partner has unlimited liability.

Silent Partner A silent partner does not play an active role, but is known to the public. A silent partner has unlimited liability.

Case Study – Roach v. Mead

Critical Thinking *Is one partner liable for the actions of the other partner?*

Flex Your Reading Note key facts in the text below and look up words you do not understand. Restate difficult ideas in your own words. Go back and reread the text quickly to make sure you did not miss any important detail. Now, you are ready to formulate an opinion.

Bad Advice? On November 1, 1979, David Berentson and Kenneth Mead formed a law partnership. One of their clients was William Roach. Mr. Roach owned a meter repair business. Mr. Berentson and Mr. Mead assisted Mr. Roach with legal issues arising from his business, including preparing his tax returns. They also represented him on various traffic infractions.

In June 1980, Mr. Roach sold his business for $50,000. In November 1980, he consulted with Mr. Mead about how to invest $20,000 of the profits. At that time, Mr. Mead needed a loan. He offered to take the money from Mr. Roach and pay him 15% interest in return. Mr. Mead drafted a promissory note that stated Mr. Mead would pay Mr. Roach $23,000 on or before November 25, 1982. Mr. Mead never paid Mr. Roach the $23,000, and Mr. Mead eventually declared bankruptcy.

Mr. Roach then sued Mr. Berentson. Mr. Roach argued that since Mr. Berentson was Mr. Mead's partner, Mr. Berentson could be held liable for Mr. Mead's actions. Mr. Roach argued that Mr. Mead had negligently given him bad legal advice by: not advising Mr. Roach to consult with an uninterested attorney when Mr. Mead took the $20,000; and not advising him that a 15% interest rate was unenforceable because it would be usury.

Roach v. Mead, 722 P.2d 1229 (Ore. 1986)

Go to **ConnectEd.mcgraw-hill.com** for more case study practice.

Dormant Partner A **dormant** partner is a general partner who takes no active part in the management of the firm and whose connection with the firm is kept secret. A dormant partner, however, still has unlimited liability.

Limited Partner A limited partner is one whose liability does not extend beyond his or her investment. Limited partnerships are discussed later in this section.

Partnership Rights

Partners share certain rights. These rights include the right to use the property, the right to manage the firm, and the right to share in the profits.

Property Rights of the Partners It is important to distinguish between property that belongs to the partnership and property that belongs to individual partners. Property contributed directly to the partnership when the partnership is created is partnership property.

The UPA and the RUPA differ on the right to use property. According to the RUPA: "A partner is not co-owner of partnership property and has no interest in partnership property which can be transferred either voluntarily or involuntarily." Partners are permitted to use partnership property, but the right to use the property is limited to partnership purposes. In contrast, the UPA states that partners are co-owners of all real and personal property included in the partnership. This co-ownership of property, called tenancy in partnership by the UPA, creates certain limitations. For example, a partner cannot personally transfer ownership of property. Also, the property cannot be taken by a partner's personal creditors.

Right to Manage the Firm Unless otherwise stated in the partnership agreement, each partner has an equal voice in managing the firm. Each partner can bind the partnership on any matter within the scope of its business affairs. In a disagreement, the decision of the majority is final. If there is an even number of partners and the vote is split, no decision can be made. If a deadlock persists, the partners might consider ending their partnership.

Right to Share in the Profits Unless otherwise stated in the partnership agreement, partners share equally in the profits, regardless of their initial capital contribution or the time devoted by each partner to the business. This right can be assigned to others. Partners also have a right to reimbursement for any money they personally spend on behalf of the partnership.

Enforcement Rights Under the UPA, partners had three enforcement rights: the right to inspect the firm's books; the right to an account; and the right to dissolve the partnership. The RUPA added a fourth right: a partner has the right to sue a partner or the partnership itself to enforce his or her rights as stated in the partnership agreement or in the RUPA.

Reading Check

Analyze *What is the difference between limited and unlimited liability?*

Partnership Duties

The RUPA states that partners have three duties: loyalty, obedience, and due care.

The Duty of Loyalty Loyalty is always the first duty because a partnership is a fiduciary relationship, or a relationship based on trust. The RUPA emphasizes loyalty more strongly than the UPA did. According to the RUPA, each partner must:

- tell the partnership about property, profits, or benefits that any partner receives for using partnership property
- avoid dealing with individuals who have any interest that somehow hurts the partnership
- avoid competing with the partnership

A partner does keep the right to look after his or her own interests before the partnership is actually formed.

The Duty of Obedience Once the partners have written the articles of partnership, the partners have the duty to obey those articles. The partners must follow the decisions made by the partners. If a partner disobeys the articles of partnership or partnership decisions, then that partner will be liable for any loss that results.

The Duty of Due Care The duty of due care means that a partner must work to the best of his or her ability, based on his or her talents, education, and experience, when that partner is working on partnership business.

Terminating a Partnership

A partnership may end in a number of ways. A partner may die, go bankrupt, become incapacitated, be expelled by the other partners, or simply wish to leave a partnership. Partners can leave a partnership any time they want to. However, they do not always have the legal right to do so. Whether a partner has the right to leave may depend on whether the partnership is a term partnership or a partnership at will. If the partner does not have the right, he or she may have to pay damages to the other partners.

Dissolution of a Partnership A dissolution is when a partnership (or any legal entity) breaks up. Dissolution is not the same as the termination of the business. Dissolution occurs at the moment one partner ceases to be associated with the firm. There are three ways dissolution can happen:

- **By the acts of the partners.** This arises when one partner decides to leave and the other partners agree; when the original agreement had a set time period or goal that has been reached; or when the majority of partners vote to expel a partner.
- **By operation of law.** This arises in cases of bankruptcy or death of a partner.

- **By a court order.** This arises when partners obtain a court order to end the partnership because of misconduct, **incompetence**, or incapacity of a partner.

Winding up a Partnership The dissolution of a partnership does not cause it to end immediately. The partnership must close down its business operations, called a winding up. During the winding up period, the business does not continue. The partners perform an accounting of the old firm's affairs, sell the partnership property, pay creditors, and divide what remains of the profits.

Dissociation of a Partnership Dissolution does not necessarily end a partnership. Other partners may want to continue the business. If so, a new agreement must be drawn up regarding the conduct of a new firm. There must be an accounting of the old firm's affairs and new financial arrangements must be made regarding the new firm. Public notice must be given to relieve retiring partners from liability for any new debts.

Under the UPA, a partnership ends automatically any time a partner leaves the partnership. The RUPA changed the law by adding a way for a partnership to continue even after a partner leaves, called a dissociation. **A dissociation, according to the RUPA, is when a partner is no longer associated with the firm.** A dissociation allows the business to continue doing business with the remaining partners or with a new partner.

Courdy v. Paycom Billing Services, Inc.
2006 WL 847212 (Cal. Ct. App. 2006)

On July 1, 1997, Edward Courdy and Paycom Billing Services, Inc. (Paycom) entered into a general partnership called Internet Commerce Solutions (ICS). According to the written partnership agreement, the purpose of the partnership was "to engage in the business of Internet Commerce." ICS provided check processing for Internet merchants by taking check information from the merchants and relaying that information to banks. After experiencing problems with the online check processing, Paycom decided to end the partnership. It gave notice on August 12, 1998, that it wished to dissolve the partnership. Six days later, Paycom then notified ICS's clients that it would be providing a new check-processing service plus a credit-card processing service. Courdy sued Paycom on a number of counts, including fraud, arguing that Paycom stole Internet Commerce from ICS when it dissolved the partnership.

Ruling and Resolution
The California Court of Appeals held that the partnership was at will; that is, it could be dissolved at any time. Courdy did not have a right to any damages from profits gained by Paycom from former ICS clients.

Critical Thinking Are partnerships at will a good thing?

Limited Partnerships Limited partners have no right to manage a partnership, but have only limited liability if the partnership is sued or goes bankrupt. *What happens to a limited partner who gets involved in running a partnership?*

Other Types of Partnerships

The business world constantly adjusts to the changing needs of the marketplace. As a result, several types of partnerships that differ from general partnerships are now legally recognized.

Limited Partnerships Limited partnerships are controlled by provisions of the Revised Uniform Limited Partnership Act (RULPA). **A limited partnership is a partnership formed by two or more persons, with one or more general partners and one or more limited partners.** The general partners of a limited partnership have the same types of duties as a general partner in a general partnership. Limited partners are investors who have no right to manage the partnership.

Limited partnerships must meet stricter formalities than general partnerships. The names of the limited partners cannot appear in the partnership name. The partners must file a certificate of limited partnership with the appropriate state or county office. The business name must indicate that it is a limited partnership. This is to warn third parties that some partners have only limited liability.

In terms of liability, the limited partnership falls between the general partnership, in which all owners have unlimited liability, and the corporation, in which all owners have limited liability. When a limited partnership ends, the assets are first distributed to creditors of the firm, and then to the partners.

Registered Limited Liability Partnerships A **limited liability partnership (LLP) is a registered partnership in which each partner is not liable for the acts of the other partners.** Partners can escape joint and several liability for the torts, wrongful acts, negligence, or misconduct of other partners by registering with the appropriate state office. The registration statement usually includes the following information:

- the name of the partnership
- the purpose of the partnership
- the number of partners in the partnership
- a statement of the intent to form an LLP
- the address of the partnership's main place of business
- the name and address of a statutory agent for service of process

All the partners, or at least the partners holding a majority interest in the partnership, must file the statement. The registration statement must be updated annually. LLPs are taxed in the same way as general partnerships.

Partnership-Type Business Organizations

Other partnership-type business organizations include limited partnership associations and joint ventures.

Limited Partnership Associations A limited partnership association is like a corporation in that it is considered an entity having an existence all its own. The participants own shares in the association and can convey their shares to another individual as long as the other participants vote to accept the new individual. The participants can lose only the amount of their initial investment. Not every state has made statutory provisions for limited partnership associations.

Joint Ventures A joint venture is a business enterprise in which two or more participants combine in order to complete a single task. There is no ongoing relationship in a joint venture, unlike a partnership.

After You Read

Summarize What are the different types of partners?

SECTION 16.1 ASSESSMENT

Self Check

1. What is a sole proprietorship?
2. What is a partnership?
3. What is a limited partnership?

Academic Connection

English Language Arts Get together with three other members of the class to form a partnership. Decide what kind of business you want to go into, what kind of partnership to create, and how much each partner will invest. Then decide how the duties of managing the business might be divided, what kind of partner each person will be, and how the profits will be split. For example, one partner might want to be a secret partner and another a dormant partner. One partner might want to focus on running the day-to-day operations of the business and the other focus on bringing in business. Write up a brief partnership agreement laying out what you decide.

Critical Thinking

Extent of Liability Suppose you are running a sole proprietorship in a building that you have just purchased. The floor collapses and injures several customers. Will your losses be limited to the amount of money in your company's business accounts?

Corporations and Limited Liability Companies

What You'll Learn

- ◆ Characterize corporations.
- ◆ Explain the different types of corporations.
- ◆ Discuss the steps involved in forming a corporation.
- ◆ Explain what a limited liability company is.
- ◆ List the steps in forming a limited liability company.

Why It's Important

Knowing how to form a corporation or limited liability company will help you if you want to expand your business.

Reading Guide

Before You Read

Connect How many different corporations can you name?

Focus on Ideas

A corporation is treated by law as a person.

Take Notes

Go to connectED.mcgraw-hill.com to download a graphic organizer you can use to take notes as you read this section

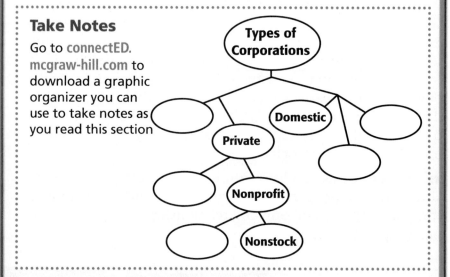

Key Terms

You will learn these legal words and expressions in this chapter. You can also find these terms in *Black's Law Dictionary* or in an online legal dictionary.

- corporation
- share
- shareholder
- articles of incorporation
- certificate of incorporation
- limited liability company (LLC)
- expropriation

Academic Vocabulary

You will find these words in your readings and in your tests. Look them up in a dictionary and familiarize yourself with them.

- domestic
- process
- similar

Corporations

Are all corporations giant multinational companies?

A corporation is an entity with the legal authority to act as a single person, distinct from its owners. Unlike a sole proprietorship or partnership, a corporation is treated by law as if it is an individual person. It can make contracts, buy and sell goods, sue, and be sued.

All corporations have the same basic form. Ownership of a corporation is divided into shares. **A share is a single unit of ownership of a corporation. A shareholder is an individual who owns shares of a corporation.** Each shareholder has one vote for each share of stock that he or she owns in the corporation. Shareholders elect a board of directors who run the corporation.

As You Read

Predict What are the disadvantages of a corporation?

Advantages and Disadvantages of a Corporation

Corporations have several advantages. A corporation can obtain a great deal of capital by selling shares, while general partnerships and sole proprietorships cannot. Each shareholder's liability is limited to the amount of money he or she paid for shares in the corporation. Corporations also have perpetual existence. This means that a corporation continues to exist after the founders, shareholders, managers, and directors are gone.

Corporations also have disadvantages. First, a corporation's income may be taxed more than once: the corporation is taxed on the profits it makes, and then the shareholders are taxed on the dividends (share of the profits) they receive. This is called double taxation. Second, corporations face numerous government regulations and are looked at very closely. Finally, the original founders of the corporation can lose control and ownership of the corporation to the shareholders or the board of directors.

Types of Corporations

Not all corporations are large. In fact, about 40 percent of all corporations have fewer than five employees. Corporations may be classified as public or private corporations, stock or nonstock corporations, and domestic, foreign, or alien corporations (see **Figure 16.1** on page 368).

Public Corporations Public corporations include incorporated political units, such as towns, villages, cities, and school districts. These entities often incorporate to obtain the protections of this form of business organization, such as limited liability.

Private Corporations Private corporations are owned by private individuals and may be for profit or nonprofit. For profit corporations are organized for the purpose of making money. A for profit corporation may be either a C corporation or an S corporation. A C corporation is a standard corporation and the type subject to double taxation: the corporation is taxed on its income and the shareholders are taxed on their dividends.

Legal Talk

De jure: *adj* Latin for as a matter of law.
De facto: *adj* Latin for as a matter of fact.

Vocabulary Builder In class, list as many words as you can think of in two minutes that come from the Latin root *jure*. Then, compare your list with the rest of the class.

Figure 16.1 Types of Corporations

Private Most corporations are privately held corporations. They are organized to make a profit and are usually owned by a small group of private individuals.

Public A public corporation is a corporation created by the federal, state, or local government for governmental purposes, or a large private corporation that sells its stock to the general public.

Nonprofit A nonprofit corporation, such as Habitat for Humanity, is formed for educational, religious, charitable, or social purposes. Membership is acquired by agreement, rather than by acquisition of stock, and no stockholder may share in the profits.

There are different types of corporations, but they all have the same form. *What is the difference between a domestic and a foreign corporation?*

An S corporation is a special type of corporation that avoids double taxation. With an S corporation, the corporation itself does not pay income tax and the shareholders pay tax on their share of the income as if they were partners. However, an S corporation has limitations on the number of shareholders it can have.

Nonprofit corporations are formed for educational, religious, charitable, or social purposes. A nonprofit corporation in which membership is acquired by agreement, rather than by the sale and acquisition of stock, is called a nonstock corporation.

Domestic, Foreign, and Alien Corporations A corporation is considered a **domestic** corporation in the state in which it is incorporated. In any other state in which it operates, a corporation is considered a foreign corporation. An alien corporation is one that is incorporated in another country but does business in this country.

Forming a Corporation

Creating a corporation requires extensive paperwork according to each state's laws. Corporations can choose any state to incorporate in, even if they do not do business in that state. Despite differences, in the requirements of different states, there are many common procedures to the incorporation **process**.

Corporate Promoters A corporate promoter is someone who organizes the new corporation. The promoter may help assemble investors, lease office and warehouse space, purchase supplies and equipment, and hire employees. Promoters are personally liable for the contracts they make in the name of the corporation.

Choosing a Corporate Name The name of a corporation must include the word *corporation*, *incorporated*, or *company*, or the abbreviation for one of these words. A corporation cannot use the name of another corporation, foreign or domestic. In some states, the name cannot be **similar** to another business name in use.

Articles of Incorporation The articles of incorporation is a legal document filed with the state to establish a corporation. It describes the corporation's organization, powers, and authority. This can sometimes be done online. There may be a requirement to have a minimum amount of capital, such as $500 to $1,000. After the application is filed and fees are paid to the office of the secretary of state, the company will receive a certificate of incorporation. A certificate of incorporation is a corporation's official authorization to do business in a state. In some states, the certificate is called a charter.

Structure of the Corporation The shareholders of a new corporation elect a board of directors. The board elects a chairman and the top officers of the corporation. The officers manage the company and carry out the board's policies and decisions. Officers can be members of the board, or they may be hired employees.

Reading Check

Discuss *What are the requirements for a corporate name?*

Vocabulary You can find vocabulary definitions in the **Key Terms** glossary and Academic Vocabulary glossary in the back of this book.

Global Law

Brazilian Corporations

In 2002, the country of Brazil updated its corporation laws by passing the New Civil Code, Law 10.406. Under that system, there are many different business organizational structures. However, there are two main forms that make up the majority of businesses.

Limitadas

A *sociedade por quotas de responsabilidade limitada (limitada)* is similar to a limited liability company, limited partnership, or closely-held company in the United States. By law, a *limitada* must have at least two partners. Partners can be either individuals or legal entities.

The articles of association for a *limitada* must state the *limitada's* name and for what period of time the business has been created. It must also state the company's main activities and the location of its main place of business.

Finally, the *limitada* can be managed by all the partners, some of the partners, or by only one partner. The only requirement is that power to run the company must be in the hands of at least one legal resident of Brazil.

Sociedade anônima

The *sociedade anônima* is like a joint-stock company or corporation in the United States. Like a *limitada,* the *sociedade anônima* requires no less than two partners. However, there are additional requirements to forming one.

For example, all the documents relating to the formation of a *sociedade anônima* must be filed at the commercial registry. It must then be published in the *Official Gazette* and in a second major newspaper in the region where the company will be located.

Finally, shareholders of stock in *sociedade anônimas* have the following rights: the right to the company's profits; the right to distribution of the company's assets, if the company is dissolved; and the right to oversee the company's management.

Across Cultures: Ethanol Fuel

As the rest of the world is struggling to get enough oil for its energy needs, Brazil has shifted its focus from petroleum to ethanol. At least 20% of Brazilian cars run on pure ethanol, which is produced in Brazil from sugar cane. Many countries are looking to follow Brazil's lead in the future.

Critical Thinking: *Is publishing the documents for forming a new corporation in a newspaper a good idea?*

Incorporation Problems

If the incorporation process has been completed, the corporation legally exists and it is known as a *de jure* corporation. However, sometimes mistakes or problems interrupt the incorporation process. Although the corporation does not legally exist, some states will still recognize it as a *de facto* corporation as long as the incorporators made a good faith attempt to incorporate.

Piercing the Corporate Veil

The corporate entity can be seen as a veil protecting the shareholders from liability. Under some circumstances, however, the court will "pierce the corporate veil" and hold shareholders personally liable. This happens when a corporation is formed to avoid paying debt or is run like a sole proprietorship. The court will also hold shareholders liable if they use corporate assets for their own purposes or commit fraud in the corporation's name.

Limited Liability Companies

Are there any other ways you could set up your own company?

A **limited liability company (LLC) is an entity with the legal authority to act as a single person, distinct from its owners, and combines the best features of a partnership and a corporation.** Like a corporation, it offers limited liability to its owners. Like the partners in a partnership, the owners of an LLC escape double taxation.

The first step in forming an LLC is to draw up the articles of organization. The LLC must have a statutory agent within the state where it is organized. Filing fees must also be paid.

The dissolution of an LLC is similar to a partnership and can occur for any of the same reasons. It must also be followed by a winding up to put the LLC officially out of business. However, a winding up need not follow a dissolution if the remaining members want to continue the LLC.

Doing Business Internationally

What do you think you would need to do to create a company abroad?

Different countries have different tax codes and different laws regarding establishing a business. For example, many countries have favorable corporate tax laws designed to attract corporations there. On the other hand, the LLC form of business does not exist in most countries. Businesses in other countries are also subject to expropriation. **Expropriation is when a government seizes a privately-owned business to be used for a public purpose.**

After You Read

Summarize What are the different types of corporations?

SECTION 16.2 ASSESSMENT

Self Check

1. What is a corporation?
2. What is the difference between a public and a private corporation?
3. What is a limited liability company?

Academic Connection

Mathematics The Miller Metal Products Corporation manufactures hand-held can openers. It plans to manufacture 750,000 can openers to be sold at $0.44 each. The fixed costs to make them are $142,570. The variable costs to make them are $0.19 each. How many can openers must Miller Metal Products sell to break even?

CONCEPT **Number and Operations:** To find the break-even point in units, use the following formula:

Total Fixed Costs ÷ (Selling Price per Unit – Variable Costs per Unit)

 For more math practice, go to the Math Appendix.

Critical Thinking

Changing Form Why might a sole proprietorship or a partnership want to incorporate?

Summary

Section 16.1 Sole Proprietorships and Partnerships

◆ A sole proprietorship is a form of business that is owned and operated by one person.

◆ A partnership is an association of two or more persons to carry on as co-owners of a business for profit.

◆ General partnerships can be formed by agreement or by proof of existence.

◆ There are five types of partners: general, secret, silent, dormant, and limited.

◆ Partners have three duties: to be loyal to the firm; to be obedient to the arrangements made by the partnership agreement; and to act with due care in carrying out the business of the firm.

◆ Partnerships can end through dissociation and dissolution.

Section 16.2 Corporations and Limited Liability Companies

◆ A corporation is an entity with the legal authority to act as a single person, distinct from its owners.

◆ A shareholder is an individual who owns shares of a corporation.

◆ A share is a single unit of ownership of a corporation.

◆ Corporations may be classified as public or private corporations, stock or nonstock corporations, and domestic, foreign, or alien corporations.

◆ A limited liability company (LLC) is an entity with the legal authority to act as a single person, distinct from its owners, and combines the best features of a partnership and a corporation.

Vocabulary Builder

1 On a sheet of paper, use each of these terms in a sentence.

Key Terms

- sole proprietorship
- unlimited liability
- partnership
- joint liability
- dissolution
- dissociation
- limited partnership
- limited liability partnership (LLP)
- corporation
- share
- shareholder
- articles of incorporation
- certificate of incorporation
- limited liability company (LLC)
- expropriation

Academic Vocabulary

- perpetual
- dormant
- incompetence
- domestic
- process
- similar

Key Points Review

Answer the following questions. Refer to the chapter for additional reinforcement.

2 What are the advantages and disadvantages of a sole proprietorship?

3 What is unlimited liability?

4 What are the advantages of forming a partnership?

5 What is the difference between a term partnership and a partnership at will?

6 What are the advantages of a corporation?

7 What are the steps in the formation of a corporation?

8 What are the articles of incorporation?

9 What is needed to form an LLC?

Standardized Test Practice

10 Read the following information about the concept of micro-enterprise development and complete questions 1 and 2.

The concept of micro-enterprise development has its roots in the recognition of a previously untapped market—skilled or motivated individuals who could provide desired services to the public but lacked access to traditional forms of credit and, in many cases, business and financial expertise. The micro-enterprise theory is simple. Loan these individuals small amounts of money for business start-up costs, make the loan terms affordable, and give them business training and support. This formula has proven to be a success.

Today the term micro-enterprise is commonly used to describe a business with up to five employees, which requires $25,000 or less in start-up capital, and does not have access to the traditional commercial banking sector. Many aspiring micro-entrepreneurs have little formal business training and varying levels of education. Training and technical assistance can often be the biggest factor in the success of a new business.

1. Which statement best describes what a micro-enterprise is?

Ⓐ a group of individuals who invest in small business concepts

Ⓑ business counselors who work with entrepreneurs to start companies

Ⓒ technical assistants who guide entrepreneurs with technology problems

Ⓓ small businesses with few employees that need minimal start-up capital

2. Often the biggest factor to the success of a micro-enterprise is the

Ⓐ ability to have an endless supply of funds

Ⓑ ability to offer training and technical assistance

Ⓒ ability to have new entrepreneurs be self-sufficient

Ⓓ ability to provide raw materials and employees

 Test-Taking Strategies Notes that are complete and well organized, with key terms defined and highlighted, will make reviewing for a test easier.

Apply and Debate

Read the following scenarios. Get together with other students in pairs or groups of three and take a position on each scenario. Debate your position in class with students taking the opposite position or prepare a written argument justifying your position.

11 **Who Owns a Name**

Mark registered the business name Crazy Cookies, but did not open his bakery right away. When Ruth later opened Crazy Cool Cookies, Mark sued her for infringing on his registered business name.

You Debate *Should Ruth be allowed to use the business name? Why or why not?*

12 **Disagreeing Partner**

Ming was one of four general partners in a business. The other partners voted to terminate a contract. Ming disagreed, fearing they might be sued. They were.

You Debate *If you were one of the other partners, would you excuse Ming from being held liable in the lawsuit as partnership law requires since he had disagreed?*

13 **Widow Partner**

Tasha's husband was a partner in a store. When he died, the other partners continued to pay Tasha for his share of the profits. Tasha eventually decided to go into the store every day to help. One day, a patron tripped in the store and sued.

You Debate *If you were the lawyer for the suing patron, would you make a case that Tasha is also one of the partners?*

14 **Lost Letter**

Luca filed to incorporate his company. He was told that the charter was in the mail. He began his business. Later, when he was sued for an accident, he learned that the state had never mailed the incorporation charter and he was not protected.

You Debate *If you were the lawyer for Luca, would you defend him by saying that he was told that his business was incorporated?*

15 **Putting on a Corporate Veil**

Your sole proprietorship company has debts of $200,000 but only $27,000 in cash. You consider incorporating to protect yourself, in case your creditors sue you for failure to pay.

You Debate *Is it legal and valid to incorporate to get the protections under law, even though you know you may not be able to pay your debts?*

Case Study Practice– Hurwitz v. Padden

16 When Does a Partnership End? In September 1991, Thomas Hurwitz and Michael Padden formed a two-person law firm. They failed to enter into a written partnership agreement, but orally agreed to share all firm proceeds on a 50-50 basis. They also agreed to split all costs and fees on a 50-50 basis. In January 1993, Mr. Hurwitz and Mr. Padden changed their firm from a partnership to a limited liability company. On February 15, 1996, Mr. Padden notified Mr. Hurwitz that he wanted to dissolve the firm effective March 1, 1996. The two men resolved all the business issues involving their relationship except for a batch of attorneys' fees from several of the firm's cases, which Mr. Padden worked on after he gave notice of termination. Mr. Padden argued that since he worked on the cases after dissolution began, he was entitled to additional fees. Mr. Hurwitz argued that during dissolution, fees are split the same as they were prior to dissolution.

Source: Hurwitz v. Padden, 581 N.W.2d 359 (Minn. Ct. App. 1998)

Practice How should the fees be split?

17 Ethics Application

Conflict of Interest? Moesha Allen is co-owner of a small restaurant in a partnership at will. She is planning on leaving the partnership and opening her own restaurant in a couple of months. Her favorite customers keep asking her about her plans for the future.

◆ Is Moesha entitled to tell her customers about her new restaurant or will it appear as if she is trying to steal customers?

18 Think back to the Legal Briefs feature you read at the beginning of the chapter. Research the business culture of a non-English speaking country to learn about that country's protocol, customs, and business etiquette. Take notes on your research, and then write one or more paragraphs to summarize your research, identifying specific things you found interesting or unusual.

17 Operating a Corporation

Legal Briefs

Corporate Social Responsibility

Good citizenship can lead to great profits.

Corporate decision makers have come to realize that the company has an impact on more than just the shareholders and managers. Corporations also have an impact on society, and that impact influences the success of the business.

Both large and small companies have come to understand that being a good corporate citizen has become increasingly important for the company's bottom line. Shareholders and the citizenry expect honesty and philanthropy from modern-day corporations.

McDonald's Corporation funds the charitable Ronald McDonald Houses that provide housing for parents of hospitalized children. The Anderson Corporation, manufacturer of windows and doors, partnered with Habitat for Humanity to build 100 homes during a five-year period.

Some companies emphasize corporate social responsibility in their company's Code of Conduct. Consider this excerpt from the Procter and Gamble Employee Code of Conduct:

"Strong performance is critical to our success, but just as important is how we go about achieving result—with honesty and respect, without taking shortcuts, and by operating ethically and with integrity in all that we do."

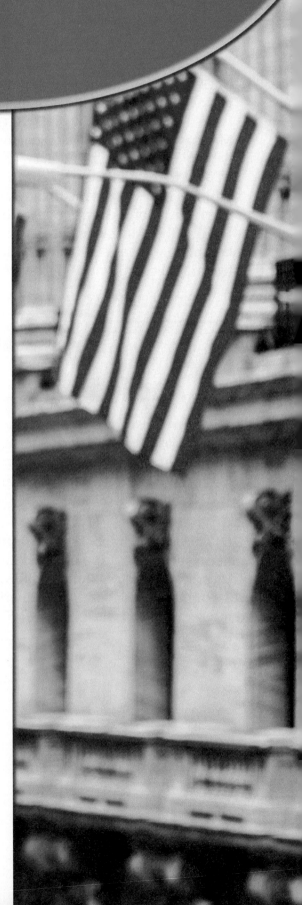

Stock Exchange Shares in U.S. and global companies are publicly traded in marketplaces called stock exchanges. *What is the most famous stock exchange in the United States?*

What You'll Learn

- Distinguish the roles of corporate directors and corporate officers.
- List the rights shareholders have.
- Explain the business judgment rule.
- Explain the fairness rule.
- Describe the liability of corporate directors and officers.

Why It's Important

If you ever manage or buy stock in a corporation, you need to know how a corporation is run and what rights shareholders have.

Reading Guide

Before You Read

Connect You have probably heard of corporations such as Bank of America, Microsoft, and Coca-Cola. Who do you think actually owns these companies?

Focus on Ideas

Owners of stock in a corporation have certain rights.

Take Notes

Go to connectED. mcgraw-hill.com to download a graphic organizer you can use to take notes as you read this section.

Rights of Shareholders

Right to Receive a Stock Certificate

Key Terms

You will learn these legal words and expressions in this chapter. You can also find these terms in *Black's Law Dictionary* or in an online legal dictionary.

- corporate director
- corporate officer
- direct suit
- derivative suit
- insider trading

Academic Vocabulary

You will find these words in your readings and in your tests. Look them up in a dictionary and familiarize yourself with them.

- proportionate
- preemptive
- exploit

Corporate Management

What is the difference between a corporate director and a corporate officer?

In a sole proprietorship or a partnership, power is concentrated in the hands of a few individuals. In a corporation, power is scattered among many individuals and institutions that make up the directors, corporate officers, and shareholders. Some key figures can also play more than one role. For example, directors can be officers and shareholders of the corporation.

As You Read

Predict Do shareholders have any say in the management of a corporation?

Corporate Directors

Corporate directors are people elected by the shareholders to make broad policy decisions in the running of a corporation. Generally, directors do not have to meet any legal qualifications unless the corporation's certificate of incorporation or its bylaws specify. For example, the bylaws might require that a director be a shareholder or a state resident. Directors usually serve for a set number of years and must be reelected by the shareholders. Directors are subject to the duty of due care and the duty of loyalty to the corporation.

Corporate Officers

Corporate officers are people chosen by the directors to run the day-to-day affairs of a corporation. The officers include a president, several vice-presidents, a secretary, a treasurer, and assistant officers. Officers are agents of the corporation. This means that the rules of agency law apply. Like directors, officers are subject to the duties of loyalty and due care.

Corporate Shareholders

Corporate shareholders, or simply shareholders, are the owners of a corporation based on the number of shares they hold. Shareholders are also called investors, but in fact they are both the investors in and owners of a corporation. Shareholders are often individual people, but partnerships, labor union retirement funds, and other corporations can also be shareholders in a corporation.

The Rights of Shareholders

What rights do shareholders of a corporation have?

Owners of stock in a corporation acquire certain rights. These include the right to:

- receive a stock certificate
- receive dividends
- examine the corporate books and records
- transfer all shares
- maintain a proportionate share of stock
- exercise a vote for each share of stock owned
- sue

Legal Talk

Dividend: *n* Portion of a corporation's profits paid to shareholders.

Proxy: *n* Person authorized to vote on behalf of shareholders.

Vocabulary Builder List five synonyms for *dividend* and five synonyms for *proxy*. If you need help, you can find synonyms in a printed or online thesaurus.

Global Law

Businesses in South Africa

All companies in South Africa are governed by the Companies Act, which is based on the English system of company law. There are specific rules and regulations to follow for forming a business. The Act is governed by the Companies and Intellectual Property Registration Office (CIPRO).

Steps to Incorporation

There are three steps for a company to follow before it can be incorporated in South Africa.

1 The company must reserve a company name.

2 The company must file a memorandum and articles of association.

3 The company must provide a written consent of auditors to act for the company.

The first and third steps are straightforward. The second step, however, requires a few more steps.

Memorandum and Articles of Association

The memorandum and articles of association must include the following:

1 the name of the company

2 the primary purpose and business of the company

3 the number of shares and the amount of capital invested in the company

In addition to registering with CIPRO, new companies usually must register with other government offices, such as tax and unemployment offices. Finally, the number of shareholders needed depends on the type of company. A private company needs only one shareholder and a director, who may be the same person. In contrast, a public company must have at least seven shareholders and at least two directors.

> #### Across Cultures: Three Capital Cities
> South Africa has three capital cities. Pretoria is the administrative capital, where the president and his cabinet reside. Cape Town is the legislative capital, where the National Assembly meets. Bloemfontein is the judicial capital, where the Constitutional Court sits.

Critical Thinking: *What is a reason for requiring at least seven shareholders and two directors for a public company?*

Right to Receive a Stock Certificate

A stock certificate proves that the shareholder owns part of the corporation. The right to receive this document is an essential shareholder's right.

Right to Receive Dividends

Dividends are profits distributed to shareholders. When a corporation has made a profit, the board of directors may declare a dividend. Dividends must be distributed proportionately among shareholders. A dividend can be in the form of shares or cash.

Directors do not automatically have to declare a dividend when the corporation has made a profit. They may instead decide to keep the profit for the benefit of the corporation.

Right to Examine Corporate Books and Records

The law requires a corporation to keep records of its business affairs, including a list of shareholders, an accounting of all transactions, and the minutes of all directors' meetings. Shareholders have a statutory right to see these records.

Right to Transfer All Shares

Shareholders have the right to transfer or sell their shares. The person who sells or transfers stock is the transferor, and the person who receives it is the transferee.

Right to Maintain a Proportionate Share of Stocks

Shareholders have the right to purchase a **proportionate** share of every new stock issue before it is offered to the public. This right is called the shareholder's **preemptive** right. The purpose of this right is to prevent directors from taking control of the corporation by issuing more shares and buying them all themselves. However, this right can be limited or denied by the corporation's certificate of incorporation, by its bylaws or regulations, or by state law.

Right to Vote for Each Share of a Stock Owned

Shareholders have voting powers as part owners. They can, therefore, be involved in a corporation's management. The incorporation statutes of most states require that a meeting of shareholders be held annually to elect the board of directors and conduct other necessary business. Such meetings typically follow parliamentary procedure. Shareholders may vote on issues put up for a vote at the meeting. However, only holders of stock called common stock have full voting rights.

Shareholders who disagree with the decisions of the board of directors may be able to get more voting power than their own shares entitle them to have. One method is called proxy voting. A proxy vote is the right to vote on behalf of other shareholders. Proxy voting arises when shareholders who believe in one position solicit other shareholders and obtain their permission to vote for them. The shareholders may then win the majority votes they need to defeat the board on an issue.

Right to Sue

There are three types of lawsuits shareholders can bring: direct suits, class action suits, and derivative suits. **A direct suit is a lawsuit a shareholder can bring against a corporation for denying his or her rights as a shareholder.** Shareholders may also bring a class action lawsuit against a corporation on behalf of all shareholders in their position. **A derivative suit is a lawsuit a shareholder can bring on behalf of the corporation to correct an injury to the corporation.**

Vocabulary You can find vocabulary definitions in the **Key Terms** glossary and Academic Vocabulary glossary in the back of this book.

Company Records Shareholders have a statutory right to see all company records. *What kind of lawsuit could a shareholder bring if the company refuses to show its records?*

Insider Trading It is illegal for corporate directors or officers to buy or sell stock based on inside information about a company not available to the public. *What kinds of outsiders could also be involved in insider trading?*

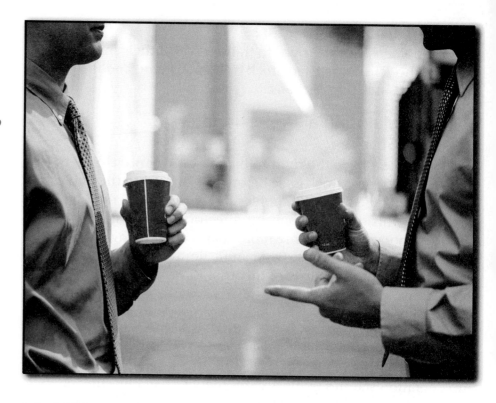

Liability of Directors and Officers

If you make a bad decision as the director of a corporation, can you be sued?

To test the decisions of corporate directors and officers, the courts have developed two standards: the business judgment rule and the fairness rule.

The Business Judgment Rule

The business judgment rule presumes that the decisions of corporate directors and officers are legal, made in good faith, with due care, and in the best interests of the corporation. However, a court will find against directors or officers if a decision involved fraud, lack of good faith, abuse of discretion, a conflict of interest, negligence, or illegality. The rule focuses not on whether a particular decision was the right decision but on how the decision was made. For example, a director who enters a deal with another corporation without doing any research could be considered negligent.

Directors and officers are not obligated to guarantee that the corporation makes a profit. If the corporation suffers a loss from a transaction the board authorized, the directors are not liable to the shareholders unless they violate the business judgment rule. Some states hold directors and officers liable only if they are grossly negligent in carrying out their duties, and some have even passed anti-liability statutes that limit the liability of directors.

The Fairness Rule

Directors and officers have a duty of loyalty to their corporation. They must not **exploit** their positions for personal gain at the expense of the corporation. Their main goal must be to act in the

Reading Check

Discuss *Is the business judgment rule too easy on corporate directors and officers?*

best interests of the corporation. They must not deliberately hurt the corporation. A director's or an officer's duty of loyalty may be questioned if he or she has a personal interest in a business decision. According to the fairness rule, if a manager profits in some way by a decision, the decision must be fair to the corporation.

Insider Trading One way directors or officers might exploit their position for personal gain is insider trading. **Insider trading is when a corporate director or officer buys or sells shares in a corporation based on firsthand information about the corporation that is not available to the public.** Insider trading gives an unfair advantage to people in a position of trust within a corporation. It also applies to passing valuable information to outsiders so they can profit from it. Under the insider trading rules, directors or officers who possess inside information must either refrain from acting on it or reveal it publicly before acting on it. Insider trading is legally considered a felony crime under the rules of the Securities and Exchange Commission (SEC).

Corporate Opportunity Doctrine The corporate opportunity doctrine is an extension of the duty of loyalty. According to this doctrine, directors and officers cannot take advantage of a business opportunity for themselves if they know that the corporation would want to take that opportunity for itself. The directors must first present the opportunity to the corporation. If the corporation turns it down, then the directors or officers can take the opportunity for themselves.

The only exception to this rule is if the director or officer knows that the corporation is financially incapable of taking the opportunity, despite its interest.

After You Read

Summarize Under the business judgment rule, for what reasons might a court find against a director for a bad decision?

SECTION 17.1 ASSESSMENT

Self Check

1. What are the differences between corporate directors and corporate officers?

2. What are the rights held by corporate shareholders?

3. What are the two standards courts have developed to test the decisions of corporate directors and officers?

Academic Connection

English Language Arts
Like corporate board meetings, many student organizations run their meetings using parliamentary procedure, also known as Robert's Rules of Order. Parliamentary procedure provides an approved and consistent format for holding meetings. It also protects majority and minority rights. Research the history, purpose, and main rules of Robert's Rules of Order. Write a brief report outlining the basic procedure for conducting a meeting.

Critical Thinking

Insider Trading What are different ways a corporate director could engage in insider trading?

SECTION 17.2 Financing, Expanding, and Dissolving a Corporation

What You'll Learn

◆ Describe the different types of corporate stock.

◆ Distinguish between a merger, a consolidation, and a conglomerate.

◆ Explain asset acquisition and stock acquisition.

◆ Identify the ways a corporation can be terminated.

Why It's Important

Knowing the laws that regulate corporate financing, expansion, and dissolution will prepare you for any dealings you might have with a corporation in the future.

Reading Guide

Before You Read

Connect Many of the corporations you come into contact with regularly are franchises. What are some franchises you can name?

Focus on Ideas

Corporations raise money by selling stocks and bonds.

Take Notes

Go to connectED. mcgraw-hill.com to download a graphic organizer you can use to take notes as you read this section.

Corporate Financing

Stocks — Bonds

Common paid last — Preferred

Key Terms

You will learn these legal words and expressions in this chapter. You can also find these terms in *Black's Law Dictionary* or in an online legal dictionary.

- merger
- consolidation
- conglomerate
- asset acquisition
- stock acquisition
- franchise

Academic Vocabulary

You will find these words in your readings and in your tests. Look them up in a dictionary and familiarize yourself with them.

- subscription
- significant
- unanimous

Corporate Financing

How do you get money to finance a corporation?

Corporations need financing to pay for their business activities, such as research, product development, office space, marketing, and advertising. Corporations can finance their activities by raising money through the sale of stocks or borrowing money through the sale of bonds.

Corporate Stocks

Corporations raise money by selling stock. Shares of stock represent a shareholder's interest or investment in a corporation.

All stock is originally sold by the corporation. At the time a corporation is organized, the promoters seek **subscriptions** from investors. These stock subscriptions are contracts to buy stock once the corporation is authorized by the state to sell stock to the public. The subscribers do not become stockholders until the organization is completed and stock certificates are issued to them. The corporation may continue to sell shares after its incorporation is complete.

Purchasers of stock may buy the stock from the corporation or from current owners who want to sell their shares. They may buy stock personally or through agents called brokers. A broker fills the purchaser's order in one of two ways. The broker may buy the stock on a stock exchange, which is a public auction in which stocks are bought and sold. The largest and best-known stock exchange is the New York Stock Exchange (NYSE). The broker may also purchase stocks over the counter, meaning outside the organized exchanges. Many stock trades today are done online, using a brokerage house that has a Web site where the public can place buy and sell orders.

As You Read

Predict Why do corporations sell stocks and bonds?

Vocabulary You can find vocabulary definitions in the **Key Terms** glossary and the Academic Vocabulary glossary in the back of this book.

Business ETHICS

Executive Pay

As President and CEO, Paul Krocker guided his company stock price from $3.23 to $81.00 per share. Now, Big Blue Technology wants to hire him away. They offer him $50 million dollars per year. He accepts and begins by cutting some jobs and reducing salaries by 25 percent, which help to make Big Blue more profitable. The share price of Big Blue shoots up 35 percent in one month.

Critical Thinking *Is it ethical for an executive to earn a huge salary while the employees lose jobs or salaries, but the stock price increases to the benefit of thousands of shareholders?*

Types of Stock There are two types of corporate stock: common stock and preferred stock. Common stock is the basic form of corporate ownership. All public corporations issue common stock. Holders of common stock have voting rights in a corporation. As a group, they elect the corporation's board of directors. Common stock sometimes pays dividends to the shareholders based on how the corporation performs. Holders of common stock are the last shareholders to be paid.

The second type of stock a corporation issues is preferred stock. Holders of preferred stock cannot vote. However, they do have the right to receive a fixed dividend. Holders of preferred stock are the first shareholders to be paid. **Figure 17.1** shows how to interpret the information in stock quotations.

Corporate Bonds

A corporation may also finance its activities through bonds. Bonds are notes issued for money that the corporation borrows. When a company makes bonds available, it is called a bond issue. Unlike stocks, bonds earn interest and must be repaid in the future. If a company files for bankruptcy, bondholders are paid before shareholders.

Corporate Expansion

How can you increase the size of a corporation?

A corporation might want to expand by acquiring new land, new manufacturing plants, new sales outlets, or entering new fields of business. A corporation can expand by buying or investing in another corporation through a merger or consolidation, by acquiring the assets or stock of another company, or by opening new franchises.

Merger and Consolidation

A merger is when two companies join together, with one company keeping its corporate identity and the other company losing its corporate identity. A consolidation is when two or more companies join together to form a new corporation. There is no significant difference between a merger and a consolidation, and the terms are often used interchangeably. Most of the time, the term merger is used to describe both scenarios. The boards of directors and shareholders of the corporations being merged must give their approval.

In some cases, companies merge or consolidate to form a conglomerate. **A conglomerate is a corporation that owns many different types of companies.** These companies do business in a variety of separate marketplaces, such as clothing, food, and entertainment. General Electric, for example, owns financial services, plastics companies, and theme parks.

Asset Acquisition

An asset acquisition is when one corporation agrees to purchase the assets, such as property, buildings, and

Reading Check

Analyze *Why do bonds pay interest but stocks do not?*

Figure 17.1 Understanding Stock Quotations

Identify the Company
Make sure you've found the quote you were looking for.

Dateline—Day, time, and time zone of this stock quote.

Company name—Official name under which the company stock is sold.

Ticker symbol—Unique short code of capital letters used to identify a specific stock

Check the Price
See how much the stock costs per share and whether the price is trending up or down.

Last—Amount in U.S. dollars and cents paid for one share when the stock was last traded.

Change—Rise or fall in the stock price in dollars and cents, and as a percentage, since the previous time it was traded.

Stock Exchange—Acronym for the exchange on which this stock is traded. This helps an investor understand where to buy or sell the stock.

Share Price over Time—A line graph showing the rise and fall in the stock price over the course of a day, month, quarter, or year. Useful for understanding how the stock is performing over the short and long term.

Understand the Details
Learn more about a company and how its stock is performing.

P/E—Short for "price/earnings ratio," the share price divided by the company's earnings per share. Investors use P/E to help determine whether a stock is a good investment.

Div Yield—Short for "dividend yield," dividends (direct annual or quarterly payments to shareholders) as a percentage of stock price. Some investors look for stocks that pay high dividends.

Market Cap—Short for "market capitalization," the total value of all shares of the company. In other words, how much the company is worth.

Open—Stock price at the beginning of the trading day of the quote.

High—Highest price paid for a share of stock on the day of the quote.

Low—Lowest price paid for a share of stock on the day of the quote.

Stock quotes help investors determine how much their stock is worth and decide whether to buy, sell, or hold. Here's how to read one.

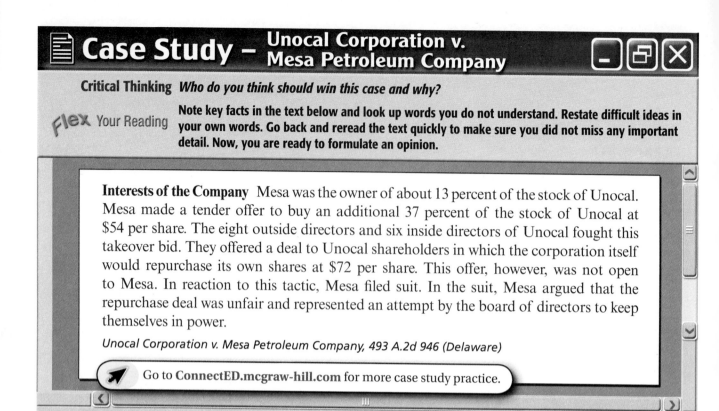

Case Study – Unocal Corporation v. Mesa Petroleum Company

Critical Thinking *Who do you think should win this case and why?*

Flex Your Reading Note key facts in the text below and look up words you do not understand. Restate difficult ideas in your own words. Go back and reread the text quickly to make sure you did not miss any important detail. Now, you are ready to formulate an opinion.

Interests of the Company Mesa was the owner of about 13 percent of the stock of Unocal. Mesa made a tender offer to buy an additional 37 percent of the stock of Unocal at $54 per share. The eight outside directors and six inside directors of Unocal fought this takeover bid. They offered a deal to Unocal shareholders in which the corporation itself would repurchase its own shares at $72 per share. This offer, however, was not open to Mesa. In reaction to this tactic, Mesa filed suit. In the suit, Mesa argued that the repurchase deal was unfair and represented an attempt by the board of directors to keep themselves in power.

Unocal Corporation v. Mesa Petroleum Company, 493 A.2d 946 (Delaware)

Go to **ConnectED.mcgraw-hill.com** for more case study practice.

equipment, of a second corporation. A corporation will buy the assets of another corporation rather than the corporation itself to avoid taking on the debts and liabilities of the other corporation. The shareholders and directors of the corporation selling the assets must approve the transaction.

Stock Acquisition

A stock acquisition is when an individual or a corporation buys enough shares of stock in another corporation to take over control of it. A stock acquisition often begins when a prospective buyer makes a tender offer. A tender offer is an offer to buy a specific number of shares at a specific price.

Tender offers are often referred to as takeover bids. The party making the offer is called the suitor. The corporation the suitor wants to take over is called the target. The suitor does not need to buy all the stock of the target. The suitor only needs to buy enough stock to control the election of directors.

Franchises

A franchise is a license a company grants to a business or individual for the right to use its name and sell its products or services. The business buying the franchise benefits from the trade name and expertise of the parent company. The corporation benefits by expanding its business without spending money or building new stores itself. McDonald's, Blockbuster, and Holiday Inn are well-known franchises.

Dissolution of a Corporation

Can shareholders end a corporation?

As with partnerships and LLCs, the end of a corporate entity is referred to as a dissolution. The dissolution of a corporation can come about in two ways: voluntarily or involuntarily.

Voluntary Dissolution

A corporation can end voluntarily through a **unanimous** vote of its shareholders. The directors can vote for its end, provided they get the support of two-thirds of the shareholders. After the decision to end the corporation has been made, a statement of intent to dissolve must be filed with the secretary of state's office. The dissolution must be reported to the government, to creditors, and to the public.

Involuntary Dissolution

An involuntary dissolution occurs when the government itself terminates a corporation. If a corporation was formed by fraud, conducted business illegally, or exceeded its authority, the secretary of state can ask the state attorney general to bring a *quo warranto* action against it. If such an action is taken, the corporation could lose its charter and would no longer be authorized to do business in the state. Grounds for bringing such an action also include failure by the corporation to file annual reports, or pay franchise taxes.

A shareholder can also seek the involuntary dissolution of a corporation. However, the shareholder must have appropriate grounds to do this. Such grounds include evidence of fraud, waste of corporate assets, and that a dissolution is necessary to protect the shareholders' rights.

After You Read

Summarize List the ways a corporation can expand its business.

SECTION 17.2 ASSESSMENT

Self Check

1. What are the differences between stocks and bonds?

2. What is a tender offer, and what else is it called?

3. On what grounds might the government bring an action to dissolve a corporation?

Academic Connection

Mathematics You bought 80 shares of Netmark Associates stock at $24 per share last year. The company had a good year and paid all of its stockholders annual dividends of $0.72 per share. How much is your total annual dividend?

THEORY **Number and Operations:** To calculate the dividend, multiply the annual dividend per share times the number of shares.

 Math For more math practice, go to the Math Appendix.

Critical Thinking

Online Trading Buying and selling stock over the Internet has become a common way of playing the stock market. Why can this be risky for small investors?

Summary

Section 17.1 Managing a Corporation

◆ Corporate directors are elected by shareholders to make broad policy decisions. Corporate officers are chosen by the directors to run the day-to-day affairs of a corporation. Corporate shareholders are the owners of a corporation based on the number of shares they hold.

◆ Shareholders rights include: (1) to receive a stock certificate; (2) to receive dividends; (3) to examine the corporate books and records; (4) to transfer all shares; (5) to maintain a proportionate share of stock; (6) to exercise a vote for each share of stock owned; and (7) to sue.

◆ The courts hold corporate directors and officers to two standards: the business judgment rule and the fairness rule.

Section 17.2 Financing, Expanding, and Dissolving a Corporation

◆ Corporations raise money by selling stocks or bonds.

◆ The public can purchase stock personally or through a stock broker.

◆ The two types of stocks corporations sell are common stock and preferred stock.

◆ Bonds are notes issued to those who lend money to the corporation. Bonds earn interest.

◆ A corporation can expand through a merger, a consolidation, an asset acquisition, a stock acquisition, or by opening new franchises.

◆ A corporation can be dissolved either voluntarily by the directors or shareholders, or involuntarily by the government.

Vocabulary Builder

1 On a sheet of paper, use each of these terms in a sentence.

Key Terms

- corporate director
- corporate officer
- direct suit
- derivative suit

- insider trading
- merger
- consolidation
- conglomerate

- asset acquisition
- stock acquisition
- franchise

Academic Vocabulary

- proportionate
- preemptive

- exploit
- subscription

- significant
- unanimous

Key Points Review

Answer the following questions. Refer to the chapter for additional reinforcement.

2 What are the two duties corporate directors and officers owe a corporation?

3 What is the difference between a direct suit and a derivative suit?

4 What is insider trading?

5 What is the corporate opportunity doctrine?

6 What are the differences between common and preferred stock?

7 What are corporate bonds and how are they different from corporate stocks?

8 What are the differences between a merger, an asset acquisition, and a stock acquisition?

9 What are the ways a corporation can be dissolved voluntarily?

Standardized Test Practice

10 Read the excerpt below about buying a franchise and complete questions 1 and 2.

Anyone who thinks about buying an existing business should know the phrase *caveat emptor*, which is Latin for let the buyer beware. It is in the seller's best interest to paint the prettiest possible picture of the business. It is in the prospective buyer's best interest to investigate the accuracy of the seller's statements. This means asking both technical and social questions.

Technical questions usually require the help of professionals such as accountants or lawyers. Are the financial records accurate? Are the legal requirements of the business in order? Was the business sued in the past?

Asking social questions means talking to the present owner, the employees, and the customers. Why is the owner selling? What is the business's reputation? How does the company compare to its competition? All of these questions need to be answered before deciding to purchase an existing business.

1. What does *caveat emptor* mean?

Ⓐ Let the seller beware.

Ⓑ Let the buyer beware.

Ⓒ Ask questions.

Ⓓ The truth is out there.

2. Which is an example of a technical question?

Ⓐ Why is the owner selling?

Ⓑ What is the business's reputation?

Ⓒ Was the business sued in the past?

Ⓓ How does the company compare to its competition?

 Test-Taking Strategies Choose a good seat to take the test. To avoid distractions, do not sit near a door or near friends.

Apply and Debate

Read the following scenarios. Get together with other students in pairs or groups of three and take a position on each scenario. Debate your position in class with students taking the opposite position or prepare a written argument justifying your position.

⑪ Insider Trading

Cyrus is an executive assistant at GenCom. His boss asks him to type a press release announcing that Gencom will soon merge with Billcom. That night, he discusses the merger with his aunt, who is a business journalist. She then buys 1,000 shares of GenCom, and, after the news is released, makes $20,000 in stock price gains.

You Debate *Did Cyrus engage in insider trading by discussing the merger?*

⑫ Conflict of Interest?

Lakefront Craft, Inc. manufactures boats. To expand the company, the board of directors decided to purchase Paddle Canoes, Inc. for $3.5 million. Lakefront's stock price rose with this news. A reporter later discovered that a cousin of Lakefront's chairperson was the owner of Paddle Canoes, and made $1 million on the sale.

You Debate *Is there a conflict of interest in this situation?*

⑬ Hurricane Loss

Scott, a shareholder, brought suit against Big Trucking, Inc. when the company lost $2 million because the senior executives failed to move 200 trucks out of the path of a hurricane that was forecast. The trucks and their contents were destroyed.

You Debate *Are executives responsible for losses arising out of natural disasters?*

⑭ Missed Market

Jackson was a shareholder in Life Pharmaceuticals, Inc. The company announced its plans to launch a new cancer drug. Jackson's stock soared. After the company delayed the drug's release due to complications in the research, his stock dropped. Jackson sued the company for mismanagement.

You Debate *Are stockholders right to sue for product delays?*

⑮ Merger Pros and Cons

Linda often shops at PayDown. When PayDown was bought out by a chain called High Quality Clothing, Inc., Linda was joyful because it carries nicer merchandise. Later, she learned her friend Sharon lost her job at PayDown.

You Debate *Is it important for a community to have better stores even though it may create job losses for some people?*

Case Study Practice – Hoschett v. TSI International Software, Ltd.

⓰ Shareholders' Meeting TSI International Software, Ltd. (TSI) was incorporated in the state of Delaware in 1993, but its headquarters is in Wilton, Connecticut. The company is a privately-held corporation. Less than 40 stockholders hold all the shares in the corporation. Fred Hoschett owns 1,200 shares of common stock, which is much less than 1% of all the stock. Since its incorporation, TSI has never had an annual meeting to elect its directors. Mr. Hoschett, as a shareholder, sued the corporation to make it hold an annual meeting. Under the Delaware Code, a Delaware corporation must have an annual meeting to elect directors, unless the by-laws of the corporation say otherwise. TSI argued that on November 16, 1995, the company received written consent from a majority of shareholders who chose five individuals as directors of TSI. Since a majority of shareholders had provided written consent, TSI argued that an annual meeting was unnecessary.

Source: Hoschett v. TSI International Software, Ltd., 683 A.2d 43 (Del. Ct. Chan. 1996)

Practice Does TSI have to hold an annual meeting?

⓱ Ethics
←?→ Application

Nonprofit Monica Edwards and Javier Perez formed a political watchdog group as a nonprofit corporation. Because of political changes, income from donations and membership dues soared in the first year. Monica and Javier gave themselves huge bonuses and took lavish, fact-finding trips because, as a nonprofit corporation, there was no need to show a profit.

◆ Are Monica and Javier entitled to do this? Why or why not?

⓲ Think back to the Legal Briefs feature you read at the beginning of the chapter. Then write one or more paragraphs to answer these questions: Do you think a corporation formed to conduct business has an ethical obligation to use some of its resources for charitable purposes? Then team up with a classmate and share your opinions and have a brief discussion about what each of you wrote.

CHAPTER 18 Business and Regulations

Legal Briefs

Doing Business in China

Why Guanxi Matters

Do you know what *guanxi* is? The literal meaning of the Mandarin Chinese word is "relationship." You might call it "networking," but it's much more. *Guanxi* is an intricate system of interpersonal relationships woven together by social ties. It's essential for doing business in China.

Building a business relationship—building *guanxi*—takes time and effort. Guanxi involves doing favors for potential clients or partners, and receiving favors in return. If that sounds like bribes or kickbacks, which are illegal in the United States, it isn't. Building guanxi isn't a payoff, but a system of reciprocity. Building a business may require giving dinner parties or delivering gifts to potential clients to strengthen ties, for example.

Guanxi develops over time. However, the time and effort you put into proving yourself an honorable person to deal with will be rewarded with trust and respect from the Chinese business establishment.

Using *guanxi* is an excellent example of how important it is to understand a country's culture if you want to succeed in a foreign market.

Environmental Impact The federal government has passed laws to conserve energy and protect the environment. *Which government agency was created to deal with pollution and toxic waste?*

What You'll Learn

◆ Explain the source of federal power in the regulation of business.

◆ Identify the laws that regulate the sale of securities.

◆ Distinguish between the laws that regulate antitrust activity.

◆ Describe what laws regulate corporate takeovers.

Why It's Important

Once you understand the background for governmental regulations, you will appreciate why the government plays a regulatory role to ensure competition and fairness.

Reading Guide

Before You Read

Connect If you have ever been someplace where you could only buy goods at one store, you are familiar with a monopoly. Name an instance where you experienced a monopoly.

Focus on Ideas

The federal government regulates corporations to make sure they do business fairly.

Take Notes

Go to connectED. mcgraw-hill.com to download a graphic organizer you can use to take notes as you read this section.

Antitrust Laws

Act	Purpose
Sherman Antitrust Act	_____
_____	_____
_____	_____
_____	_____

Key Terms

You will learn these legal words and expressions in this chapter. You can also find these terms in *Black's Law Dictionary* or in an online legal dictionary.

- Commerce Clause
- security
- registration statement
- prospectus
- monopoly

Academic Vocabulary

You will find these words in your readings and in your tests. Look them up in a dictionary and familiarize yourself with them.

- commerce
- administer
- certify

Business and the Constitution

What gives the federal government the right to regulate businesses?

The federal government gets its power to regulate business from the Commerce Clause of the United States Constitution. **The Commerce Clause is a statement in Article I of the Constitution giving Congress the power to regulate commerce among the states.** Over the last two hundred years, the U.S. Supreme Court has enlarged the government's power to regulate business. Now the federal government can regulate any business activity that affects interstate **commerce**, even one that occurs completely within the borders of a single state.

The individual states also have laws to regulate commerce. However, all state laws must abide by the Constitution. For example, the U.S. Supreme Court has ruled that a state violates the Commerce Clause when it creates a law that treats in-state and out-of-state businesses differently when the different treatment hurts the out-of-state business.

There are three major areas in which governments regulate commerce:

- securities (sale of stocks)
- antitrust (unfair competition)
- corporate takeovers

Securities Regulation

In October 1929 the stock market collapsed in what became known as the Great Crash or the Crash of '29. The crash led to a severe worldwide economic depression. Experts identified the sale of worthless securities as a major cause of the collapse. **A security is a monetary investment that seeks to make a profit solely because of another's efforts.** Corporate stocks, interests in savings and loans, interests in racehorses or sports teams, and even the sale of coins are types of securities.

The Securities Act of 1933 To prevent another stock market crash, Congress passed the Securities Act of 1933. The Securities Act is designed to protect investors by making sure they can learn about the securities they buy. It also provides a way to uncover fraud and unfair practices.

The Securities and Exchange Commission The Securities Exchange Act of 1934 created the Securities and Exchange Commission (SEC). The SEC is an independent federal agency set up to **administer** federal securities law. It consists of five commissioners appointed by the President. The SEC also employs lawyers, accountants, and securities analysts who oversee the sale of securities and the brokers, dealers, and bankers who sell them.

The Registration Requirement One way the SEC ensures that investors know what they are buying is through the registration

As You Read

Predict For what reasons do you think the government tries to regulate certain aspects of business?

Vocabulary You can find vocabulary definitions in the **Key Terms** glossary and **Academic Vocabulary** glossary in the back of this book.

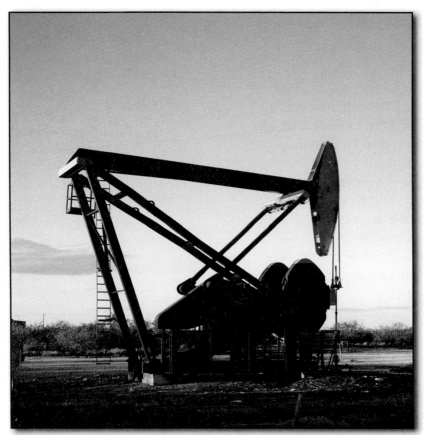

Antitrust In 1911 the Supreme Court ruled that Standard Oil had violated the Sherman Antitrust Act by using devious means to drive its competition out of business. *What did the Supreme Court make Standard Oil do?*

requirement. This requires companies to file a registration statement and a prospectus with the SEC before they offer securities for sale. **The registration statement is a general description of the securities and of the company making the offer. The prospectus is a document that contains a detailed explanation of the stock offering for potential investors.** These documents further prevent the sale of fraudulent securities. A firm caught selling securities without SEC approval can be punished with fines or imprisonment.

Sarbanes-Oxley Act Following a series of corporate failures in the 1990s, Congress passed the Sarbanes-Oxley Act. The Act requires all chief executive officers (CEOs) and chief financial officers (CFOs) to **certify** periodic company reports filed with the SEC. It prohibits most corporate loans to directors and executive officers. The law also places an affirmative duty on the board of directors to make certain that their company is conforming to all legal requirements.

Antitrust Law

In the nineteenth century a popular way for someone to gain control of several companies was to form a trust. In a trust, the voting power of the stock for all the companies was given to one person, or trustee. Today, this type of trust is usually called a monopoly. **A monopoly is a business situation in which one person, company, or group of companies controls the market for a product or service.** Antitrust laws were created to prevent monopolies.

The Sherman Antitrust Act In 1890 Congress passed the Sherman Antitrust Act, which made monopolies illegal. However, a Supreme Court ruling that said contracts or combinations were illegal only if they formed an "unreasonable restraint of trade" undermined the Sherman Act.

The Clayton Antitrust Act In 1914 Congress passed the Clayton Antitrust Act. The Clayton Act makes specific business practices illegal. For example, a business cannot sell goods to one company for less than the price it charges another company if it harms competition. It also makes it illegal to sell goods on the condition that a buyer cannot buy products from a competitor.

Reading Check

Analyze How does the Williams Act control takeover bids to ensure fairness to shareholders?

The Federal Trade Commission Act Congress passed the Federal Trade Commission Act in 1914 to protect businesses from the wrongful acts of other businesses. It allows the courts to determine unfair methods of competition. The act also created the Federal Trade Commission (FTC). The FTC prevents businesses from violating the Federal Trade Commission Act.

The Robinson-Patman Act The Robinson-Patman Act is an amendment to the Clayton Act. It says companies cannot sell goods at lower prices to large purchasers without offering the same discount to smaller purchasers. It also outlaws unfair behavior, such as setting up a delivery schedule that helps one seller but hurts another.

Regulation of Corporate Takeovers

Starting in the 1980s, many large corporations took over smaller corporations in what became known as merger mania. The deals were often valued in the billions of dollars and created huge conglomerates and multinational corporations. As a result, Congress, state legislatures, and the courts became involved in regulating the corporate takeover process.

Federal Regulation The Williams Act strictly controls takeover bids. Under this act, when a suitor offers to acquire more than five percent of a target's stock, the suitor must file a statement with the SEC indicating where the money for the takeover is coming from, why the suitor is purchasing the stock, and how much of the target the suitor owns. The goal is to make certain shareholders know the qualifications and the intentions of the suitor.

State Regulation State legislatures have passed anti-liability statutes to protect corporate directors whose companies are

Legal Talk

Prospectus: *n* Latin for *view, outlook.*

Monopoly: *n* From Greek *mono* = one + *polein* = seller: one seller.

Vocabulary Builder The prefix *mono* means one in Greek. List and define five words that begin with this prefix in terms of its meaning. For example, *monochrome* means one color.

📄 **Case Study –** Centex-Winston v. Edward Hines Lumber Co.

Critical Thinking *Is Centex-Winston right in this case? Why or why not?*

Flex Your Reading — Note key facts in the text below and look up words you do not understand. Restate difficult ideas in your own words. Go back and reread the text quickly to make sure you did not miss any important detail. Now, you are ready to formulate an opinion.

Preferential Treatment After being hired to build homes, the Centex-Winston Corporation contracted to purchase lumber, for resale, from Edward Hines Lumber Company. Hines consistently failed to deliver orders on time due to its preferential treatment of several Centex-Winston competitors. Centex-Winston sued Hines, claiming the preferential delivery violated the Robinson-Patman Act.

Centex-Winston v. Edward Hines Lumber Co., 447 F.2d 585 (7th Circuit)

➤ Go to **ConnectEd.mcgraw-hill.com** for more case study practice.

involved in takeovers. Several state legislatures have also enacted anti-takeover statutes to discourage suitors from targeting companies within their states.

Judicial Scrutiny Sometimes, a corporation's directors and officers who successfully resist a takeover bid are sued by dissatisfied shareholders who may complain that the suitor's takeover would have been more profitable for them. In such lawsuits, the courts must evaluate the decisions made by the corporation's directors and officers. One question courts must ask is whether the business judgment rule should apply. Recall that the business judgment rule (Chapter 17) presumes a director acts with due care. However, the business judgment rule does not apply if the director acts illegally or if there is a conflict of interest.

Operating a Business Internationally

Several organizations regulate international business dealings. The International Law Commission (ILC) is an agency within the United Nations responsible for the codification of international law dealing with relations among countries. The U.N. Commission on International Trade Law (UNCITL) codifies a set of international laws that regulate international trade among private businesses. The World Trade Organization (WTO) is not a U.N. agency, but a separate international organization that drafts rules dealing with trade among member nations. The WTO tries to limit or remove trade barriers. The rules drafted by all three organizations are enacted in the United States through the treaty process, and if Congress approves the rules, they become valid laws on par with Federal statutes.

After You Read

Summarize List the three major acts passed by Congress to help regulate unfair business practices.

SECTION 18.1 ASSESSMENT

Self Check

1. What is the federal government's authority to regulate business based on?

2. What are securities and what are some examples of them?

3. What is a monopoly?

Academic Connection

English Language Arts
Economist Alan Greenspan argues that the very existence of antitrust laws discourages businessmen from some activities that might be socially useful out of fear that their business actions will be determined illegal and dismantled by government. In his essay entitled "Antitrust," Greenspan says: "No one will ever know what new products, processes, machines, and cost-saving mergers failed to come into existence, killed by the Sherman Act before they were born. No one can ever compute the price that all of us have paid for that Act which, by inducing less effective use of capital, has kept our standard of living lower than would otherwise have been possible."

Write a one-to-two-page essay explaining why you agree or disagree with Alan Greenspan.

Critical Thinking

Monopoly Why is it a bad thing if one company controls the entire market for a particular product?

Environmental Laws

What You'll Learn

◆ Describe the laws that regulate the environment.

◆ Identify the federal and state agencies that regulate the environment.

◆ Identify the federal and state agencies that are responsible for regulating energy.

◆ Describe the impact of international law on energy regulation and conservation.

Why It's Important

If you ever go into business, you need to know that there are environmental and energy laws you have to obey.

Reading Guide

Before You Read

Connect Have you ever noticed days when the sky is brown with smog? Name some of the sources that you think might be responsible for the smog.

Focus on Ideas

To ensure a higher quality of life for its citizens, federal and state governments have passed laws to protect the environment and conserve energy.

Take Notes

Go to connectED.mcgraw-hill.com to download a graphic organizer you can use to take notes as you read this section.

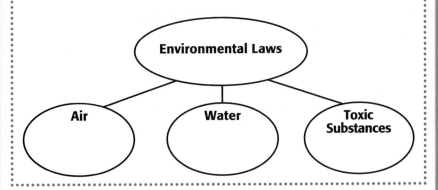

Key Terms

You will learn these legal words and expressions in this chapter. You can also find these terms in *Black's Law Dictionary* or in an online legal dictionary.

- Environmental Protection Agency (EPA)
- Federal Energy Regulatory Commission (FERC)
- Nuclear Regulatory Commission (NRC)

Academic Vocabulary

You will find these words in your readings and in your tests. Look them up in a dictionary and familiarize yourself with them.

- comply
- emissions
- proactive

As You Read

Predict When were the first environmental laws created?

Environmental Protection

What does the federal government do to make sure our air and water are not polluted?

In the nineteenth century, the rapid rise of industrialism led to an increase in factory-produced waste which polluted the land, air, and water. The only environmental laws that existed were based on common law, such as nuisance claims. For example, if a farmer had a feed lot that was a nuisance to its neighbors, the matter could be taken to court. By the mid-twentieth century, as the damage caused by industrialization to the environment and human health became apparent, the government recognized the need to pass laws specifically designed to protect the environment (see **Figure 18.1**).

The Environmental Protection Agency

In 1969 Congress passed the National Environmental Policy Act, which established the Environmental Protection Agency. **The Environmental Protection Agency (EPA) is the federal agency responsible for protecting the environment.** It is an independent agency that is a part of the executive branch. The EPA was set up to establish a national policy to combat pollution.

Regulatory Responsibilities The EPA can make regulations involving environmental policies, including laws that deal with air, water, solid waste, toxic substances, and noise pollution. Such regulations must be written in clear and unambiguous language to give fair notice of the regulations to individuals and institutions affected by them.

Research, Administrative, and Support Responsibilities The EPA can do research, create and administer pollution control guidelines, and support programs designed to make sure that pollution standards are met. The agency can also administer grants to help eliminate pollution under state-run programs.

Enforcement The EPA prefers that businesses voluntarily comply with its standards. However, if businesses do not comply, the EPA can bring action against them for polluting the environment, even if the pollution is unintentional.

Current Legislation Congress has continued to increase the EPA's power to deal with new environmental challenges. For instance, the EPA was given the authority to deal with major oil spills using funds provided under the Oil Pollution Act. This allowed the EPA to compel oil storage plants to be built and to fund the development of strategies for dealing with oil-related accidents.

The Clean Air Act

There are actually several Clean Air Acts, each of which was an attempt to improve upon the preceding act. The first clean air act, the Air Pollution Control Act, was passed by Congress in 1955 to provide funds for research into the problems of air pollution. It also recognized that air pollution was a national problem.

Vocabulary You can find vocabulary definitions in the **Key Terms** glossary and Academic Vocabulary glossary in the back of this book.

Figure 18.1 Environmental Regulations

The Environmental Protection Agency was created by the federal government in response to the growing public demand for cleaner water, air, and land. The EPA's tasks include repairing the damage already done to the environment, creating guidelines for controlling pollution, and promoting the use of more environmentally friendly sources of green energy, such as wind and solar power.

The purpose of the Clean Water Act is to protect the nation's waterways, wetlands, and drinking water. One of the biggest environmental problems is the illegal or negligent dumping of waste materials into lakes and rivers by mining operations.

The Clean Air Act identified automobile emissions as a major source of air pollution and created emission standards for motor vehicles. It also regulates the level of pollutants that can be emitted by factories and even common household items such as house paints. Corporate officers who knowingly violate the Clean Air Act are subject to criminal penalties, including imprisonment.

Before laws such as the National Environmental Policy Act were passed, the federal government was not equipped to deal with pollutants that harm human health and the environment. *What are some of the problems businesses have with environmental laws?*

Global Law

Environmental Law in Cambodia

In 1992, the country of Cambodia created a new constitution. Since that time, a system of laws has been created to provide for peaceful resolutions. This system is not too different from the one in the United States and consists of five levels of laws:

1. The Constitution

2. Laws passed by the National Assembly

3. Decrees issued by the Council of Ministers

4. Implementing legislation enacted by the Ministries

5. Decree Laws, or laws passed before the 1992 Constitution

Constitutional Environmental Protections

Cambodia passed a series of laws to permanently protect the environment. Article 59 of the Constitution states:

The State shall protect the environment and balance of abundant natural resources and establish a precise plan of management of land, water, air, wind, geology, ecologic system, mines, energy, petrol and gas, rocks and sand, gems, forests and forestrial products, wildlife, fish and aquatic resources.

In November 1996, the Cambodian National Assembly passed the Law on Environmental Protection and Natural Resource Management. This law's goals are:

- Reduce and control pollution

- Establish the Environmental Impact Assessment system

- Ensure the sustainable use of resources

- Make the public aware and eager to participate

- Stop activities that are detrimental to the environment

Across Cultures: Civil War

In the 1970s and 1980s, the economy of Cambodia was destroyed by civil war. In the 1990s, however, the economy began to recover as Cambodia began to export rice, rubber, and timber.

Critical Thinking *Should the United States amend the Constitution to provide for environmental protections?*

The Clean Air Act of 1963 The Clean Air Act of 1963 was the first statute passed by Congress to use the words *clean air*. The act set aside funds that state and local programs could use to fight air pollution. The act also identified automobiles as a major source of air pollution and set automobile **emissions** standards.

The Clean Air Acts of 1970 and 1977 The Clean Air Act of 1970 set up the National Ambient Air Quality Standards to further improve air quality. Unfortunately, the standards were difficult, if not impossible, to meet. As a result, the act was amended once again in 1977 to establish more practical guidelines.

The Clean Water Act

The Clean Water Act is also known as the Federal Water Pollution Control Act. It was passed by Congress to guard against water pollution in the United States. The act set up guidelines for dealing with the risks involved in dumping pollutants into the nation's waterways. The act also provides money to help cities develop sewage treatment plants. The act encourages state and national cooperation in the effort to clean up the waterways.

The Toxic Substance Control Act

The Toxic Substance Control Act authorizes the EPA to police the production, use, and importation of industrial chemicals. The act gives the EPA the power to order the assessment of certain chemical agents and to outlaw the development of harmful chemical substances. Under the act, the EPA has authority over the production and use of existing chemical agents and over the introduction and use of newly developed chemical substances.

State Legislation and Regulation

The EPA encourages state and local governments to enforce actions in their own regions. Many states have passed their own state laws and standards to deal with environmental concerns. Massachusetts, for example, has established its own Department of Environmental Protection, which enforces air and water quality standards within the state. California has passed vehicle emissions standards that are stricter than the federal standards.

International Influences on Environmental Regulation

Environmental concerns are among the most serious problems facing the global community today. In response to these problems, the nations of the world have held a variety of international conferences over the last two decades. Some of these conferences have produced protocols or procedures for dealing with these concerns. For instance, a United Nations conference held in Kyoto, Japan, produced a set of protocols for the gradual reduction of greenhouse gases such as carbon dioxide. Many countries have passed the Kyoto Protocol into law; however, the United States has not.

Reading Check

Discuss *Can environmental laws be too strict?*

Solar Energy The government offers tax breaks to individuals and businesses who install solar panels. *What are some of the advantages and disadvantages of using solar energy?*

Qwest Communications Corp. v. The City of Berkeley
146 F.Supp.2d 1081 (N.D. Cal. 2001)

Qwest Communications Corp. (Qwest) is a telecommunications company authorized to do business in the state of California. The California Public Utilities Commission granted Qwest the power to do public projects using public rights-of-way. In December 1999, Qwest was contracted to provide faster telecommunications, including higher-speed Internet, to the Lawrence Berkeley National Laboratory. To complete the project, Qwest needed to lay new fiber optic cable in the City of Berkeley's right-of-way. The City of Berkeley refused to let Qwest use the right-of-way. Qwest sued to use the right-of-way. Among the reasons Berkeley refused permission was that Qwest had to be certified under the California Environmental Quality Act to create the 4,300-foot trench needed for the cable.

Ruling and Resolution
The Federal District Court in California held that under the California Environmental Quality Act, construction projects must receive certification. A project is defined as any activity that causes direct physical change in the environment. However, the court was not persuaded that a single 4,300-foot trench could be considered a project under the law.

Critical Thinking How detailed should environmental regulations be?

Energy Regulation and Conservation
Why do we need laws to regulate energy?

Up until the early 1970s, Americans were accustomed to a seemingly endless supply of cheap gasoline. Then, in 1973, the oil-producing countries of the Mideast cut off the supply of oil to many nations in the West, including the U.S., creating a major gas shortage. As a result of the 1973 oil crisis, the U.S. government recognized the need to conserve and regulate its energy resources.

Federal Agencies
In 1977, the federal government created the Department of Energy (DOE). Although it was created in 1977, the roots of the DOE go back to World War II and the Manhattan Project, which developed the first nuclear weapons. To control this new form of energy, the government created the Atomic Energy Commission (AEC), the forerunner of the DOE.

The DOE has a dual function. First, the DOE develops and implements a national policy on energy resources. Second, the DOE has responsibility for the nation's nuclear energy program.

The Federal Energy Regulatory Commission The **Federal Energy Regulatory Commission (FERC), which is part of the DOE, regulates electricity and natural gas.** FERC controls the wholesale price of natural gas and electricity sold for use in interstate (between states) commerce and the interstate transportation of electricity and natural gas. Intrastate (within a state) prices are regulated by state utility agencies. FERC is also responsible for regulating oil pipeline rates.

The Nuclear Regulatory Commission The Nuclear Regulatory Commission (NRC), which is also part of the DOE, regulates nuclear energy. It regulates the licensing, constructing, and opening of nuclear power plants. The NRC also handles the possession, use, transportation, and disposal of nuclear material.

State Agencies

Every state in the United States now has an energy office to deal with energy-related concerns. Although the names of these agencies differ, the functions are the same. These functions are to improve energy regulation, to promote energy-efficient technologies, and to reduce the cost of energy development and production. Some states are more **proactive** than others in promoting and financing the development of alternative energy sources, such as solar power, wind power, and hydropower.

International Influences on Energy Regulation

The International Energy Agency (IEA) is the main worldwide group established to research energy conservation. The IEA is made up of 26 nations, including the United States. Originally, the IEA focused on planning for unanticipated oil shortages. Today, it has expanded its scope to include wide-ranging energy issues, including the development of alternate forms of energy and the creation of strategies for dealing with shifts in the Earth's climate.

After You Read

Summarize List the federal acts that deal with clean air and clean water.

SECTION 18.2 ASSESSMENT

Self Check

1. What federal agency is responsible for combating pollution?

2. What was the Federal Energy Regulatory Commission (FERC) created to do?

3. What are the goals of the International Energy Agency (IEA)?

Academic Connection

Social Studies The Resource Conservation and Recovery Act of 1976 (RCRA) gave the EPA the authority to control hazardous waste from cradle to grave. This includes the generation, transportation, treatment, storage, and disposal of hazardous waste. The RCRA also set forth a framework for the management of non-hazardous wastes. The RCRA was amended in 1986 to enable the EPA to address environmental problems that could result from underground tanks storing petroleum and other hazardous substances. The RCRA focuses only on active and future facilities and does not address abandoned or historical sites. Read about the Resource Conservation and Recovery Act. Then write an environmental act proposal to address a current environmental issue you are interested in.

Critical Thinking

A Matter of Jurisdiction What is the difference between interstate commerce and intrastate commerce and why is the distinction important?

Chapter 18 Review and Assessment

Summary

Section 18.1 Corporate Regulations

◆ The federal government gets its power to regulate business from the Commerce Clause of the United States Constitution, which gives Congress the power to regulate commerce among the states.

◆ Congress passed the Securities Act of 1933 and the Securities Exchange Act of 1934 to protect investors in securities from fraud and unfair practices.

◆ Congress has passed a series of antitrust laws to prevent monopolies from controlling the market for a product or service.

◆ Congress, state legislatures, and the courts have created various laws to regulate the corporate takeover process.

Section 18.2 Environmental Laws

◆ Federal laws passed to protect the environment include the National Environmental Policy Act, the Clean Air Act, the Clean Water Act, and the Toxic Substances Control Act.

◆ Many states have created their own state laws and standards to deal with environmental concerns.

◆ The Department of Energy (DOE), the Federal Energy Regulatory Commission (FERC), and the Nuclear Regulatory Commission (NRC) were created to develop an energy policy and regulate the energy industry.

◆ Every state in the U.S. has an energy office to deal with energy-related concerns, such as improving energy regulation, promoting energy efficient technologies, and reducing the cost of energy development and production.

Vocabulary Builder

1 On a sheet of paper, use each of these terms in a sentence.

Key Terms

- Commerce Clause
- security
- registration statement
- prospectus
- monopoly
- Environmental Protection Agency (EPA)
- Federal Energy Regulatory Commission (FERC)
- Nuclear Regulatory Commission (NRC)

Academic Vocabulary

- commerce
- administer
- certify
- comply
- emissions
- proactive

Key Points Review

Answer the following questions. Refer to the chapter for additional reinforcement.

2 What is the function of the Securities and Exchange Commission (SEC)?

3 Why were antitrust laws created?

4 What was the Federal Trade Commission Act designed to do?

5 What is the goal of the Williams Act?

6 Why did Congress pass the National Environmental Policy Act?

7 What does the Toxic Substances Control Act do?

8 What is the role of the Department of Energy?

9 What is the difference between the Federal Energy Regulatory Commission (FERC) and the Nuclear Regulatory Commission (NRC)?

Standardized Test Practice

10 Read the following excerpt about energy law and complete problems 1 and 2.

Within the framework of energy laws, governments establish their policies, rules and regulations concerning ownership, exploitation, development, and use of energy resources within the boundaries of their jurisdiction. Some countries have comprehensive energy laws which regulate resource exploration, development, production, transport, purchase, and distribution of energy for one or more than one energy carrier. Other countries have issued separate laws for each type of fuel governing resource ownership, exploration rights, and trade regulations as well as supply and pricing rules. In most countries, energy supply systems, and electricity supply in particular, remain in the domain of the public sector. Due to the strategic and economic importance of energy, private sector activity in this field also remains highly regulated. However, conventional energy laws typically focus on the development and management of the energy resource and supply side, and do not normally provide specific guidelines concerning energy use or demand management.

1. In most countries, who controls the energy supply systems?

Ⓐ government agencies
Ⓑ public and private sectors
Ⓒ private corporations
Ⓓ the public sector

2. Conventional energy laws typically focus on

Ⓐ energy use
Ⓑ development and management of the energy resource
Ⓒ demand management
Ⓓ resource ownership

Test-Taking Strategies Always pace yourself when taking a test and avoid spending too much time on a single passage or question.

Apply and Debate

Read the following scenarios. Get together with other students in pairs or groups of three and take a position on each scenario. Debate your position in class with students taking the opposite position or prepare a written argument justifying your position.

⑪ Downstream Pollution

Country A has a river running through it which flows into Country B. A lumber mill in Country A that makes plywood for needed housing is located on the river. When pollutants from the mill end up in Country B, it demands that it be closed down.

You Debate · *Do you think that Country B has a right to ask Country A to close the lumber mill that supplies jobs and housing materials to the people in its country?*

⑫ Family History

The Jeffersons have owned a manufacturing company for over 100 years. They incorporated it in 2003. Now Merkson Industries is attempting a hostile takeover. But the board chairman, a descendant of the founder, refuses to sell.

You Debate · *Do shareholders have a right to insist that the company be sold?*

⑬ Assessing a Primary Motive

After purchasing Italian eyewear company Ugo, Cambria Eye Glasses, Inc. lost money for years. The shareholders sued when they learned that Cambria's chairman had taken 12 lavish trips to Italy in two years and purchased a villa there.

You Debate · *Does the evidence prove that the chairman acted solely in self-interest?*

⑭ Model Airplanes

Allied, Inc. manufactures model airplanes. Whenever their best customer, Flying Toys, calls to order 1,000 models, Allied ships them in 24 hours. But whenever Rich's Models places its usual 500 model order, Allied says it takes two weeks to ship.

You Debate · *Could Rich's Models sue Allied for infringing on the Robinson-Patman Act guaranteeing them equal service?*

⑮ Grocery Store Fireplace

Dick Heeley has owned a cozy grocery store in Vermont for ten years. In the winter, hundreds of neighbors come in to sit by the wood-burning stove to chat. One day, a town resident complains to Dick that the stove pollutes the air. She insists that he halt its usage.

You Debate · *Should the owner stop using the wood-burning stove?*

Case Study Practice – Community Group v. City of San Diego

16 Exempt from Environmental Laws? Developers in San Diego wanted to construct a 14-unit residential building with an underground parking garage. The site of the project was a 10,247-square-foot vacant lot. Across the street is Balboa Park, an 1,100-acre urban park that contains theaters, museums, restaurants, and other public facilities.

In January 2004, the City of San Diego issued a building permit for the parking garage. Banker's Hill, Hillcrest, Park West Community Preservation Group (Community Group) filed a petition to stop the construction project. The Community Group argued that the developers had not obtained an environmental review as required under California Environmental Quality Act (CEQA). Under CEQA, developers can be exempt from CEQA, if the project qualifies as urban in-fill. Urban in-fill is defined as an area that: is surrounded by urban structures; has no value to endangered species; would not result in significant traffic or noise; and would be adequately serviced by already installed utilities.

Source: Banker's Hill, Hillcrest, Park West Community Preservation Group v. City of San Diego, 2006 WL 1216918 (Cal. Ct. App. 2006)

Practice Can the City exempt the project from CEQA?

17 Ethics ←?→ Application

Who Is Responsible? Margaret works for a furniture refinishing company. She notices that the chemicals used in the process are rinsed into the floor drains, which flow into the city's sewer system. She tells her boss he should dispose of the chemicals in a safe manner. He tells her that it is too costly, and the chemicals are not that dangerous.

◆ Does Margaret have an ethical duty to report the problem to the Environmental Protection Agency, or is it the responsibility of her boss or the company?

18 Think back to the Legal Briefs feature you read at the beginning of the chapter. Then write one or more paragraphs to explain your opinion on guanxi. Do you think it is important to have confidence that the businesses you deal with are honorable? What aspects of guanxi do not align with American business practices?

19 Cyberlaw and E-Commerce

Legal Briefs

Smartphone Wars

Focus on Intellectual Property Rights

Apple and Samsung are not only competitors in business; they are also competitors in the courts, protecting their innovations. The court cases among these two powerful companies center on intellectual property rights (IP) such as copyrights, trademarks, and trade secrets.

Both companies have filed various patent infringement suits against each other. For example, Apple filed against Samsung, claiming that Samsung copied the iPhone® and iPad® design. Samsung filed against Apple, claiming that Apple violated several of Samsung's patents, including the one for emailing photos from a camera phone.

With all the innovations in the smartphone industry, Apple and Samsung are bound to come up with some of the same ideas, but how far can either company take the idea before stealing the other's intellectual property? That's where the courts come in. In one lawsuit, a jury decided that Samsung did infringe on an Apple patent, which diluted Apple products, but that Apple did not infringe on any Samsung patents.

Critics argue the patents are too broad, whereas patent holders claim they deserve protection for all the money and effort that went into research.

Internet Insecurity The Internet has made doing business much faster and easier but has also brought with it the risk of Internet fraud and identity theft. *What are some of the things you can do to protect yourself online?*

What You'll Learn

- ◆ Explain the nature of a cybercrime.
- ◆ List different types of cybercrimes.
- ◆ Describe the nature of a cybertort.
- ◆ Distinguish between cyberdefamation and cyberinvasion of privacy.

Why It's Important

Learning how the law deals with computer-related crimes and torts will help you keep up with new technology.

Reading Guide

Before You Read

Connect If you have ever received an e-mail with a virus in it, you know what cybercrime is. What are some cybercrimes that you have experienced?

Focus on Ideas

Technology has created new areas of law to prosecute criminals who use computers to commit crimes.

Take Notes

Go to connectED. mcgraw-hill.com to download a graphic organizer you can use to take notes as you read this section.

Cyberlaw
- Types of Cybercrimes—
- Types of Cybertorts—

Key Terms

You will learn these legal words and expressions in this chapter. You can also find these terms in *Black's Law Dictionary* or in an online legal dictionary.

- cyberlaw
- cybercrime
- cybertrespass
- cyberspoofing
- cyberpiracy
- cyberblackmail
- identity theft
- cybervandalism
- cybertort
- cyberdefamation
- cyberinvasion of privacy

Academic Vocabulary

You will find these words in your readings and in your tests. Look them up in a dictionary and familiarize yourself with them.

- simulate
- infrastructure
- sabotage

The Development of Cyberlaw

Are there laws that control your use of a computer?

The interaction of the law and the world of computers is so new that new words have had to be invented. The field is now called cyberlaw. **Cyberlaw is the area of the law which concerns computers and computer-related crimes.** Some people also call it computer law, electronic law, or e-law. Cyberlaw merges concepts, doctrines, and principles from many legal fields—criminal law, tort law, intellectual property law, and contract law—and puts them into the context of computers. Cyberlaw is intended to deal with cybercrimes. **A cybercrime is any criminal activity associated with a computer.** Legal experts at the federal and state levels have developed two approaches for creating cyberlaws to deal with the new area of cybercrime.

As You Read

Predict How does the government keep our laws current with new technology that is used to commit crimes?

The Cybertrespass Approach

Some states have dealt with the problem of covering cybercrimes by adding cybertrespass statutes to the traditional criminal code. **Cybertrespass, or computer trespass, is any illegal activity already in the criminal code committed by using a computer.** Under the cybertrespass approach, states do not define each individual cybercrime.

Rewriting of Criminal Code

Some state legislatures have dealt with cybercrime by writing individual statutes for every crime that can possibly be committed by using a computer. This approach is difficult because every new statute must be individually created. Some state legislators prefer this approach because criminal law statutes must be very specific

Business ETHICS

Czech Investments

As a recent immigrant to the United States from the Czech Republic, you are trying to start a new life as a business owner. Back in the Czech Republic, you owned and operated a successful stock brokerage firm. Since moving to the U.S., you have realized that many people are interested in investing in Czech companies. The easiest thing for you to do is to set up an Internet investment company that would link American investors with the Czech stock market. U.S. law limits promoting stock for sale on the Internet, but Czech law does not. You want to send mass e-mails out to a lot of people promoting your new service.

Critical Thinking: *What kinds of issues should you be concerned about in using the Internet to link American investors with the Czech stock market?*

Legal Talk

Trespass: *v* Unlawful act committed against a person or person's property. From Latin *trans* = beyond + *passer* = pass.

Extort: *v* To obtain from a person by force. From Latin *ex* = out + *tort* = twist: to twist out.

Vocabulary Builder List three words each that begin with the prefix *ex* and the prefix *trans*.

Vocabulary You can find vocabulary definitions in the **Key Terms** glossary and Academic Vocabulary glossary in the back of this book.

Reading Check

Differentiate *What is the difference between cyberpiracy and cyberspoofing?*

---

in detailing an outlawed behavior. Otherwise, when the statute is used to prosecute a cyberdefendant, the court might decide that the statute is void because it is too vague.

Cybercrimes

What kinds of crimes can be committed using computers?

Cybercrimes include both crimes directed at people using a computer and crimes directed at other computers.

Cyberspoofing

Cyberspoofing is a crime in which a cybercriminal falsely adopts the identity of another computer user or creates a false identity on a computer Web site in order to commit fraud. One of the most common types of cyberspoofing is called *phishing*. This involves creating a phony Web site that **simulates** a real bank, credit card agency, or retail store. The criminals then broadcast false e-mails in the name of the business with a link to the phony Web site. They attempt to lure people into believing the Web site is real and attempt to obtain from the victims their private information such as credit card and bank account numbers, personal ID numbers (PINs), and passwords.

Cyberspoofers also use online auction sites, such as eBay, to deceive legitimate buyers. They pretend to have goods for sale that they do not actually have. After the consumers purchase the goods, the criminals pocket the money and do not deliver any goods.

Cyberpiracy

Cyberpiracy is a crime that involves using a computer to steal computer data stored in a digital format. Cyberpiracy often involves the theft of intellectual property, such as downloading software programs or transmitting them to others without payment or permission. To combat this, Congress passed the Digital Millennium Copyright Act (DMCA). The DMCA makes it illegal to pirate copyrighted computer programs using methods that bypass software copyright protection systems. The penalties for violating the DMCA are very severe, reaching as high as ten years in prison for second time offenders. The DMCA also allows individual plaintiffs to bring civil lawsuits against cyberpirates who violate its provisions.

Cyberblackmail

Cyberblackmail, sometimes called cyberextortion, is the use of information unlawfully obtained by computer to pressure a victim into granting a payoff to the blackmailer. Generally, the criminal threatens to reveal some sort of illegal or embarrassing conduct gathered about the person. Computer users who spend time in chat rooms are especially vulnerable to this type of crime. The cyberblackmailer often befriends a person, learns damaging information, then uses it to extort money from the victim.

Identity Theft

Identity theft is using a computer to steal financial, employment, educational, medical, and personal data. Identity thieves attempt to obtain credit card numbers, financial data, passwords, PINs, Social Security numbers, and access codes. They then use the data to empty bank accounts, run up credit card bills, steal cash, and generally disrupt the target's personal life. It is important to be aware of all activity on your accounts to prevent identity theft because once your identity is stolen it can take years to fix the problem.

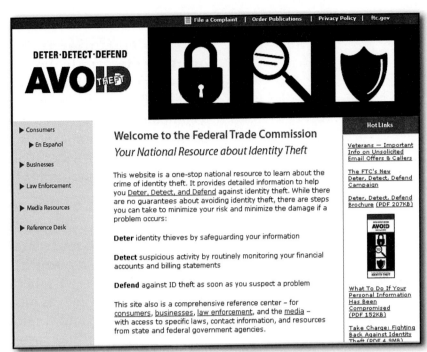

Cyberterrorism

Cyberterrorism is committed when someone operating a computer disrupts part of the national electronic **infrastructure**. This includes power grids, the air traffic control system, and the national defense system, among others. It also includes disrupting corporate computer systems, such as banks, brokerages, and telecommunications.

Cybervandalism

Cybervandalism is disrupting, damaging, or destroying a Web site or computer network. Cybervandals, also called hackers, might attack a business or government computer system as an act of **sabotage** or revenge. Although many people commit cybervandalism as a prank, to gain attention, or to show off, cybervandalism is still a crime and cybervandals are criminals.

Cybergerm Warfare

Cybergerm warfare involves transmitting computer viruses to people to destroy their computer system or files. Like cybervandals, perpetrators transmit viruses as a prank or to show off, but others use viruses intentionally to commit crimes, such as cyberterrorism or cybervandalism. Firewalls and anti-virus software can block many viruses.

Cybercrime The advent of computer technology and the Internet created new ways of communicating and doing business. Unfortunately, it also created new opportunities for criminals. *What crimes have computers and the Internet made it much easier to commit?*

Cybertorts

What is the difference between a tort and a cybertort?

A tort is a private wrong committed by one person against another. **A cybertort is the invasion, theft, falsification, misuse, or deletion of data stored in a computer to commit a tort.** The two most common cybertorts are cyberdefamation and cyberinvasion of privacy.

Cyberdefamation

Cyberdefamation is the communication via computer or other electronic device of false data that damages a person's reputation. Cyberdefamation may involve sending out e-mails or text messages that contain false information about a company that ruins its name in the public. Congress recently passed the Communications Decency Act (CDA) that protects Internet Service Providers (ISPs) from being held liable for any cyberdefamation performed by users on these services.

Cyberinvasion of Privacy

Cyberinvasion of privacy is an unwelcome intrusion into the private matters of an individual carried out or sustained by a computer. Cyberinvasion of privacy often involves employees who, because of their jobs, work closely with confidential files, such as medical records, financial records, scholastic records, and employment records.

The government has passed several laws to protect the privacy of individuals and their computer records. The Fair Credit Reporting Act protects records kept by credit bureaus. The law says that credit bureaus must tell people about their files and must send corrections to anyone who might have been misled by false reports. The Right to Financial Privacy Act states that financial institutions cannot open customer records to a government official without the customer's permission, unless there is a court order. The Electronic Communications Privacy Act restricts the unauthorized access of e-mail and instant messaging. However, employers can monitor the e-mail transmissions of employees if the employees consent to it.

After You Read

Summarize List the four types of crimes in which the computer is the victim.

SECTION 19.1 ASSESSMENT

Self Check

1. What is a cybercrime?
2. What is a cybertort?
3. What is the difference between cyberdefamation and cyberinvasion of privacy?

Academic Connection

English Language Arts
You are a small business owner who conducts business internationally via the Internet. You are concerned that this may expose your computer system to cybervandalism and cybergerm warfare. To combat this, you wish to upgrade your anti-virus software. Research three brands of anti-virus software, such as Norton and EZAntivirus. Create a chart comparing and contrasting the various features offered by each brand and determine which product best suits your needs. Write a brief report stating your reasons for choosing this software application.

Critical Thinking

Cyberterrorism
Since 9/11 the federal government has become much more involved in combating the threat of cyberterrorism. What are some of the concerns about what cyberterrorists could do?

Internet Transactions

Reading Guide

Before You Read

Connect What are some of the problems with doing business over the Internet you do not usually have doing business face-to-face, by phone, or by mail?

Focus on Ideas

The government has been very careful to balance the rights of the Internet buyer with those of the Internet seller.

Take Notes

Go to connectED.mcgraw-hill.com to download a graphic organizer you can use to take notes as you read this section.

Key Terms

You will learn these legal words and expressions in this chapter. You can also find these terms in *Black's Law Dictionary* or in an online legal dictionary.

- e-commerce
- digital signature
- domain name

Academic Vocabulary

You will find these words in your readings and in your tests. Look them up in a dictionary and familiarize yourself with them.

- tangible
- broadcast
- duplicate

What You'll Learn

- ◆ Explain intellectual property and copyright for digital products.
- ◆ Explain the importance of trademarks.
- ◆ Identify the characteristics of a patentable invention.
- ◆ Recognize two unsettled issues in e-commerce law.
- ◆ Explain new laws regarding digital signatures and documents.

Why It's Important

Knowing the laws that affect e-commerce will help you whenever you download music or movies, or buy goods on the Internet.

E-Commerce Laws

How does e-commerce save you time?

As You Read

Predict Can a software program be copyrighted just like a book or song?

E-commerce, short for electronic commerce, is the process of conducting business using electronic means, especially the Internet. E-commerce includes purchasing products by using electronic credit or debit cards, extracting money from a checking account at the local ATM, and transferring funds electronically between financial institutions. These new electronic forms of business have raised jurisdictional issues, taxation issues, and authentication problems, as well as intellectual property rights issues (see **Figure 19.1**).

Jurisdictional Issues

Doing business over the Internet raises the question of which state has jurisdiction in a case when the user or buyer does not reside in the same state as the seller. The courts have recognized two principles on this matter:

- Just because a Web site can be accessed in a state does not, by itself, give jurisdiction to that state.
- A state may gain jurisdiction over an e-commerce transaction when a Web site allows users to purchase merchandise on that site. The merchandiser Amazon.com is an example. In such cases, the state in which the buyer resides has jurisdiction, even though the physical home of the seller is another state.

Tax Issues

The jurisdictional issue above is important because it plays a role in determining which state has the right to tax Internet sites that sell goods. The courts have ruled that sellers who do not have a store, office, or wholesale shop within a state cannot be taxed by that state. However, the buyer may be taxed at the buyer's location, such as a sales tax. At this time, Internet sales are governed by the Internet Tax Freedom Act.

Authentication Issues and the E-Sign Act

One difficulty with buying and selling on the Internet is making certain that the buyer and the seller really are who they claim to be. This is referred to as authentication. To manage this problem, Congress passed the E-sign Act, a short name for the Electronic Signatures in Global and National Commerce Act. This act ensures that any cybercontract is considered as legal as a paper equivalent if the parties have agreed to use digital signatures. **A digital signature is an encoded message that appears at the end of a contract created online.** The signature can be verified by a confidential password, by a special smart card, or by electronic equipment that can identify a person by scanning his or her fingerprints or retina.

Figure 19.1 Issues in Cyberlaw

View Your Accounts

Log in to your account online:

User Name:

Enter user name

Password:

Forgot password?　[GO]

New user sign up

🔒 Why this is secure

Taxation Charging and collecting sales taxes on Internet transactions is complicated in e-commerce because Internet transactions routinely cross state lines and sales tax rates differ from state to state.

Internet Security Encryption makes Internet transactions secure by encoding data sent over the Internet in such a way that only authorized persons can decode it.

Copyright Protection Trademarks, trade names, and domain names on the Internet receive the same kinds of protection as other types of intellectual properties.

🔼 E-commerce has made it easy for someone in Texas to buy something from a company in New York without ever leaving his or her chair, but it has raised questions regarding issues such as jurisdiction, security, and taxation. *What does a cybercontract require to be considered completely legal?*

Cyberlaw and Intellectual Property

Is there any way to protect intellectual property on the Internet?

Reading Check

Analyze *How can an author or songwriter keep track of whether people are illegally copying their works on the Internet?*

Vocabulary You can find vocabulary definitions in the **Key Terms** glossary and Academic Vocabulary glossary in the back of this book.

Another new legal area is cyberprotection law. This involves laws that protect people and businesses that create or invent any of the following:

- products that can be distributed digitally using computers, such as music and movies
- new computer products and inventions, such as hardware devices
- products that use or work with computers, such as software

New cyberprotection laws have been created in three areas: copyrights, trademarks, and patents. These types of laws allow writers, artists, inventors, and businesses to protect their ideas, products, and trade names from having other people imitate, copy, use, or sell them without permission and/or payment.

Copyrights

A copyright is a legal protection that has been available in the United States for literary, artistic, and scientific works since 1790. Under the federal Copyright Act, the originator of a work in a "fixed **tangible** medium of expression" is granted the exclusive authority to publish, reproduce, and sell his or her work. The Computer Software Copyright Act of 1980 added computer software programs to the types of work to which copyright protection can be extended.

Copyrighting a work is done by registering it at the Copyright Office in Washington, D.C., although a formal registration is no longer required to obtain protection. As soon as a work exists in tangible form, the owner is protected. A copyright extends for the creator's life plus 70 years. If the originator is a corporation, the copyright lasts 120 years from when it was first written or 95 years from its first publication. After the copyright period is over, the work goes into the public domain where it may be copied by others.

Another new area of copyright law concerns the **broadcast** of artistic works over the Internet. Millions of computer users can get free access to a protected literary or artistic work if just one person illegally publishes it on a Web site. As a result, Congress passed the No Electronic Theft Act (NET Act) in 1997. This statute provides prison terms and fines for anyone

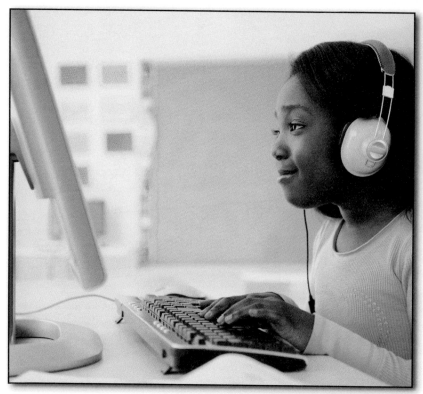

Electronic Copying Federal laws have given computer programs the same copyright protection as literary works and made it illegal to make electronic duplicates of them. *What exceptions are there to the law?*

Critical Thinking *Can a corporation be sued for antitrust violations when the actions involve an Internet company it invested in?*

Flex Your Reading **Note key facts in the text below and look up words you do not understand. Restate difficult ideas in your own words. Go back and reread the text quickly to make sure you did not miss any important detail. Now, you are ready to formulate an opinion.**

Antitrust Violations? Medical Supply Chain, Inc. (MSC) provided an e-commerce marketplace for suppliers and purchasers of hospital supplies. Its two main competitors, Neoforma and GHX, controlled 80 percent of the hospital supply market. MSC looked for a location for its commercial offices and found a place in Blue Springs, Missouri. The office space, however, was already leased to GE Transportation Systems Global Signaling, LLC, a subsidiary of General Electric Co. (GE). MSC decided to buy the whole building. It sought financing from GE Capital Business Asset Funding Corporation (GE Capital), another GE subsidiary.

Everything seemed to be going fine, until GE Capital refused to provide financing to MSC. MSC discovered that GE was an investor in GHX and sued GE for antitrust violations. MSC argued that GE was trying to create or maintain a monopoly in hospital supply e-commerce by refusing to provide financing to MSC, thus preventing MSC from becoming a competitor of GHX.

Medical Supply Chain, Inc. v. General Electric Co., 144 Fed.Appx. 708 (10th Cir. 2005)

Go to **ConnectED.mcgraw-hill.com** for more case study practice.

---

who creates an electronic **duplicate** of a copyrighted work for commercial profit or private financial gain. The Digital Millennium Copyright Act (DMCA) also outlaws pirated copies of software made by disabling the internal protection system of the software.

Trademarks and Domain Names

A trademark is a distinctive name, word, symbol, image or slogan used by a business to identify and distinguish its goods from products sold by others. Trademarks are registered with the United States Patent and Trademark Office in Washington, D.C. Many hardware and software companies trademark their name and the name of their products.

A domain name is the Internet address of a business. Domain name disputes arise when one party has registered a domain name that uses a famous person's name, a trademark, or a trade name that is registered by another user. In some cases, cybersquatters register a person's name, a trademark, or a trade name as a domain name with no intent to actually use it. Instead, the cybersquatter holds on to the name until the real holder of the name, the trademark, or the trade name appears to claim the name.

Global Law

Internet Privacy Laws in Taiwan

In 1995, the Taiwanese legislature passed the Computer-Processed Personal Data Protection Law 1995. This law covers the privacy of information collected over the Internet.

Who the Law Covers

The law only applies to the public sector and some industries within the private sector. The private sector categories only include:

- credit information organizations
- hospitals
- schools
- telecommunications businesses
- bank and financial institutions
- securities businesses
- insurance companies
- mass communications

Government Regulation

The law provides regulations for the transmission of private information from Taiwan to other locations in the world. There are four reasons the government can block a transmission:

1 to protect Taiwan's national interest

2 where an international treaty or agreement prohibits the transfer

3 where the receiving country lacks sufficient laws or regulation to protect personal information

4 the indirect transmission of information to a third country to get around Taiwan's laws

> **Across Cultures: Convenience Store Culture**
>
> Taiwan boasts more convenience stores per person than any other country. There are over 8,000 convenience stores in Taiwan. Because they are so prevalent, the stores provide a number of services, such as collection of parking fees, utility bills, and credit card payments. Eighty percent of Taiwan's urban population visits a convenience store weekly.

Critical Thinking *How much should the government do to control private information sent over the Internet?*

The cybersquatter then asks for an enormous amount of money to sell the name back to the real owner.

To deal with this tactic, Congress passed the Anticybersquatting Consumer Protection Act. The object of the act is to provide a shield for the real owners of trademarks and trade names.

Patents

A patent is a property right that inventors can acquire to protect their right to make, use, and sell their inventions for a number of years as set by law. In order for an invention to be patentable, it must meet three requirements. The invention must fit within the statute as "patentable subject matter." The invention must consist of some nonobvious, new, and useful feature. The application designed for the invention must be so specific that, from its detail, the invention could be reproduced by experts in the field.

For many years, lawmakers debated whether stand-alone computer programs were patentable. Once lawmakers determined that software programs are indeed a process, or a means of doing something, they agreed that they qualify as patentable subject matter. Another software programmer must invent a different way to do the same thing as the one who owns the patent.

The patent application process requires documenting in detail the plans, structure, and operation of the invention. The document is then filed at the United States Patent and Trademark Office. If approved, the inventor is given a number that must be placed on the invention along with the word *patent* or the abbreviation *pat.*

Cybercontract Law

What is the difference between a contract and a cybercontract?

Cybercontract law deals with the buying and selling of computers and computer programs. One area of cybercontracts involves the sale of custom-programmed software. For example, a company might hire a programmer to come to its business to develop a new program. The legal issue in this matter is the question of who owns the source code, which is the actual code behind the software.

The Uniform Computer Information Transactions Act

The Uniform Computer Information Transactions Act (UCITA) governs the law for cybercontracts such as software agreements and licenses, software formulation contracts, and software maintenance contracts. Once the parties to a cybercontract have entered an agreement using electronic means, the agreement will be just as binding as a similar one negotiated outside of the Web. The UCITA is a default statute, which means that the parties can use it to resolve any issues not covered by their own contracts.

After You Read

Summarize List three issues of law that e-commerce has raised.

SECTION 19.2 ASSESSMENT

Self Check

1. What kinds of products and property do cyber-protection laws cover?

2. What is a domain name dispute?

3. What is the purpose of the No Electronic Theft Act?

Academic Connection

Mathematics Appleton Wholesale Grocers, Inc. plans to construct a new building at a cost of $875,000 to house the new computer installation.

Appleton hires an architect, a systems analyst, and a computer programmer. The architect charges seven percent of the total cost of the building. The system analyst charges a flat fee of $6,000. The computer programmer charges $30 an hour and works 150 hours. What is the total cost of the professional services?

THEORY **Number and Operations:** To calculate the total cost of professional services, find the sum of consultants' fees using the formula:

(Cost of Building × 7%) + Systems Analyst Fee + (Computer Programmer Rate × Total Hours)

For more math practice, go to the Math Appendix.

Critical Thinking

The Future of Cyberlaw
What are some of the legal challenges you can imagine facing lawmakers in the future?

Summary

Section 19.1 Cyberlaw and Cybercrime

◆ Cyberlaw is the area of the law which concerns computers and computer-related crimes.

◆ A cybercrime is any criminal activity associated with a computer.

◆ Some states have dealt with cybercrimes by adding cybertrespass statutes to the traditional criminal code.

◆ Some states have dealt with cybercrimes by writing individual statutes for every crime that can be committed by using a computer.

◆ Cybercrimes include cyberblackmail, cyberspoofing, cyberpiracy, cyberterrorism, identity theft, cybervandalism, and cybergerm warfare.

◆ Cybertorts include cyberdefamation and cyberinvasion of privacy.

Section 19.2 Internet Transactions

◆ E-commerce is the process of conducting business using electronic means, especially the Internet.

◆ E-commerce has raised jurisdictional issues, taxation issues, and authentication problems.

◆ Cyberprotection laws protect intellectual property that can be distributed using computers, new computer products and inventions, and products that use or work with computers.

◆ No Electronic Theft Act provides prison terms and fines for anyone who creates an electronic duplicate of a copyrighted work for commercial profit or private financial gain.

◆ The Uniform Computer Information Transactions Act (UCITA) governs software agreements and licenses, software formulation contracts, and software maintenance contracts.

Vocabulary Builder

1 On a sheet of paper, use each of these terms in a sentence.

Key Terms

- cyberlaw
- cybercrime
- cybertrespass
- cyberspoofing
- cyberpiracy
- cyberblackmail
- identity theft
- cybervandalism
- cybertort
- cyberdefamation
- cyberinvasion of privacy
- e-commerce
- digital signature
- domain name

Academic Vocabulary

- simulate
- infrastructure
- sabotage
- tangible
- broadcast
- duplicate

Key Points Review

Answer the following questions. Refer to the chapter for additional reinforcement.

2 What two approaches have states used to cover cybercrimes?

3 What is cyberspoofing?

4 How do identity thieves work?

5 What is a cybertort?

6 What are the two principles courts use to decide jurisdiction in e-commerce sales?

7 What is a digital signature and how can it be verified?

8 What did the Computer Software Copyright Act of 1980 do?

9 What is the purpose of the Anticybersquatting Consumer Protection Act?

Standardized Test Practice

10 Read the following excerpt about efforts to combat cybercrime internationally and complete questions 1 and 2.

In May 2006, representatives of the Group of Eight (G8) industrialized nations, including France, Japan, and the U.S., met in Paris and agreed to boost cooperation to fight cybercrime. Participants there confirmed their support of the France-based Council of Europe's efforts to finalize a Convention on Cybercrime, which will be the first international treaty to deal with the different forms of criminal activity in cyberspace. The treaty would require countries to approve and enforce laws regarding interception of data, interference with computer systems, fraud, and forgery via the Internet. It also requires them to provide national law enforcement with the authority to carry out computer searches and seizures of computer data. "Everyone realizes that we are at a point where business is in transition, technology is in transition, and there is a legal transition as well," says Randy Picker, a law professor at the University of Chicago. "The reality is, the legal clock is a lot slower than the business or technology clock."

1. The first international treaty to deal with cybercrime will allow:

Ⓐ the G8 to represent the world in technology

Ⓑ laws to meet the needs of technology

Ⓒ methods to deal with cyberspace crimes

Ⓓ ability to search and seize computer data

2. The treaty would require countries to approve and enforce laws regarding:

Ⓐ fraud, forgery, interception of computer data, and overuse of the Internet

Ⓑ forgery, interception of data, fraud, and computer system interference

Ⓒ search and seizures, computer data, fraud, forgery, and cyberspace

Ⓓ cybercrime, technology, forgery, fraud, and computer system interference

 Test-Taking Strategies Do not cram the night before a test. Plan to get a full eight hours of sleep.

Apply and Debate

Read the following scenarios. Get together with other students in pairs or groups of three and take a position on each scenario. Debate your position in class with students taking the opposite position or prepare a written argument justifying your position.

11 **Computer Hacker Dilemma**

A computer hacker, Raoul, broke into computer systems at several businesses for fun. He did not do any damage, but he was caught and put on probation. After a year, he was hired to work at a computer security firm helping to stop hackers.

You Debate · *Does it send the wrong message to computer hackers that they can get good jobs after committing crimes?*

12 **Web Site with Music**

Tina is a candle maker and sells her candles on a Web site. The site also contains photos of famous celebrities and the caption: "These stars would love my candles." Tina found the photos on the Internet.

You Debate · *Is it fair that Tina uses photos of famous people to help sell her products?*

13 **Online Purchase Fairness**

To avoid paying sales tax, Jack buys his big purchases online from sellers located outside his state. Jack's friend's TV store loses sales because it must charge sales tax.

You Debate · *Is it fair that some Internet-based companies are able to avoid charging sales tax when local stores must charge it?*

14 **A Smart Programmer**

Nick is a programmer. A company hired him to develop software that translates Web sites into French. While doing this, he also figured out how to translate the Web sites into Italian, German, and Russian. Nick claims he owns the extra programs.

You Debate · *Do you think programmers own the rights to software programs they create that go beyond what they were hired to do?*

15 **Fake Internet Order?**

Juicy Oranges, Inc. received an e-mail from Alison Adams providing her credit card number and ordering five crates of oranges, worth $272. When the shipment was delivered, Alison claimed she never sent the e-mail and refused to pay.

You Debate · *If you were the judge in this case, would you rule in favor of Alison or Juicy Oranges, Inc.?*

Case Study Practice – See, Inc. v. Imago Eyewear Party, Ltd.

16 Does the Court Have Jurisdiction? See, Inc. is an American corporation that sells eyewear over the Internet on its Web site, seeeyewear.com, which it registered as a domain name in 1998. See, Inc. owns federal trademarks on SEE and SEE SELECTIVE EYEWEAR ELEMENTS. See, Inc. has also filed for a trademark on SEE EYEWEAR.

The Defendant, Imago Eyewear Party, Ltd., is an Australian company that also sells eyewear over the Internet. Imago uses the Web site "seeyewear.com" to sell its products. This Web site domain name was registered in 2002. Image has filed for a United States trademark on SEEYEWEAR. See, Inc. sued Imago Eyewear in Michigan Federal Court. See, Inc. claimed that Imago, by using the Web site seeyewear.com, had violated Federal trademark law and Michigan's unfair trade practices statutes.

Imago argued that there is no jurisdiction for See, Inc. to sue in Michigan. Imago argued that See, Inc. is an Australian corporation and that, although Michigan residents can access its Web site on the Internet, no Michigan resident has every contacted See, Inc. via its Web site. Therefore, a U.S. Court does not have jurisdiction to hear this case.

Source: See, Inc. v. Imago Eyewear Party, Ltd., 167 Fed.Appx. 518 (6th Cir. 2006)

Practice Can See, Inc. sue Imago Eyewear in Michigan?

17 Ethics ←?→ Application

Is It Ever Okay to Copy CDs? Five students from your school who graduated two years ago are in a band. They just cut a CD and began selling it. You love the music and buy a copy. Your two closest friends also love the music and ask you to make copies of the CD for them.

◆ Is it ethical for you to copy this CD and give it to other people? Explain your position.

18 Think back to the Legal Briefs feature you read at the beginning of the chapter. Think about the fact that you recognize many products by the trademark. For example, you're likely to be very familiar with the Apple brand because of the unique design and logo on their products. Companies rely on their trademarks for customers to recognize the brand and for protection under the law. Conduct research to identify a lawsuit over the use of a logo. Write two or more paragraphs to explain the lawsuit. Tell both sides of the story. Conclude with your opinion on the matter.

Patrick A. McNutt
Antitrust Consultant

What do you do at work?

"My job as a strategic antitrust consultant involves the preparation of advices for private clients, liaison with lawyers, and representations before competition agencies. On a larger scale it has involved the implementation of competition in a jurisdiction, drafting the legislation, and recruitment of staff. My work also involves quite a bit of travel, lecturing, and participating as a speaker at international conferences."

What skills are most important to you?

"The skills set includes an ability to communicate effectively, an ability to understand the client's problem from the client's perspective, and an ability to work in teams or alone depending on the nature of the assignment. Up-to-date knowledge of the law is taken for granted."

What kind of training do you recommend?

"I would recommend a primary degree in law and economics with an elective in antitrust economics and competition law. Early in one's career, one could work as a paralegal in a law firm or join an economic consultancy firm in order to gain experience. Alternatively, one could gain experience as a case handler, either as a lawyer or economist with a national competition agency, and then move later in your career to the private sector as a consultant."

What is your key to success?

"It is important to showcase a combination of hard work and dedication to the job without necessarily sacrificing a personal life. The key to this is developing good time management skills. Prioritizing and meeting deadlines reflects well on your professional image. Listening to clients and understanding the issue at hand from their idiosyncratic perspective also aid in the steps needed to move a successful professional relationship forward."

Resume Builder

Academic Skills

- Above average analytical skills
- Good speaking, listening, and negotiating skills

Education and Training

Obtain a bachelor's degree in business administration, law, and economics as well as augment these with specifics in the industry of interest. The following high school and college courses will help develop the necessary background knowledge:

- Business Management
- Business law courses
- Communication
- English Language Arts (rhetoric and composition)
- Introduction to Business
- U.S. Government
- Social Studies

Critical Thinking

How can quality performance and time management skills impact your career?

Personal Essay Practice

The Particulars of a Dream Four college graduates come up with the dream of starting their own cultural magazine on music, literature, and art. They envision running the magazine full time and drawing salaries as the owners and editors of the magazine. One of the friends, a business major, brings up the real-world details of accomplishing their dream. They should form their business as a 501(c)(3) nonprofit corporation. They could then hold fundraisers, write grant proposals, and seek out funding from businesses, the government, and other sources. First, they will need to find out how to propose a budget, create an accounting system, and write a grant.

Assignments

Research Find out what it takes to form a nonprofit corporation in your state. Be sure to examine the federal laws as well as state laws.

Write Consider the situation above and write a personal essay about the nonprofit company you would want to start.

Writing Tips Before you start writing your personal essay, remember that it should:

✓ represent the writer's point of view
✓ reflect the writer's life and interests

✓ share a life lesson with the reader or talk about a relevant past experience

Discuss the specific details of how to start a nonprofit, and explain why you think there is a need in the marketplace for your idea. What makes you so passionate about your idea? Why would individuals, corporations, or organizations want to invest in your idea?

Essay Test Strategies CollegeBoard, a not-for-profit membership association, recommends the following tips on essay writing: read the entire assignment before writing; do not oversimplify; and support your idea with facts and figures.

Thematic Project

Protecting Social and Environmental Concerns

For this project, you will use what you have learned to prepare an informational guide on an environmental law affecting society at large, as well as business. You can work on this project alone or with a partner.

Here is a checklist of the skills that you will need to complete this project. Your teacher will consider these skills when evaluating your work.

Evaluation Rubric

Academic Skills		
1. Online and library research	1.	10 points
2. Reading for information	2.	10 points
3. Note-taking	3.	5 points
4. Estimation and computation of facts/figures you discover	4.	10 points
5. English composition to summarize findings	5.	15 points
Legal Skills		
6. Researching laws that protect the environment	6.	15 points
7. Knowledge of federal laws that set precedent for businesses	7.	15 points
8. Analysis of essential legislative acts governing businesses	8.	15 points
9. Use of technology	9.	5 points
		Total 100 Points

Step 1: Preparation

① Write a proposal for an area of environmental protection law you plan to research.

② Use all you have learned in this unit and library or Internet resources as tools.

③ Complete this project in a format that is acceptable for adding to your portfolio.

Step 2: Procedure

❶ Review the text in this unit and make a list of the environmental protection laws that pertain to your specific area of interest, such as air pollution, oil spills, global warming, disposing of nuclear waste, etc.

❷ List all the legal terms you come across in your research. What laws protect the public and regulate business? How are these laws enforced?

❸ Write an informational guide about the legal terms and documents that a business owner would need to know about the law you chose. Use the Internet to research and download important documents. Make enough copies so your classmates can review and annotate your guide.

❹ Describe a real-world situation in which a business violated the laws in your area of interest. Explain the impact of the violation not only on the business, but on the public and on the environment as well. Present your guide and conclusion to your classmates.

Step 3: Create an Analysis Report

As a class, compare and contrast the information presented in each guide. See if any of the guides stand out, and if so what makes the information presented most interesting. After comparing the guides, answer the following questions:

❶ How many and what areas of environmental laws were presented?

❷ Did the guides presented include all the necessary information needed to understand the importance of federal environmental legislation?

❸ If not, what should have been added to make the information easier to use?

❹ How was your guide similar to and different from the other guides presented?

Community Connection

Research current environmental laws that are being debated by politicians, businesses, and environmental organizations either on a local, national, or international level. Decide who has the most to win and who has the most to lose if the law is passed.

Competitive Event Prep

New Business Venture

Situation: Assume the role of a high school business law student. A college student friend is a landscaping major who is planning to open a new landscaping and lawn service business. Your friend is concerned about the type of business ownership that should be established. Your friend has cared for lawns on a casual basis without a formally established business. This new venture will require the purchase of equipment and hiring help.

Activity: You must explain the different types of business ownership to your friend, with an emphasis on the pros and cons of each.

Broz v. Cellular Information Systems, Inc.
Delaware Supreme Court 673 A.2d 148 (1996)

Read Critically As you read this case, ask yourself the following questions:

1. What companies did Mr. Broz have a responsibility to?
2. Why did CIS sue Mr. Broz?
3. What legal doctrine applies to his case?
4. What did the Delaware Supreme Court hold with regard to Mr. Broz?

Assignment Write a short summary of the situation. Include the court's decision and a couple of sentences about why or how the court reached its decision.

Facts **Board Member** Robert Broz was the president and sole stockholder of RFB Cellular, Inc. (RFBC), a Delaware corporation that provided cellular phone service. Mr. Broz was also a member of the board of directors of Cellular Information Systems, Inc. (CIS), a publicly-held Delaware corporation that was a competitor of RFBC.
License Availability Among the service areas it covered, RFBC had a license for service in the Michigan-4 area. In 1994, a license for service in the Michigan-2 area became available. This area was right next to Michigan-4. The owner of the Michigan-2 license, Mackinac Cellular Corp. (Mackinac) contacted Mr. Broz about selling the license to RFBC. Mackinac did not contact CIS to see whether it was interested in the license because CIS had just emerged from bankruptcy. At the same time, PriCellular, Inc. expressed an interest in buying the license from Mackinac. RFBC won a bidding war and bought the license.

CIS Financial Struggles At the time Mr. Broz was interested in buying the Michigan-2 license, CIS was going through financial problems. In fact, CIS was negotiating with PriCellular, Inc. for PriCellular to buy CIS. However, PriCellular was having trouble financing the purchase, and it took several months before it was able finally to do so. PriCellular finalized the purchase nine days after RFBC bought the Michigan-2 license.
Lawsuit Commencement After RFBC bought the license and PriCellular bought CIS, CIS sued Mr. Broz and RFBC. CIS argued that Mr. Broz should have notified the board of CIS about the availability of the Michigan-2 license to see if CIS was interested in buying the license. CIS argued that the actions of Mr. Broz constituted an "impermissible usurpation of a corporation opportunity" belonging to CIS.

Opinion **Delaware Court of Chancery Proceedings** The Delaware Court of Chancery held that the actions of Mr. Broz did constitute a usurpation of a corporate opportunity that belonged to CIS. The Court found that CIS could have required Mr. Broz to abstain from the purchase out of deference to the CIS board, and that if Mr. Broz had notified the CIS board, the board could have notified PriCellular about the pending purchase.

Corporate Opportunity Doctrine In making its decision, the Delaware Supreme Court first had to define the law that applied. The Court had previously defined the corporate opportunity doctrine in the case *Guth v. Loft, Inc.* as follows:

A corporate officer or director may not take a business opportunity for his/her own if:

(1) the corporation is financially able to exploit the opportunity;

(2) the opportunity is within the corporation's line of business;

(3) the corporation has an interest or expectancy in the opportunity; and

(4) by taking the opportunity for his own, the corporate fiduciary will thereby be placed in a position inimical to his duties to the corporation.

A director or officer may take a corporate opportunity if:

(1) the opportunity is presented to the director or officer in his individual and not his corporate capacity;

(2) the opportunity is not essential to the corporation;

(3) the corporation holds no interest or expectancy in the opportunity; and

(4) the director or officer has not wrongfully employed the resources of the corporation in pursuing or exploiting the opportunity.

Applying the Corporate Opportunity Doctrine Under the doctrine, CIS must have been in a financial position to buy the license from Mackinac to keep Mr. Broz from pursuing the opportunity to do so himself. The testimony of board members was that CIS was emerging from bankruptcy and was not in a position to buy any additional licenses. Further, PriCellular had not yet bought CIS, so even if PriCellular had the money it could not be considered by the court.

In addition, CIS must have an interest or expectancy in the opportunity. By the time CIS had emerged from bankruptcy, it no longer held cellular phone licenses in the area. The testimony of board members in court was that CIS's business plan after bankruptcy did not include getting any additional licenses.

Finally, CIS argued that, in applying the doctrine, it was an implicit requirement that Mr. Broz, as a board member, must present the opportunity to the full board of CIS so that the board can officially discuss the opportunity for its own benefit.

Holding The Delaware Supreme Court held that the Delaware Court of Chancery had improperly applied the corporate opportunity doctrine. The Supreme Court found that CIS was in no position to acquire or expect the license. The Court further held that board members are not required to present an opportunity to a full board, if such a presentation would result in the board's rejection of the offer, as was the case in this situation.

TRIAL PREP

The National High School Mock Trial Association organizes competitions at the local, regional, and national levels where teams of high school or college students prepare and argue fictional legal cases before practicing attorneys and judges. Mock Trial team members are each assigned a role as either an attorney or witness. Each team must develop a courtroom strategy, legal arguments, and a presentation style.

Family Law

Looking Ahead Once you finish your education, you may look forward to traveling, getting a good job, or buying a home. *What are some of the aspects of life that require long-term planning?*

Health Insurance Legislation

As you read this unit, use this checklist to prepare for the unit project:

✓ List the laws and the legislation governing health care.

✓ Compare advantages and disadvantages of a health care legislation policy.

✓ Explain why a particular aspect of health care has been contentious.

✓ Determine the outcome of an issue in the health care debate.

Legal Portfolio When you complete the Unit Thematic project, you will have a guide to the politics of health care law for your portfolio.

Ask

AN EXPERT

Manage Your Finances

Q: I notice that there are now credit cards for students. Should I get one?

A: Credit cards can be more convenient to carry than cash and they can be useful in an emergency. If you use them wisely, they can help you build a strong credit rating that will make it easier to get a car or home loan later. However, you should not accept just any credit card offer. Shop around first and read the fine print on the applications. Look for cards that have low interest rates and no annual fees. Do not be fooled by cards with low introductory rates that go way up after a few months. Do not use a credit card to borrow cash: the interest rates for cash are much higher than they are for store purchases. If you cannot pay off the card every month, pay as much as you can. Credit card balances continue to accumulate interest charges. If you only make the minimum monthly payment, it can take years to pay off the card and cost thousands of dollars in interest.

Legal Briefs

Parental Responsibility Laws

Should parents be held liable for the acts of their children?

Do parents have to pay for what their children do? The answer is, "Usually, but not always." Here are a few examples.

Most of the time, parents are liable for their children's actions, so businesses often require an adult co-signer when minors enter a contract. For example, when a minor takes out a loan for an item, such as a vehicle or computer, a responsible adult may have to co-sign to assure the loaner the loan will get paid.

If a minor commits a tort—causes harm or damages—the child is responsible, but only in some states. In many states the parents are responsible if they weren't supervising the child properly.

Parents are held legally responsible for providing their children with the basic necessities of life, including food, clothing, and shelter. Thus, parents can be held responsible for some contracts a minor enters into. For example, if a minor uses a parent's credit card to buy necessary food, the parents must pay the bill. The minor may have signed the credit slip, but the parent must honor the contract.

Age of Consent A marriage is a personal relationship, but it is also a civil contract.
How old do you have to be to get married without parental consent?

SECTION 20.1 Marriage Laws

What You'll Learn

- ◆ Name the rights and duties involved in marriage.
- ◆ Describe the different types of marriages.
- ◆ Explain the types of marriages that are prohibited by law.
- ◆ List the requirements of a legal marriage.

Why It's Important

If you ever get married, you need to know what the rights, responsibilities, and requirements of marriage are.

Reading Guide

Before You Read

Connect A wedding is the final step in a long process. What are some decisions a couple should make before they marry to avoid problems in the future?

Focus on Ideas

Marriage is a legal contract that binds the parties to specific legal rights and obligations.

Take Notes

Go to connectED. mcgraw-hill.com to download a graphic organizer you can use to take notes as you read this section.

Marriage Rights and Duties

Rights	Duties
Support	_____
_____	_____
_____	_____
_____	_____
_____	_____

Key Terms

You will learn these legal words and expressions in this chapter. You can also find these terms in *Black's Law Dictionary* or in an online legal dictionary.

- marriage
- prenuptial agreement
- common-law marriage
- bigamy
- polygamy
- consanguinity
- affinity

Academic Vocabulary

You will find these words in your readings and in your tests. Look them up in a dictionary and familiarize yourself with them.

- spouses
- status
- ceremony

Understanding Marriage Law

What is legally considered a marriage?

Marriage is considered the basis of the family unit and vital to the preservation of traditional values and culture. **Marriage is defined by most states and the federal government as the legal union of one man and one woman as husband and wife.**

The Marriage Contract

Is an engagement ring a kind of contract?

Marriage is not just a personal relationship between two people. It is also a contract. The engagement represents the offer and acceptance of the contract. The consideration is the promise to give up one's right to remain single. During engagement, the marriage contract is in its executory stage. It is fully executed when the wedding occurs.

In some states, a man is entitled to the return of the engagement ring when an engagement is called off. The legal theory holds that the ring is a contingent gift, dependent upon carrying out the marriage. In other states, the courts have allowed a woman to keep the ring if the man ended the engagement.

Prenuptial Agreements

Before marrying, soon-to-be **spouses** sometimes create a prenuptial, or premarital agreement. **A prenuptial agreement is a written and signed legal contract couples make before getting married dealing with property and support issues.**

As You Read

Predict Does every state have the same laws about marriage?

Vocabulary You can find vocabulary definitions in the **Key Terms** glossary and Academic Vocabulary glossary in the back of this book.

Ureneck v. Cui
798 N.E.2d 305 (Mass. App. Ct. 2003)

Joseph Ureneck runs Rainbow International Marriage Service, Inc. (Rainbow), a Massachusetts company, from a hotel in Beijing, China. Rainbow maintained a Web site that was marketed as "a personal and convenient way to meet your marriage partner." Clients paid Rainbow a fee of $700 to put their profiles on the Internet. If a match led to a marriage, clients agreed to pay Rainbow a second fee of $7,500 within 60 days of getting married. On May 20, 1995, Ping Cui paid her registration fee, and her profile was placed on the Web site. On November 28, 1997, John Choma met Ms. Cui on the Web site. On May 18, 1998, Ms. Cui sent a letter to Rainbow, stating she was unemployed and could not pay the $7,500 fee if she found love, and requesting that her profile be removed from the Web site. Ms. Cui and Mr. Choma were married in Massachusetts on April 24, 1999. Ms. Cui did not pay the $7,500 fee, so Rainbow sued for breach of contract.

Ruling and Resolution
The Massachusetts Appeals Court held that marriage brokerage contracts, where a third party is paid to negotiate or procure a marriage, are void as a matter of public policy in Massachusetts. Therefore, Rainbow could not sue for breach of contract because the contract was void.

Critical Thinking Should marriage brokerage contracts be legal?

This agreement lists the assets of each party, the rights each party has to control their property, and the division of property upon separation, divorce, and death. This formal agreement becomes effective upon marriage.

Marriage Rights and Obligations

Marriage changes a couple's legal **status**. The law gives them new rights and obligations as a married couple. This is not true for people who live together without being married. Marriage includes the right to:

- support by your spouse when necessary
- inheritance from your deceased spouse
- property if the marriage ends
- compensation to continue your standard of living if the marriage ends
- file a joint income tax return

Global Law

Marriage Laws in Kenya

The Kenyan Constitution recognizes five systems of marriage and grants all systems equal importance under the law. The five systems are: Customary Law, Islamic Law, Hindu Law, Christian Law, and Civil Law. The Christian Law and Civil Law systems are identical when it comes to marriage laws.

Civil & Christian Law:

- Civil law is based on the English legal and Christian belief systems.
- Marriages must be monogamous.
- Both the man and the woman must be at least 18 years of age.

Muslim Law:

- Muslim law is based on the Islamic faith and teachings of the Koran.
- In Muslim law a man may have as many as four wives at any given time.
- There is no minimum age for marriage; rather a party can marry once puberty is reached. However, a guardian can give permission for a prepubescent child to marry.

Hindu Law:

- Hindu law is based on the Hindu faith.
- Marriages are monogamous under Hindu law.
- The groom must be at least 18 years of age, while the bride need only be 16. If the bride is 16 to 18 years old, then permission must be granted by a guardian or by a court of justice.

Customary Law:

- Customary law is based on the traditional Kenyan tribal law.
- Under customary law, a man may have as many wives as he wishes.
- Like Muslim law, minimum age to marry is linked to reaching puberty.

Across Cultures: The Kenyan National Motto

The national motto of Kenya is *harambee*, which in Swahili means to pull together. Volunteers nationwide have taken that motto to heart and built numerous schools and hospital clinics throughout the country, and pooled money to send Kenyan children to study abroad.

Critical Thinking *Should different religious and ethnic groups be allowed to follow their own laws, even though their members are citizens of a particular country?*

The primary obligation of marriage is the duty of the spouses to be faithful to each other. This duty cannot be surrendered, even by agreement. In addition, all people, married or not, are obligated to refrain from causing bodily harm to those with whom they live. The law does not tolerate the physical abuse of spouses or children. Doing so is a criminal offense, punishable by imprisonment and the loss of the custody of one's children. In addition, all parents have the duty to support their children.

Reading Check

Enumerate *List the marriage rights that spouses are entitled to receive from each other.*

Types of Marriage

If two people simply claim they are married, are they legally married?

Each state has its own laws regulating the types of marriage it will recognize.

Common-Law Marriage

In the English common law system, people did not need a formal **ceremony** to be married. They could simply agree that they were married in a common-law marriage. **A common-law marriage is an informal type of marriage created by the parties themselves.** Today, 11 states and the District of Columbia still allow common-law marriages. In the remaining 39 states, only ceremonial marriage is recognized. However, under the U.S. Constitution's Full Faith and Credit clause, every state must treat as valid common-law marriages that originated in other states. States that continue to allow common-law marriage require that the parties agree, by words in the present tense, that they are husband and wife. There is no such thing as a common-law divorce.

Ceremonial Marriage

In early colonial times, a marriage ceremony had to be performed by a cleric or magistrate in a specific manner. Today, most states still require some kind of ceremony to formalize the marriage, but no particular form need be followed. However, the parties must declare that they are married in the presence of a person authorized by state law to conduct marriages.

Proxy Marriage

The Uniform Marriage and Divorce Act allows a proxy marriage. A proxy marriage occurs when one or both of the parties cannot be present for the wedding ceremony. Instead, an agent acts on behalf of the absent party.

Covenant Marriage

The covenant marriage, adopted in Arkansas, Arizona, and Louisiana, is an attempt to reduce divorce and protect children. The parties must have counseling before the wedding and during the marriage to solve conflicts. In most cases, the couple can divorce only after a period of separation.

Legal Talk

Bigamy: *n* The state of being married to two people at the same time. From Latin *bi* = two + Greek *gamos* = marriage.

Polygamy: *n* The state of being married to multiple people at the same time. From Greek *poly* = many + *gamos* = marriage.

Vocabulary Builder The Greek root *poly* means *many*. List and define five words that contain this root word.

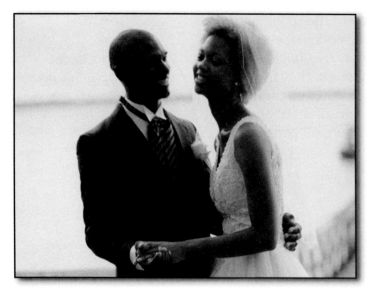

Making Wedding Plans
Preparing for marriage
includes meeting certain legal
requirements, such as obtaining
a marriage license. *Where can
you obtain a marriage license?*

Marriages Performed Internationally

If Americans get married abroad, those marriages are usually recognized in the United States as valid, as long as the marriages are legal in those foreign countries. Similarly, most marriages in the United States are recognized in other countries.

Prohibited Marriages

Is it illegal for first cousins to marry?

Certain types of marriages are prohibited in every state of the country, while others are prohibited in just some states.

Bigamy and Polygamy

Bigamy and polygamy are crimes under the laws of every state in this country. **Bigamy is the illegal act of having two spouses at the same time. Polygamy is the illegal act of having more than two spouses at the same time.** Thus, any marriage that occurs while one party is already married is void in every state. Any children born of a man and woman whose marriage is void are considered illegitimate. In some states, if one of the parties married without knowing the other party was already married, the second marriage becomes valid upon the death or divorce of the partner to the first marriage.

Marriage between Relatives

Some states have statutes that prohibit marriage between persons related by consanguinity or by affinity. **Consanguinity means related by blood. Affinity means related by marriage.** For example, many states prohibit the marriage of first cousins. Almost half the states do not have a law against marriages between persons related by affinity, such as the brother of one spouse marrying the sister of the other spouse.

Requirements of a Legal Marriage

Why do you have to go through a waiting period before you get married?

Depending on the state, there are various requirements that must be followed in order for a marriage to be legal.

Age Requirement

In nearly every state except Mississippi and Nebraska, you can marry at age 18. Teens younger than 18 can marry only with the consent of a parent or guardian. Laws requiring parental permission are intended to prevent minors from entering into unsuitable or coerced marriages.

However, marriage age differs around the world. Some countries allow children to be married as young as age 13.

Marriage License

You must get a marriage license before you can get married. This is a certificate issued by a government office giving permission to marry. Once issued, the license becomes effective after any waiting period required by state law. The license will expire if the couple does not marry during the prescribed time period. A common-law marriage does not require a license.

Waiting Period

Most states require a waiting period to give the couple time to reconsider their decision. Also, a waiting period may allow evidence of fraud, force, or jest to be uncovered. Moreover, the delay gives interested parties, such as the parents, an opportunity to object on other grounds.

Blood Test/Physical Examination

Some states require a blood test before a marriage license is issued. Such tests screen prospective spouses for AIDS, venereal disease, sickle cell anemia, rubella (German measles), and infectious tuberculosis.

Use of Names

After marriage, the parties may use any name provided they do not commit fraud. A wife does not have to adopt her husband's surname. Today, many married women continue to use their maiden name, or they hyphenate their name with their husband's surname.

After You Read

Summarize List the requirements the parties must fulfill in a legal marriage.

SECTION 20.1 ASSESSMENT

Self Check

1. What is the primary obligation of marriage?
2. What types of marriages are prohibited by law?
3. What is required in most states for a marriage to be legal?

Academic Connection

English Language Arts
More and more couples are signing prenuptial marriage agreements before they marry. A prenuptial marriage agreement is a contract that spells out how a couple will handle the financial aspects of their marriage. Although not very romantic, having this honest financial discussion before a wedding can be a very positive experience. Review samples of prenuptial agreements available on the Internet and use them as a guide to write your own. In class, compare your agreement with other students' agreements and discuss what you would and would not change.

Critical Thinking Activity

Surnames Although it is traditional when people get married for the wife to take the husband's surname (last name), many women today choose to keep their own surname. Why do you think this is?

Divorce and Its Legal Consequences

Reading Guide

What You'll Learn

◆ Describe the differences between an annulment, a legal separation, and a divorce.

◆ Identify the common grounds for divorce.

◆ Explain the issues involved in a divorce settlement.

Why It's Important

Before you ever consider getting a divorce, you need to know what the legal grounds and consequences of divorce are.

Before You Read

Connect Almost one-half of all marriages end in divorce today. Can you think of ways to help reduce the divorce rate?

Focus on Ideas

In a divorce, issues of alimony, child support and custody, and division of property must be legally settled.

Take Notes

Go to connectED.mcgraw-hill.com to download a graphic organizer you can use to take notes as you read this section.

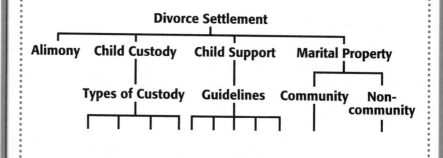

Key Terms

You will learn these legal words and expressions in this chapter. You can also find these terms in *Black's Law Dictionary* or in an online legal dictionary.

- annulment
- divorce
- adultery
- no-fault divorce
- alimony

Academic Vocabulary

You will find these words in your readings and in your tests. Look them up in a dictionary and familiarize yourself with them.

- persistent
- reconciliation
- capacity

How Marriages End

Is divorce the only way a marriage can end?

A marriage comes to an end in one of three ways: the death of a spouse, annulment, or divorce. Couples can also become legally separated, without a divorce or annulment. Annulment and divorce are subject to specific state laws.

Annulment

An annulment is a declaration by the court that a marriage was never valid. To have a marriage annulled, the parties must go before a probate court judge and prove certain grounds. Proof varies from state to state, but two common grounds the courts accept are duress and fraud. Duress is when someone is forced to marry against his or her will. Examples of fraud include being below the state's legal age to marry, secretly intending never to have children, or concealing pregnancy by someone other than the husband.

Legal Separation

A legal separation, also called a limited divorce or a separation from bed and board, is a court judgment ending the right to cohabitation. In making a separation judgment, the court will temporarily decide the issues of child custody and support. The two people remain married until there is a final divorce, which does not need to follow immediately.

Divorce

A divorce (called dissolution of marriage in some states) is a declaration by the court that a valid marriage has come to an end. The procedure for obtaining a divorce varies from state to state. The process may be contested by the parties, or they may agree to the divorce.

Grounds for Divorce

Do you have to prove anything in court to get a divorce?

States differ on the grounds they accept for divorce. The most common grounds are explained below.

Adultery

Adultery is when one spouse has sexual relations with someone outside of the marriage. It is a crime in some states, in addition to being grounds for divorce. Because of its private nature, criminal adultery is difficult to prove beyond a reasonable doubt. Without solid proof, the injured spouse must show convincing circumstantial evidence that the other spouse had the opportunity to commit adultery and the inclination to do so.

As You Read

Predict Is an annulment of a marriage the same as a divorce?

Cruelty

To prove cruelty, a spouse must show that there was personal violence that endangered his or her life or health. Usually, more than one act of violence is required. Sometimes, a spouse can claim cruelty due to mental suffering, not physical violence.

Other Grounds

Other grounds include desertion, alcohol or drug addiction, and nonsupport. Desertion is the unjustified separation of one spouse from the other with the intent of not returning. The length of separation to qualify as desertion is one year in most states. Alcohol or drug addiction must be confirmed, **persistent**, voluntary, and excessive. Divorce can be based on nonsupport if one spouse can show that the other had the ability to provide economic support but willfully failed to do so. Husbands, as well as wives, may claim nonsupport as grounds for divorce. Many states allow a divorce if one spouse is convicted of a felony or imprisoned for a certain number of years after the marriage occurs.

No-Fault Divorce

Almost all states now have a no-fault divorce law. **A no-fault divorce is a divorce granted without either party having to prove the other party guilty of misconduct.** The parties simply agree that they have a personality conflict so deep that there is no chance for **reconciliation**. Many states require that the spouses live apart for a period of time before the divorce is finalized. Some states have reconciliation bureaus that attempt to save the marriages through counseling.

Divorce Settlement

How do courts decide who gets custody of the children?

The parties in a divorce must come to a legal settlement regarding the issues of alimony, child custody and support, and distribution of property (see **Figure 20.1**).

Alimony

Alimony is an allowance for support paid to one person by the former spouse in a divorce. In an at-fault divorce, the spouse who is found to have been at fault will not be awarded alimony. In determining alimony, each person's age, income, and financial resources are considered. Their obligations and number of dependents are taken into account. Also examined are each spouse's future earning **capacity** and separate property owned. Software is often used to make alimony calculations today.

Child Custody and Support

Parents are considered to be joint guardians of any offspring born during their marriage. Upon divorce, each parent has an equal right to custody of the children. Most states divide custody into two parts:

Figure 20.1 Divorce Settlement

Marital Property In non-community property states, assets gained during marriage are usually divided according to how much each spouse contributed. In community property states, assets gained during marriage are usually divided in half.

Child Custody Most states divide custody into legal custody and physical custody. Legal custody determines a parent's right to make major decisions about the child's health, education, and welfare. Physical custody deals with the daily living arrangements of the child.

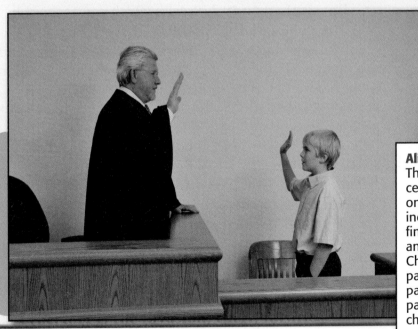

Alimony and Child Support The amount a spouse receives in alimony is based on factors such as the income, earning capacity, financial resources, health, and age of the spouses. Child support is usually paid by the noncustodial parent to the custodial parent and must cover a child's basic needs.

Federal regulations require every state to adopt child support guidelines. *What information do you think should be in a mathematical formula to determine parents' support obligations?*

Case Study – Adlakha v. Adlakha

Critical Thinking *Should Mr. Adlakha receive alimony? Why?*

Flex Your Reading   Note key facts in the text below and look up words you do not understand. Restate difficult ideas in your own words. Go back and reread the text quickly to make sure you did not miss any important detail. Now, you are ready to formulate an opinion.

Divorce Settlement Mr. and Ms. Adlakha were married in India in 1984. Immediately after getting married, Ms. Adlakha requested a divorce. She decided to stay in India while Mr. Adlakha moved to the United States. Ms. Adlakha then changed her mind and moved to the United States to study medicine. Between 1985 and 1995, Mr. and Ms. Adlakha lived together for a total of three years. Ms. Adlakha became a doctor, while Mr. Adlakha worked as a nuclear engineer. After Mr. Adlakha lost his job, the two parties lived together from 1996 until 2002. The couple separated in 2002. At the time divorce proceedings began, Mr. Adlakha worked as a salesperson for $10 per hour. In the divorce decree, the judge determined that Mr. Adlakha would receive $731,283 in marital assets, plus $600 per month in alimony for two years. Ms. Adlakha would receive $504,461 in marital assets and their house in Massachusetts. Ms. Adlakha appealed, arguing Mr. Adlakha deserved no alimony. Mr. Adlakha appealed, arguing that there should be no time limit on his alimony.

Adlakha v. Adlakha, 844 N.E.2d 700 (Mass. App. Ct. 2006)

Go to **ConnectEd.mcgraw-hill.com** for more case study practice.

- **Legal custody** deals with a parent's right to make major decisions about the child's health, education, and welfare.
- **Physical custody** deals with which parent the child will live.

Courts can declare sole or joint custody. Sole custody gives all parental rights, duties, and powers to one parent. The children live with that parent and the noncustodial parent has visitation rights. In contrast, joint custody gives both parents rights and duties. Children may live with each parent at different times. In awarding custody, the court attempts to determine the best interests of the child. Some states favor awarding custody to the primary caretaker, that is, the parent who spent the most time caring for the child. Many states give great weight to the child's personal wishes.

Child Support Guidelines Child support is a basic obligation of every parent. This obligation exists regardless of which parent has custody. Federal regulations require every state to adopt child support guidelines, following these principles:

- Both parents should share responsibility for child support in proportion to their income.
- The financial needs of each parent should be considered, but each parent must contribute more than zero.
- Child support must cover a child's basic needs and ensure that the child shares in a parent's standard of living.

- Each child has an equal right to share in a parent's income, the income of a current spouse, and other dependents.
- Each child is entitled to support, even if the parents were not married at the time of the child's birth.

Enforcement of Child Support Child support is enforced using a legal order obtained from a judge or from an administrative hearing officer. If a parent moves out of state, the support order must be enforced in any other state. Support orders can be registered in different states so that parents who do not pay can be found. Out-of-state employers can withhold support payments from an employee's paycheck. Federal and state income tax refunds can be garnished to pay for support. Liens can be placed on out-of-state real estate. Passports may also be denied to enforce child support orders.

Marital Property

State law and judges determine property distribution. Some states are non-community property states. In these states, the assets and earnings gained during marriage are divided proportionately. For example, the higher wage earner might take two-thirds of the assets while the lower wage earner receives only one-third. In contrast, in community property states, each spouse is entitled to a one-half interest in property acquired during the marriage. This applies regardless of which spouse purchased the property or if only one spouse worked. There are exceptions in community property states for property a spouse owned before marriage or received as a gift.

After You Read

Summarize What are the issues that a divorce settlement must cover?

SECTION 20.2 ASSESSMENT

Self Check

1. What are the two common grounds for annulment?
2. What are the most common grounds for divorce?
3. Explain the difference between sole custody and joint custody.

Academic Connection

Mathematics Jay and Kay were married for six years when they got a divorce. They have two children, ages 2 and 4. After taking into account the finances of Jay and Kay, and granting Kay primary custody of the children, the court ordered Jay to pay 10% of his net income to Kay in alimony for one-half the length of the marriage, and 15% of his net income to Kay for child support until the children are 18. Jay's net income is $40,000 per year. How much does Jay pay in combined alimony and child support the first four years?

CONCEPT **Number and Operations: Using Multiple Operations** Calculate the amount for alimony and for child support by multiplying the net income times the percentage for each. Then multiply the amount for each by the number of years. Keep in mind that Jay pays alimony only for half the length of the marriage.

 For more math practice, go to the Math Appendix.

Critical Thinking

No-Fault Divorce Why do you think most states have a no-fault divorce law?

Summary

Section **20.1** Marriage Laws

◆ Most states and the federal government define marriage as the union of one man and one woman.

◆ Marriage changes a couple's legal status and gives them new rights and obligations as a married couple.

◆ The primary obligation of marriage is the duty of the spouses to be faithful to each other.

◆ Types of marriage include common-law marriage, ceremonial marriage, proxy marriage, and covenant marriage.

◆ Prohibited marriages include bigamy and polygamy, and marriage between relatives.

◆ For a marriage to be legal requires a marriage license, a waiting period, a blood test, and a minimum age of 18 in most states.

Section **20.2** Divorce and Its Legal Consequences

◆ A marriage comes to an end in one of three ways: the death of a spouse, annulment, or divorce.

◆ An annulment is a declaration by the court that the marriage was never effective and was void from the beginning.

◆ A divorce is a declaration by the court that a valid marriage has come to an end.

◆ Common grounds for divorce include adultery, cruelty, desertion, alcohol or drug addition, and nonsupport.

◆ Almost all states have a no-fault divorce law.

◆ The parties in a divorce must come to a legal settlement regarding the issues of alimony, child custody and support, and distribution of property.

Vocabulary Builder

1 On a sheet of paper, use each of these terms in a sentence.

Key Terms

- marriage
- prenuptial agreement
- common-law marriage
- bigamy

- polygamy
- consanguinity
- affinity
- annulment

- divorce
- adultery
- no-fault divorce
- alimony

Academic Vocabulary

- spouse
- status

- ceremony
- persistent

- reconciliation
- capacity

Key Points Review

Answer the following questions. Refer to the chapter for additional reinforcement.

2 When does the marriage contract actually come into existence? Explain your answer.

3 What is a prenuptial agreement?

4 List five rights that are given by law to people when they marry.

5 What is a common-law marriage and how widely recognized is it?

6 What is the difference between an annulment and divorce?

7 What is a no-fault divorce?

8 What is the difference between legal custody and physical custody of a child?

9 How is marital property divided in community and noncommunity property states?

Standardized Test Practice

10 Read the following legal excerpt regarding marriage and the rights afforded through a legalized marriage, and then complete questions 1 and 2.

Marriage is the legal union of two people in which a ceremony is performed. Non-religious ceremonies, called civil ceremonies, must be performed by a judge, justice of the peace, or court clerk who has legal authority to perform marriages, or by a person given temporary authority by a judge or court clerk to conduct a marriage ceremony. Religious ceremonies must be conducted by a clergy member (priest, minister, or rabbi). Native American weddings may be performed by a tribal chief or by another official, as designated by the tribe. Federal laws regarding marriage and divorce are listed in the Uniform Marriage and Divorce Act. When you are married, your responsibilities and rights toward your spouse concerning property and support are defined by the laws of the state in which you live.

1. Marriage can best be defined as:

Ⓐ the legal union of two people in which a ceremony has been performed

Ⓑ two people agreeing to be married and sharing all their assets and debts

Ⓒ a legal agreement between two people that is witnessed to be married

Ⓓ the legal union of two people that is not witnessed or no ceremony is performed

2. Marriage responsibilities and rights between the spouses are defined by the:

Ⓐ Uniform Marriage and Divorce Act

Ⓑ state in which the couple resides

Ⓒ spouses in their prenuptial agreement

Ⓓ adopted customs and practices of society

 Test-Taking Strategies As you prepare to answer a question, first identify the verbs or words in the question that give you direction.

Apply and Debate

Read the following scenarios. Get together with other students in pairs or groups of three and take a position on each scenario. Debate your position in class with students taking the opposite position or prepare a written argument justifying your position.

11 Broken Engagement and the Ring

Despite Betty's warning him that she would break off their engagement, Rick took a ten-day fishing trip with his buddies. When Betty broke off the engagement, Rick asked for his ring back, but Betty refused, saying he caused the breakup.

You Debate *Assume the couple lives in a state that allows the woman to keep the ring if the man breaks off the engagement. Is Betty entitled to keep the ring?*

12 Premarital Agreement Difficulties

Reta, a wealthy heiress, fell in love with Darnell. Their premarital agreement allowed him nothing if he divorced her before 24 months, but after that he would be entitled to $1 million. Darnell asked for a divorce 25 months after the wedding.

You Debate *Do you think Darnell is entitled to the $1 million?*

13 A Long Separation

Dan and Vicki were married for 12 years. Due to incompatibility, they obtained a legal separation but never divorced. Ten years later, Vicki wanted the divorce and felt entitled to half of the assets Dan acquired after the separation.

You Debate *Assume the couple lives in a community property state. Do you think that Vicki is right to ask for one-half of Dan's assets?*

14 Who Takes the Children?

Luana and Dang have two sons and live in Texas. They are divorcing. Luana wants to move to Idaho to live with her parents. Dang, a wealthy executive who often travels, wants the sons with him. He is remarrying to a woman who will care for the boys.

You Debate *Which parent do you think should get custody of the sons?*

15 Dogs, Cats, and Divorce

Selma has acquired six dogs and eight cats since she and Sam got married. Sam now wants a divorce on grounds of irreconcilable differences. He cannot stand living with so many animals.

You Debate *If you were the judge in this case, would you suggest the couple seek counseling or would you agree to let them divorce?*

Case Study Practice – Lukich v. Lukich

16 Divorce or Annulment? In March 1985, George and Phyllis Lukich were married. They lived together as a married couple for 19 years. On August 21, 2002, Ms. Lukich filed for legal separation and an award of alimony, alleging that Mr. Lukich was physically cruel and adulterous. Prior to a decree of divorce, Mr. Lukich began to suspect that Ms. Lukich had never legally divorced her first husband, Charles Havron, whom she had married in 1973. The South Carolina authorities were able to provide a copy of the marriage certificate issued for Ms. Lukich and Mr. Havron. However, there was no evidence that they ever received a divorce decree. On September 25, 2003, Mr. Lukich filed for an annulment of his marriage to Ms. Lukich on the grounds that Ms. Lukich was a bigamist. Prior to a hearing on Mr. Lukich's motion, on October 21, 2003, Ms. Lukich filed for an annulment of her marriage to Mr. Havron on the grounds that they were married while they were intoxicated and that they had never actually lived together after they were married. Ms. Lukich was granted her annulment against Mr. Havron on October 31, 2003, so in the eyes of the law, Ms. Lukich was never married to Mr. Havron.

Source: Lukich v. Lukich, 627 S.E.2d 754 (S.C. Ct. App. 2006)

Practice Can Mr. Lukich still get an annulment of his marriage to Ms. Lukich?

17 Ethics ←?→ Application

Green Card Marriage Rodney, an American, met Zuzana, a woman from Slovakia, in college. After graduating, Zuzana asked Rodney to help her become a permanent resident of the United States by marrying her. Rodney likes her, but is not sure he loves her. He knows that a fraudulent marriage is illegal, but that it is also difficult to prove. He wants to help his friend. The marriage would only be for two or three years.

◆ Do you think it is ethical for Rodney to marry Zuzana to help her gain U.S. citizenship?

18 Think back to the Legal Briefs feature you read at the beginning of the chapter. Discuss the following with a small group: Jordan, a responsible 17-year-old junior works part time after school and on weekends. For a year, she's been saving money to buy a car, but she is short by $2,500. She talked to her bank about a loan, and they require a co-signer. Do you think Jordan should be able to get the loan without a co-signer? Why or why not?

Legal Briefs

Interest Rates and Your Estate

How they influence the value of your investments.

Estate planning is complicated. Many factors affect *what* a person leaves to others and *how* they leave it. Death and inheritance taxes, changing laws, and interest rates all must be considered.

Take interest rates. Whether interest rates are high or low helps determine an estate planning strategy. The key interest rate to watch is the IRS's Code Sec. 7520 rate, which changes monthly.

Here's a look at trusts that do better under higher and lower interest rates.

Higher Interest Rates

Qualified Personal Residence Trusts—QPRTs freeze a home's value and lower gift taxes.

Retained Income Trusts—GRITs benefit unmarried couples, and those leaving assets to distant relatives (aunts, cousins, etc.).

Charitable Remainder Annuity Trusts—CRATs involve leaving money to charities and take advantage of the tax deduction for that.

Lower Interest Rates

Grantor Retained Annuity Trusts—GRATs are good if assets are expected to increase in value before they are inherited.

Family loans—These must be loans that charge an interest rate, though it can be lower than on commercial loans.

The best advice is to be very informed, pay close attention to the 7520 rate, and invest wisely.

Uninsured Many people do not have any kind of health insurance. *What can you do if you get injured unexpectedly and do not have health insurance?*

SECTION 21.1 Insurance

What You'll Learn

- Explain the meaning and purpose of insurance.
- Describe the different types of property insurance.
- Distinguish between types of life insurance.
- Identify the different types of health insurance.

Why It's Important

Knowing the different types of insurance that are available will help you protect your property and your health.

Reading Guide

Before You Read

Connect If you drive, you probably have car insurance. What other kinds of insurance are there?

Focus on Ideas

People and businesses buy insurance to protect themselves against the loss of their property, income, health, or life.

Take Notes

Go to connectED.mcgraw-hill.com to download a graphic organizer you can use to take notes as you read this section.

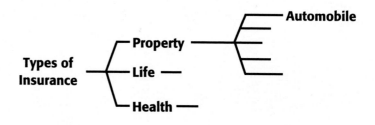

Key Terms

You will learn these legal words and expressions in this chapter. You can also find these terms in *Black's Law Dictionary* or in an online legal dictionary.

- insurance
- premium
- beneficiary
- insurable interest
- straight life insurance
- term life insurance

Academic Vocabulary

You will find these words in your readings and in your tests. Look them up in a dictionary and familiarize yourself with them.

- comprehensive
- endowment
- routine

What Is Insurance?

Can you insure your iPod?

Insurance is an agreement in which one party (the insurer) compensates another party (the insured) for any losses. The purpose of insurance is to protect individuals and businesses against losses by spreading the risks of loss among a large number of people. Every state has its own set of laws that governs the various types of insurance offered in that state.

Insurance Basics

An insurance policy is the written contract between a person or business buying insurance and an insurance company. The buyer of the insurance policy is called the policyholder. **The premium is the amount of money an insured pays for insurance coverage.** The proceeds are payments by insurance companies for losses covered by a policy. **The beneficiary is the person named in a life insurance policy to receive the proceeds.**

To acquire an insurance policy, an insurable interest in the person or property insured is required. **An insurable interest is the financial interest (or its possible loss) that a policyholder has in the insured person or property.** For life insurance, the insurable interest must exist at the time you buy the insurance. For property insurance, the insurable interest must exist at the time of loss.

As You Read

Predict How is insurance a type of contract?

Global Law

Russian Automobile Insurance

In 2003, the Russian legislature passed the OSAGO law, requiring all drivers to have liability insurance. Russian car owners must pay a minimum of 1,980 rubles per year (about $75). However, factors such as car model, location, and driver's experience can push the sum up to 3,760 rubles (about $140) or more.

Since the law was passed, there have been many complaints. From 2003 to 2005, the insurance companies received 89.6 billion rubles in premiums, but only paid out 26.3 billion rubles in claims, meaning they made 63.6 billion rubles in profits.

Another complaint is that to receive an insurance settlement, persons involved in an accident must have a police report. However, the police do not often respond quickly to an accident, causing

drivers to get frustrated and leave the scene rather than wait to make a police report.

Finally, there is an active black market for fake insurance certificates. People buy the black market certificates to get out of paying for the OSAGO insurance. When one person is in an accident with someone who has a black market certificate, there is no coverage by the OSAGO insurance company.

Across Cultures: Business Etiquette in Russia

There are things you should keep in mind when doing business in Russia. In Russia, meetings begin on time and negotiations can be lengthy. The exchange of business cards is very important. Have one side translated into Russian.

Critical Thinking *Should the government require everyone to buy car insurance?*

Property Insurance

Does homeowner's insurance cover your losses due to flooding?

Property insurance is a contract that covers damage or destruction of property. Buyers can purchase property insurance on such items as cars, homes, boats, and personal items. A special type of property insurance is a floater policy. It insures property that constantly changes value or location, such as a bicycle or an iPod.

Liability insurance covers claims for damages or injuries made against a policyholder. For example, if you hit another car while driving and injure the occupants, your liability insurance pays for the injuries. Vehicle, homeowner's, and renter's insurance policies usually cover both physical property and liability. Businesses can buy insurance to protect against commercial liability.

Automobile Insurance

Most states legally require drivers to carry liability insurance to cover any physical injuries or property damage they might cause. There are other types of insurance drivers should also carry.

Collision insurance covers damage to your vehicle if it is in an accident, regardless of who was at fault. **Comprehensive** insurance covers damage to your vehicle from sources other than collision, such as fire, theft, flood, and vandalism. Uninsured motorist insurance provides protection when the insured's auto is in an accident caused by a driver who has no insurance.

Vocabulary You can find vocabulary definitions in the **Key Terms** glossary and Academic Vocabulary glossary in the back of this book.

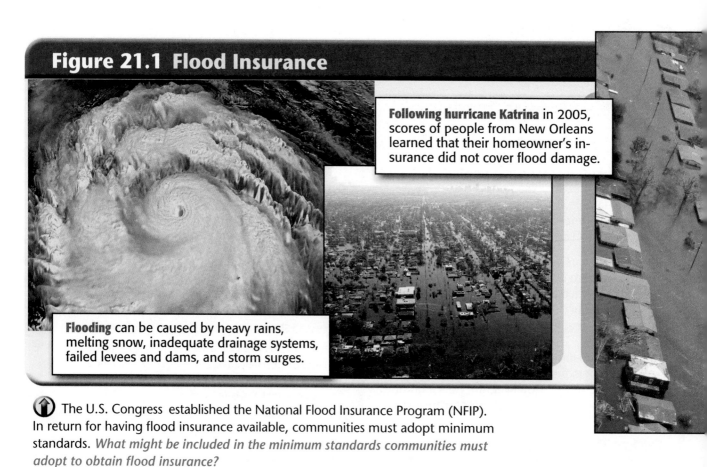

Figure 21.1 Flood Insurance

Following hurricane Katrina in 2005, scores of people from New Orleans learned that their homeowner's insurance did not cover flood damage.

Flooding can be caused by heavy rains, melting snow, inadequate drainage systems, failed levees and dams, and storm surges.

The U.S. Congress established the National Flood Insurance Program (NFIP). In return for having flood insurance available, communities must adopt minimum standards. *What might be included in the minimum standards communities must adopt to obtain flood insurance?*

Many states settle auto accident claims under no-fault insurance law. Regardless of who causes an accident, all drivers involved collect any money due from their own insurance company, rather than going to court to determine responsibility.

Homeowner's and Renter's Insurance

Homeowner's insurance protects against losses of both real and personal property related to home ownership. These include fire, windstorm, vandalism, burglary, and injuries suffered by others while on the property. Homeowner's policies also cover personal property anywhere in the world. Mortgage lenders usually require anyone with a mortgage to carry homeowner's insurance so their investment in the home is covered if something happens. Renter's insurance protects renters against loss of personal property and liability for a visitor's personal injury.

Flood Insurance

Homeowner's policies ordinarily do not cover flood damage, and special flood insurance must be obtained (see **Figure 21.1**). Almost all flood insurance is backed by the National Flood Insurance Program (NFIP) established by Congress. Communities that agree to manage flood hazard areas can participate in the NFIP. Communities that do not agree cannot receive flood insurance. Banks that are federally regulated or insured require flood insurance on property located in Special Flood Hazard Areas (SFHAs).

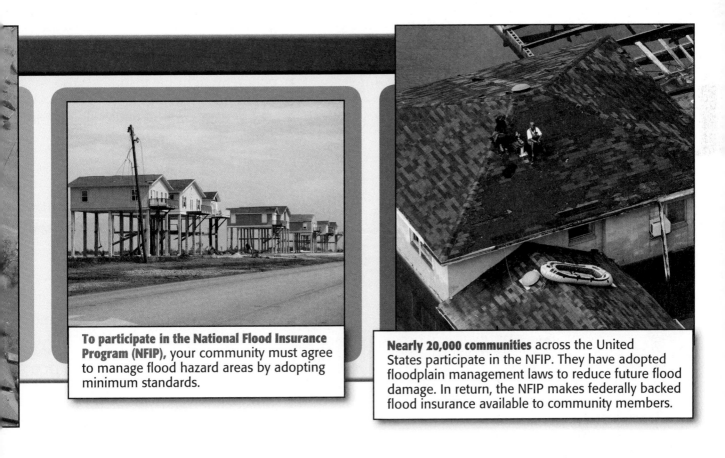

To participate in the National Flood Insurance Program (NFIP), your community must agree to manage flood hazard areas by adopting minimum standards.

Nearly 20,000 communities across the United States participate in the NFIP. They have adopted floodplain management laws to reduce future flood damage. In return, the NFIP makes federally backed flood insurance available to community members.

Fire Insurance

Many businesses purchase fire insurance to cover losses resulting directly from a fire, and damages resulting from smoke and from water used to put out the fire. Damages caused by soot, smoke, water, or heat from a nearby burning building may also be covered.

Marine Insurance

Marine insurance is one of the oldest forms of insurance and dates back to old Venetian traders who sailed the Mediterranean Sea. It covers property that is transported and the means of transportation. Today, ocean marine insurance covers goods shipped at sea. Inland marine insurance covers goods moved by trains, trucks, and airplanes.

Life Insurance

What is the least expensive kind of life insurance you can buy?

Life insurance is an insurance contract that provides compensation for losses due to a person's death. Because the cost of insurance is based on risk, it is less expensive to buy life insurance when you are young because the death rate for young people is low so they are considered low risk.

Straight Life Insurance

Straight life insurance, also called ordinary life or whole life, is life insurance that requires the payment of premiums until the face value is reached or the insured is deceased. The face value is the amount of protection stated in the policy. Straight life insurance also builds up a cash and loan value, which is an amount you can cash the policy in for or borrow on.

Term Life Insurance

Term life insurance is life insurance issued for a particular period, usually five or ten years. It is the least expensive kind of life insurance because it has no cash or loan value. Premiums for term insurance increase at the end of each term because the insured is older and is considered a greater risk.

Other Types of Life Insurance

Limited-payment life insurance allows you to stop paying premiums after a stated length of time, usually 20 or 30 years. The beneficiary

Reading Check

Enumerate *List five types of property insurance.*

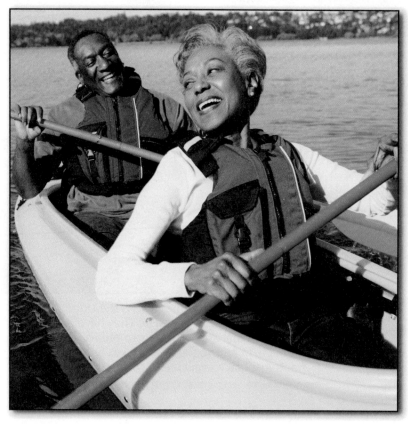

Life Insurance Term insurance is the least expensive kind of life insurance. *Why do the premiums for term insurance increase at the end of each term?*

Business ETHICS

Health Insurance Benefits

You are the chief executive of a nine-person architecture company in a small town. Under your state's labor laws, companies with 15 or more employees must provide health insurance to their employees. At this time, your company has made the decision not to offer health insurance. However, due to an increase in home building in your area, your company could make much more money if you hired five more architects. You know that you will attract better applicants if you can offer them health benefits.

Critical Thinking: *Should you offer health insurance?*

receives the amount of the policy upon the death of the insured, even if it occurs before the payment period is over.

Endowment insurance is insurance that provides protection for a stated time period and pays the proceeds either when the period is up or at death, whichever occurs first. Endowment policies are typically written for periods of ten, 20, or 30 years.

An annuity is a guaranteed retirement income that is purchased by paying either a lump-sum premium or by making periodic payments to an insurer. You may choose to receive a reduced income for a certain fixed number of years, with a beneficiary receiving whatever remains in the annuity when you die. You may choose to receive full payments as long as you live, but should you die before using up the annuity, your heirs receive nothing.

Health Insurance

What can you do if you cannot afford health insurance?

Two major categories of health insurance are basic and major medical. Major medical coverage typically pays only for long-term hospitalization and the cost of catastrophic illness. It does not cover **routine** medical care and prescriptions. In contrast, basic health insurance includes additional coverage, such as inpatient and out-patient hospital care, physician care, surgery, and prescription drugs.

Individual and Group Insurance

Many people get their health insurance through a group insurance plan where they work. Insurance companies can offer lower premiums to large groups because more people are sharing the expense of medical care. Employers often pay part of the premium and employees pay the remainder. People who work for themselves or for a company that does not offer health insurance may purchase their own individual health insurance. Individual insurance is more expensive than group insurance.

After You Read

Summarize What is the difference between a group health policy and an individual health insurance policy?

Two of the most common types of health insurance plans today are HMOs and PPOs. A Health Maintenance Organization (HMO) is a health care organization that contracts with doctors to provide services for its members. Members pay monthly premiums and must choose from a list of doctors provided by the HMO. A Preferred Provider Organization (PPO) is a group of doctors or hospitals that provide care for employees at reduced rates. PPOs are usually sponsored as part of an employer's group health plan.

Government Health Care Plans

Medicare is a federally funded health insurance program for people who are covered by Social Security. Medicare has two parts. Part A helps pay for inpatient hospital care. Part B pays for 80 percent of doctors' visits and certain other medical services. Many people buy an additional policy, called Medigap insurance, to cover the 20 percent not covered by Medicare. Another government health insurance program is called Medicaid. Medicaid is a health care plan for low-income people, administered by each state government and funded by both state and federal funds. Most states also offer health care plans to cover children from low-income families.

Disability Insurance

Disability insurance pays benefits if the policyholder cannot work because of a disability. Many employers purchase disability insurance for their employees. A long-term disability plan pays if a person cannot perform normal job duties for a year or longer. A short-term disability plan pays for a few months of being disabled.

SECTION 21.1 ASSESSMENT

Self Check

1. What is the purpose of insurance?

2. What is the difference between a policyholder and a beneficiary?

3. What is the difference between straight life insurance and term life insurance?

Academic Connection

Social Studies For every type of risk there is some form of insurance coverage. For example, Fred Astaire, the famous dancer, had his legs insured for $650,000. Employers can buy insurance for employees who quit if they win the lottery. You can even buy alien abduction insurance. One company offers insurance not only for alien abductions, but for injury caused by an asteroid or a piece of a falling satellite.

Go to the library or on the Internet and research unusual insurance policies and claims, past and present. Share your findings with the class.

Critical Thinking

Life Insurance Why do you think you cannot take out insurance on anyone you want?

Transformations

A transformation is a movement of a geometric figure. There are several types of transformations. In a translation, also called a slide, a figure is slid from one position to another without turning it. Every point of the original figure is moved the same distance and in the same direction. In a reflection, also called a flip, a figure is flipped over a line to form a mirror image. Every point of the original figure has a corresponding point on the other side of the line of symmetry. In a rotation, also called a turn, a figure is turned around a fixed point. A figure may be rotated 90° clockwise, 90° counterclockwise, or 180°. A dilation transforms each line to a parallel line whose length is a fixed multiple of the length of the original line to create a similar figure that will be either larger or smaller.

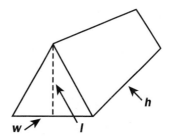

► *Use visualizations, spatial reasoning, and geometric modeling to solve problems*

Two-Dimensional Representations of Three-Dimensional Objects

Three-dimensional objects can be represented in a two-dimensional drawing in order to more easily determine properties such as surface area and volume. When you look at the triangular prism, you can see the orientation of its three dimensions, length, width, and height. Using the drawing and the formulas for surface area and volume, you can easily calculate these properties.

Another way to represent a three-dimensional object in a two-dimensional plane is by using a net, which is the unfolded representation. Imagine cutting the vertices of a box until it is flat then drawing an outline of it. That's a net. Most objects have more than one net, but any one can be measured to determine surface area. Below is a cube and one of its nets.

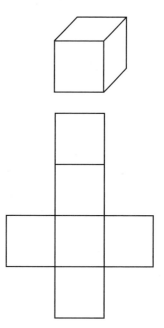

Measurement

▶ *Understand measurable attributes of objects and the units, systems, and processes of measurement*

Customary System

The customary system is the system of weights and measures used in the United States. The main units of weight are ounces, pounds (1 equal to 16 ounces), and tons (1 equal to 2,000 pounds). Length is typically measured in inches, feet (1 equal to 12 inches), yards (1 equal to 3 feet), and miles (1 equal to 5,280 feet), while area is measured in square feet and acres (1 equal to 43,560 square feet). Liquid is measured in cups, pints (1 equal to 2 cups), quarts (1 equal to 2 pints), and gallons (1 equal to 4 quarts). Finally, temperature is measured in degrees Fahrenheit.

Metric System

The metric system is a decimal system of weights and measurements in which the prefixes of the words for the units of measure indicate the relationships between the different measurements. In this system, the main units of weight, or mass, are grams and kilograms. Length is measured in millimeters, centimeters, meters, and kilometers, and the units of area are square millimeters, square centimeters, square meters, and square kilometers. Liquid is typically measured in milliliters and liters, while temperature is in degrees Celsius.

Selecting Units of Measure

When measuring something, it is important to select the appropriate type and size of unit. For example, in the United States it would be appropriate when describing someone's height to use feet and inches. These units of height or length are good to use because they are in the customary system, and they are of appropriate size. In the customary system, use inches, feet, and miles for lengths and perimeters; square inches, square feet, and square miles for area and surface area; and cups, pints, quarts, gallons or cubic inches and cubic feet (and less commonly miles) for volume. In the metric system use millimeters, centimeters, meters, and kilometers for lengths and perimeters; square units of millimeters, centimeters, meters, and kilometers for area and surface area; and milliliters and liters for volume. Always use degrees to measure angles.

▶ *Apply appropriate techniques, tools, and formulas to determine measurements*

Precision and Significant Digits

The precision of measurement is the exactness to which a measurement is made. Precision depends on the smallest unit of measure being used, or the precision unit. One way to record a measure is to estimate to the nearest precision unit. A more precise method is to include all of the digits that are actually measured, plus one estimated digit. The digits recorded, called significant digits, indicate the precision of the measurement. There are special rules for determining significant digits. If a number contains a decimal point, the number of significant digits is found by counting from left to right, starting with the first nonzero digit. If the number does not contain a decimal point, the number of significant digits is found by counting the digits from left to right, starting with the first digit and ending with the last nonzero digit.

Surface Area

The amount of material needed to cover the surface of a figure is called the surface area. It can be calculated by finding the area of each face and adding them together. To find the surface area of a rectangular prism, for example, the formula $S = 2lw + 2lh + 2wh$ applies. A cylinder, on the other hand, may be unrolled to reveal two circles and a rectangle. Its surface area can be determined by finding the area of the two circles, $2\pi r^2$, and adding it to the area of the rectangle, $2\pi rh$ (the length of the rectangle is the circumference of one of the circles), or $S = 2\pi r^2 + 2\pi rh$. The surface area of a pyramid is measured in a slightly different way because the sides of a pyramid are triangles that intersect at the vertex. These sides are called lateral faces and the height of each is called the slant height. The sum of their areas is the lateral area of a pyramid. The surface area of a square pyramid is the lateral area $\frac{1}{2}$ bh (area of a lateral face) times 4 (number of lateral faces), plus the area of the base. The surface area of a cone is the area of its circular base (πr^2) plus its lateral area (πrl, where l is the slant height).

Volume

Volume is the measure of space occupied by a solid region. To find the volume of a prism, the area of the base is multiplied by the measure of the height, $V = bh$. A solid containing several prisms can be broken down into its component prisms. Then the volume of each component can be found and the volumes added. The volume of a cylinder can be determined by finding the area of its circular base, πr^2, and then multiplying by the height of the cylinder. A pyramid has one-third the volume of a prism with the same base and height. To find the volume of a pyramid, multiply the area of the base by the pyramid's height, and then divide by 3. Simply stated, the formula for the volume of a pyramid is $V = \frac{1}{3}bh$. A cone is a three-dimensional figure with one circular base and a curved surface connecting the base and the vertex. The volume of a cone is one-third the volume of a cylinder with the same base area and height. Like a pyramid, the formula for the volume of a cone is $V = \frac{1}{3}bh$. More specifically, the formula is $V = \frac{1}{3}\pi r^2 h$.

Upper and Lower Bounds

Upper and lower bounds have to do with the accuracy of a measurement. When a measurement is given, the degree of accuracy is also stated to tell you what the upper and lower bounds of the measurement are. The upper bound is the largest possible value that a measurement could have had before being rounded down, and the lower bound is the lowest possible value it could have had before being rounded up.

Data Analysis and Probability

▶ *Formulate questions that can be addressed with data and collect, organize, and display relevant data to answer them*

Histograms

A histogram displays numerical data that have been organized into equal intervals using bars that have the same width and no space between them. While a histogram does not give exact data points, its shape shows the distribution of the data. Histograms also can be used to compare data.

1 to 20
21 to 40
41 to 60
61 to 80

Box-and-Whisker Plot

A box-and-whisker plot displays the measures of central tendency and variation. A box is drawn around the quartile values, and whiskers extend from each quartile to the extreme data points. To make a box plot for a set of data, draw a number line that covers the range of data. Find the median, the extremes, and the upper and lower quartiles. Mark these points on the number line with bullets, then draw a box and the whiskers. The length of a whisker or box shows whether the values of the data in that part are concentrated or spread out.

Scatter Plots

A scatter plot is a graph that shows the relationship between two sets of data. In a scatter plot, two sets of data are graphed as ordered pairs on a coordinate system. Two sets of data can have a positive correlation (as *x* increases, *y* increases), a negative correlation (as *x* increases, *y* decreases), or no correlation (no obvious pattern is shown). Scatter plots can be used to spot trends, draw conclusions, and make predictions about data.

Perfect Positive Correlation

Randomization

The idea of randomization is a very important principle of statistics and the design of experiments. Data must be selected randomly to prevent bias from influencing the results. For example, you want to know the average income of people in your town but you can only use a sample of 100 individuals to make determinations about everyone. If you select 100 individuals who are all doctors, you will have a biased sample. However, if you chose a random sample of 100 people out of the phone book, you are much more likely to accurately represent average income in the town.

Statistics and Parameters

Statistics is a science that involves collecting, analyzing, and presenting data. The data can be collected in various ways—

through a census or by making physical measurements, for example. The data can then be analyzed by creating summary statistics, which have to do with the distribution of the data sample, including the mean, range, and standard error. They can also be illustrated in tables and graphs, like box-plots, scatter plots, and histograms. The presentation of the data typically involves describing the strength or validity of the data and what they show. For example, an analysis of ancestry of people in a city might tell you something about immigration patterns, unless the data set is very small or biased in some way, in which case it is not likely to be very accurate or useful.

Categorical and Measurement Data

When analyzing data, it is important to understand if the data is qualitative or quantitative. Categorical data is qualitative and measurement, or numerical, data is quantitative. Categorical data describes a quality of something and can be placed into different categories. For example, if you are analyzing the number of students in different grades in a school, each grade is a category. On the other hand, measurement data is continuous, like height, weight, or any other measurable variable. Measurement data can be converted into categorical data if you decide to group the data. Using height as an example, you can group the continuous data set into categories like under 5 feet, 5 feet to 5 feet 5 inches, over 5 feet 5 inches to 6 feet, and so on.

Univariate and Bivariate Data

In data analysis, a researcher can analyze one variable at a time or look at how multiple variables behave together. Univariate data involves only one variable—height in humans, for example.

You can measure the height in a population of people then plot the results in a histogram to look at how height is distributed in humans. To summarize univariate data, you can use statistics like the mean, mode, median, range, and standard deviation, which is a measure of variation. When looking at more than one variable at once, you use multivariate data. Bivariate data involves two variables. For example, you can look at height and age in humans together by gathering information on both variables from individuals in a population. You can then plot both variables in a scatter plot, look at how the variables behave in relation to each other, and create an equation that represents the relationship, also called a regression. These equations could help answer questions such as, for example, does height increase with age in humans?

▶ Select and use appropriate statistical methods to analyze data

Measures of Central Tendency

When you have a list of numerical data, it is often helpful to use one or more numbers to represent the whole set. These numbers are called measures of central tendency. Three measures of central tendency are mean, median, and mode. The mean is the sum of the data divided by the number of items in the data set. The median is the middle number of the ordered data (or the mean of the two middle numbers). The mode is the number or numbers that occur most often. These measures of central tendency allow data to be analyzed and better understood.

Measures of Spread

In statistics, measures of spread or variation are used to describe how data are distributed. The range of a set of data is the difference between the greatest and the least values of the data set. The quartiles are the values that divide the data into four equal parts. The median of data separates the set in half. Similarly, the median of the lower half of a set of data is the lower quartile. The median of the upper half of a set of data is the upper quartile. The interquartile range is the difference between the upper quartile and the lower quartile.

Line of Best Fit

When real-life data are collected, the points graphed usually do not form a straight line, but they may approximate a linear relationship. A line of best fit is a line that lies very close to most of the data points. It can be used to predict data. You also can use the equation of the best-fit line to make predictions.

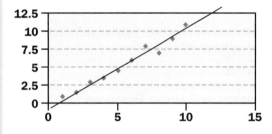

Stem and Leaf Plots

In a stem and leaf plot, numerical data are listed in ascending or descending order. The greatest place value of the data is used for the stems. The next greatest place value forms the leaves. For example, if the least number in a set of data is 8 and the greatest number is 95, draw a vertical line and write the stems from 0 to 9 to the left of the line. Write the leaves from to the right of the line, with the corresponding stem. Next, rearrange the leaves so they are ordered from least to greatest. Then include a key or explanation, such as 1|3 = 13. Notice that the stem-and-leaf plot below is like a histogram turned on its side.

```
0|8
1|3 6
2|5 6 9
3|0 2 7 8
4|0 1 4 7 9
5|1 4 5 8
6|1 3 7
7|5 8
8|2 6
9|5
```
Key: **1|3 = 13**

▶ Develop and evaluate inferences and predictions that are based on data

Sampling Distribution

The sampling distribution of a population is the distribution that would result if you could take an infinite number of samples from the population, average each, and then average the averages. The more normal the distribution of the population, that is, how closely the distribution follows a bell curve, the more likely the sampling distribution will also follow a normal distribution. Furthermore, the larger the sample, the more likely it will accurately represent the entire population. For instance, you are more likely to gain more representative results from a population of 1,000 with a sample of 100 than with a sample of 2.

Validity

In statistics, validity refers to acquiring results that accurately reflect that which is being measured. In other words, it is important when performing statistical analyses, to ensure that the data are valid in that the sample being analyzed represents the population to the best extent possible. Randomization of data and using appropriate sample sizes are two important aspects of making valid inferences about a population.

▶ Understand and apply basic concepts of probability

Complementary, Mutually Exclusive Events

To understand probability theory, it is important to know if two events are mutually exclusive, or complementary: the occurrence of one event automatically implies the non-occurrence of the other. That is, two complementary events cannot both occur. If you roll a pair of dice, the event of rolling 6 and rolling doubles have an outcome in common (3, 3), so they are not mutually exclusive. If you roll (3, 3), you also roll doubles. However, the events of rolling a 9 and rolling doubles are mutually exclusive because they have no outcomes in common. If you roll a 9, you will not also roll doubles.

Independent and Dependent Events

Determining the probability of a series of events requires that you know whether the events are independent or dependent. An independent event has no influence on the occurrence of subsequent events, whereas, a dependent event does influence subsequent events. The chances that a woman's first child will be a girl are $\frac{1}{2}$, and the chances that her second child will be a girl are also $\frac{1}{2}$ because the two events are independent of each other. However, if there are 7 red marbles in a bag of 15 marbles, the chances that the first marble you pick will be red are $\frac{7}{15}$ and if you indeed pick a red marble and remove it, you have reduced the chances of picking another red marble to $\frac{6}{14}$.

Sample Space

The sample space is the group of all possible outcomes for an event. For example, if you are tossing a single six-sided die, the sample space is {1, 2, 3, 4, 5, 6}. Similarly, you can determine the sample space for the possible outcomes of two events. If you are going to toss a coin twice, the sample space is {(heads, heads), (heads, tails), (tails, heads), (tails, tails)}.

Computing the Probability of a Compound Event

If two events are independent, the outcome of one event does not influence the outcome of the second. For example, if a bag contains 2 blue and 3 red marbles, then the probability of selecting a blue marble, replacing it, and then selecting a red marble is $P(A) \times P(B) = \frac{2}{5} \times \frac{3}{5}$ or $\frac{6}{25}$.

If two events are dependent, the outcome of one event affects the outcome of the second. For example, if a bag contains 2 blue and 3 red marbles, then the probability of selecting a blue and then a red marble without replacing the first marble is $P(A) \times P(B$ following $A) = \frac{2}{5} \times \frac{3}{4}$ or $\frac{3}{10}$. Two events that cannot happen at the same time are mutually exclusive. For example, when you roll two number cubes, you cannot roll a sum that is both 5 and even. So, $P(A$ or $B) = \frac{4}{36} + \frac{18}{36}$ or $\frac{11}{18}$.

Math Appendix

The Constitution of the United States

PREAMBLE

We the People of the United States, in Order to form a more perfect Union, establish Justice, insure domestic Tranquility, provide for the common defence, promote the general Welfare, and secure the Blessings of Liberty to ourselves and our Posterity, do ordain and establish this Constitution for the United States of America.

* Text of the Constitution printed in gray and crossed out indicates that it has been ammended and is no longer in effect.

ARTICLE I

Section 1 ■ All legislative Powers herein granted shall be vested in a Congress of the United States, which shall consist of a Senate and House of Representatives.

Section 2 ■ The House of Representatives shall be composed of Members chosen every second Year by the People of the several States, and the Electors in each State shall have the Qualifications requisite for Electors of the most numerous Branch of the State Legislature.

No Person shall be a Representative who shall not have attained to the Age of twenty five Years, and been seven Years a Citizen of the United States, and who shall not, when elected, be an Inhabitant of that State in which he shall be chosen.

*Representatives and direct Taxes shall be apportioned among the several States which may be included within this Union, according to their respective Numbers, which shall be determined by adding to the whole Number of free Persons, including those bound to Service for a Term of Years, and excluding Indians not taxed, three fifths of all other Persons. The actual Enumeration shall be made within three Years after the first Meeting of the Congress of the United States, and within every subsequent Term of ten Years, in such Manner as they shall by Law direct. The Number of Representatives shall not exceed one for every thirty Thou-sand, but each State shall have at Least one Representative; and until such enumeration shall be made, the State of New Hampshire shall be entitled to chuse three, Massa-chusetts eight, Rhode-Island and Provi-dence Plantations one, Connecti-cut five, New-York six, New Jersey four, Pennsylvania eight, Delaware one, Maryland six, Virginia ten, North Carolina five, South Carolina five, and Georgia three.

When vacancies happen in the Representation from any State, the Executive Authority thereof shall issue Writs of Election to fill such Vacancies.

The House of Representatives shall chuse their Speaker and other Officers; and shall have the sole Power of Impeachment.

Section 3 ■ The Senate of the United States shall be composed of two Senators from each State, chosen by the Legislature thereof, for six Years; and each Senator shall have one Vote.

Immediately after they shall be assembled in Consequence of the first Election, they shall be divided as equally as may be into three Classes. The Seats of the Senators of the first Class shall be vacated at the Expiration of the second Year, of the second Class at the Expiration of the fourth Year, and of the third Class at the Expiration of the sixth Year, so that one third may be chosen every second Year;

and if Vacancies happen by Resignation, or otherwise, during the Recess of the Legislature of any State, the Executive thereof may make temporary Appointments until the next Meeting of the Legislature, which shall then fill such Vacancies.

No Person shall be a Senator who shall not have attained to the Age of thirty Years, and been nine Years a Citizen of the United States, and who shall not, when elected, be an Inhabitant of that State for which he shall be chosen.

The Vice President of the United States shall be President of the Senate, but shall have no Vote, unless they be equally divided.

The Senate shall chuse their other Officers, and also a President pro tempore, in the Absence of the Vice President, or when he shall exercise the Office of President of the United States.

The Senate shall have the sole Power to try all Impeachments. When sitting for that Purpose, they shall be on Oath or Affirmation. When the President of the United

States is tried, the Chief Justice shall preside: And no Person shall be convicted without the Concurrence of two thirds of the Members present.

Judgment in Cases of Impeachment shall not extend further than to removal from Office, and disqualification to hold and enjoy any Office of honor, Trust or Profit under the United States: but the Party convicted shall nevertheless be liable and subject to Indictment, Trial, Judgment and Punishment, according to Law.

Section 4 ■ The Times, Places and Manner of holding Elections for Senators and Representatives, shall be prescribed in each State by the Legislature thereof; but the Congress may at any time by Law make or alter such Regulations, except as to the Places of chusing Senators.

The Congress shall assemble at least once in every Year, and such Meeting shall be on the first Monday in December, unless they shall by Law appoint a different Day.

Section 5 ■ Each House shall be the Judge of the Elections, Returns and Qualifications of its own Members, and a Majority of each shall constitute a Quorum to do Business; but a smaller Number may adjourn from day to day, and may be authorized to compel the Attendance of absent Members, in such Manner, and under such Penalties as each House may provide.

Each House may determine the Rules of its Proceedings, punish its Members for disorderly Behaviour, and, with the Concurrence of two thirds, expel a Member.

Each House shall keep a Journal of its Proceedings, and from time to time publish the same, excepting such Parts as may in their Judgment require Secrecy; and the Yeas and Nays of the Members of either House on any question shall, at the Desire of one fifth of those Present, be entered on the Journal.

Neither House, during the Session of Congress, shall, without the Consent of the other, adjourn for more than three days, nor to any other Place than that in which the two Houses shall be sitting.

Section 6 ■ The Senators and Representatives shall receive a Compensation for their Services, to be ascertained by Law, and paid out of the Treasury of the United States. They shall in all Cases, except Treason, Felony and Breach of the Peace, be privileged from Arrest during their Attendance at the Session of their respective Houses, and in going to and returning from the same; and for any Speech or Debate in either House, they shall not be questioned in any other Place.

No Senator or Representative shall, during the Time for which he was elected, be appointed to any civil Office under the Authority of the United States, which shall have been created, or the Emoluments whereof shall have been encreased during such time; and no Person holding any Office under the United States, shall be a Member of either House during his Continuance in Office.

Section 7 ■ All Bills for raising Revenue shall originate in the House of Representatives; but the Senate may propose or concur with Amendments as on other Bills.

Every Bill which shall have passed the House of Representatives and the Senate, shall, before it become a Law, be presented to the President of the United States; If he approve he shall sign it, but if not he shall return it, with his Objections to that House in which it shall have originated, who shall enter the Objections at large on their Journal, and proceed to reconsider it.

If after such Reconsideration two thirds of that House shall agree to pass the Bill, it shall be sent, together with the Objections, to the other House, by which it shall likewise be reconsidered, and if approved by two thirds of that House, it shall become a Law. But in all such Cases the Votes of both Houses shall be determined by Yeas and Nays, and the Names of the Persons voting for and against the Bill shall be entered on the Journal of each House respectively. If any Bill shall not be returned by the President within ten Days (Sundays excepted) after it shall have been presented to him, the Same shall be a Law, in like Manner as if he had signed it, unless the Congress by their Adjournment prevent its Return, in which Case it shall not be a Law.

Every Order, Resolution, or Vote to which the Concurrence of the Senate and House of Representatives may be necessary (except on a question of Adjournment) shall be presented to the President of the United States; and before the Same shall take Effect, shall be approved by him, or being disapproved by him, shall be repassed by two thirds of the Senate and House of Representatives, according to the Rules and Limitations prescribed in the Case of a Bill.

Section 8 ■ The Congress shall have Power To lay and collect Taxes, Duties, Imposts and Excises, to pay the Debts and provide for the common Defence and general Welfare of the United States; but all Duties, Imposts and Excises shall be uniform throughout the United States;

To borrow Money on the credit of the United States;

To regulate Commerce with foreign Nations, and among the several States, and with the Indian Tribes;

To establish an uniform Rule of Naturalization, and uniform Laws on the subject of Bankruptcies throughout the United States;

To coin Money, regulate the Value thereof, and of foreign Coin, and fix the Standard of Weights and Measures;

To provide for the Punishment of counterfeiting the Securities and current Coin of the United States;

To establish Post Offices and post Roads;

To promote the Progress of Science and useful Arts, by securing for limited Times to Authors and Inventors the exclusive Right to their respective Writings and Discoveries;

To constitute Tribunals inferior to the supreme Court;

To define and punish Piracies and Felonies committed on the high Seas, and Offences against the Law of Nations;

To declare War, grant Letters of Marque and Reprisal, and make Rules concerning Captures on Land and Water;

To raise and support Armies, but no Appropriation of Money to that Use shall be for a longer Term than two Years;

To provide and maintain a Navy;

To make Rules for the Government and Regulation of the land and naval Forces;

To provide for calling forth the Militia to execute the Laws of the Union, suppress Insurrections and repel Invasions;

To provide for organizing, arming, and disciplining, the Militia, and for governing such Part of them as may be employed in the Service of the United States, reserving to the States respectively, the Appointment of the Officers, and the Authority of training the Militia according to the discipline prescribed by Congress;

To exercise exclusive Legislation in all Cases whatsoever, over such District (not exceeding ten Miles square) as may, by Cession of particular States, and the Acceptance of Congress, become the Seat of the Government of the United States, and to exercise like Authority over all Places purchased by the Consent of the Legislature of the State in which the Same shall be, for the Erection of Forts, Magazines, Arsenals, dock-Yards, and other needful Buildings; And

To make all Laws which shall be necessary and proper for carrying into Execution the foregoing Powers, and all other Powers vested by this Constitution in the Government of the United States, or in any Department or Officer thereof.

Section 9 ■ The Migration or Importation of such Persons as any of the States now existing shall think proper to admit, shall not be prohibited by the Congress prior to the Year one thousand eight hundred and eight, but a Tax or duty may be imposed on such Importation, not exceeding ten dollars for each Person.

The Privilege of the Writ of Habeas Corpus shall not be suspended, unless when in Cases of Rebellion or Invasion the public Safety may require it.

No Bill of Attainder or ex post facto Law shall be passed.

No Capitation, or other direct, Tax shall be laid, unless in Proportion to the Census or Enumeration herein before directed to be taken.

No Tax or Duty shall be laid on Articles exported from any State.

No Preference shall be given by any Regulation of Commerce or Revenue to the Ports of one State over those of another: nor shall Vessels bound to, or from, one State, be obliged to enter, clear, or pay Duties in another.

No Money shall be drawn from the Treasury, but in Consequence of Appropriations made by Law; and a regular Statement and Account of the Receipts and Expenditures of all public Money shall be published from time to time.

No Title of Nobility shall be granted by the United States: And no Person holding any Office of Profit or Trust under them, shall, without the Consent of the Congress, accept of any present, Emolument, Office, or Title, of any kind whatever, from any King, Prince, or foreign State.

Section 10 ■ No State shall enter into any Treaty, Alliance, or Confederation; grant Letters of Marque and Reprisal; coin Money; emit Bills of Credit; make any Thing but gold and silver Coin a Tender in Payment of Debts; pass any Bill of Attainder, ex post facto Law, or Law impairing the Obligation of Contracts, or grant any Title of Nobility.

No State shall, without the Consent of the Congress, lay any Imposts or Duties on Imports or Exports, except what may be absolutely necessary for executing its inspection Laws: and the net Produce of all Duties and Imposts, laid by any State on Imports or Exports, shall be for the Use of the Treasury of the United States; and all such Laws shall be subject to the Revision and Controul of the Congress.

No State shall, without the Consent of Congress, lay any Duty of Tonnage, keep Troops, or Ships of War in time of Peace, enter into any Agreement or Compact with another State, or with a foreign Power, or engage in War, unless actually invaded, or in such imminent Danger as will not admit of delay.

ARTICLE II

Section 1 ■ The executive Power shall be vested in a President of the United States of America. He shall hold his Office during the Term of four Years, and, together with the Vice President, chosen for the same Term, be elected, as follows

Each State shall appoint, in such Manner as the Legislature thereof may direct, a Number of Electors, equal to the whole Number of Senators and Representatives to which the State may be entitled in the Congress: but no Senator or Representative, or Person holding an Office of Trust or Profit under the United States, shall be appointed an Elector.

The Electors shall meet in their respective States, and vote by Ballot for two Persons, of whom one at least shall not be an Inhabitant of the same State with themselves. And they shall make a List of all the Persons voted for, and of the Number of Votes for each; which List they shall sign and certify, and transmit sealed to the Seat of the Government of the United States, directed to the President of the Senate. The President of the Senate shall, in the Presence of the Senate and House of Representatives, open all the Certificates, and the Votes shall then be counted. The Person having the greatest Number of Votes shall be the President, if such Number be a Majority of the whole Number of Electors appointed; and if there be more than one who have such Majority, and have an equal Number of Votes then the House of Representatives shall immediately chuse by Ballot one of them for Presi-dent; and if no Person have a Majority, then from the five highest on the List the said House shall in like Manner chuse the President.But in chusing the President, the Votes shall be taken by States, the Representation from each State having one Vote; A quorum for this Purpose shall consist of a Member or Members from two thirds of the States, and a Majority of all the States shall be necessary to a Choice.In every Case, after the Choice of the President, the Person having the greatest Number of Votes of the Electors shall be the Vice Pres-ident. But if there should remain two or more who have equal Votes, the Senate shall chuse from them by Ballot the Vice President.

The Congress may determine the Time of chusing the Electors, and the Day on which they shall give their Votes; which Day shall be the same throughout the United States.

No Person except a natural born Citizen, or a Citizen of the United States, at the time of the Adoption of this Constitution, shall be eligible to the Office of President; neither shall any Person be eligible to that Office who shall not have attained to the Age of thirty five Years, and been fourteen Years a Resident within the United States.

In Case of the Removal of the President from Office, or of his Death, Resignation, or Inability to discharge the Powers and Duties of the saidOffice, the Same shall devolve on the Vice President, and the Congress may by Law provide for the Case of Removal, Death, Resignation or Inability, both of the President and Vice President, declaring what Officer shall then act as President, and such Officer shall act accordingly, until the Disability be removed, or a President shall be elected.

The President shall, at stated Times, receive for his Services, a Compensation, which shall neither be encreased nor diminished during the Period for which he shall have been elected, and he shall not receive within that Period any other Emolument from the United States, or any of them.

Before he enter on the Execution of his Office, he shall take the following Oath or Affirmation: "I do solemnly swear (or affirm) that I will faithfully execute the Office of President of the United States, and will to the best of my Ability, preserve, protect and defend the Constitution of the United States."

Section 2 ■ The President shall be Commander in Chief of the Army and Navy of the United States, and of the Militia of the several States, when called into the actual Service of the United States; he may require the Opinion, in writing, of the principal Officer in each of the executive Departments, upon any Subject relating to the Duties of their respective Offices, and he shall have Power to grant Reprieves and Pardons for Offences against the United States, except in Cases of Impeachment.

He shall have Power, by and with the Advice and Consent of the Senate, to make Treaties, provided two thirds of the Senators present concur; and he shall nominate, and by and with the Advice and Consent of the Senate, shall appoint Ambassadors, other public Ministers and Consuls, Judges of the supreme Court, and all other Officers of the United States, whose Appointments are not herein otherwise provided for, and which shall be established by Law: but the Congress may by Law vest the Appointment of such inferior Officers, as they think proper, in the President alone, in the Courts of Law, or in the Heads of Departments. The President shall have Power to fill up all Vacancies that may happen during the Recess of the Senate, by granting Commissions which shall expire at the End of their next Session.

Section 3 ■ He shall from time to time give to the Congress Information of the State of the Union, and recommend to their Consideration such Measures as he shall judge necessary and expedient; he may, on extraordinary Occasions, convene both Houses, or either of them, and in Case of Disagreement between them, with Respect to the Time of Adjournment, he may adjourn them to such Time as he shall think proper; he shall receive Ambassadors and other public Ministers; he shall take Care that the Laws be faithfully executed, and shall Commission all the Officers of the United States.

Section 4 ■ The President, Vice President and all civil Officers of the United States, shall be removed from Office on Impeachment for, and Conviction of, Treason, Bribery, or other high Crimes and Misdemeanors.

ARTICLE III

Section 1 ■ The judicial Power of the United States, shall be vested in one supreme Court, and in such inferior Courts as the Congress may from time to time ordain and establish. The Judges, both of the supreme and inferior Courts, shall hold their Offices during good Behaviour, and shall, at stated Times, receive for their Services, a Compensation, which shall not be diminished during their Continuance in Office.

Section 2 ■ The judicial Power shall extend to all Cases, in Law and Equity, arising under this Constitution, the Laws of the United States, and Treaties made, or which shall be made, under their Authority; to all Cases affecting Ambassadors, other public Ministers and Consuls; to all Cases of admiralty and maritime Jurisdiction;—to Controversies to which the United States shall be a Party;—to Controversies between two or more States; between a State and Citizens of another State;—between Citizens of different States, between Citizens of the same State claiming Lands under Grants of different States, and between a State, or the Citizens thereof, and foreign States, Citizens or Subjects.

In all Cases affecting Ambassadors, other public Ministers and Consuls, and those in which a State shall be Party, the supreme Court shall have original Jurisdiction. In all the other Cases before mentioned, the supreme Court shall have appellate Jurisdiction, both as to Law and Fact, with such Exceptions, and under such Regulations as the Congress shall make.

The Trial of all Crimes, except in Cases of Impeachment, shall be by Jury; and such Trial shall be held in the State where the said Crimes shall have been committed; but when not committed within any State, the Trial shall be at such Place or Places as the Congress may by Law have directed.

Section 3 ■ Treason against the United States, shall consist only in levying War against them, or in adhering to their Enemies, giving them Aid and Comfort. No Person shall be convicted of Treason unless on the Testimony of two Witnesses to the same overt Act, or on Confession in open Court.

The Congress shall have Power to declare the Punishment of Treason, but no Attainder of Treason shall work Corruption of

Blood, or Forfeiture except during the Life of the Person attainted.

ARTICLE IV

Section 1 ▪ Full Faith and Credit shall be given in each State to the public Acts, Records, and judicial Proceedings of every other State. And the Congress may by general Laws prescribe the Manner in which such Acts, Records and Proceedings shall be proved, and the Effect thereof.

Section 2 ▪ The Citizens of each State shall be entitled to all Privileges and Immunities of Citizens in the several States.

A Person charged in any State with Treason, Felony, or other Crime, who shall flee from Justice, and be found in another State, shall on Demand of the executive Authority of the State from which he fled, be delivered up, to be removed to the State having Jurisdiction of the Crime.

No Person held to Service or Labour in one State, under the Laws thereof, escaping into another, shall, in Consequence of any Law or Regulation therein, be discharged from such Service or Labour, but shall be delivered up on Claim of the Party to whom such Service or Labour may be due.

Section 3 ▪ New States may be admitted by the Congress into this Union; but no new State shall be formed or erected within the Jurisdiction of any other State; nor any State be formed by the Junction of two or more States, or Parts of States, without the Consent of the Legislatures of the States concerned as well as of the Congress.

Clause 2: The Congress shall have Power to dispose of and make all needful Rules and Regulations respecting the Territory or other Property belonging to the United States; and nothing in this Constitution shall be so construed as to Prejudice any Claims of the United States, or of any particular State.

Section 4 ▪ The United States shall guarantee to every State in this Union a Republican Form of Government, and shall protect each of them against Invasion; and on Application of the Legislature, or of the Executive (when the Legislature cannot be convened) against domestic Violence.

ARTICLE V

The Congress, whenever two thirds of both Houses shall deem it necessary, shall propose Amendments to this Constitution, or, on the Application of the Legislatures of two thirds of the several States, shall call a Convention for proposing Amendments, which, in either Case, shall be valid to all Intents and Purposes, as Part of this Constitution, when ratified by the Legislatures of three fourths of the several States, or by Conventions in three fourths thereof, as the one or the other Mode of Ratification may be proposed by the Congress; Provided that no Amendment which may be made prior to the Year One thousand eight hundred and eight shall in any Manner affect the first and fourth Clauses in the Ninth Section of the first Article; and that no State, without its Consent, shall be deprived of its equal Suffrage in the Senate.

ARTICLE VI

All Debts contracted and Engagements entered into, before the Adoption of this Constitution, shall be as valid against the United States under this Constitution, as under the Confederation.

This Constitution, and the Laws of the United States which shall be made in Pursuance thereof; and all Treaties made, or which shall be made, under the Authority of the United States, shall be the supreme Law of the Land; and the Judges in every State shall be bound thereby, any Thing in the Constitution or Laws of any State to the Contrary notwithstanding.

The Senators and Representatives before mentioned, and the Members of the several State Legislatures, and all executive and judicial Officers, both of the United States and of the several States, shall be bound by Oath or Affirmation, to support this Constitution; but no religious Test shall ever be required as a Qualification to any Office or public Trust under the United States.

ARTICLE VII

The Ratification of the Conventions of nine States, shall be sufficient for the Establishment of this Constitution between the States so ratifying the Same.

Done in Convention by the Unanimous Consent of the States present the Seventeenth Day of September in the Year of our Lord one thousand seven hundred and Eighty seven and of the Independence of the United States of America the Twelfth In witness whereof We have hereunto subscribed our Names,

> G. O. Washington—Presidt.
> and deputy from Virginia
>
> [Signed also by
> the deputies of twelve States.]

AMENDMENT I

Congress shall make no law respecting an establishment of religion, or prohibiting the free exercise thereof; or abridging the freedom of speech, or of the press; or the right of the people peaceably to assemble, and to petition the Government for a redress of grievances.

AMENDMENT II

A well regulated Militia, being necessary to the security of a free State, the right of the people to keep and bear Arms, shall not be infringed.

AMENDMENT III

No Soldier shall, in time of peace be quartered in any house, without the consent of the Owner, nor in time of war, but in a manner to be prescribed by law.

AMENDMENT IV

The right of the people to be secure in their persons, houses, papers, and effects, against unreasonable searches and seizures, shall not be violated, and no Warrants shall issue, but upon probable cause, supported by Oath or affirmation, and particularly describing the place to be searched, and the persons or things to be seized.

AMENDMENT V

No person shall be held to answer for a capital, or otherwise infamous crime, unless on a presentment or indictment of a Grand Jury, except in cases arising in the land or naval forces, or in the Militia, when in actual service in time of War or public danger; nor shall any person be subject for the same offence to be twice put in jeopardy of life or limb; nor shall be compelled in any criminal case to be a witness against himself, nor be deprived of life, liberty, or property, without due process of law; nor shall private property be taken for public use, without just compensation.

AMENDMENT VI

In all criminal prosecutions, the accused shall enjoy the right to a speedy and public trial, by an impartial jury of the State and district wherein the crime shall have been committed, which district shall have been previously ascertained by law, and to be informed of the nature and cause of the accusation; to be confronted with the witnesses against him; to have compulsory process for obtaining witnesses in his favor, and to have the Assistance of Counsel for his defence.

AMENDMENT VII

In suits at common law, where the value in controversy shall exceed twenty dollars, the right of trial by jury shall be preserved, and no fact tried by a jury, shall be otherwise reexamined in any Court of the United States, than according to the rules of the common law.

AMENDMENT VIII

Excessive bail shall not be required, nor excessive fines imposed, nor cruel and unusual punishments inflicted.

AMENDMENT IX

The enumeration in the Constitution, of certain rights, shall not be construed to deny or disparage others retained by the people.

AMENDMENT X

The powers not delegated to the United States by the Constitution, nor prohibited by it to the States, are reserved to the States respectively, or to the people.

AMENDMENT XI

The Judicial power of the United States shall not be construed to extend to any suit in law or equity, commenced or prosecuted against one of the United States by Citizens of another State, or by Citizens or Subjects of any Foreign State.

AMENDMENT XII

The Electors shall meet in their respective states and vote by ballot for President and Vice-President, one of whom, at least, shall not be an inhabitant of the same state with themselves; they shall name in their ballots the person voted for as President, and in distinct ballots the person voted for as Vice-President, and they shall make distinct lists of all persons voted for as President, and of all persons voted for as Vice-President, and of the number of votes for each, which lists they shall sign and certify, and transmit sealed to the seat of the government of the United States, directed to the President of the Senate; the President of the Senate shall, in the presence of the Senate and House of Representatives, open all the certificates and the votes shall then be counted; The person having the greatest number of votes for President, shall be the President, if such number be a majority of the whole number of Electors appointed; and if no person have such majority, then from the persons having the highest numbers not exceeding three on the list of those voted for as President, the House of Representatives shall choose immediately, by ballot, the President. But in choosing the President, the votes shall be taken by states, the representation from each state having one vote; a quorum for this purpose shall consist of a member or members from two-thirds of the states, and a majority of all the states shall be necessary to a choice.

And if the House of Representatives shall not choose a President whenever the right of choice shall devolve upon them, before the fourth day of March next following, then the Vice-President shall act as President, as in case of the death or other constitutional disability of the President.

The person having the greatest number of votes as Vice-President, shall be the Vice-President, if such number be a majority of the whole number of Electors appointed, and if no person have a majority, then from the two highest numbers on the list, the Senate shall choose the Vice-President; a quorum for the purpose shall consist of two-thirds of the whole number of Senators, and a majority of the whole number shall be necessary to a choice. But no person constitutionally ineligible to the office of President shall be eligible to that of Vice-President of the United States.

AMENDMENT XIII

Section 1 ▪ Neither slavery nor involuntary servitude, except as a punishment for crime whereof the party shall have been duly convicted, shall exist within the United States, or any place subject to their jurisdiction.

Section 2 ▪ Congress shall have power to enforce this article by appropriate legislation.

AMENDMENT XIV

Section 1 ▪ All persons born or naturalized in the United States, and subject to the jurisdiction thereof, are citizens of the United States and of the State wherein they reside. No State shall make or enforce any law which shall abridge the privileges or immunities of citizens of the United States; nor shall any State deprive any person of life, liberty, or property, without due process of law; nor deny to any person within its jurisdiction the equal protection of the laws.

Section 2 ▪ Representatives shall be apportioned among the several States according to their respective numbers, counting the whole number of persons in each State, excluding Indians not taxed. But when the right to vote at any election for the choice of electors for President and Vice-President of the United States, Representatives in Congress, the Executive and Judicial officers of a State, or the members of the Legislature thereof, is denied to any of the male inhabitants of such State, being twenty-one years of age, and citizens of the United States, or in any way abridged, except for participation in rebellion, or other crime, the basis of representation therein shall be reduced in the proportion which the number of such male citizens shall bear to the whole number of male citizens twenty-one years of age in such State.

Section 3 ▪ No person shall be a Senator or Representative in Congress, or elector of President and Vice-President, or hold any office, civil or military, under the United States, or under any State, who, having previously taken an oath, as a member of Congress, or as an officer of the United States, or as a member of any State legislature, or as an executive or judicial officer of any State, to support the Constitution of the United States, shall have engaged in insurrection or rebellion against the same, or given aid or comfort to the enemies thereof. But Congress may by a vote of two-thirds of each House, remove such disability.

Section 4 ▪ The validity of the public debt of the United States, authorized by law, including debts incurred for payment of pensions and bounties for services in suppressing insurrection or rebellion, shall not be questioned. But neither the United States nor any State shall assume or pay any debt or obligation incurred in aid of insurrection or rebellion against the United States, or any claim for the loss or emancipation of any slave; but all such debts, obligations and claims shall be held illegal and void.

Section 5 ▪ The Congress shall have the power to enforce, by appropriate legislation, the provisions of this article.

AMENDMENT XV

Section 1 ▪ The right of citizens of the United States to vote shall not be denied or abridged by the United States or by any State on account of race, color, or previous condition of servitude.

Section 2 ▪ The Congress shall have the power to enforce this article by appropriate legislation.

AMENDMENT XVI

The Congress shall have power to lay and collect taxes on incomes, from whatever source derived, without apportionment among the several States, and without regard to any census or enumeration.

AMENDMENT XVII

The Senate of the United States shall be composed of two Senators from each State, elected by the people thereof, for six years; and each Senator shall have one vote. The electors in each State shall have the qualifications requisite for electors of the most numerous branch of the State legislatures.

When vacancies happen in the representation of any State in the Senate, the executive authority of such State shall issue writs of election to fill such vacancies: *Provided,* That the legislature of any State may empower the executive thereof to make temporary appointments until the people fill the vacancies by election as the legislature may direct.

This amendment shall not be so construed as to affect the election or term of any Senator chosen before it becomes valid as part of the Constitution.

AMENDMENT XVIII

Section 1 ▪ After one year from the ratification of this article the manufacture, sale, or transportation of intoxicating liquors within, the importation thereof into, or the exportation thereof from the United States and all territory subject to the jurisdiction thereof for beverage purposes is hereby prohibited.

Section 2 ▪ The Congress and the several States shall have concurrent power to enforce this article by appropriate legislation.

Section 3 ▪ This article shall be inoperative unless it shall have been ratified as an amend-ment to the Constitution by the legislatures of the several States, as provided in the Constitu-tion, within seven years from the date of the submission hereof to the States by the Congress.

AMENDMENT XIX

The right of citizens of the United States to vote shall not be denied or abridged by the United States or by any State on account of sex. Congress shall have power to enforce this article by appropriate legislation.

AMENDMENT XX

Section 1 ▪ The terms of the President and the Vice President shall end at noon on the 20th day of January, and the terms of Senators and Representatives at noon on the 3d day of January, of the years in which such terms would have ended if this article had not been ratified; and the terms of their successors shall then begin.

Section 2 ▪ The Congress shall assemble at least once in every year, and such meeting shall begin at noon on the 3d day of January, unless they shall by law appoint a different day.

Section 3 ▪ If, at the time fixed for the beginning of the term of the President, the President elect shall have died, the Vice President elect shall become President. If a President shall not have been chosen before the time fixed for the beginning of his term, or if the President elect shall have failed to qualify, then the Vice President elect shall act as President until a President shall have qualified; and the Congress may by law provide for the case wherein neither a President elect nor a Vice President shall have qualified, declaring who shall then act as President, or the manner in which one who is to act shall be selected, and such person shall act accordingly until a President or Vice President shall have qualified.

Section 4 ▪ The Congress may by law provide for the case of the death of any of the persons from whom the House of Representatives may choose a President whenever the right of choice shall have devolved upon them, and for the case of the death of any of the persons from whom the Senate may choose a Vice President whenever the right of choice shall have devolved upon them.

Section 5 ■ Sections 1 and 2 shall take effect on the 15th day of October following the ratification of this article.

Section 6 ■ This article shall be inoperative unless it shall have been ratified as an amendment to the Constitution by the legislatures of three-fourths of the several States within seven years from the date of its submission.

AMENDMENT XXI

Section 1 ■ The eighteenth article of amendment to the Constitution of the United States is hereby repealed.

Section 2 ■ The transportation or importation into any State, Territory, or Possession of the United States for delivery or use therein of intoxicating liquors, in violation of the laws thereof, is hereby prohibited.

Section 3 ■ This article shall be inoperative unless it shall have been ratified as an amendment to the Constitution by conventions in the several States, as provided in the Constitution, within seven years from the date of the submission hereof to the States by the Congress.

AMENDMENT XXII

Section 1 ■ No person shall be elected to the office of the President more than twice, and no person who has held the office of President, or acted as President, for more than two years of a term to which some other person was elected President shall be elected to the office of President more than once. But this Article shall not apply to any person holding the office of President when this Article was proposed by Congress, and shall not prevent any person who may be holding the office of President, or acting as President, during the term within which this Article becomes operative from holding the office of President or acting as President during the remainder of such term.

Section 2 ■ This article shall be inoperative unless it shall have been ratified as an amendment to the Constitution by the legislatures of three-fourths of the several States within seven years from the date of its submission to the States by the Congress.

AMENDMENT XXIII

Section 1 ■ The District constituting the seat of Government of the United States shall appoint in such manner as Congress may direct:

A number of electors of President and Vice President equal to the whole number of Senators and Representatives in Congress to which the District would be entitled if it were a State, but in no event more than the least populous State; they shall be in addition to those appointed by the States, but they shall be considered, for the purposes of the election of President and Vice President, to be electors appointed by a State; and they shall meet in the District and perform such duties as provided by the twelfth article of amendment.

Section 2 ■ The Congress shall have power to enforce this article by appropriate legislation.

AMENDMENT XXIV

Section 1 ■ The right of citizens of the United States to vote in any primary or other election for President or Vice President, for electors for President or Vice President, or for Senator or Representative in Congress, shall not be denied or abridged by the United States or any State by reason of failure to pay poll tax or other tax.

Section 2 ■ The Congress shall have power to enforce this article by appropriate legislation.

AMENDMENT XXV

Section 1 ■ In case of the removal of the President from office or of his death or resignation, the Vice President shall become President.

Section 2 ■ Whenever there is a vacancy in the office of the Vice President, the President shall nominate a Vice President who shall take office upon confirmation by a majority vote of both Houses of Congress.

Section 3 ■ Whenever the President transmits to the President pro tempore of the Senate and the Speaker of the House of Representatives his written declaration that he is unable to discharge the powers and duties of his office, and until he transmits to them a written declaration to the contrary, such powers and duties shall be discharged by the Vice President as Acting President.

Section 4 ■ Whenever the Vice President and a majority of either the principal officers of the executive departments or of such other body as Congress may by law provide, transmit to the President pro tempore of the Senate and the Speaker of the House of Representatives their written declaration that the President is unable to discharge the powers and duties of his office, the Vice President shall immediately assume the powers and duties of the office as Acting President.

Thereafter, when the President transmits to the President pro tempore of the Senate and the Speaker of the House of Representatives his written declaration that no inability exists, he shall resume the powers and duties of his office unless the Vice President and a majority of either the principal officers of the executive department or of such other body as Congress may by law provide, transmit within four days to the President pro tempore of the Senate and the Speaker of the House of Representatives their written declaration that the President is unable to discharge the powers and duties of his office. Thereupon Congress shall decide the issue, assembling within forty-eight hours for that purpose if not in session. If the Congress, within twenty-one days after receipt of the latter written declaration, or, if Congress is not in session, within twenty-one days after Congress is required to assemble, determines by two-thirds vote of both Houses that the President is unable to discharge the powers and duties of his office, the Vice President shall continue to discharge the same as Acting President; otherwise, the President shall resume the powers and duties of his office.

AMENDMENT XXVI

Section 1 ■ The right of citizens of the United States, who are eighteen years of age or older, to vote shall not be denied or abridged by the United States or by any State on account of age.

Section 2 ■ The Congress shall have power to enforce this article by appropriate legislation.

AMENDMENT XXVII

No law, varying the compensation for the services of the Senators and Representatives, shall take effect, until an election of representatives shall have intervened.

The Declaration of Independence

IN CONGRESS, JULY 4, 1776. THE UNANIMOUS DECLARATION OF THE THIRTEEN UNITED STATES OF AMERICA.

When in the Course of human events, it becomes necessary for one people to dissolve the political bands which have connected them with another, and to assume among the powers of the earth, the separate and equal station to which the Laws of Nature and of Nature's God entitle them, a decent Respect to the Opinions of Mankind requires that they should declare the causes which impel them to the separation.

We hold these truths to be self-evident, that all men are created equal, that they are endowed by their Creator with certain unalienable Rights, that among these are Life, Liberty and the Pursuit of Happiness. That to secure these rights, Governments are instituted among Men, deriving their just powers from the consent of the governed, that whenever any Form of Government becomes destructive of these Ends, it is the Right of the People to alter or to abolish it, and to institute new Government, laying its foundation on such principles, and organizing its Powers in such form, as to them shall seem most likely to effect their Safety and Happiness. Prudence, indeed, will dictate that Governments long established should not be changed for light and transient causes; and accordingly all experience hath shewn, that mankind are more disposed to suffer, while evils are sufferable, than to right themselves by abolishing the forms to which they are accustomed. But when a long train of abuses and usurpations, pursuing invariably the same Object, evinces a design to reduce them under absolute Despotism, it is their right, it is their duty, to throw off such Government, and to provide new Guards for their future security. Such has been the patient Sufferance of these Colonies; and such is now the necessity which constrains them to alter their former Systems of Government. The history of the present King of Great Britain is a history of repeated injuries and usurpations, all having in direct object the Establishment of an absolute Tyranny over these States. To prove this, let Facts be submitted to a candid world.

He has refused his Assent to Laws, the most wholesome and necessary for the public good.

He has forbidden his Governors to pass Laws of immediate and pressing importance, unless suspended in their operation till his Assent should be obtained; and when so suspended, he has utterly neglected to attend to them.

He has refused to pass other Laws for the accommodation of large districts of people, unless those people would relinquish the right of Representation in the Legislature, a right inestimable to them, and formidable to tyrants only.

He has called together legislative bodies at places unusual, uncomfortable, and distant from the depository of their public Records, for the sole purpose of fatiguing them into compliance with his measures.

He has dissolved Representative Houses repeatedly, for opposing with manly firmness his invasions on the rights of the people.

He has refused for a long time, after such dissolutions, to cause others to be elected; whereby the Legislative powers, incapable of the Annihilation, have returned to the People at large for their exercise; the State remaining in the mean time exposed to all the dangers of invasion from without, and the convulsions within.

He has endeavoured to prevent the population of these States; for that purpose obstructing the Laws for Naturalization of Foreigners; refusing to pass others to encourage their migrations hither, and raising the conditions of new Appropriations of Lands.

He has obstructed the Administration of Justice, by refusing his Assent to Laws for establishing Judiciary powers.

He has made Judges dependent on his Will alone, for the Tenure of their offices, and the amount and payment of their salaries.

He has erected a multitude of New Offices, and sent hither swarms of Officers to harrass our people, and eat out their substance.

He has kept among us, in times of peace, Standing Armies, without the Consent of our Legislatures.

He has affected to render the Military independent of and superior to the Civil power.

He has combined with others to subject us to a jurisdiction foreign to our constitution, and unacknowledged by our laws; giving his Assent to their Acts of pretended Legislation:

For quartering large bodies of armed troops among us:

For protecting them, by a mock Trial, from punishment for any Murders which they should commit on the Inhabitants of these States:

For cutting off our Trade with all parts of the world:

For imposing Taxes on us without our Consent:

For depriving us, in many Cases, of the benefits of Trial by Jury:

For transporting us beyond Seas to be tried for pretended Offences:

For abolishing the free System of English Laws in a neighbouring Province, establishing therein an Arbitrary government, and enlarging its Boundaries so as to render it at once an example and fit instrument for introducing the same absolute rules into these Colonies:

For taking away our Charters, abolishing our most valuable Laws, and altering fundamentally the Forms of our Governments:

For suspending our own Legislatures, and declaring themselves invested with power to legislate for us in all cases whatsoever.

He has abdicated Government here, by declaring us out of his Protection and waging War against us.

He has plundered our Seas, ravaged our Coasts, burnt our towns, and destroyed the lives of our people.

He is at this time transporting large Armies of foreign Mercenaries to compleat the works of death, desolation, and tyranny, already begun with circumstances of Cruelty and perfidy scarcely paralleled in the most barbarous ages, and totally unworthy the Head of a civilized nation.

He has constrained our fellow Citizens taken Captive on the high Seas to bear Arms against their Country, to become the executioners of their friends and Brethren, or to fall themselves by their Hands.

He has excited domestic insurrections amongst us, and has endeavoured to bring on the inhabitants of our frontiers, the merciless Indian Savages, whose known rule of warfare, is an undistinguished destruction, of all ages, sexes and conditions.

In every stage of these Oppressions we have Petitioned for Redress in the most humble terms: Our repeated Petitions have been answered only by repeated injury. A Prince, whose character is thus marked by every act which may define a Tyrant, is unfit to be the ruler of a free people.

Nor have We been wanting in attentions to our British brethren. We have warned them from time to time of attempts by their legislature to extend an unwarrantable jurisdiction over us. We have reminded them of the circumstances of our emigration and settlement here. We have appealed to their native justice and magnanimity, and we have conjured them by the ties of our common kindred to disavow these usurpations, which, would inevitably interrupt our connections and correspondence. They too have been deaf to the voice of justice

and of consanguinity. We must, therefore, acquiesce in the necessity, which denounces our Separation, and hold them, as we hold the rest of mankind, Enemies in War, in Peace, Friends.

We, therefore, the Representatives of the United States of America, in General Congress, Assembled, appealing to the Supreme Judge of the world for the rectitude of our intentions, do, in the Name, and by Authority of the good People of these Colonies, solemnly publish and declare, That these United Colonies are, and of Right ought to be, Free and Independent States; that they are absolved from all Allegiance to the British Crown, and that all political connection between them and the State of Great Britain, is and ought to be totally dissolved; and that as Free and Independent States, they have full Power to levy War, conclude Peace, contract Alliances, establish Commerce, and to do all other Acts and Things which Independent States may of right do. And for the support of this Declaration, with a firm reliance on the protection of divine Providence, we mutually pledge to each other our Lives, our Fortunes, and our sacred Honor.

Signed by Order and in Behalf of the Congress,
JOHN HANCOCK, PRESIDENT.

Attest. CHARLES THOMSON, Secretary.

Philadelphia: Printed by JOHN DUNLAP.

Key Terms Glossary

acceptance The second party's unqualified willingness to go along with the first party's proposal

accord and satisfaction A legal way to settle contractual disputes by which one party agrees to accept less than the amount due as full payment

actual authority The real power a principal gives to an agent

actual notice A formal notice given directly to a party, usually using certified mail with a receipt

adhesion contract A take-it-or-leave-it offer made by a party who holds most of the power in a bargaining session

administrative law The body of rules created by government agencies

adultery When one spouse has sexual relations with someone outside of marriage

affinity Related by marriage

agency A type of working relationship in which one person represents another person in a business transaction with a third party

agency by estoppel When the principal's actions lead the third party to believe that the agent is working for the principal

agent The person who has been authorized to do the work

agent's agent An agent who is appointed by another agent without the principal's authority to do so

alimony An allowance for support paid to one person by the former spouse in a divorce

Alternative dispute resolution Parties try to resolve disagreements outside of the usual court system, by mediation, arbitration, conciliation, and negotiation

annual percentage rate (APR) The true interest rate of the loan

annulment A declaration by the court that a marriage was never valid

apparent authority Authority that a third party believes an agent has while acting on behalf of the principal

appellate court The U.S. courts of appeals in the federal system; hears appeals and reviews cases from the lower courts

arraignment A formal hearing during which the defendant is read the indictment or information and is asked to plead guilty or not guilty

arrest Occurs when a person is legally deprived of his or her freedom

articles of incorporation A legal document filed with the state to establish a corporation

assault Attempt to commit a battery

asset acquisition When one corporation agrees to purchase the assets, such as property, buildings, and equipment, of a second corporation

assignment The transfer of a right under contract

assumption of risk A defense against negligence that is raised when the plaintiff knew of the risk and still took the chance of being injured

bail Money or other property that is left with the court to assure that a person who has been arrested, but released, will return to trial

bailment The transfer of possession and control of personal property to another with the intent that the same property will be returned later

bankruptcy The legal process by which a debtor can make a fresh start through the sale of assets to pay off creditors

battery The unlawful touching of another person

beneficiary The person named in an insurance policy to receive the proceeds of the policy

bigamy The illegal act of having two spouses at the same time

bilateral contract A contract that contains two promises: one party promises to do something in exchange for the other's promise to do something else

bill of sale Formal evidence of ownership

breach of contract When one party to a contract fails to perform the duties spelled out by the contract

burglary Breaking and entering a house or other structure to commit a felony

capacity The legal ability to enter into a contract

carrier A business that transports persons, goods, or both

certificate of incorporation A corporation's official authorization to do business in a state

Chapter 7 bankruptcy A type of bankruptcy that allows individual debtors to discharge all their debts and make a fresh start; ordinary bankruptcy

Chapter 11 bankruptcy A type of bankruptcy that allows businesses to reorganize their financial affairs and still remain in business

Chapter 12 bankruptcy A form of bankruptcy that lets family farmers, and fishing businesses, create a plan for debt repayment that allows them to keep their operations running

Chapter 13 bankruptcy A form of bankruptcy that permits individual debtors to reorganize their debts and develop payment plans

class action suit A lawsuit shareholders with a common claim can bring as a group against a corporation

collateral The property that is offered as a security interest

collective bargaining A process in which union and management representatives get together to work out issues such as wages, working conditions, and hiring and firing policies

Commerce Clause A statement in Article I of the Constitution giving Congress the power to regulate commerce among the states

common carrier A carrier that is compensated for providing transportation to the general public

common law A set of laws made by the courts that provide a series of consistent rules that later courts must follow

common-law marriage An informal type of marriage created by the parties themselves

comparative negligence A defense against negligence which is raised when the carelessness of each party is compared to the carelessness of the other party

compensation Fair payment for the job performed

conglomerate A corporation that owns many different types of companies

consanguinity Related by blood

consideration The exchange of benefits and detriments by the parties to a contract

consolidation When two or more companies join together to form a new corporation

constitution A country's formal document that spells out the principles by which its government operates

Consumer Credit Protection Act A federal law that requires creditors to inform consumers of the costs and terms of credit; Truth in Lending Act

Key Terms Glossary

Key Terms Glossary

contract Any agreement enforceable by law

contributory negligence A defense against negligence when the defendant can show the victim did something to help cause his or her own injuries

copyright A right granted to an author, composer, photographer, or artist to publish and sell an artistic or literary work

corporate director A person elected by shareholders to make broad policy decisions in the running of a corporation

corporate officer A person chosen by the directors to run the day-to-day affairs of a corporation

corporation An entity with a legal authority to act as a single person distinct from its owners

counteroffer A response to an offer in which the terms of the original offer are changed

credit An arrangement in which one may receive cash, goods, or services now and pay in the future

creditor The party who sells the goods on credit or lends the money

crime An offense committed against the public good, or society

cyberblackmail The use of information unlawfully obtained by computer to pressure a victim into granting a payoff to the blackmailer

cybercrime Any criminal activity associated with a computer

cyberdefamation The communication via computer or other electronic device of false data that damages a person's reputation

cyberinvasion of privacy An unwelcome intrusion into the private matters of an individual carried out or sustained by a computer

cyberlaw The area of law that concerns computer and computer-related crimes

cyberpiracy A crime that involves using a computer to steal computer data stored in a digital formal

cyberspoofing A crime in which a cybercriminal falsely adopts the identity of another computer user or creates a false identity on a computer Web site in order to commit fraud

cybertort The invasion, theft, falsification, misuse, or deletion of data stored in a computer

cybertrespass Any illegal activity already in the criminal code committed by using a computer

cybervandalism Disrupting, damaging, or destroying a Web site or computer network

damages Payment recovered in court by a person who has suffered an injury

debtor The party who buys the goods on credit or borrows money

deed A written instrument that transfers title of ownership of property

default A failure in making timely payments on a loan

defendant A person who is accused of a crime

delegation Transferring of a duty under a contract

derivative suit A lawsuit a shareholder can bring on behalf of the corporation to correct an injury to the corporation

detention hearing A court session during which the judge tries to learn whether there are good reasons to keep an accused juvenile in custody

digital signature An encoded message that appears at the end of a contract created online

direct suit A lawsuit a shareholder can bring against a corporation for denying his or her rights as a shareholder

disaffirm To show the intent not to live up to a contract

discharge by agreement The act of ending contracts by mutual agreement

discrimination The unequal treatment of individuals based on sex, age, race, nationality, or religion

disparate impact When an employer has an employment policy that appears neutral on its surface, but has an unfair impact on members of a protected class

disparate treatment When an employer intentionally discriminates against an individual or a group of individuals belonging to a protected class

dissociation When a partner is no longer associated with a firm

dissolution The breakup of a partnership or any legal entity

divorce A declaration by the court that a valid marriage has come to an end; sometimes called dissolution of marriage

domain name The Internet address of a business

double representation When an agent works simultaneously for two competing principals

draft An order to a third party to pay money

drawee The person to whom an order is given to pay money in a draft

drawer The person who orders money to be paid in a draft

duress The act of destroying somebody's free will by force, threat of force, or bodily harm

easement An irrevocable right to the limited use of another's land

e-commerce (Electronic commerce) The process of conducting business using electronic means, especially the Internet

electronic fund transfer (EFT) A computerized system for transferring funds electronically rather than by writing checks

emancipation Freeing someone from the control of another; especially a parent's relinquishing authority and control over a minor child

eminent domain The right of the government to take private land for a public purpose

employment-at-will Based on the principle that each party should be free to end the employment relationship at any time without penalty

Environmental Protection Agency (EPA) The federal agency responsible for protecting the environment

Equal Credit Opportunity Act (ECOA) Makes it illegal for banks and businesses to discriminate against credit applicants on the basis of their gender, race, marital status, national origin, religion, age, or because they get public assistance income

equal pay rule A standard that states that employers working in interstate commerce must pay women the same rate of pay as men holding the same type of job

estate The interest or right that a person has in real property

ethics The rules used to determine the difference between right and wrong

eviction Occurs when a landlord deprives a tenant of the possession of the premises

executor/executrix The person named to carry out the terms of a will (executor—male; executrix—female)

express authority Comes from the orders, commands, or instructions a principal explicitly gives an agent

Key Terms Glossary

express contract A contract statement that may be oral or written

express warranty An oral or written statement, promise, or other representation about the quality of a product

expropriation When a government seizes a privately-owned business to be used for a public service

Fair Credit Billing Act Requires creditors to correct billing errors brought to their attention

Fair Credit Reporting Act A federal law that grants people the right to know what is contained in their credit reports

Fair Debt Collection Practices Act (FDCPA) Prohibits certain practices by debt collectors

Federal Energy Regulatory Commission (FERC) Part of the Department of Energy, this agency regulates electricity and natural gas

felony A major crime

fiduciary relationship A relationship based on trust

finance charge The cost of the loan in dollars and cents

firm offer A merchant's written promise to hold an offer open for the sale or lease of goods

fixtures Items of personal property attached in such a way that they become real property

forbearance The act of not doing what you have the right to do

forgery The fraudulent making or material alteration of a writing

franchise A license a company grants to a business or individual for the right to use its name and sell its products or services

fraud A deliberate deception intended to secure an unfair and unlawful gain

full warranty An assurance that a defective product will be repaired or replaced without charge within a reasonable time

garnishment The legal procedure through which a worker's earnings are withheld for payment of a debt

general agent An agent who has authority to perform any act within the scope of a business

genuine agreement An agreement that is true and genuine: a valid offer is met by a valid acceptance

gratuitous bailment A bailment for the sole benefit of the bailor

holder A person who possesses a negotiable instrument payable to "the order of" the person holding it or to "bearer"

holder in due course A holder who takes an instrument for value, in good faith, and without notice that the instrument is defective

identity theft Using a computer to steal financial, employment, educational, medical, and personal data

implied authority Additional authority that allows an agent to perform reasonable acts necessary to carry out the express authority

implied contract A contract that comes about from the actions of the parties; a contract that exists when an employer has said, written, or done something to lead an employee to reasonably believe that he or she is not an at-will employee

implied covenant A legal argument that holds that any employment relationship is based on an implied promise that the employer and employee will be fair and honest with one another

implied warranty A guarantee of quality imposed by law

impossibility of performance When one of three situations prevent the performance of a service contract: a death or illness that prevents the performance of a personal service contract; the destruction of the exact subject matter, or the means for performance; and illegality

indemnification Payment for losses suffered by an agent because of a principal's instructions

independent contractor A person who works for a proprietor to perform a particular task using his or her own tools and deciding the best way to do the job

indorsement The act of placing one's signature on an instrument, usually on the back, to transfer it to another

infraction A minor offense that is usually punishable with a fine and not with jail time

injunction A court order that prevents a party from performing a specific act

insider trading When a corporate director or officer buys or sells shares in a corporation based on firsthand information about the corporation that is not available to the public

insurable interest The financial interest a policyholder has in the person or property that is insured

insurance An agreement in which one party (the insurer) compensates another party (the insured) for any losses

intellectual property An original work fixed in a tangible medium of expression

intentional tort Actions that hurt, embarrass, or scare other people

interest A fee charged by creditors for lending money or extending credit

intestate To be without a will

invitations to negotiate Invitations to deal, trade, or make an offer

involuntary bankruptcy When creditors begin the proceeding instead of the debtor

joint liability Liability shared by two or more people

jurisdiction A court's power to hear a case and make a judgment

justice Treating people fairly and equally

larceny The unlawful taking of someone's personal property with the intent to keep the property away from that person

law A system of rules of conduct established by a country's government to maintain stability and justice according to the values that are relevant to that country

lease The contract between a tenant and a landlord

lessee The tenant in a lease

lessor The landlord in a lease

license A temporary, revocable right to the limited use of another's land

lien A legal claim against another person's property as a security for a debt or loan to ensure it will be paid

limited liability company (LLC) An entity with the legal authority to act as a single person distinct from its owners and combines the best features of a partnership and a corporation

limited liability partnership (LLP) A registered partnership in which each partner is not liable for the acts of the other partners

limited partnership A partnership formed by two or more persons, with one or more general partners and one or more limited partners

limited warranty Any written warranty that does not meet the requirements of a full warranty

majority The status of reaching the age of adulthood, 18 in most states

manslaughter Voluntary or involuntary killing of another person without intending to do so

maker The person who promises to pay money in a note

marriage Defined by most states and the federal government as the legal union of one man and one woman as husband and wife

merger When two companies join together, with one company keeping its corporate identity and the other company losing its corporate identity

minor A person who has not yet reached the age of adulthood

mirror image rule The terms stated in the acceptance must exactly mirror or match the terms of the offer

misdemeanor A less-serious crime

monopoly A business situation in which one person, company, or group of companies controls the market for a product or service

morality The values that govern a group's ideas about right and wrong

murder The intentional killing of another person

mutual benefit bailment A bailment in which both the bailor and bailee receive benefits

negligence A tort that results when one person carelessly injures another

negotiable instrument A written document giving legal rights that may be passed to others by endorsement or delivery; commercial paper

negotiation The transfer of an agreement in such a way that the transferee becomes a holder

no-fault divorce A divorce granted without either party having to prove the other party guilty of misconduct

nondelegable duty A duty that cannot be delegated, or transferred, to another party

note A written promise to pay money; promissory note

notice by publication Notice usually given by publishing a notice in a local newspaper

Nuclear Regulatory Commission (NRC) Part of the Department of Energy, this agency regulates nuclear energy

Occupational Safety and Health Administration (OSHA) The federal government agency that regulates health and safety standards for companies in the United States

offer A proposal by one party to another intended to create a legally binding agreement

partnership An association of two or more persons to carry on as co-owners of a business for profit

patent A grant giving an inventor the exclusive right to make, use, or sell an invention for a period set by Congress

payee The person to whom the promise is made in a note

pension plan A program established by an employer or a union to provide income to employees after they retire

personal property Everything, other than real property, that can be owned

plaintiff The party that accuses a person of a crime

polygamy The illegal act of having more than two spouses at the same time

power of attorney Any writing granting someone authority to act as an agent

premium The amount of money an insured pays for insurance coverage

prenuptial agreement A written and signed legal contract couples make before getting married dealing with property and support issues

principal The person who authorizes someone to represent his or her interests

probate The process of validating and executing a will

promissory estoppel The principle that a promise made without consideration may nonetheless be enforced to prevent injustice

prosecutor The government official who brings the case against the defendant

prospectus A document that contains a detailed explanation of the stock offering for potential investors

proximate cause When the link between negligent conduct and injury is strong enough to be recognized by the law

public policy A legal principle that holds that nobody should be allowed to do something that harms the public

public policy tort A legal theory that permits a discharged employee to bring a wrongful discharge lawsuit against a former employer based on the argument that the firing somehow hurts the public at large

punitive damages Money payments for damages that go beyond what the innocent party actually lost and that are designed to punish the wrongdoer

ratification The act of agreeing to go along with a contract that could have been avoided

real property The ground and everything permanently attached to it

registration statement A general description of the securities and of the company making the offer

reimbursement Payment for money spent by an agent on behalf of a principal

rejection A refusal of an offer by the offeree that brings the offer to an end

remedy A legal means of enforcing a right or correcting a wrong

repossession When a creditor reclaims property on which it has a lien if the debtor does not make payment

respondeat superior A legal doctrine that holds that the master is responsible for the torts of his or her servants

revocation The taking back of an offer by the offeror

Key Terms Glossary

risk of loss The responsibility for loss or damage to goods

robbery The wrongful taking of someone's property by threatening or using violence

secured loan A loan which is backed up by property that the creditor can take if the loan is not repaid

security A monetary investment that seeks to make a profit solely because of another's efforts

security interest A creditor's right to use collateral to recover a debt

self-dealing When agents make deals that benefit themselves rather than their principal

share A single unit of ownership in a corporation

shareholder An individual who owns shares of a corporation

Social Security A government program that provides continuing income to workers and their dependents when their earnings stop or are reduced because of retirement, disability, or death

sole proprietorship A form of business that is owned and operated by one person

special agent An agent whose authority is restricted to accomplishing only a specific job or purpose; limited agent

special bailment A bailment for the sole benefit of the bailee

statute A law passed by a government body that has been made for the purpose of creating laws

Statute of Frauds A state law that requires that certain contracts be in writing so that there is evidence that the contract exists and that it has certain definitive terms

statute of limitations Establishes a time limit for suing in a civil case, based on the date when the breach occurred or was discovered

stock acquisition When an individual or a corporation buys enough shares of stock in another corporation to take over control of it

straight life insurance Life insurance that requires the payment of premiums until the face value is reached or the insured is deceased; also called ordinary life or whole life

strict liability A legal doctrine that says some activities are so dangerous that liability will always follow any injury that results from those activities

subagent An agent lawfully appointed by another agent

sublease The transfer of part of the term of a lease, but not the remainder of it, to someone else

substantial performance A situation in which a party has, in good faith, completed the major requirements of a contract, leaving only a few minor details unfinished

tenancy An interest in the real estate they lease; leasehold estate

tender An offer to do what you have agreed to do under a contract

term life insurance Life insurance issued for a particular period, usually five or ten years

testamentary capacity The mental ability (being of sound mind) to create a will

testamentary intent The intention that the document is meant to be a last will and testament

testator/testatrix A person who dies with a will (testator—male; testatrix—female)

third party The person with whom the agent does business on behalf of the principal

title The right of ownership to goods

tort A private wrong committed by one person against another

tortfeasor A person who commits a tort

trust A legal device by which property is held by one person for the benefit of another

trustee A person who holds title to the property for another's benefit

unconscionable contract An agreement in which the consideration is so out of line with the actual value of the subject matter and so unfair that shocks the court's conscience

undue influence An action or series of overly persuasive actions that make inappropriate use of one person's position of power over another person to create an agreement that is very favorable to the person with all the power

unemployment compensation A system of government payments to people who are out of work and looking for a job

Uniform Commercial Code (UCC) A collection of laws that governs various types of business transactions

unilateral contract A contract that contains a promise by only one person to do something, if and when the other party performs some act

union An organization of employees formed to promote the welfare of its members

unlimited liability A legal duty placed on a business owner that requires the owner to be responsible for all losses experienced by the business

usury law A law restricting the amount of interest that can be charged

vandalism Willful or malicious damage to property

voidable title A title that may be canceled if the injured party chooses to do so

voluntary bankruptcy When a debtor files for bankruptcy to eliminate or reduce the burden of debt

warranty A guarantee, usually by a seller to a buyer, that a product will perform as promised

warranty of fitness for a particular purpose An implied warranty that goods will be fit for a specific use

warranty of merchantability An implied warranty that goods are fit for the ordinary purpose for which the goods are sold

will A document that is signed during your lifetime that provides for the distribution of your property upon death

workers' compensation An insurance program that provides income for workers who are injured on the job or develop a disability or disease as a result of their job

Academic Terms Glossary

acquired Gained possession of

adhere To carry out a plan, or an operation without deviation; to stick to

administer To manage or direct

advantage Benefit, profit, or gain

affected Influenced by

alternative A situation presenting a choice between two mutually exclusive possibilities

apparent Appearing as such, seeming

assets Property, tangible and intangible, including cash, inventories, and property rights

assign To transfer to another

assume To take on; adopt

assumption Something taken for granted or accepted as true without proof

benefit Something that promotes well-being; a useful aid

broadcast To send out or communicate, especially by radio, television, or the Internet

capacity Ability to perform or produce

ceremony A formal act performed as prescribed by ritual or custom

certify To confirm formally as true or genuine

commerce The exchange or buying and selling of goods on a large scale

compensate To make up for a loss

comply To act in accordance with another's command or request

comprehensive Covering completely or broadly

conduct To direct, manage, control, or carry out

confidential Communicated or entrusted in secret

consent To give approval

contain To have as component parts; include or comprise

contempt Open disrespect or willful disobedience of a court or legislative body

cooperation The act of working together toward a common end or purpose

corruption Impairment of integrity, morals, and honesty; promoting wrong by improper or illegal means

definite Unquestionable; certain; precise

determine To decide or settle conclusively or definitely

directive An order or instruction, especially one issued by a central authority

discharge To set aside; annul

disclose To make known

dispensing Distributing; dealing out in portions

distress Anxiety or mental suffering

domestic Relating to home or household, or to a specific state or country

dominant Exercising the most influence or control

dormant Inactive

download Transfer data from a computer to another device

duplicate Identically copied from an original

effective In force; in effect

elective A choice; an option

emission A substance that is discharged

empathy Understanding, being sensitive to

endowment The act of furnishing with an income

exaggerate To enlarge beyond the truth; overstate

exceed To go beyond the limits of; surpass

exception Something omitted, excluded, or neglected

exclude To prevent from being included, considered, or accepted; reject

exclusive Not divided or shared with others

expire To come to an end; terminate

exploit To make use of unfairly for one's own advantage

extent The degree to which something is stretched out

foreseeable To see or know beforehand

genuine Actually possessing the apparent attribute or character; authentic

gratuitous Given or received without cost or obligation; free.

impersonate To assume the character or appearance of, especially fraudulently

impose To force; to establish as compulsory; to apply by authority

impulse An impelling force; an urge that prompts an unpremeditated act or feeling

incidental Of a minor, casual, or subordinate nature

incompetence Lack of physical or intellectual ability or qualifications

indicating Serving as a sign, symptom, or token of; signifying

informal Appropriate to ordinary, casual, or familiar use

infrastructure The basic facilities, services, and installations needed for the functioning of a community, society, or a system such as the national electronic system

intent Purpose; meaning; significance

involved Connected by participation or association

irrevocable Impossible to take back

jeopardy Exposure to loss or injury

Academic Terms Glossary

loyal Faithful to a person, ideal, custom, cause, or duty

malicious Deliberately harmful; spiteful

mediator One who intervenes between conflicting parties to bring about an agreement

motive A need or desire that causes a person to act

mutual Possessed in common; having the same relationship

objective Uninfluenced by emotions or personal prejudices; factual

obligation Something one is bound to legally or morally

option The act of choosing; choice

permissible Allowable

permission Formal consent

perpetual Continuing forever

persistent Existing or remaining in the same state for an indefinitely long time; enduring

petition A formal written application requesting a court for a specific judicial action

preemptive Undertaken or initiated to deter or prevent an anticipated situation or occurrence

prevalent Generally or widely accepted, practiced, or favored; widespread

proactive Controlling a situation by causing something to happen rather than waiting to respond to it after it happens

process A series of actions, changes, or functions bringing about a result

proportionate Properly related in size, degree, or other measurable characteristics; corresponding

provision A measure or requirement made beforehand

random Having no specific pattern, purpose, or objective

reasonable Moderate, fair, rational

reconcile To make compatible or consistent; to balance, as a bank statement

reconciliation Reestablishment of a relationship

register To set down in writing; record; enter in a record

require To impose an obligation on; compel

revoke To void or annul by recalling, withdrawing, or reversing

routine Habitual; regular

sabotage Destruction of property or obstruction of normal operations

schedule A plan for performing work or achieving an objective, specifying the order and allotted time for each part

signature A distinctive mark, characteristic indicating identity

significant Having or likely to have a major effect; important

similar Having the same or some of the same characteristics

simulate To have or take on the appearance, form, or sound of; imitate

solicit To seek to obtain by persuasion, entreaty, or formal application

specify To state in detail or as a condition

spouse A marriage partner; a husband or wife

standard A model, measure, or criterion

status The legal character or condition of a person or thing

subscription The completion of a legal instrument (such as a contract or deed) by signing it so that it becomes legally binding and enforceable

subsidize Supported materially or financially

substitute Something that takes the place of another; a replacement; a copy

supplement Something added to complete a thing, make up for a deficiency, or extend or strengthen the whole.

tangible That which can be valued monetarily or touched; real

unanimous Having the agreement of all

unauthorized Not having official permission or approval

unconditional Without conditions or limitations; absolute

uniform Conforming to one principle, standard, or rule; consistent

usury Charging more than the maximum legal interest rate

vacate To make legally void

voluntary Done or undertaken of one's own free will

waiver Intentional relinquishment of a right, claim, or privilege

Case Index

Index

Index

Index

Index

Index

Index